Jesus, Justice, and the Reign of God

Jesus, Justice, and the Reign of God

A Ministry of Liberation

William R. Herzog II

Westminster John Knox Press
Louisville, Kentucky

Scripture cited is the author's translation.

Book design by Sharon Adams
Cover design by PAZ Design Group
Cover art courtesy Erich Lessing/Art Resource, NY

First edition
Published by Westminster John Knox Press
Louisville, Kentucky

This book is printed on acid-free paper that meets the American National Standards Institute Z39.48 standard. ∞

PRINTED IN THE UNITED STATES OF AMERICA

00 01 02 03 04 05 06 07 08 09 — 10 9 8 7 6 5 4 3 2 1

Library of Congress Cataloging-in-Publication Data
Herzog, William R.
    Jesus, justice, and the reign of God : a ministry of liberation / William R. Herzog II.
        p.   cm.
    Includes bibliographical references and index.
    ISBN 0-664-25676-7 (pbk. : alk. paper)
    1. Jesus Christ—Historicity.   2. Jesus Christ—Prophetic office.
I. Title.
BT303.2.H44   1999
232.9'08—dc21   99-36579

To my mother and father
Helen M. Herzog
C. Chester Herzog
of blessed memory

CONTENTS

Contents

Contents

INTRODUCTION

The first quest for the historical Jesus was not launched by Enlightenment scholars, as we are apt to assume because we have been so profoundly influenced by Albert Schweitzer's *Quest of the Historical Jesus*. The first quest for the historical Jesus was launched by anonymous followers of Jesus who remembered his words and circulated reports of his mighty acts. Their efforts eventually yielded the first written fruits of the quest, the Gospels of Mark, Matthew, Luke, and John. They may have been itinerant radicals, as Gerd Theissen supposes,[1] or they may have been peasant villagers, incorporating the wisdom of Jesus into the little tradition that shaped village life. The first questers included both the inner core of disciples, who journeyed with Jesus from the beginning of his work in Galilee to its end in Jerusalem, and the outer periphery of demoniacs, who met Jesus for one life-transforming moment and then were gone.

From the beginning of the quest for the historical Jesus, the problem has not been too little information but too much, a situation that made the painful but essential tasks of selection and ordering necessary. The author of the fourth Gospel said it best: "Now Jesus did many other signs in the presence of his disciples, which are not written in this book. But these are written so that you may believe that Jesus is the Christ, the Son of God, and that, through believing, you may have life in his name" (John 20:30–31). Not an innocent statement, because it indicates that John's quest was pursued with an agenda, another inescapable condition of any quest for the historical Jesus. More recent studies might paraphrase John's programmatic statement so that it reads, "these things are written that you might surrender your belief and, through unbelief, might have freedom to do empirical research unencumbered by church dogma."[2] Schweitzer would call it simply "the problem."[3] Whatever form the confession takes, it must be made if the quest is to be taken seriously. In this matter, everyone falls short of the glory of the quest.

This study of Jesus as a prophet of the justice of the reign of God is like every other example of the quest for the historical Jesus. I have pursued it with an agenda, and that agenda will be plain to anyone who attends to chapters that follow. In brief, I am persuaded that Jesus of Nazareth cannot be fully understood unless we understand the world in which he conducted his public work and comprehend the prophetic role he played in that world. This means that the task of understanding the politics, kinship networks, economics, social life, symbolic world, and systems of meaning of ancient Palestine is an indispensable part of any quest for the historical Jesus. It is only by understanding Jesus in his context that we can glimpse how he came to transcend his original setting and what that transcendence means for us.

As the author of the fourth Gospel knew so well, it is impossible to study the historical Jesus without doing theology. All study of the historical Jesus involves Christology, whether it be the orthodox Christology of the creeds or the heterodox Christology of the scholars. This study is no different. Throughout this quest, I have attempted to weave together politics and theology, the material conditions of life as a context for making sense out of God's covenant, the hard fate of peasants struggling to survive as a context for understanding Jesus' portrayal of God, and the way he assumed a public role as God's broker to a broken world.

No investigation is done alone. The endnotes and bibliography of this volume will provide some indication of the great cloud of witnesses that surrounded me and contributed to this work. I hope that I have treated my conversational partners with respect, even when I have disagreed with them. I am indebted to generations of students at Colgate Rochester Divinity School/Crozer Theological Seminary/Baptist Missionary Training School for their eager interest in rediscovering the historical Jesus. In addition to the students at my home divinity school, I have been fortunate to work, in summer school sessions, with students at Central Baptist Seminary in Kansas City and The Graduate Theological Union in Berkeley. My time at the G.T.U. was made possible by the faculty and administration of The American Baptist Seminary of the West in Berkeley, who invited me to teach in the common G.T.U. Summer School. All of these students have contributed to this work.

I have been fortunate to be associated with the Context Group, a gathering of scholars interested in learning how the social sciences can contribute to the interpretation of biblical texts. I owe a special debt to Scott Bartchy, Jack Elliott, K. C. Hanson, Bruce Malina, Jerry Neyrey, Doug Oakman, and Richard Rohrbaugh, whose work continues to inspire me and judge the inadequacy of my own. I am indebted to my faculty colleagues in Rochester, especially my biblical studies colleagues Tom Haverly, Werner Lemke, and Richard Middleton, who were kind enough to read and comment on portions of the manuscript. Their careful work spared me many embarrassing errors and enabled me to rethink critical assumptions I had made. Needless to say, they are not responsible for any errors that remain. Those are solely my responsibility.

In my seminary years, I was most fortunate to have Dr. David Wallace as my New Testament professor. He taught us not only the hard work involved in biblical interpretation but also the sheer joy that accompanies the task. His goal was to educate every student to be a "worker who need not be ashamed, cutting straight to the heart of the word of truth" (2 Tim. 2:15). I suspect that he would agree with very little in this work, but I hope that he can see the evidence of his influence and his love of the word of truth in this effort.

I thank the Trustees of Colgate Rochester Divinity School/Crozer Theological Seminary/Baptist Missionary Training School for granting me a sabbatical leave during the spring semester of 1998. The leave enabled me to do much of the research needed to begin writing this book. I continue to appreciate the many ways in which the divinity school encourages research and writing.

I owe a special debt of gratitude to my editor at Westminster John Knox, Dr. Carey Newman. His obvious interest and engagement with the project were encouraging, and his skill as an editor has greatly improved the quality of this work. His advice and help have been invaluable.

With grace and loving support, my family has endured the usual changes in routine that accompany a writing project. They have been kind and understanding throughout the long days and evenings. I want to express special gratitude to Mary, my wife, and our two teenagers, Dan and Catherine.

This book is dedicated to the memory of my mother and my father. My mother was my first biblical teacher, who taught me to read the Bible with care, never assuming that I knew what it meant. My father showed me the sustaining power of the Word during his long illness. The lessons of their lives continue to sustain and nurture me.

ABBREVIATIONS

AJS	*American Journal of Sociology*
ANRW	Hildegard Temporini and Wolfgang Haase, *Aufsteig und Niedergang der Römischen Welt*
ARA	*Annual Review of Anthropology*
ATR	*Anglican Theological Review*
Ant.	Josephus, *Jewish Antiquities*
BA	*Biblical Archaeologist*
BAGD	Walter Bauer, William F. Arndt, F. Wilbur Gingrich, Frederick W. Danker, *A Greek English Lexicon of the New Testament and Other Early Christian Literature*
BAR	*Biblical Archaeology Review*
BASOR	*Bulletin of the American Society for Oriental Research*
BibRes	*Biblical Research*
BR	*Bible Review*
BTB	*Biblical Theology Bulletin*
CA	*Current Anthropology*
CBQ	*Catholic Biblical Quarterly*
HST	Rudolf Bultmann, *History of the Synoptic Tradition*
HTR	*Harvard Theological Review*
HUCA	Hebrew Union College Annual
IDB	*Interpreter's Dictionary of the Bible*
IEJ	*Israel Exploration Journal*
JAAR	*Journal of the American Academy of Religion*
JBL	*Journal of Biblical Literature*
JBibRel	*Journal of Bible and Religion*

JJS	*Journal of Jewish Studies*
JR	*Journal of Religion*
JRS	*Journal of Roman Studies*
JSNT	*Journal for the Study of the New Testament*
LCL	Loeb Classical Library
Life	Josephus, *The Life*
LuthQ	*Lutheran Quarterly*
NTS	*New Testament Studies*
NovT	*Novum Testamentum*
PacTheolRev	*Pacific Theological Review*
PEQ	*Palestine Exploration Quarterly*
PJ	*Perkins Journal*
PrinSem Bull	Princeton Seminary Bulletin
RL	*Religion in Life*
SBLSP	Society of Biblical Literature Seminar Papers
SBT	Studies in Biblical Theology
SJT	*Scottish Journal of Theology*
T&L	*Theology and Life*
TDNT	G. Kittel and G. Friedrich, eds., *Theological Dictionary of the New Testament*
TheolRev	*Theological Review*
TheolToday	*Theology Today*
TrinitySemRev	*Trinity Seminary Review*
TS	*Theological Studies*
USQR	*Union Seminary Quarterly Review*
War	Josephus, *The Jewish War*

PART 1

The Continuing Quest for the Historical Jesus

Since the author of the Gospel of Mark sat down to write a story of Jesus' public work, church leaders have been engaged in the quest for the historical Jesus. Since the Enlightenment the church has been joined by others who share their curiosity about Jesus, if not their beliefs. It would be impossible for any study of the historical Jesus to ignore this long and venerable tradition in the church and outside the church.

Part 1 of this study contains three chapters. Chapter 1 surveys the scholarly quest for the historical Jesus, as it has unfolded during the course of the twentieth century. It develops a convenient typology for organizing the efforts of the past century. The "old quest," sometimes called the first quest, began in 1778 and lasted until 1906, when Schweitzer published his epoch-making study of it. The "old quest" was succeeded by a period called "the no quest," since scholars, discouraged by Schweitzer's outlook, abandoned the attempt to seek the historical Jesus and turned their efforts to defining the kerygma (preaching) of the early church. The skepticism did not last, and a "new quest" for the historical Jesus was launched in the early 1950s. It was followed, in turn, by a "third quest," beginning in the 1970s and continuing to the present.

Chapter 2 examines the models and methods used in the current quest. The chapter includes a discussion of the so-called criteria of authenticity and asks how these criteria are influenced by larger models for understanding who Jesus was. It would seem that the larger gestalt that researchers bring to their task exercises a significant influence on the way they evaluate the bits and pieces of the Jesus tradition.

This is why chapter 3 proposes to view Jesus as a prophet of the justice of the reign of God, and through this gestalt, to approach the materials of the Synoptic tradition. This way of proceeding is contrary to the supposedly inductive method of evaluating Gospel materials made popular by the Jesus Seminar and used by scholars throughout this century.

Taken together, the three chapters lay the groundwork for the interpretation of Jesus that will inform the remainder of this study.

1

The "Third Quest" in Context

The current scholarly discussion of the historical Jesus has been called "the third search for the Jew of Nazareth,"[1] and, like most scholarly conversations, it has a distinctive history, in this case one that spans the twentieth century. In the first decade of this century, Albert Schweitzer announced the death of the quest for the historical Jesus and wrote its obituary.[2] After Schweitzer completed his survey of the "first quest," no one from Hermann Reimarus to Wilhelm Wrede had to ask for whom the bell tolled; it tolled for anyone foolhardy enough to attempt the impossible quest. Yet, during the final three decades of this same century, scholars have resumed the once moribund quest, suggesting a paraphrase of Mark Twain's famous line, "reports of its death have been greatly exaggerated." How could such a reversal have occurred?

The answer to that question can be found, in part, by tracing the four distinctive stages through which scholarly interest in Jesus has passed from Schweitzer to the present. The first quest, which lasted from 1778 through 1901, was eulogized by Schweitzer in 1906. From 1906 to 1953, in the German world and on the continent generally, the quest was, for all practical purposes, abandoned in favor of a search for the kerygma of the early church. This has been called the period of the "no quest" for the historical Jesus.[3] But, beginning in 1953 and lasting for a decade and a half, German scholars launched a "new quest for the historical Jesus"[4] which expired shortly after it had made its singular but limited contribution to the ongoing discussion. Just when it seemed that the new quest had reached a dead end, North American scholars launched a third quest beginning around 1970, but becoming a major movement from 1980 to the present. Since these first three epochs form the context for the current discussion of the historical Jesus, it will be useful to survey their results.

1906: THE QUEST FOR THE HISTORICAL JESUS AND THE DISCOVERY OF THE APOCALYPTIC JESUS

In 1906, Albert Schweitzer published one of the most influential books of the twentieth century. The stated purpose of the work was to trace "the attempt to form a historical conception of the life of Jesus" beginning with Hermann Samuel Reimarus's work, *The Goal of Jesus and His Disciples* (1778), and concluding with Wilhelm Wrede's work, *The Messianic Secret in the Gospels* (1901).[5] Those dates, 1778–1901, defined the first era of scholarly efforts to identify the aim and purpose of the life of Jesus, shorn of church doctrine and pious trappings. When Schweitzer's book was translated into English in 1910, its publisher entitled it *The Quest of the Historical Jesus,* and since its appearance, the English title of Schweitzer's work has come to describe a distinctive area of New Testament studies.

Schweitzer's achievement was to provide an interpretive framework for understanding the initial quest for the historical Jesus while defining its persistent and unresolved hermeneutical impasses. Reduced to its essentials, the first quest had discovered and defined three crucial issues, posed in the form of alternatives. David Friedrich Strauss had proposed the first, "either purely historical or purely supernatural"; the Tübingen School and Heinrich Holtzmann had proposed the second, "either the Synoptics or John," while Johannes Weiss, Wrede, and Schweitzer had together defined the third, "either eschatological or uneschatological."[6] For Schweitzer, the third was by far the most significant, because the greatest obstacle blocking the road to understanding the historical Jesus was the tendency to spiritualize Jewish eschatology, thereby assimilating it to the liberal spirit of the age and, in the process, stripping it of its unique explanatory power. In essence, therefore, all three alternatives finally met in the last one, according to Schweitzer.

> There is, on the one hand, the eschatological solution, which at one stroke, raises the Marcan account as it stands, with all its disconnectedness and inconsistencies, into genuine history; and there is, on the other hand, the literary solution, which regards the incongruous dogmatic element as interpolated by the earliest Evangelist into the tradition and therefore strikes out the Messianic claim altogether from the life of Jesus. (337)

To spiritualize the eschatological Jesus was to replace the historical Jesus with "a construction artificially planted into history"(309) in order to suit the tastes of the interpreter and present a Jesus compatible with the spirit of the age. By contrast, to reconstruct the historical Jesus on the bedrock of his eschatological proclamation was to create a figure who would inevitably be a "stranger and an enigma" to the modern age. This authentic Jesus "passes by our time and returns to His own" but remains significant for us because of the "mighty spiritual force that streams forth from Him and flows through our time also" (399).

Schweitzer's solution created something like a psychotic break between the historical Jesus and the mystical Jesus whose spirit continually encounters us in history. The historical Jesus was a deluded and self-deceived apocalyptic fanatic who thought he could by the sheer exercise of his will force God's hand and create a new age. Schweitzer's vivid description bears repeating, for it has lost none of its shocking power.

> There is silence all around. The Baptist appears and cries: "Repent, for the kingdom of heaven is at hand." Soon after that comes Jesus and in the knowledge that he is the coming Son of Man lays hold of the wheel of the world to set it moving on that last revolution which is to bring all ordinary history to a close. It refuses to turn, and he throws himself upon it. Then it does turn; and crushes him. Instead of bringing in the eschatological conditions; He has destroyed them. The wheel rolls onward, and the mangled body of the one immeasurably great Man, who was strong enough to think of Himself as the spiritual ruler of humankind and to bend history to His purpose, is hanging upon it still. That is his victory and His reign. (370f).

Thus ends the historical Jesus, but it is not the historical Jesus who is important for Schweitzer; rather it is "Jesus as spiritually arisen within men [and women] who is significant for our time" (401). This is the Jesus who meets us as he met the disciples of old by the lake and calls us to follow, and as we pass through the toils of that journey we shall enter into his "ineffable mystery" and learn who he is (403). The appeal is to a form of Jesus mysticism. It is as though, for Schweitzer, retelling the story of the historical Jesus in all its unvarnished truth would liberate the enormous but misguided energy of Jesus so that it could survive his death and continue to touch men and women throughout history.

Schweitzer's volume accomplished far more than summarizing the results of the first quest for the historical Jesus and critiquing them by focusing on their inadequate handling of the problem of eschatology. In a small introductory chapter innocently entitled "The Problem," Schweitzer identified the three persistent hermeneutical difficulties that continue to stalk and haunt the quest to the present day (1–12). First, he noted the self-involving nature of the study.

> Thus each successive epoch of theology found its own thoughts in Jesus: that was indeed the only way it could make Him live. But it was not only that each epoch found its reflection in Jesus; each individual created him in accordance with his [or her] own

character. There is no historical task which so reveals a [person's] true self as the writing of a Life of Jesus. (4)

All historical research involves projection, but none more so than the attempt to write a life of Jesus. No interpreters of the historical Jesus can afford to ignore the degree to which their study reflects their own internalized values, convictions, and perspectives. Objectivity is not possible in historical Jesus studies. In turn, this problem was compounded by a second, the use of the study of the historical Jesus to subvert the power of ecclesiastical hierarchies that controlled orthodox views of Jesus and punished dissent. Or, as Schweitzer put it, the quest "turned to the Jesus of history as an ally in the struggle against the tyranny of dogma" (4). In other words, the quest was, from the beginning, both historical inquiry and political polemic, and it was as inherently agenda-laden as it was iconoclastic. This explains why so many lives of Jesus were seen as radical documents, and why so many lives were constructed upon an unformulated version of "the criterion of dissimilarity."[7] The more offensive and outrageous a portrayal of Jesus was, the more likely it was to be historically true. The very historical context in which the quest arose either encouraged the writing of radical lives or intimidated researchers into writing domesticated lives of Jesus aimed at mollifying the demands of ecclesial orthodoxy while retouching the evangelical portraits found in the Gospels.

Finally, Schweitzer identified a third equally complex problem, the nature of the sources, the Synoptic Gospels, on which the quest was based. The Gospels reveal two tendencies, neither of which helps the historian. First, they lack "any thread of connexion in the material which they offer us,"[8] an insight that anticipated the results of form criticism. Instead, they seem to be composed of strings of anecdotes in place of a connected and coherent narrative. This led Schweitzer to pose the third problem:

> From these materials, we can only get a Life of Jesus with yawning gaps. How are these gaps to be filled? At the worst with phrases, at the best with historical imagination. There is really no other means of arriving at the order and inner connexion of the facts of the life of Jesus than the making and testing of hypotheses. (7)

But the problem is not merely with the disconnected and anecdotal nature of the sources. To make matters worse, the Gospels reveal a second tendency. They are infused with their own messianic reading of Jesus' life, even though sober historical assessments of Jesus had concluded that he exhibited no messianic consciousness. This dilemma requires that historians form a conception of Jesus that uses the Gospel materials but shows how Jesus could have acted "otherwise than as the Evangelists describe" (10–11). Such a course of action could only be pursued through the use of the historical imagination, and this is what Schweitzer believed he had accomplished by his thoroughgoing eschatological reading of the historical Jesus.

However, Schweitzer was not primarily interested in supplanting earlier liberal lives of Jesus with his own. His project was much more radical; it intended to repudiate all reconstructions of the historical Jesus because they all finally reduced Jesus to the size of the age in which they were done and actually erected a barrier between the will of the spiritual Jesus and the present age.[9] This is why his book ends on the note it does. Having shown the futility of all reconstructions of the historical Jesus, Schweitzer can present the spiritual Jesus risen in the experience of men and women, an intuitive appeal based on the ethical vitality of Jesus, which is capable of renewing the will even of modern men and women living in a degenerate age.[10] Seen in this light, Schweitzer's study intended the demise of all further quests of the historical Jesus.

Schweitzer's work intended to discredit all further attempts to write a life of Jesus because the "lives of Jesus" so produced made Jesus conform to the canons of modern psychology. In this way, they created a believable Jesus who could inhabit the world of nineteenth century Europe by sharing the worldview and religious outlook of other moderns. To make Jesus in their image, his liberal interpreters had to reconstruct the course of his inner life and development as well as explain his behavior. It was this effort that Schweitzer hoped to put to an end because it necessarily reduced Jesus to the lowest common denominator and utterly disguised or repressed his apocalyptic intensity. The very task of writing a biography of Jesus was flawed by virtue of the assumptions made by the biographer.[11] To demonstrate the futility of that task, Schweitzer wrote a "biography" of Jesus that presented him as an alien in a bizarre world of fanatic zeal and fantastic expectations, an actor in his own drama guided by a script so distant from modern worldviews and philosophies that it effectively isolated Jesus from the world of bourgeois values and banal moralism. He wrote the biography that would shatter all future biographies, the life of Jesus that would render all future lives of Jesus irrelevant or domesticated frauds, and his study of the first quest had provided him with a model for this very project in the work of Reimarus.

In Reimarus, Schweitzer found a student of the historical Jesus who was able to use the Gospel traditions to sketch a Jesus who acted otherwise than as the Gospel writers describe, a Jesus whose mission was entirely natural, not supernatural. Reimarus may have dismissed the apocalyptic elements, but he still provided the model Schweitzer needed.

After Schweitzer, scholars would routinely disclaim any attempt to write a "life of Jesus" or biography of Jesus. They knew the materials of the Synoptic tradition would not permit it, and they knew that such attempts would merely impose some other form of modern psychological understandings on Jesus. But this dismissal still left open important questions stimulated by Schweitzer's own reconstruction. Was it possible to reconstruct the teachings of Jesus, however strange they might sound to the modern ear? Was it possible to construct scenarios other than the one Schweitzer had created for understanding Jesus' public actions and teachings? If one could not compose a full biography, could one reconstruct the public work and activity of Jesus? How was one to interpret the apocalyptic or eschatological elements of the Gospel traditions? Was Schweitzer's reading definitive and final?

1906–1953: THE ABANDONED QUEST FOR THE HISTORICAL JESUS AND THE SEARCH FOR THE KERYGMA OF THE EARLY CHURCH

Schweitzer's description of the problem and his thoroughgoing eschatological solution were discouraging enough to dissuade two generations of scholars from continuing the quest. The period of the "old quest" was replaced by a period called the "no quest," extending from the publication of Schweitzer's book to the early 1950s. The period of the "no quest" was dominated by Rudolf Bultmann, whose work brought together the practice of form criticism, the hermeneutics of demythologizing, and the application of existentialist philosophy to interpret the Gospel traditions. Three works established the basic premise of this period of Jesus studies. In 1919, Martin Dibelius published *From Tradition to Gospel*, and two years later Bultmann published his masterful study, *History of the Synoptic Tradition*.[12] Both works applied the tools of form criticism to the Jesus traditions. The results of their studies confirmed Schweitzer's apprehension about the nature of the Synoptic Gospels. They were little more than collections of oral traditions written down and reshaped to speak to the issues of the early church. In their present form, Dibelius and Bultmann concluded, the Synoptic materials conveyed almost nothing about the historical Jesus. The Jesus who appeared in them was little more than a cipher for the concerns of the early church, and the debates found in the Gospels were anachronistic retrojections of the debates of the early church onto the ministry of Jesus. The third work that contributed to defining the task was Karl Ludwig Schmidt's *Der Rahmen der Geschichte Jesu* (1919; never translated into English but bearing the title, *The Framework of the History of Jesus*).[13] Schmidt concluded that all the connective tissue in the Gospel accounts was the product of the evangelists themselves and, as such, it reflected their efforts to connect isolated pericopes in order to write a coherent narrative. However, if the connections were the creations of the Gospel writers, then it was impossible to know anything more than individual pericopes of the Jesus tradition. No chronology was possible since the connecting framework was a later fabrication, not a reflection of historical sequence, and without chronology it was impossible to construct a biography or life of Jesus. Schmidt's work reinforced what Dibelius had already argued: the Gospels were examples of *kleines Literatur,* or folk literature, not the kind of sources from which history is fashioned.[14] In the view of the early form critics, the evangelists were less authors than collectors of anecdotes and other bits and pieces of oral tradition that they strung together or stitched together using either perfunctory phrases or stock summaries devoid of historical value. All of this meant that it was impossible to use the Gospels as historical sources for discovering the historical Jesus. Going even further, the work of these figures demolished the two-source hypothesis on which the original quest had been built, namely, the priority of Mark and the importance of Q, the sayings source behind Matthew and Luke, but their work particularly undermined any confidence in Mark and the historical framework that his Gospel seemed to provide. C. H. Dodd argued that the Markan framework, relying as it did on prior tradition, does represent "in broad lines . . . a genuine succession of events," even if one could not discern "the precise sequence of the narrative in detail."[15]

Instead of viewing the Gospels as historical sources for a life of Jesus, Bultmann and his disciples saw them as sources for reconstructing the kerygma, or preaching, of the early church. The word *kerygma* came to have two meanings: (1) the act of preaching in the early church; and (2) the content of that preaching.[16] Both are implied throughout this discussion. The important point to note is that the research of the form critics had produced a conundrum. As Schweitzer had shown, the historical Jesus had proclaimed an apocalyptic gospel announcing the end of the world while the early church proclaimed a Risen Lord reigning at the right hand of glory. In Ernst Käsemann's apt phrase, "the preaching of Jesus [became] the preaching about Jesus,"[17] or the proclaimer became the proclaimed. In light of this, the no-questers saw only discontinuity and distance between Jesus of Nazareth and the Christ of the church. This disjunction became even more evident when the teaching of Jesus was examined closely. He was, as Schweitzer had guessed, a Jewish apocalypticist whose proclamation was confined to the alien thought world of a distant time. It was simply not possible to build a bridge between the proclamation of Jesus and the kerygma of the early church.

This premise dominated the period of the "no quest," from 1906 through the early 1950s. In 1926, Bultmann did write a volume simply entitled *Jesus* (1926), published in America under the title *Jesus and the Word* (1934).[18] But he made it clear in his introduction on "view point and method" that his work was no attempt to return to the task of finding the historical Jesus.

> I do indeed think that we can now know almost nothing concerning the life and personality of Jesus, since the early Christian sources show no interest in either, are moreover fragmentary and often legendary; and other sources about Jesus do not exist. (8)

After Schweitzer's critique of previous attempts to write a life of Jesus, Bultmann knew that no biography of Jesus could be written without recreating Jesus in the author's own image. But by shifting his attention to reproducing the teaching of Jesus, Bultmann hoped to avoid the trap that had ensnared earlier interpreters. The novel effort produced familiar results, and Bultmann's work quite predictably reconfirmed the validity of Schweitzer's insight, as the following summary will show.

When Bultmann turned to Jesus' teachings, he discovered in them the dead words of a Jewish apocalypticist that could be revivified if they were demythologized and re-presented as an interpretation of human existence. In this way, Jesus' teachings became an ancient version of Martin Heidegger's existentialist philosophy expressed through the mythological worldview of first-century Palestine. So the kingdom of God that Jesus proclaimed was neither apocalyptic speculation (contra Wrede and Schweitzer) nor the highest value of humankind (contra classic liberal theology), but the wholly other that confronts us in the moment and demands decision, "decision between good and evil, decision for God's will or [one's] own will" (84). The decision required of humans arises from the fact they stand before God, unable to draw on the resources of their past and incapable of charting a future course. However, in the crisis of decision, people can still comprehend what is demanded in the concrete moment and obey, much as the Samaritan did on the Jericho road. Since each decision is an all-or-nothing choice, Jesus teaches neither individual nor social ethics; indeed, "he teaches no ethics at all" (84). Jesus has neither a doctrine of duty nor a definition of right.

This can only mean that the kingdom of God is "no ideal social order. Subversive ideas and revolutionary utterances are lacking in Jesus" (103). Jesus was indifferent to all political, social, and economic conditions because they simply detract people's attention from the necessity of decision in which they stand at each moment of their lives. Jesus unswervingly calls people to the necessity of decision for authentic or inauthentic existence in the now, the present moment, suspended between past and future alike. This was his proclamation.

As even this brief summary reveals, Bultmann managed to construct a form of the kerygma compatible with his evaluation of the Gospel traditions. If the tradition cannot be reconstructed beyond the individual pericope or unit of tradition, that is sufficient, for each Gospel pericope can still contain isolated glimpses of the moment in which human beings face the crisis of decision. As each moment of decision is detached from past and future, so each unit of Gospel tradition is detached from what precedes and what follows. Indeed, each story or saying can convey the same existential necessity, and to do so, nothing more than an individual unit of tradition is needed.

Although he failed in his effort to present the teachings of Jesus, Bultmann did create a Jesus for his own time. Bultmann's Jesus no longer walks the countryside and villages of rural Galilee but steps into the alienated landscape, devastated cities, and horrendous battlefields of Europe after the great war to end all wars. It may well be that people living in the interregnum between the rubble of the nineteenth century and the unknown world of the twentieth century stood in a moment of decision, unable either to recall a glad past or to conjure a hopeful future, but the people of Palestine lived differently. They lived in a world dominated by the memory of their past enacted in the pilgrimage festivals in the temple each year or captured in prophetic traditions like those about Elijah and Elisha and their hopeful anticipation for the future enshrined in their sacred texts. Perhaps the people of postwar Europe could construct neither personal nor social ethics, but Jesus lived in a world where the Torah of Moses and the social vision of the prophets supplied both. Bultmann's Jesus was, as Schweitzer could have predicted, created in the image of Bultmann and his contemporaries to inhabit the Europe of the 1920s, the era of the lost generation. This situation is captured poignantly by Friedrich Gogarten's essay, "Between the Times" (German, "Zwischen den Zeiten," 1920), in which he writes:

> It is the fate of our generation that we stand between the times. We never belonged to the time that is today reaching its end. Will we ever belong to the time that will come? . . . The times fell apart and now time stands still. It is here that the decision must be made.[19]

Bultmann's effort to avoid the problem seen so clearly by Schweitzer had failed, and it would be thirty years before a major German scholar would again try to write a critical study of Jesus. The silence of the "no quest" period would continue almost without interruption except in England, where scholars such as William Manson and Vincent Taylor, among others, would continue to write full-length studies of the historical Jesus using form criticism as an ally in the task of sifting and sorting the Gospel traditions.[20]

During the "no quest" period, scholars generally assumed that the quest for the historical Jesus was invalid because it was pursued primarily for the purpose of writing "lives of Jesus," and Schweitzer had demolished the epistemological foundation on which such lives had been based. When Bultmann published his study of Jesus, he created the possibility of undertaking a more modest task, explicating the teachings of the historical Jesus, even though this more limited task was subject to the same hermeneutical pitfalls that attended the attempt to write lives of Jesus. Yet even the more limited attempt to study aspects of the historical Jesus was viewed with suspicion because scholars assumed a radical historical discontinuity between the historical Jesus and the theology of the early church, a discontinuity so great that it amounted to an impassable chasm and an insurmountable problem. It seemed to many as though form criticism led directly to historical skepticism, that is, until Joachim Jeremias changed the terms of the debate. If form criticism could be used to show that the Gospel traditions contained the theology of the early church, it could also be used as a guide for identifying materials that traced to the historical Jesus. Toward the close of the no-quest period, Jeremias published his groundbreaking study, *Parables of Jesus,* which used form criticism as a tool for unearthing the words of the historical Jesus.[21] In a chapter that shared the title of Schweitzer's famous chapter, "The Problem," Jeremias argued that each parable reflects a specific situation in the ministry of Jesus and "hence to recover this is the task before us."[22] In part 2 of his study, Jeremias detailed the pitfalls involved in that task, and in part 3, he applied the method to the study of specific parables.

After Jeremias, it was no longer possible to assume that form criticism revealed only discontinuity between the historical Jesus and the shaping of his words by the early church. A path of continuity could be traced so clearly that it was possible to discern the shadowy figure of Jesus of Nazareth even in the Gospel materials that expressed his significance for the early church. Using the very historical-critical tool that had been used to demolish the quest, Jeremias had laid the foundation for resuming it. Of course, Jeremias was not the lone figure arguing the case. Dodd's study of the parables had made a similar argument twelve years earlier,[23] but Jeremias had shown in more painstaking detail how the method worked to yield results different from those envisioned by Dibelius and Bultmann. There were other problems with the historical skepticism promulgated by Bultmann, and his students were beginning to reflect on them. The absolute disjuncture between the historical Jesus and the Christ of faith, posited by Bultmann, disturbed his students and led directly to the next phase of historical Jesus studies. The silence was nearly over.

1953–1970: THE NEW QUEST FOR THE HISTORICAL JESUS AND THE DISCOVERY OF THE EXISTENTIALIST JESUS

When the silence was finally broken in the 1950s, it was at first by only one or two voices crying in the wilderness. What was significant was not that the voices were finally speaking but whose voices they were. All of them were students of Bultmann, the master of the silence imposed on the period of the "no quest." In 1953, Ernst Käsemann presented a paper to a gathering of "old Marburgers," former students of Bultmann. He entitled his remarks, "The Problem of the Historical Jesus."[24] The problem, he noted, lies in the fact that the Gospels that offer us the historical Jesus do so only through the medium of the kerygma, the preaching of the early church. This means that all of our sources are compromised as historical sources. But, even in the face of these difficulties, it would be unthinkable to abandon the search for the historical Jesus, because to do so would be to unmoor the kerygma from history and retreat into mythology. The outcome would be not only the loss of the historical Jesus but the gain of a docetic imposter in his place, clearly an intolerable situation for the church.

But where do the kerygma of the early church and historical words of Jesus come together, and how is it possible to move from the former to the latter? Käsemann proposed to examine the first, second, and fourth antitheses of the Sermon on the Mount as a test case for solving this dilemma (Matt. 5:21–30, 38–42). The antitheses fulfill the criterion of dissimilarity, because they exceed the claims of any rabbi. The criterion of dissimilarity asserts that sayings of Jesus are more likely to be authentic when they contain materials found in neither the Judaism of Jesus' day nor the theology of the early church. When Jesus says, "but I say unto you," he makes an implicit claim to supersede both Moses and the Torah. No rabbi could make this claim and remain a rabbi. These sayings, therefore, must stamp Jesus as something more, and that "something more" became the basis of the kerygma, the proclaimer became the proclaimed, "the preaching of Jesus" became "the preaching about Jesus" (20). In this way, Käsemann explains how the teachings of Jesus could form the basis of the kerygma of the early church, or how a narrow path of continuity could be carved out of a forest of discontinuity. Käsemann devoted less attention to the other test of the criterion of dissimilarity, namely, that the teaching of Jesus should also differ from the teaching of the early church, because to do so would have imperiled his project, for if the teaching of Jesus were not found in the teaching of early Christianity, it would be impossible to establish the connection between Jesus' words and the kerygma of the church. The "something more" had to count as establishing the dissimilarity between Jesus and the early church while providing a bridge on which he could move from one to the other.

In spite of the troubles mentioned, Käsemann had taken a subtle, but noteworthy, step beyond Bultmann, who deemed it impossible to peer behind the kerygma to find enough of the historical Jesus to make such a step either practical or productive. Käsemann thought it possible to identify teachings of Jesus so distinctive that they became the basis of the kerygma itself. As Käsemann put it, "we must look for the distinctive element of the earthly Jesus in his preaching and interpret both his other activities and his destiny in light of this preaching" (44). To summarize using Käsemann's own memorable phrase, "history is only accessible to us through tradition and comprehensible to us through interpretation" (18). Once the tradition had been identified, Käsemann could apply his existential interpretation to the tradition to disclose its understanding of existence.

In spite of his tentative efforts to discern glimpses of the historical Jesus, Käsemann was quick to disclaim any attempt to construct a life of Jesus. It was adequate, he surmised, to be able to recapture enough of the historical Jesus to save the kerygma from docetism. This was an urgent assignment because a gospel without a historical Jesus was an anonymous gospel that would produce moralism or mysticism, but little else. The particularity of the gospel remained an important issue, as did the centering of that particularity on Jesus of Nazareth.

Three years after Käsemann ventured his tentative suggestions, a second Marburger, Ernst Fuchs, delivered a lecture at the University of Zurich entitled "The Question of the Historical Jesus."[25] Following a path somewhat different from the one proposed by Käsemann, Fuchs proposed to ground knowledge of the historical Jesus in a correlation between his conduct and teachings. For example, Fuchs found in the parable of the prodigal son (Luke 15:11–32) an attempt by Jesus to defend his own conduct in receiving sinners and enjoying table companionship with them. Read in this way, the parable implies that "Jesus' conduct explains the will of God, by means of a parable drawn from that very conduct" (53). Jesus conducts himself as though he were acting in God's stead, a form of behavior so audacious that he was eventually put to death. It is not difficult to detect in Fuchs's argument the influence of Jeremias's interpretation of the parables of Jesus.

Unlike Käsemann, who sought to find the basis for the kerygma in Jesus' distinctive teaching, Fuchs looked to Jesus' distinctive conduct to provide the "framework of his proclamation" (21). Fuchs then located places in the Gospels where he could find congruence between Jesus' words and conduct. When he put these pieces together, he found that Jesus was neither a prophet nor a wisdom teacher but a man who acts in God's place by drawing sinners to himself. Jesus demands repentance of his hearers in the moment of decision and, in this way, grasped "the time of the rule of God in a new way; he could attempt to make the time of the rule of God his own" (23).

Six months after Fuchs delivered his guest lecture at the University of Zurich (May 25, 1956), Günther Bornkamm, a professor of New Testament Exegesis at Heidelberg University, published the first, and only, book-length study of the historical Jesus to come out of the new quest. It was entitled simply *Jesus of Nazareth*.[26] In many ways, it was unremarkable. It organized the teachings of Jesus into familiar themes, such as the reign of God, the call to repentance, the nature of the will of God, and the call and demands of discipleship. Perhaps his most significant chapter is one least noted. It was called "Period and Environment," and it devoted about twenty-five pages to explicating the context of Jesus' public work, focusing on the situation of the Jewish people—their religion, factions, and movements—and the figure of John the Baptist.

Once Bornkamm settled into the task of presenting Jesus, however, his synthesis seemed less than original, and he began to echo familiar themes. Even his attempt to place Jesus in the setting of first-century Galilee reflects a well-worn theme.

> Thus the world in which Jesus appears is a world between past and future; it is so strongly identified with the one and with the other that . . . the immediate present is practically non-existent. . . . All time is time between. (55)

In this world caught between past and future, Jesus brings a message of unprecedented immediacy and embodies an unmistakable otherness. Neither fixated on past traditions nor preoccupied by future speculation, Jesus alone restores the power of the present by bringing the unmediated presence of God in word and deed. As Bornkamm puts it:

> To make the reality of God present: this is the essential mystery of Jesus. This making-present of the reality of God signifies the end of the world in which it takes place. This is why the scribes and Pharisees rebel, because they see Jesus' teaching as a revolutionary attack upon law and tradition. This is why the demons cry out, because they sense an inroad upon their sphere of power "before the time" (Mt. viii, 29). This is why his own people think him mad (Mk. iii, 21). The story told by the Gospels signifies the end of the world, although not, it is true, in the sense of an obvious drama and a visible catastrophe. (62)

Bornkamm then surveys the types of characters in the Gospels who approach Jesus, from scribes and Pharisees to lepers and demoniacs, noting what they all have in common.

> In each case a world has come to its end, be it for salvation or judgment. Its past is called into question. Its future [is] no longer secure. . . . Its time has ended. . . . In the encounter with Jesus, time is left to no one; the past whence he comes is no longer confirmed, and the future he dreams of no longer assured. But this is precisely why every individual is granted his own new present. (62–63)

From this yarn, Bornkamm spins his version of the familiar tale of the existential Jesus whose understanding of existence became the basis of the kerygma of the early church.

Bornkamm's Jesus, like the Jesus identified by Käsemann and Fuchs, was an apolitical existentialist. Bornkamm's study was released during the height of the Cold War, and in a section devoted to the new righteousness found in the Sermon on the Mount, he pauses to explain why Jesus directed his remarks against those who would try to contain his new teaching in old political wineskins. Jesus directed his teachings against

> the front of fanatics who wish to claim Jesus for their own as a great revolutionary, as a prophet of a new world order, as the bringer of a new era, to which must be sacrificed all that has gone before . . . they are obsessed by a picture of the future of the world. (101–2)

Bornkamm then proceeds to excoriate Marxists and Bolshevists for daring to appropriate Jesus for their agenda. It was enough that Jesus called for decision in the moment. No prophetic impulse was required.

In 1959, James M. Robinson published the scholarly monograph that summarized the emergence of this new movement among the intellectual inheritors of the Bultmannian tradition. He titled his work *A New Quest of the Historical Jesus,* and in it he sought to summarize the intent of the "new quest," while distinguishing it from the old.[27] Unlike the old quest, which was built upon a fallacious nineteenth-century historiography, the new quest is made possible by the startling coincidence that one can find in the indisputably authentic materials of the Jesus tradition (as determined by form criticism) an understanding of Jesus' selfhood and historical existence analogous to that found in the kerygma itself. This congruence grows directly out of the demythologizing of the kerygma, so that "in the process of demythologizing, the objectified language of the kerygma loses its own concreteness, and becomes, so to speak, transparent, so that its existential meaning can be grasped" (80). Once the understanding of existence proclaimed in the kerygma has been grasped, it is possible to turn to the Gospel traditions and scrutinize the authentic Jesus materials by disengaging them from their kerygmatic coloring. As one must demythologize the kerygma, so one must dekerygmatize the Gospel traditions in order to remove the interpretive hand of the early church. But since the kerygma is framed in mythological terms as fully as are Jesus' teachings, the two tasks amount to much the same thing and yield much the same results. Having arrived at "an understanding of Jesus' historical action and existential selfhood," one can compare it to the kerygma itself (94). When one does, one discovers a common understanding of existence in the moment, although it can be stated in familiar Christian language. Robinson summarizes the vision of Christian existence in the following way:

Grace continues to reside in judgment, life in death, revelation in historical ambiguity. It is in this dialectical movement from the old [person] to the new that one finds the distinctive characteristic of Christian existence. (98)

One can illustrate this method by examining the passion predictions in the Gospels (Mark 8:31; 9:31; 10:33f. and par.). There they are portrayed as Jesus' own words, although they actually are the later interpretations of his death by the early church. But they still reveal an understanding of Christian existence:

Thus the deeper meaning of Jesus' message is: in accepting one's death there is life for others; in suffering there is glory; in submitting to judgment one finds grace; in accepting one's finitude resides the only transcendence. (123)

The Easter event was "the revelation of Jesus' transcendent selfhood to his disciples," and as a result of Easter, the selfhood of Jesus was translated into the kerygma.

Robinson believed that the hermeneutical path traced above was made possible by a remarkable coincidence or stroke of good fortune.

The kind of material that the 'kerygmatizing' process would leave *unaltered* is the kind of material which fits best the needs of research based upon the modern view of history and the self. For the kerygmatic interest of the primitive Church would leave unaltered precisely those sayings and scenes in which Jesus made his intention and understanding of existence most apparent to them. (69)

Although it evidently did not occur to Robinson, it is equally possible to suggest that an interpreter engaged in demythologizing the kerygma and dekerygmatizing the Gospel traditions using the same lens provided by Heidegger's existentialism might reasonably be expected to find that same philosophical outlook in both bodies of New Testament materials. The coincidence can be traced less to the nature of the materials than to the unified philosophical outlook of the interpreter. So the unity is found in the prior commitment of the interpreter, not in the peculiar nature of the materials themselves. Robinson made Schweitzer, once again, look like a prophet. Hermeneutically speaking, the scholars of the new quest failed to escape the pitfalls of the old quest; they simply changed the terms of engagement from German liberal theology to German existential philosophy.

By 1960, the terms of the debate had been set, but the decade of the '60s was devoted to arguing the details, not enlarging the synthesis. Bornkamm's work remained the only major study of the historical Jesus to emerge from the movement known as the "new quest," and, by the late 1960s, the inability of the movement to generate any serious or substantial studies of the historical Jesus was evident. The new quest was becoming old hat. The burst of activity seemed to have accomplished nothing more than hardening the debate between the continuing advocates of the old quest, such as Ethelbert Stauffer and Jeremias, and the proponents of the new quest. The quest for the historical Jesus had stalled once again.[28]

In part, the movement stalled because it had narrowed its interest in the historical Jesus almost to a point, the place where the teachings of the historical Jesus and the kerygma intersected, or the point where one could infer the one from the other. The new quest needed only enough of the historical Jesus to insure the possibility of contact between kerygma and Jesus. It was the theological import of the historical Jesus that interested the advocates of the new quest. As Käsemann's work on the antitheses suggests, it was less the content of Jesus' teachings that mattered than the "something more" that could be inferred from them. This strategy reduced interest in the historical Jesus to a minimum. However, Käsemann and Fuchs had provided alternative ways to approach the minimalist historical Jesus, Käsemann following the traditional path through his teaching while Fuchs charted another course beginning with Jesus' "conduct" or actions. Both of these paths would be pursued in the third quest.

Finally, Bornkamm had demonstrated that it was feasible to pursue a full-length study of Jesus of Nazareth without resorting to writing a biography or life of Jesus. Although his work was largely a restatement of familiar theological themes and existential insights, it provided a model for undertaking a study of the larger scope of the historical Jesus, and however incompletely, Bornkamm's study recognized the importance of contextualizing Jesus in his "period and environment," an issue that would become a major theme of the third quest. Nonetheless, Bornkamm's work also illustrated the liability of providing an interpretation of Jesus compatible with modern perspectives, and in the process, revealed just how distorting the lens of existentialism could be, because, in a single stroke, it divorced Jesus from his Jewish environment and the political, social, and economic realities of his world. If his Jesus fit the "criterion of dissimilarity," he did so at the unacceptable cost of being removed from the world in which he lived. In this respect, Bornkamm revealed the risk involved in advancing any contemporary interpretation of Jesus; it may produce nothing more than another anachronistic reading of Jesus.

1970–PRESENT: THE THIRD QUEST FOR THE HISTORICAL JESUS, DIVERSE METHODS, AND A FRAGMENTED SYNTHESIS

The origins of what has come to be known as the "third quest" for the historical Jesus are not easily traced.[29] The mid-1960s through the mid-1970s served as a bridge between the end of the new quest and the beginning of the third quest, and during this decade, it is possible to find precursors to many of the issues that would emerge more clearly after 1980. Yet it was possible for Leander Keck to summarize the tenor of the times and necessary for him to justify his concerns for the future of the historical Jesus by observing, "it may readily appear foolhardy to propose that the future lies with the historical Jesus, for it is widely assumed that 'the search for the real Jesus' . . . is a dead-end street."[30] In the middle of the transitional decade, the movement toward a renascence of interest in Jesus was not obvious to all, perhaps not even to many, but the sterility of the new quest was evident to most observers.

Jesus and the Zealots: A Preview of Coming Attractions

Not all was quiet on the Western front of biblical studies. The decade did witness one major debate, which was triggered by S. G. F. Brandon's *Jesus and the Zealots*.[31] Since the debate anticipated many later developments, it may be useful to summarize and analyze it briefly.

Brandon's work established a contrast between two views of Jesus. The traditional version of Jesus promulgated by the Gospel writers Brandon called "the pacific Christ," by which he seems to mean the pacifist Christ.[32] Against this view he proposed that Jesus was an active political figure with possible sympathetic ties to the Zealots, whose proclamation of the coming reign of God was a simultaneous critique of Roman occupation and priestly collaboration. This image of Jesus led Brandon to view, in a different light, events narrated in the Gospels. The entry into Jerusalem, for example, was a carefully planned messianic demonstration in which Jesus claimed royal power for himself, and his "cleansing of the temple" was an attack on the compromised sacerdotal aristocracy. Both events reflect Jesus' belief, shared by the Zealots, that Yahweh alone should be sovereign over the land. Brandon speculates that the temple cleansing was part of a coordinated insurrection in which the Zealots (e.g., Barabbas) participated but which was put down by Roman soldiers. If true, this means that the incident was much larger and more threatening than depicted in the Gospels; it included Jesus' followers as well as sympathetic portions of the crowd and, most likely, involved "violence and pillage."[33] The Gospel writers were forced to minimize the event in order to portray a Jesus who was less threatening to Roman power.

Brandon understood the "Zealots" to be a long-standing nationalist liberation movement active from the death of Herod the Great through the fall of Jerusalem. Jesus was crucified as a *lēstēs* between two other *lēstai,* that is, as a zealot between two other zealots. When the hostile takeover of the temple failed, Jesus and his armed followers retreated to the Garden of Gethsemane, where they were betrayed by an informer. Jesus was captured, interrogated by the temple authorities, and turned over to the Romans to be executed for sedition, a charge that, it turns out, was well deserved. Jesus knew that the sacerdotal aristocracy and the Roman colonial presence were the two major obstacles that had to be removed to make way for the coming kingdom of God. Realizing the threat he posed, the reigning authorities eliminated Jesus.

Throughout his study, Brandon readily admitted that the Gospels did not portray the Jesus he had uncovered. He had to work through the cover story perpetrated by the Gospel writers, namely, that Jesus was executed by the perfidy of the Jews against the reluctant wishes of the Romans. This point of view allowed the evangelists to promulgate the early church's vision of the "pacific Christ" who died for the sins of the world while remaining serenely uninvolved in politics.

Brandon's historical reconstruction required reading the Gospels until they yielded the outlines of another, quite different story. This is, of course, what Schweitzer had recognized long ago. But Brandon drew upon a resource ignored by Schweitzer, the writings of Josephus, and used those writings both to sketch the political and social dynamics of the first century and to construct his picture of the Zealots.

The first part of the thesis, which associated Jesus with a violent militarist liberation movement, generated refutations by Oscar Cullmann and Martin Hengel.[34] Ironically, Hengel's own investigation of the Zealots had contributed to Brandon's thesis by portraying the Zealots in much the same way as Brandon had done.[35] Hengel had formulated "the Zealot hypothesis," but did not agree with Brandon's application of it.[36] The nature of both Cullmann's and Hengel's refutations illustrates the division created by Brandon's bold work. Cullmann was forced to acknowledge that there were two sets of texts to which an interpreter could appeal, one that was pro-Zealot and another than was anti-Zealot. This situation indicated that Jesus' relationship to the Zealots might be a complex one. But Cullmann believed that the key to reading the complexity generated by both sets of texts was to be found in Jesus' "radical eschatological expectation."[37] Jesus proclaimed the imminent end of the world, a conviction from which both sets of texts arise. All human institutions are part of a world that is passing away; therefore, they cannot have lasting value or enduring significance. So Jesus could not have been fixated on institutional or systemic injustice as an end in itself. Jesus criticized institutional injustice as a platform to appeal for a radical change of heart. In no way was Jesus political. It is more likely that Jesus' eschatological radicalism depoliticized his actions and aims. This is why it is the individual character of Jesus' teachings that stands out; when he calls for change, it is a change of heart that matters more than any change of unjust institutions. Why was he crucified? It was "the result of a judicial error."[38] The Romans could not understand Jesus' "eschatological attitude," and they mistook it for a political challenge. Using the episode of Peter's confession to illustrate his contention, Cullmann goes so far as to suggest that Jesus considered zealotic messianic views as a satanic temptation.[39]

Hengel's answer to the question, "Was Jesus a revolutionist?" is a resounding, "No!" True, Jesus' teachings attack greed and descry the gap between rich and poor, but his teachings are not political. They appeal to the individual. The temple cleansing was a prophetic demonstration directed at the commercialization of the temple and those who profited from it, not a revolutionary provocation. Jesus didn't arm his disciples for military action. To be sure, Jews typically carried knives or small swords to protect themselves from brigands or wild animals when they traveled, and Jesus' disciples were no different. But the single sword thrust in Gethsemane hardly qualifies as a revolutionary attack. Jesus is no Che! In his second attempt at refuting Brandon, *Victory over Violence,* Hengel placed Jesus' ministry in the context of the use of force from the days of Hellenistic imperialism (the Ptolemies and Seleucids) through the Hasmonean, Herodian, and Roman periods. The Zealot movement may have seen itself as a latter-day Hasmonean liberation movement, but Jesus saw his movement quite differently. In Jesus' proclamation, violence is overcome by love, and only the changed heart can transform the world. This is because, for Jesus, evil resided in the human heart, not in the world of "transsubjective social and political" situations, such as Roman hegemony or priestly collusion.[40] In the context of resistance to Roman rule, Jesus' teaching of love of enemies and forgiveness was an offense. To confuse this teacher of love with a Zealot is incomprehensible and wrong-headed.

The debate sparked by Brandon's study was continued by the work of John Howard Yoder, which could equally well have been entitled "the pacifist Jesus," a work largely dependent on the earlier work of André Trocmé.[41] Both Yoder and Trocmé made an important contribution to the impasse created by Brandon, Cullmann, and Hengel, all of whom had posed the issue in terms of a false alternative: Jesus was either a Zealot or an apolitical teacher. Yoder proposed that Jesus was an active pacifist who preached and acted out a form of "nonviolent resistance."[42] Jesus was a politically active pacifist. In effect, this created a new path for understanding how Jesus could be understood as a political figure, without remaking him in the image of a Zealot. Yoder also proposed that Jesus announced "jubilee" and sought to develop an ethic out of the arrival of jubilee.[43] Throughout the discussion, the central issue seemed to be whether Jesus was best understood as an advocate of violent change or a nonviolent pacifist, a theme very much at home in the turbulent 1960s and early 1970s when these works were written.

This debate contained many elements that would emerge as part of the third quest for the historical Jesus. Brandon's provocative thesis had been an attempt to place Jesus in the context of first-century Judaism, but whereas previous studies usually saw Jesus as a Pharisee, rabbi, or prophet, Brandon interpreted Jesus in terms of the Zealot movement. But Brandon did more than contextualize Jesus within the dynamics of Judaism. He made him into a political figure, involved in the social and political issues of his time. This may have been the most important byproduct of the discussion. The refutations of Brandon put forward by Cullmann and Hengel indicate what a sensitive nerve Brandon had touched. Brandon was able to make his case as forcefully as he did because of his extensive use of Josephus to sketch the political landscape of Galilee and Judea, but he lacked the richness of social-scientific models to nuance his discussion and place first-century forms of political protest in larger frameworks. This left him dependent on Hengel's "scholarly construct" of the Zealots to explain the politics of the time. But for all his limitations, Brandon placed the political Jesus in the center of the discussion and inaugurated a trend that would continue to the present.

In pursuing his reconstruction of a Jesus with zealotic sympathies, Brandon knew that he had to distinguish between the story told by the Gospels and the one he was composing, because the two were incompatible. In following this course, he affirmed Schweitzer's insight that researchers had to use the Gospels to show how Jesus could have acted otherwise than the Gospels show him acting. Brandon crystallized the difference by contrasting the "pacific Christ" with Christ the Zealot, and he knew that he could not simply read the Gospels at face value. There was a cover story as well as an underlying tale that might not be so tame. Once again, Brandon anticipated many of the works that would follow in the 1980s and beyond, for they too would offer interpretations of Jesus that conflicted with the portraits of Jesus found in the Gospels and church tradition. The refutations by Cullmann and Hengel also anticipate the more traditional responses that these later studies would generate, and the conversation established among Brandon, Cullmann, Hengel, and Yoder anticipates later studies. Cullmann, Hengel, and Yoder in their distinctive ways reaffirm more traditional views of Jesus as a rabbi and sage who teaches the way of the reformed heart and transformed life. Yoder adds a spice of social ethics to the mix, but all three distance themselves from Brandon's political Jesus.

Brandon relied not so much on the teaching of Jesus as he did on the actions of Jesus, placing great emphasis on the triumphal entry, the so-called cleansing of the temple, and the trial and crucifixion. He begins with actions and reads Jesus' teachings in light of them. By contrast, Cullmann and Hengel begin with Jesus' teachings and move to his actions. This familiar divide was proposed during the new quest for the historical Jesus and would reappear during the period of the third quest. Where does one begin, with teachings or actions? How are they to be related to each other?

The debate illustrates once again what Schweitzer knew, namely, that the Synoptic Gospels are problematic sources for historical reconstruction. Since the Gospels are filled with gaps and disconnects, those who would seek the historical Jesus must use their historical imagination. It may seem more evident in the case of Brandon than in the case of Cullmann, but both scholars have a gestalt of Jesus that informs their work on specific texts. The same can be said of Hengel and Yoder. All of the participants work with their historical imagination in order to create or confirm their view of the historical Jesus.

Finally, the debate suggests how important it was to develop interdisciplinary approaches to the first century. Brandon was too limited in his reading of the Zealots, and as a result, he focused the discussion on false alternatives. Beginning in the 1980s, the situation began to change as interdisciplinary approaches and parallel inquiries, like Sean Freyne's work on Galilee,[44] began to enrich the discussion and broaden the menu of options. Finally, it could be said that the debate about Jesus the zealot served as an expiration date for the new quest. The terms in which the new quest had been conducted were utterly incapable of comprehending the issues joined by Brandon. The existentialist emphasis on the moment was rendered irrelevant by the introduction of the larger social and political world of the first century. The more specific the engagement with that world, the more useless and dated the new quest became. To be sure, the debate begun by Brandon reflected its time as well as the time of Jesus, but that is an inescapable condition of doing engaged historical research.

The Emergence of a Third Quest:
Diverse Discoveries from Divergent Methods

By the mid-1980s, it was apparent that a rejuvenated quest for the historical Jesus was underway. In an article entitled "From Barren Mazes to Gentle Rappings: The Emergence of Jesus Research," James Charlesworth noted rather dramatically, "Jesus research commenced around 1980."[45] He seems to mean that the current wave of Jesus research, as opposed to the old quest and the new quest, began in earnest around 1980. Indeed it is true that, during the 1980s, tributaries of research beginning in many disparate headwaters finally came together to form a great river of inquiry into the historical Jesus. The emergence was duly noted in scholarly articles and books, and it inspired more popular treatments as well.[46] Unlike the new quest, however, the third quest is united by neither a common philosophical outlook nor a methodological consensus and, unlike the old quest, the third quest is not attempting to reconstruct lives of Jesus but has opted for more modest and varied goals. Others have canvassed the scope of literature produced by the third quest, and so there is no need to repeat their work here.

It may be helpful to note three trends prominent in the third quest, since they all play an important role in this study. They are: (1) the study of the relationship of Jesus to first-century Judaism; (2) the character of the continuing discussion of the political character of Jesus' public work; and (3) the models employed for understanding the kind of figure Jesus embodied in his public role. What gestalt or whole image of Jesus do we use to interpret the pieces of the Jesus tradition? This question continues to occupy a critical place in the ongoing discussion. Underlying all three issues remains the larger question of how interpreters construe the first-century world in which Jesus lived and moved and had his being. How does Jesus fit into the world of Roman colonial occupation, Herodian client rule, and the hegemony of the temple state? These issues will be addressed later in chapters designed to explore those questions more directly, but they remain in the background of these first three issues.

Jesus and Judaism

The third quest continues to assess how Jesus fits into the rich and varied world of first-century Judaism.[47] It is understood that prerequisite to placing Jesus in the context of Judaism is a clear knowledge of the complexity and ferment at work in the rich and varied strands of formative Judaism. It is no exaggeration to say that one great gain of these studies has been to retrieve a more nuanced and complex view of first-century Judaism as well as to understand how Jesus fit into the spectrum of the Judaism of his time.

The work of E. P. Sanders may illustrate the gains and quandaries posed by such an approach.[48] Sanders has proposed that any study of Jesus and Judaism should begin with what we can know about Jesus' actions, rather than a study of his sayings. Whoever begins with the sayings always ends in a quagmire of differing evaluations and judgments about their authenticity. Moreover, the sayings may tell us less about Jesus' intentions than an analysis of his undisputed actions, the facts about the historical Jesus. Sanders proposed two lists of such facts that can be known about Jesus. In *Jesus and Judaism,* he listed eight "indisputable facts."

1. Jesus was baptized by John the Baptist.
2. Jesus was a Galilean who preached and healed.

3. Jesus called disciples and spoke of there being twelve.
4. Jesus confined his activity to Israel.
5. Jesus engaged in a controversy about the temple.
6. Jesus was crucified outside Jerusalem by Roman authorities.
7. After his death, Jesus' followers continued as an identifiable movement.
8. At least some Jews persecuted at least parts of the new movement.[49]

When he returned to the same task eight years later, he produced a similar list divided into two parts, the first outlining Jesus' life, the second covering the aftermath of his life. All facts on both lists are taken to be secure and well attested.

> Jesus was born c. 4 B.C.E., near the time of the death of Herod the Great:
> He spent his childhood and early adult years in Nazareth, a Galilean village.
> He was baptized by John the Baptist.
> He called disciples.
> He taught in towns, villages, and countryside of Galilee (but not cities).
> He preached the "kingdom of God."
> About the year 30 he went to Jerusalem for Passover.
> He created a disturbance in the temple area.
> He had a final meal with his disciples.
> He was arrested and interrogated by Jewish authorities, specifically the high priest.
> He was executed on the orders of the Roman prefect, Pontius Pilate.[50]

The secure aftermath may be summarized as follows:

> His disciples fled at first.
> They saw him (in what sense is not certain) after his death.
> As a consequence, they believed that he would return to found the kingdom.
> They formed a community to await his return and sought to win others to faith in him as God's Messiah.

The most important "fact" for Sanders is Jesus' action in the temple, because it provides the essential clue for interpreting his public work by revealing him as a prophet of "restoration eschatology."[51] He engaged in a symbolic destruction of the old temple as a preparation for the coming of a new temple. It is his role as a restoration prophet that makes sense of the facts of Jesus' life that we can recover. Jesus chose the Twelve as another symbolic gesture signaling his role as the restorer of Israel. This is why he confined his activity to Israel, and this is why he was crucified. Although Sanders's first list emphasizes the Romans' role in executing Jesus, his second list indicates the collusion of Jewish authorities, perhaps because he has developed more clarity about their motivations. It was their response to the prophet who pronounced doom on the Second Temple as a preparation for the new temple and who claimed to speak for God in his singular role as prophet. Sanders also believes that his reconstruction of Jesus makes the most sense of subsequent "Christian" history, explaining both the tensions between church and synagogue as well as the continuities between the time of Jesus and the history of the early church.

In both his scholarly monograph and his more popular treatment of Jesus, Sanders tries to narrow the gap between Jesus and Judaism that has been assumed in so much Protestant scholarship and to portray Jesus as a religious figure who can be contained within formative Judaism, especially with regard to his teaching about the law and his attitude toward the temple. Jesus himself neither transgressed the law nor counseled others to do so (with one possible exception), although he did not view the law as final.[52] His teaching falls well within the parameters of first-century Torah debate. Jesus' action in the temple is best understood as one act in an intra-Jewish drama focused on the role of the temple in Jewish life and its place in a restored Israel. On this stage, Jesus is a prophet of "restoration eschatology," for whom the coming reign of God implies the need for a new temple. Jesus, therefore, did proclaim an eschatological message but focused on the renewal of Israel.

Throughout these discussions, Sanders accompanies his interpretation of Jesus with a polemic against reading Jesus in political terms. Especially in the later volume, he takes pains to minimize the impact of Roman authority and Herodian rule.[53] His view of the temple and the debate around restoration eschatology assumes that religion is a free-standing area of first-century society and thereby fails to note that the temple itself is an institution embedded in politics and kinship.[54] This means that the polemic against the political dimensions of Roman occupation and Herodian rule reinforces the erroneous view that the temple can be dealt with as though it were a religious institution, and Jesus as though he were solely a religious figure. The scholarship of the third quest has uncovered too much knowledge about how agrarian societies and aristocratic empires work to perpetuate these omissions.

Sanders is not the only scholar to concern himself with the relationship between Jesus and Judaism. Beginning in 1973, Geza Vermes produced three major studies of aspects of the historical Jesus in which he discovered a historical Jesus quite different from the one discovered by Sanders.[55] Vermes found a Jesus who was not concerned with the restoration of Israel by means of rebuilding a new temple in Judea, but who was a Galilean *ḥasid* or charismatic holy man in the tradition of Elijah and Elisha. Vermes understands Jesus as a product of the *sui generis* territory of Galilee. Isolated from Judea by history and circumstance and the beneficiary of an "unsophisticated simplicity of . . . life [that] is likely to have nourished the pride and independence of its inhabitants," Galilee nurtured a respect for the idiosyncratic holy man and wonder worker, like Ḥoni the Circle Drawer and Ḥanina ben Dosa.[56] Jesus was a product of this rural environment, and his parables reflect the agricultural life of the area and its villages. Of course, the very features that encouraged the emergence of figures like Jesus also account for the rabbis' depiction of Galileans as unsophisticated rubes, ignorant of the Torah and unlearned in the ways of purity, a land filled with *amme ha-aretz*. It was in part these dynamics that account for the hostility between Jesus and the Pharisees; it was a characteristic expression of the structural and systemic conflict between the defenders of the temple and Torah, on the one hand, and the charismatic outsider, careless of purity but filled with the Spirit, on the other hand. In a subsequent volume, Vermes would devote more attention to Jesus' relationship to the Torah and to an analysis of "scriptural" and "charismatic" authority in the teaching of Jesus.[57]

Although Vermes's portrayal of Jesus is marred by an overly simplistic view of Galilee, he did introduce the question of Galilean regionalism into the discussion of the historical Jesus. For Vermes, Jesus and Galilee represent a cultural and religious fit. Jesus is understandable within Galilean traditions and by comparison with other figures from the same locale. He also raised the question about the loyalty of Galileans to the temple in Judea and the halakah of the Pharisees being perpetuated from Jerusalem. For all his insights into Jesus the Jew, Vermes, like Sanders before him, also assumed that Jesus was a religious figure and, therefore, he portrayed the conflict between *ḥasid* and Pharisee as a religious squabble. Even though he perceived the conflict between styles of authority, he failed to pursue the political implications of his own conclusions.

Sanders placed the temple in the center of the discussion of the historical Jesus, and Vermes raised the significance of Galilee as a context for Jesus' work. Both issues are important and will be addressed in the current study but using a different framework that emphasizes the role of the temple as an institution embedded in politics and kinship and takes seriously the styles of authority operating in Galilee and Judea.

The Political Jesus

The third quest has not ignored the political and economic dimensions of Jesus' public work.[58] The approach to Jesus is not new. What Ernst Bammel called "the revolution theory"[59] traces at least to Reimarus, whose fragments were published posthumously from 1774 to 1778, though written at least a decade earlier. If the lengthy discussion of Brandon and his critics has provided a glimpse into the benefits of this approach, the major portion of this work will explore it in even more detail. The most remarkable development in studies of Jesus' activity has been the elaboration of the political Jesus. Building upon Yoder's earlier work, Richard Horsley portrays a Jesus at work in the renewal of community life at the local level, all part of his strategy for a "non-violent social revolution."[60] The great gain over Yoder in Horsley's work is his detailed knowledge of Galilee and of social models for interpreting the knowledge he brings to the task. Horsley abandons "the unhistorical quest for the apolitical Jesus" in order to depict a Jesus at work in the "imperial situation" of Roman Palestine.[61] Since so much of the present work pursues this approach, it will be sufficient simply to note its importance here.

The Jesus Seminar and the Problem of Models for Understanding the Historical Jesus

Undoubtedly, the most controversial group to arise during the third quest has been the Jesus Seminar, begun in 1985 under the guiding hand of Robert Funk. The seminar was composed of thirty to forty North American scholars who gathered into a data base all of the known sayings attributed to Jesus in canonical and extracanonical sources from the ancient world and then argued their authenticity or nonauthenticity in open debate. The debates ended with a vote in which four colors of beads were used to express varying degrees of probability about whether the sayings can be attributed to the historical Jesus.[62] The votes were taken by casting beads using the following four-color scheme:

red	=	"that's Jesus"
pink	=	"sure sounds like Jesus"
gray	=	"well, maybe"
black	=	"there's been a mistake."

Translated into less-colorful language, red means that a statement can confidently be attributed to the historical Jesus while black means that the statement is most likely the product of the early church.

The Jesus Seminar was a self-selected group, not a representative body. This is not necessarily negative; it is inherently useful to know what any gathering of scholars thinks about a particular saying of Jesus. The problem arises when a group portrays itself as representative when it is not, and the Jesus Seminar has been criticized on this point. Given the present diversity of New Testament scholars, it is increasingly difficult to know just what would constitute a representative group. Of course, it is not necessary that the Jesus Seminar be representative in order to have its findings taken seriously, although in his critique Luke Johnson attempted to make the composition of the seminar an issue.[63] In any event, the character of the group does not invalidate its findings; it simply puts them in perspective.

As Luke Johnson and Ben Witherington III have both noted, and as Funk clearly stated, the Jesus Seminar was never a neutral attempt at objective inquiry.[64] In truth, scholarship rarely is, so this should not be surprising. It was, in part and by design, an attempt to make public a consensus of a particular strand of critical biblical scholarship by grabbing headlines and wresting control of the media from fundamentalists and conservatives. The resulting sound bites, headlines, and media events publicized the iconoclastic nature of the enterprise, reflecting the way the mass media normally work. The seminar publicized its findings in such a way as to emphasize their shock value. So the public learned, for instance, that, in the view of the Jesus Seminar, the Lord's Prayer does not go back to Jesus and that "less than 25% of the words attributed to Jesus were actually his."[65] The parable of the rich man and Lazarus is "banal," and the resurrection was a collective hallucination of the disciples.[66] It is hard to avoid the conclusion that the Jesus Seminar shares common roots with the polemical intent of many of the productions of the first quest, a tendency noted by Schweitzer.

Given the controversial nature of their work, it will be more useful to critique the methodology of the Jesus Seminar rather than enumerate the outrageous comments of its leaders. The members of the seminar presented themselves as doing inductive, scientific work. They assembled a data base, examined it according to criteria for authenticity, and finally voted to determine the consensus of the group. It sounds like scientific research combined with democratic theory, a sort of reconstitutional convention, but it is not. What guided the members of the seminar as they voted on individual sayings or parables? The criteria they listed? Hardly. Both Marcus Borg and John Dominic Crossan, for example, declare that the criterion of multiple attestation is one of the most important in evaluating a saying. Yet the parable of the good Samaritan made the cut. Why? In part, because Funk has devoted his career to interpreting this parable, and it is a favorite of Crossan's as well. So on the slender thread of a single, late attestation, the parable made the cut. Of course, the members would say that the theology of the parable was congruent with other materials established by using the criterion of multiple attestation, but this rationalization does not lessen the critique.

What was likely to be at work? Both Funk and Crossan held prior complete images of Jesus, and on the basis of this unacknowledged but determinative gestalt, they cast their ballots. They, like other members of the seminar, had already determined who Jesus was on the basis of previous work (for no one comes to this task as a tabula rasa), and on the basis of that previously held whole image of Jesus, they determined which sayings fit into which category. Witherington puts it this way:

> What is perhaps most striking about the work of the Jesus Seminar is that while each participating scholar no doubt has a story about the life of Jesus in mind into which he [or she] believes these various sayings of Jesus fit, this framework is never discussed.[67]

This is, from my point of view, the fundamental dishonesty or oversight of the Jesus Seminar. Had the seminar members openly discussed the views of Jesus they brought to the table (Jesus as itinerant cynic, holy man, subversive sage, etc.), then the scholars gathered around the table could have generated an interesting and pointed discussion. Their votes would have been based on whether they modified their gestalt of who Jesus was, not whether a saying fit predetermined but indifferently applied criteria. In other words, the members of the Jesus Seminar should have heeded Schweitzer's dictum, "there is no historical task which so reveals a man's true self as the writing of a Life of Jesus."[68] Schweitzer demonstrated how it applied to individual authors, while the Jesus Seminar has shown that it applies to committees as well. They portrayed themselves as doing inductive science because they courted the aura of authority associated with the scientific method. However, they were in fact doing deductive, and at times intuitive, historical work all along. For example, Borg was already working on his noneschatological hypothesis well before the Jesus Seminar was formed. In an article written in 1984 ("An Orthodoxy Reconsidered: The 'End of the World Jesus'"; it was published in 1987), a year before the Jesus Seminar was formed, Borg reassessed the role of eschatology in understanding the historical Jesus.[69] He published his article "A Temperate Case for a Noneschatological Jesus" in the journal of the Jesus Seminar in September 1986, long before the seminar had surveyed enough sayings to make such judgments possible.[70] It is more likely that Borg brought his perspectives to the seminar and cast his votes with his developing convictions already in mind. Borg himself described this very process but applied it to others when he noted that "a Gestalt or image becomes a lens," but he was referring to the eschatological gestalt that had become the lens through which the Jesus tradition was seen.[71] True enough, but the same argument could be applied to Borg's and the seminar's own procedure. This, they apparently failed to see.

All of this means that it is important to clarify the whole image of Jesus' work that informs each study of the historical Jesus, for this image will influence work on specific texts or incidents from Jesus' life. An example may further clarify this point. Sanders believes that Jesus called twelve disciples, in part to signify his reconstituting the whole of Israel.[72] Crossan argues that the references to the Twelve represent the early church's retrojection. The church adopted the Twelve to capture the significance of Jesus' work in symbolic fashion.[73] Why the differing evaluations? One reason is the whole image each scholar brings to the evaluation of the tradition. Sanders, seeing Jesus as a restoration prophet, finds the selection of twelve as an appropriate and historically defensible action. But Crossan views Jesus as an "itinerant Jewish cynic" without a desire to plan a movement and without interest in reconstituting another "Israel." This example could be replicated many times over, but one instance will have to suffice to make the larger hermeneutical principle, namely, that the whole significantly influences the evaluation of the parts. If the Jesus Seminar has brought this matter to the attention of the third quest, it has served a useful purpose.

A Postmodern Quest?

If the Jesus Seminar, which brought together some of the better minds in New Testament studies, failed to discover the historical Jesus, what factors give confidence that the entire third-quest movement will not simply repeat the past? Four are worth mentioning.

First, if one could select a single trait characteristic of many of the works constituting the third quest, it would be their interdisciplinary approach. As Bernard Brandon Scott noted, "the historical quest for the historical Jesus has ended; the interdisciplinary quest for the historical Jesus has begun."[74] In particular, the use of the social sciences has provided new ways of viewing the world of Jesus as an advanced agrarian society, an aristocratic empire, and as a peasant society, to enumerate just three points of view. Each lens allows us to see things in a different way, broadening the baseline of approaches taken to the Gospel materials. The application of these tools has illumined the materials of the Gospels in new ways. Now it is possible to understand the dynamics of biblical texts that earlier seemed disconnected and puzzling. The chapters of this study will be filled with examples of how the reading of specific texts can be enhanced through the use of the social sciences.

In addition to illuminating specific texts, the social sciences can propose larger models for understanding systemic relations in agrarian society, such as the relationship between city and countryside, the modes of production, the typical ways that centralized or tributary economies work, the relation of peasants to the various layers of masters who controlled their lives, and what factors lead to revolt and violence, to name just a few. The value of social models is great, because we have a finite amount of information about the first century. Models allow us to screen old information through new lenses, and the results can be fruitful. Long ago, John Gager argued that the use of the social sciences permitted us to generate new information from old data because we were viewing the old data in such different ways.[75] Used judiciously, models can also be used to fill gaps where information is missing. Scholars, using judgment and informed guesswork, can fill in the picture of first-century Palestine with a probable idea of what was happening.

A second factor enriching historical Jesus studies is the development of parallel inquiries. In 1980, Sean Freyne published his superb study of Galilee,[76] prompting a biblical scholar to observe that the quest for the historical Jesus had become the quest for the historical Galilee. Interest in Galilee has continued to the present, as witnessed by the recent publication of Horsley's *Galilee, History, Politics, People* (1995). Freyne's work contributed to a discussion of Galilean regionalism and opened the door to an interdisciplinary discussion by historical Jesus scholars and archaeologists. Studies of Galilee might seem to have little to do with Jesus of Nazareth, but the more we can know of his world, the better we will understand the context of his work. Of course, such studies often identify questions more readily than answering them. For instance, what was the relation of Galilee and the temple? How observant were Galileans with regard to the Torah? How does Jesus fit into the larger picture being sketched? Even when the issues cannot be resolved, they can inform portrayals of the historical Jesus.

A third factor that informs historical Jesus studies is the effort to read Jesus as a political and public figure concerned with the issues that impacted the lives of the rural peasants, artisans, the unclean and degraded, and the expendables with whom he spent so much of his time. The impetus for such a reading really began in the third world. It is no coincidence that the rise of liberation theology almost exactly parallels the rise of the third quest. Gustavo Gutiérrez's *Theology of Liberation* was published in English in 1974. A decade later Juan Luis Segundo published *The Historical Jesus of the Synoptics* (1985), a year after Hugo Echegaray's *The Practice of Jesus* (1984). Jon Sobrino's more recent *Jesus the Liberator: A Historical-Theological View* (1993) continues the trend. The interest expressed in these works has been matched by North American studies by Horsley, Horsley and Hanson, Borg, and Oakman, to name just a few. These studies address one of the most consistently overlooked dimensions of the historical Jesus, the political aspects of his work. It would seem likely that it was his political activity that led to the cross, which was, after all, a form of political execution reserved for enemies of the empire. Any study of the historical Jesus that fails to account for the cross or portrays the cross as a motiveless mistake is inadequate. This is a lesson ignored by both of the earlier quests.

A fourth factor informing historical Jesus studies is the absence of a cultural synthesis such as those that supported the first and new quests. The first quest grew out of the cultural synthesis of the Enlightenment which we call modernity, and the new quest was held together by a clear hermeneutical program that drew its inspiration from Heidegger. The third quest knows no such synthesis. The lack of such an organizing philosophy or theology promotes diversity and exploration. This can be readily seen in the varied projects that have contributed to the third quest. It is in this respect a postmodern quest.

CONCLUSION

The promise of the third quest is that it will illumine the historical Jesus in new ways, yielding better views of Jesus than we have had before and providing especially clear glimpses of Jesus in areas previously neglected, such as Jesus the political figure. If the third quest were to end tomorrow, it would already have yielded a rich harvest of publications and explorations in the historical Jesus. As John Meier has noted in the introduction to volume 2 of his magisterial work, *A Marginal Jew,* the quest of the historical Jesus does not even attempt to define the whole reality of Jesus of Nazareth, only what it can discern through the use of scholarly tools and historical sources.[77] The real Jesus is greater by far than even the most complete presentations of the historical Jesus. The third quest also promises to produce studies relevant to our historical context, although as many have noted, "nothing is as irrelevant as immediate relevance," or as John Meier put it so succinctly, "nothing ages faster than relevance."[78] But such an awareness can instill modesty and humility in the third quest, a quiet acknowledgment of limits.

The peril of the current quest is that, having failed to learn the limits of its task, it will repeat the follies of its predecessors. We shall know we have been ensnared in this trap when a new Schweitzer who perhaps at this moment is "slouching toward Bethlehem to be born" arises to write another volume chronicling the follies of our era and our failures to notice, or once noticed, to heed, the hermeneutical circle in which we are caught. Then again, maybe that would not be such a bad thing after all, for in the process of seeking the historical Jesus for our age, we have accomplished enough. It is not our call to write for the ages but to speak to our particular and peculiar age. If we can use the third quest for the historical Jesus to remind us of our vocation in our time, we will have accomplished enough. What more could we ask of any quest for the historical Jesus? What more could we ask of ourselves?

2

Models and Methods in the
Quest for the Historical Jesus

The quest for the historical Jesus imposes conditions on those who undertake it. Those conditions reflect the nature of historical reconstruction as well as the peculiar problems attending the reconstruction of Jesus' public activity and the critical use of the Synoptic Gospels.

THE JESUS OF THE GAPS

In the quest for the historical Jesus, no one begins at the beginning. One must work backward in time from the present to the past, using a variety of critical tools that are themselves the product of modern scholarly inquiry. This situation applies equally to the social sciences and the tools of the historical-critical method. The danger, of course, is that such methods are so laden with contemporary assumptions and values that they will distort, rather than clarify, any effort to reconstruct the past. Since the scholars using these tools also bring their own preconceptions and agenda, both hidden and obvious, to the task, they increase the risk that such studies will yield little more than another harvest of anachronistic studies of the historical Jesus.

If one turns to the other end of the temporal spectrum, the first century, the situation is little improved. The materials used in any quest for the historical Jesus are themselves the end product of a historical process in which oral tradition has been committed to writing. The elevation of Matthew, Mark, Luke, and John to canonical status by the early church complicates the matter even more, since other Gospel-like documents or fragments of Jesus material have survived, raising questions of influence, provenance, and sequence among the documents.[1] These are not idle matters but matters that have serious consequences for any study of the historical Jesus. The Jesus Seminar, for example, has insisted on an early date for the Gospel of Thomas,[2] placing it prior to Mark and roughly contemporaneous with Q, the putative sayings source behind Matthew and Luke.[3] Clearly, any such decision regarding sequence or priority of sources will influence the outcome of historical reconstruction. If Q and Thomas become primary sources, then Jesus will emerge as a talking head and teacher of wisdom with little or no emphasis on his public activity, and since Q and Thomas are essentially collections of sayings without narrative framework, Jesus will be seen as a picaresque figure moving from one saying to another without any connecting framework. Jesus the wandering Cynic is one logical outcome of these choices, as the works of Burton Mack and Crossan illustrate.[4]

Not only is there the gap between the twentieth century and the first century, but that gap, especially since the time of Reimarus, has been filled with a succession of scholarly quests, many of which have left their mark on the continuing project. Most studies of the historical Jesus eventually proposed some large paradigm for understanding who Jesus was, and these reconstructions continue to influence current practitioners of the quest. Over time, the cumulative result of these efforts has posed disturbing questions, because the efforts led not to a growing consensus but rather to a chaotic diversity of options and a seemingly endless number of contradictory opinions. By virtue of its sheer size and variability, this body of research on the historical Jesus forces one to consider questions of method and criteria. How does one sort the Jesus traditions in order to determine what counts toward reconstructing the historical Jesus and what does not? What criteria can be applied to ensure the historical reliability of the materials used to depict Jesus? What controls prevent the enterprise from degenerating into total subjectivity and arbitrary speculation? How does one move from the evaluation of individual units of tradition to a larger gestalt? What is the relationship between the parts and the whole? The numerous portraits of Jesus that have emerged from historical Jesus studies raise all of these questions and many more. Neither the first quest nor the third quest has produced a consensus about how they are to be approached or answered.

In summary, three gaps then are inescapable in the quest for the historical Jesus. First is the gap between the modern interpreter and the ancient figure, a gap that is not only temporal but social, cultural, economic, and political as well. The world of Jesus is not our world. Its institutions and values are not those of a late–twentieth-century democratic, capitalist, postmodern society. This fact requires some understanding of the kind of world in which Jesus lived and a disciplined effort on the part of the modern seeker to distinguish between the world of first-century Palestine and the contemporary world. The second gap is between the time of Jesus and the time of the Gospel writers and others who recorded and recast traditions about him. This gap calls for the use of critical tools to sift the layers of tradition that may be deposited in a single text and stands as a reminder that modern scholars have no unmediated traditions about Jesus. The third gap is between the parts of the tradition and the whole image of Jesus. From Schweitzer and Bultmann to the present, scholars have recognized that the Gospel materials cannot provide a complete picture of the historical Jesus. At best, they can reveal momentary glimpses into the historical figure. Ultimately, it is the interpreter who provides the larger paradigm in which the details make sense and can be related to each other. This hiatus requires some method that clearly defines the whole and the parts before articulating how they are related, and it reflects a basic condition of historical inquiry.

THE SEARCH FOR CRITERIA AND METHOD

Scholars have been well aware of the gaps just discussed and, in an effort to bring order out of chaos, have developed criteria for gauging the authenticity of the materials used to reconstruct the historical Jesus. The Jesus Seminar itself has been keenly aware of the problem, as illustrated by Funk's essay, "Rules of Evidence."[5] There Funk enumerates six kinds of evidence: (1) "the wit and wisdom of Jesus," (2) "oral evidence," (3) "written evidence," (4) "attestation," (5) "narration," and (6) "general rules" (29). The essay provides a reasonable summary of current thinking on the matter and illustrates its problems. The first category, "the wit and wisdom of Jesus," will serve to make the point. Funk discerns eight tests that define the first rule of evidence. They are as follows:

1. The oral test: "Jesus said things that were short, provocative, and memorable."
2. The form test: "Jesus' best remembered forms of speech were aphorisms and parables."
3. Distinctive talk: "Jesus' talk was distinctive."
4. Against the grain: "Jesus' sayings and parables cut against the social and religious grain."
5. Reversal and frustration: "Jesus' sayings and parables surprise and shock; they characteristically call for a reversal of roles or frustrate ordinary, everyday expectations."
6. Extravagance, humor, and paradox: "Jesus' sayings and parables are often characterized by exaggeration, humor, and paradox."
7. Vivid images, unspecified application: "Jesus' images are concrete and vivid, his sayings and parables customarily metaphorical and without explicit application."

8. The serene self-efffacing sage: "Jesus does not as a rule initiate dialogue or debate, nor does he offer to cure people;
   Jesus rarely makes pronouncements or speaks about himself in the first person." (30–35)

It is obvious that these are less criteria than conclusions about who the
historical Jesus was; they are not simply rules of thumb for conducting
the search or sorting the evidence. These eight tests reflect Funk's conclusions about Jesus and the gestalt of the historical Jesus he already believes to be true and brings to the task of assessing evidence. In addition
to masking conclusions as criteria, Funk's rules of evidence pose other
problems. If Jesus' talk was memorable and distinctive but without "explicit application," then how can he know it was characteristic of Jesus
to call for "a reversal of roles" or that he frustrated "ordinary, everyday
expectations"? Both role reversals and frustration of expectations are
"explicit applications" of Jesus' talk. And if Jesus indulged in parable for
parable's sake and metaphor for metaphor's sake, then how can Funk
know that his sayings and parables "cut against the social and religious
grain," since this too is an application of Jesus' teaching? Indeed, if we
were to take Funk's eight tests at face value, we would conclude that
Jesus taught vividly about nothing of social, political, or economic consequence. Neither is the form of Jesus' teaching as clear as Funk would
have us believe. He first states that Jesus taught in short, memorable
forms of speech, but when he speaks about the reversal of roles and frustration of expectations, he invokes the "great narrative parables," which
are decidedly not "short," pithy forms of speech.

The implied portrait of the historical Jesus underlying these eight "criteria" is even more problematic when Jesus is placed in the context of a
traditional agrarian society. In his third criterion, Funk implies a contrast
between proverb and aphorism. The proverb reflects collective, com-
monplace wisdom, while the aphorism reflects "personal insight, individual authority" (31). Marcus Borg develops this notion into a contrast
between conventional wisdom communicated through proverbs and
subversive wisdom communicated through parables and aphorisms.[6]
One problem with this approach is that it fails to consider the nature of
the society in which Jesus lived and taught. An individual and distinctive
voice was not valued and would have been little heeded. What contemporary scholars scorn as "conventional wisdom" is what first-century
Galileans would have prized far above a deviant individualistic voice.
This may be why some of the scholars of the Jesus Seminar imagine Jesus
as a Cynic sage whose distinctive voice placed him on the margins of
society. But Jesus moved through the villages and towns of Galilee,

peasant havens, where the voice of conventional wisdom and the habits of immemorial custom shaped the course of life. If Jesus were to be heard in such settings, his authority would come from his immersion in the "little tradition"[7] of the villages and towns or perhaps as a mediator of the "great tradition" of the Torah on their behalf. The master of the one-liner whose hit-and-run style we so admire or the genius of the comedic monologue with its punch lines and extravagant jokes to whom we listen after the eleven o'clock news are modern figures that have little in common with the ancient world of Palestine. To conform Jesus to a familiar, modern mold may yield a Jesus comfortable to some inquirers but fails to account for the historical Jesus of Galilee and Judea. Whatever else may be said of this section of Funk's work, it vividly illustrates the problem of the relationship between the whole and the parts and reveals how foolhardy it is to discuss the parts without first making clear the whole image that informs the evaluation of the individual pieces of the tradition.

A more discerning approach to the question of criteria has been pursued by Dennis Polkow, who distills a total of twenty-five criteria out of recent writings before combining similar criteria and reorganizing them hierarchically.[8] This hierarchy yields three levels of criteria, the "preliminary criteria," the "primary criteria," and the "secondary criteria" (342). Diagramed, the criteria appear as follows:

Preliminary Criteria:	1. discounting redaction
	2. discounting tradition
Primary Criteria:	1. dissimilarity
	2. coherence
	3. multiple attestation
Secondary Criteria:	1. Palestinian context
	2. style
	3. scholarly consensus[9]

The preliminary criteria are essentially twofold. The first task is to examine the Gospel texts and discount the redaction of the evangelists ("discounting redaction"). The second step is to determine "the middle layer of tradition between the redaction level and the Jesus level" ("discounting tradition"), a complex and uncertain task involving oral transmission and perhaps written sources as well. Once one has completed these two tasks, one has reached the earliest recoverable form of the Jesus tradition (342–46).

The next phase of work is to apply the "primary criteria" to the materials so analyzed, the first of which is the criterion of "dissimilarity" (346–51). Bultmann identified three aspects of this criterion. The materials must reflect Jesus' eschatological outlook and, therefore, contrast with Jewish morality while exhibiting no distinctive features of Christian teaching from the early church.[10] Norman Perrin modified the criterion by suggesting that the materials so revealed would "be dissimilar to *characteristic* emphases" in both Judaism and the early church.[11] Applied rigorously, the criterion of dissimilarity was thought to ensure an authentic core of Jesus materials, although, by its nature, the criterion produces "a very narrow view of the historical Jesus" which could well preclude some of his typical teaching and theological emphases.[12]

The application of the second primary criterion, the principle of coherence, was intended to enlarge the secure core by identifying materials that would not in themselves pass the test of dissimilarity but cohered with materials that did. But this is a problematic formulation. Does coherence mean identity? That is, are the materials to be added to the core merely restatements of the "dissimilar" materials? If so, then they would neither enlarge the baseline of authentic Jesus materials nor add to our understanding of Jesus. They would merely provide alternative ways in which Jesus said the same things already established by the criterion of dissimilarity. Although this might be inherently interesting and provide insight into Jesus' communication skills, it would not add to the core of materials established by the criterion of dissimilarity. However, if these "coherent" materials are more than restatements of the authentic "dissimilar" core, then how does one decide when the coherent materials are expanding and actually changing its nature by smuggling in sayings, aphorisms, parables, or proverbs that suit the interpreter's preexistent view of Jesus but cannot pass the test of dissimilarity? Under such circumstances, the criterion of coherence may be little more than a convenient means to enlarge a small core of materials in order to confirm what the quester already believes to be true but cannot establish on the basis of the criterion of dissimilarity alone.

The third of the primary criteria is the criterion of multiple attestation. Materials found in more than one source or more than one form of the tradition are more likely to be authentic Jesus materials. Of course, materials appearing in multiple traditions may not be original to the historical Jesus, so the criterion must be used in concert with others.

Once material has passed at least one of the primary criteria, it may be tested against the three secondary criteria.[13] The first test is "Palestinian context." Materials from the historical Jesus should reflect his Palestinian context. This criterion was, at first, taken to refer to the language of the tradition. Did Greek phrases bear traces of Jesus' Aramaic (Aramaisms or Semiticisms)? But Charles Carlston expanded the application of the criteria to include Jesus' cultural and social world: "An authentic parable will reflect or fit into the conditions (social, political, ecclesiastical, linguistic, etc.) prevailing during the earthly ministry of Jesus, rather than (or, in some cases as well as) conditions which obtained in the post-resurrection church."[14]

The next secondary criterion refers to "style." It was applied by Jeremias, who attempted to identify the "characteristics of the *ipsissima vox Jesu*,"[15] and has been used by many scholars subsequent to him. James Breech, for example, applied the criterion to reconstruct the original form of Jesus' parables,[16] and Funk appealed to the same criterion in his discussion of the "wit and wisdom of Jesus." Like most of the criteria, it can involve circular reasoning, and those who use it run the risk of positing a distinctive style of Jesus and then using what has been assumed as a criterion to sort the Jesus tradition.

The final secondary criterion is scholarly consensus. Is the saying widely accepted as authentic by scholars using a variety of approaches? If so, then the saying gains some credibility from this fact. Two difficulties attend the use of this criterion. First, what counts as a consensus (how many scholars and out of what total sample of scholars?), and second, how does one evaluate the constant shifts of consensus characteristic of scholarly work? What seems an "assured result" of scholarship in one generation can become a focal point of debate in the next.[17]

Polkow's article is as lucid as it is problematic. It assumes that the process of establishing "authentic" Jesus material is an inductive procedure based on sound criteria. One problem with such a procedure is that it does not wrestle with the relationship between the part and the whole; that is, it fails to recognize that those who apply these criteria do so with a complete construct of the historical Jesus informing their decisions. If this gestalt of the historical Jesus is never examined, it will exercise an unacknowledged influence on their use of criteria and application of them. But the part and whole relationship can be taken in other ways. If the use of the social sciences and the pursuit of specialized studies (e.g., on Galilee) have enabled modern scholars to construct a macro-view of ancient Palestine, then the criterion of Palestinian context may be more germane than suggested in Polkow's approach. It may well be that the larger picture of Palestine will provide a framework for helping to assess individual units of the tradition by indicating how they could fit into that setting, an especially pertinent task since language assumes meaning in relationship to social systems. This means, in part, that scholars reconstructing the public work of the historical Jesus or evaluating a piece of tradition need to place their work in a larger cultural and social framework, but this presupposes an understanding of the time and place in which events occur or sayings are uttered.

The effort to reconstruct the world of Jesus, in other words, illustrates a problem similar to the one that haunts the use of the criteria. The criterion of dissimilarity, for example, assumes a comprehensive knowledge of Judaism and the theology of the early church. Both are very large areas of knowledge, but the interpreter must form some view of them if she or he is to judge "dissimilarity." Dissimilarity is, after all, dissimilar to something, and that something has to be spelled out. So even the use of specific criteria requires the knowledge of larger wholes, whether of Judaism, the early church and its theology, or the world of first-century Palestine. In spite of the fact that these larger chunks of knowledge are necessary to the application of the criteria, they are rarely discussed and more likely to be invoked than examined. Even the application of an apparently more manageable criterion, such as discounting redaction, requires an overview and knowledge of the evangelist's theology and tendencies. In the case of particular Gospels, there is often no consensus on these matters, as the work of redaction critics testifies. All of this means that the use of criteria is a complicated task involving more than the detailed analyses of specific texts and application of particular criteria to them. It involves the use of large overviews that may or may not be acknowledged. This means that any quest for the historical Jesus must be interdisciplinary. The very nature of the materials demands it. The risk is obvious. Each of the disciplines used is also the preserve of specialists who may judge the interdisciplinary work lacking in depth or accuracy. But any effort to portray Jesus of Nazareth will require just such work and will, presumably, justify such risks.

Even if the difficulties just discussed were overcome or at least coped with, what would be the expected outcome of the use of criteria? Will the materials so analyzed yield the *ipsissima verba Jesu* (the very words of Jesus), provide echoes of the *ipsissima vox Jesu* (the very voice of Jesus) or reveal what Scott calls the *ipsissima structura Jesu* (the originating structure of Jesus' oral speech)?[18] Funk addresses the same issue by speaking of "one core, different performances."[19] This assumes that the disciples or others remembered "only the core or gist" of Jesus' sayings and parables, but not Jesus' exact words. Furthermore, in an oral culture, teachers often develop a similar theme on a number of different occasions and in a variety of oral formats, so that there might not actually be an "original version" of a parable or aphorism but only a first oral performance suited to a particular situation.

Even the more tentative outcomes annunciated by Funk may imply too ambitious a goal. After all is said and done, what do the criteria yield in the way of historical Jesus materials? Very little! One is tempted to say, nothing, nothing at all, particularly when the one using the criteria proceeds with a methodological skepticism toward the tradition. Perhaps the most that the criteria can yield is the earliest stratum of the tradition, which may or may not be contemporary with the historical Jesus. For example, even after interpreters have applied the preliminary criteria by discounting redaction and discounting tradition (both of which are themselves speculative enterprises), they have reached older traditional materials but cannot be certain that even such early tradition reflects the historical Jesus. Similarly, multiple attestation may yield a likelihood that material traces back to an early stage of the tradition, but there is no certainty that it traces to Jesus. Early layers of tradition do not necessarily equate with authentic historical Jesus materials.

The criterion of style might seem to be on firmer ground. If it is possible to detect Aramaisms or Semiticisms in sayings of Jesus, then such speech, it would seem, must take us back to Jesus. But this is not necessarily the case at all; it may only transport us as far back as the early Aramaic communities in which Jesus' sayings were remembered and retold.

The criterion that seemed to ensure the most reliable core, the criterion of dissimilarity, likewise provides no guarantee that it can certify specific materials as tracing to Jesus. The criterion begs the question by requiring a historical judgment that a saying is in fact dissimilar to formative Judaism and the early church, and it presumes to solve the riddle of when the discontinuities found in the midst of all historical continuities crystallize into "dissimilarity." What good would it do to reconstruct a Jesus alien to both the world of Judaism and the world of the early church? He would be nothing more than a historical version of a docetic Jesus, so unworldly that he fits into none of the social worlds and cultural scenes of his day. In an ironic way, the Jesus created by the criterion of dissimilarity is a theological figure more akin to the second person of the Trinity than to the stage of history. Why should such a figure be taken seriously as a historical person? Would such a figure represent anything more than an anachronistic retrojection of modern values back onto the historical Jesus, such as Jesus the wit, the master of the zinger? But if scholars reconstruct a Jesus who fits into the world of Judaism and makes sense to the early church, then why use the criterion of dissimilarity at all?

The criteria of coherence and consensus have obvious flaws as well. Of what good is the criterion of coherence when the materials in relationship to which coherence is measured are themselves established on such weak ground? Scholarly consensus is little more than shifting sand and certainly not a criterion on which to base historical certitude.

A PART OF THE WHOLE JESUS

Where does this discussion leave anyone wishing to enter the quest? What way of proceeding remains open? One approach would be to identify the larger gestalt with which one begins the quest as a proposal to be tested against the materials of the Jesus tradition. This would acknowledge the problem that Schweitzer identified so long ago. "There is really no other means of arriving at the order and inner connexion of the facts of the life of Jesus than the making and testing of hypotheses."[20] Schweitzer knew that all research into the historical Jesus necessitated the use of a paradigm in order to make understanding possible; this is what he referred to as a hypothesis. Even if the goal of such a procedure would not be "to arrive at the order and inner connexion of the facts of Jesus' life," because that sounds too much like an attempt at biography, it could still yield fruitful results.[21] But the necessity of positing a "hypothesis" about the historical Jesus and then testing it by analyzing the pieces of the Jesus tradition in the context of recent work on ancient Palestine would keep the relationship between the parts and the whole at the center of the inquiry.

What would be the outcome of such a study? Would it produce a full picture of "the historical Jesus"? Hardly. Meier has distinguished between "the historical Jesus" and "the total reality of Jesus of Nazareth" or "the real Jesus."[22] The historical Jesus is that small portion of the total life of Jesus of Nazareth that can be reconstructed through the sifting of early source materials by using critical tools. This Jesus is, therefore, a "scientific construct, a theoretical abstraction of modern scholars that coincides only partially with the real Jesus of Nazareth."[23]

The best one can hope to produce is a part of the whole historical Jesus, and this study attempts to produce just such a modest result. It will propose a view of the historical Jesus (hypothesis) and test it by analyzing some materials of the Jesus tradition in light of it. The scrutiny of the parts may alter the initial gestalt, and the gestalt will also act as a lens for analyzing the pieces of the tradition. Borg has already applied this interpretive approach to the question of the eschatological Jesus. The gestalt of eschatology, he argued, became a lens through which Jesus' proclamation was interpreted and the materials of the Jesus tradition were seen. "That is, a hunch (the hypothesizing of a particular interpretive context) flows out of the evidence and then begins to affect how evidence is seen. Gestalt becomes lens."[24]

However, Borg clings to the belief that this process proceeds in inductive fashion. As historians examine the evidence, they begin to form a whole image as "the data begins to constellate itself into a Gestalt, an image of the whole, and the Gestalt then becomes a lens, that is, an overall hypothesis or particular interpretive context within which one attempts to see the rest of the data."[25] Data does not "constellate itself" as though it had a mind of its own; interpreters construe data as they examine it through the lens of working hypotheses and incorporate it into larger frameworks of meaning. It seems more likely, therefore, that a gestalt is already present as a strainer through which the data is being sifted. As long as the gestalt remains tentative and open to alteration in light of constant work with individual pieces of tradition, then it can serve a heuristic function, but it does seem important to abandon the notion that such work is inductive science applied to the Gospel traditions. A more honest approach would acknowledge the investments already present in the portfolios of the investigators as they come to the task, the "hypotheses," to use Schweitzer's word, that guide their detailed work. The relationship between part and whole will be dialectic, each influencing the other and each subtly changing the other while being changed as well. The result of such a project will be partial, even when judged against the totality of what scholars can reconstruct as probable historical Jesus scenarios. But it will offer a partial view of the whole Jesus.

If this approach is to work, then the first step in this study should be to identify the larger paradigm for understanding Jesus' public work that informs this study. What image of the historical Jesus informs this work? Image here can mean gestalt, paradigm, or larger view of Jesus, although in light of Meier's qualifications, it is probably best not to use the phrase "whole image" of Jesus, because that would claim too much. An *eikōn* is not so much a fully blown representation as a profile (Mark 12:16 and par.). However one chooses to name the initial paradigm, it seems important to acknowledge that it is neither possible nor desirable to separate Jesus from the theological and religious readings of his work found in the Gospels, although they may not always be helpful for reconstructing the historical Jesus. More to the point, history and theology are not mutually incompatible terms, for theological convictions are also historically rooted and conditioned.

THE REJECTION OF THE MISGUIDED QUEST

The alternative to undertaking this quest is well illustrated in the work of Johnson, who would declare all quests "misguided" because they abandon the framework of the Gospel narratives and substitute for them other constructs, often those borrowed from the social sciences (a particularly offensive source of insight for Johnson).[26] Once the Gospel framework is removed, all that scholars can do is to authenticate a particular saying or deed of Jesus. But individual sayings and deeds do not provide a portrait of the historical Jesus because they are without context and without interpretive controls. Only the canonical Gospels can provide that narrative context and control. As Johnson summarizes: "My point is, however, that whether plausible or implausible, all such constructions lack any real claim to historical probability once the given narrative framework has definitively been abandoned" (125).

44

At first glance, this conclusion seems odd in light of the fact that Johnson has argued rather extensively that the Gospels themselves do not provide historically reliable materials for any quest of a historical Jesus (81–104). Indeed, the Gospels are valuable primarily because they provide a common pattern for understanding the life of Jesus, a pattern that Johnson summarizes as "radical obedience to God and selfless love toward other people" (158).[27] This pattern acts as a control to the unbridled speculation that often accompanies modern quests for the historical Jesus. It is authoritative not because it is historical, but because it reflects the creeds and canon of the church. The creed and canon of the church provide Johnson the gestalt through which he reads the Jesus of the Gospels and arrives at "the real Jesus." Johnson's work, therefore, combines a radical skepticism toward the Gospel traditions as historical sources with a belief in their nearly infallible power as a guide to the real Jesus. Any study of Jesus that wanders beyond the boundaries of the Gospel narrative framework is invalid the moment it transgresses those bounds.

> It is *not* legitimate on the basis of demonstrating the probability of such items [what Jesus purportedly said and did] to then connect them, arrange them in sequence, infer causality, or ascribe special significance to any combination of them. . . . Once the narrative control is gone, the pieces can be (and have been) put together in multiple ways.[28]

The reason for this sweeping judgment appears to be the simple fact that the versions of the historical Jesus derived from such historical reconstruction are not identical with the real Jesus derived from the implicit meta-narrative supplied by canon and creed, a nonhistorical Jesus who remains the norm or canon (the measuring rod) against which all versions of the historical Jesus are to be measured. Johnson's argument assumes that the four Gospels do present a common pattern, even though that pattern can only be derived through the use of the very processes he has just condemned, that is, selecting materials from the Gospels, connecting them by arranging them in sequence, ascribing special significance to them, including theological causality. In other words, "the real Jesus" was reconstructed in a manner analogous to the way scholars reconstruct "the historical Jesus." Why then does Johnson believe that he has reached some unassailable high ground from which he can judge others?

In a strange way, Johnson has illustrated one contention advanced in this study. It is necessary to identify the gestalt or paradigm with which one begins the task. However, Johnson has advanced the claim that his gestalt is *the* orthodox gestalt that invalidates all others and thereby renders the quest superfluous. He is quite right in observing that, if scholars abandon the narrative frameworks supplied by the Gospel writers, they will reconstruct others, perhaps even using the social sciences to assist in the task. The results will not yield the uniformity that Johnson evidently values, but they will reflect engagement with the Gospel materials. Johnson is wrong to conclude, "*There are no controls;* there is only imagination hitched to an obsessive need, somehow, anyhow, to do history."[29]

CONCLUSION: THE NECESSITY OF THE CONTINUING QUEST

By contrast, Crossan understands the reason and need for the ongoing quest when he observes, "No generation ever gets it right forever. The best we can do, and it is more than enough, is to get it adequately right for here and now. This is not personal or individual humility but structural and systemic destiny."[30] Without the quest for the historical Jesus, we would be limited to the four canonical portraits of Jesus forever. But the canonical portraits contain elements that suggest other dimensions to the historical Jesus than those so prominently displayed in the four Gospels, and the canon includes not only the final form of the documents but all the traditions that have been folded into that final form, including the subversive memories that linger on the margins of the narratives and the silenced voices that whisper through the narrator's speech.

Uncomfortable though it may be, the quest for the historical Jesus is both a historical and theological necessity whose purpose is not to supplant the canonical portraits of Jesus but to supplement them. The historical Jesus of the canonical Gospels is a figure inhabiting "world creating" and "world maintaining" documents. But what of the "world subverting" figure who was executed as a political enemy of the temple state and Roman colonial rule?[31] The Gospels also speak of a Jesus not easily contained in the canon-and-creed Jesus whom Johnson calls "the real Jesus." Will such a Jesus reflect the use of the historical imagination? Of course, but no less than "the real Jesus" reflects the use of the theological imagination. The use of imagination and creativity, no less than critical analysis and reflection, are required for the work of historical reconstruction. This yields multiple results. But the results reflect the ambiguities and uncertainties inherent in the process itself. They testify to its strength, not its weakness. Provisional results may even have the advantage of avoiding the temptation to cling to incorrect certainties rather than accepting the correct uncertainties that are so much a part of the human condition.

In the next chapter I will identify some of the larger perspectives that inform this inquiry into a part of the whole historical Jesus. I will address the question, What is the gestalt that will become the lens of this study?

3

Prophet of the Justice of the Reign of God:

An Approach to the Historical Jesus

One way to interpret Jesus' public activity is to view him as a prophet of the justice of the reign of God. In an earlier study of the parables, I argued that Jesus could be understood as a pedagogue of the oppressed who used parables to illumine the dark world of oppression and intimate the kinds of options available to those trapped in it.[1] One of the persistent criticisms of that book is that it eliminated all theological dimensions from Jesus' work, and, in effect, reduced theology to sociology. Although the theological implications of that study seemed clear to me, they were not evident to others. This work is intended to address that inadequacy. Jesus the prophet is a figure akin to the one delineated in the book on the parables but with the theological underpinnings of his public activity made clearer by connecting him to the prophetic traditions of Israel. It was also noted that my study of the parables implied a larger view of Jesus' ministry than was articulated in that work, and this study will begin to delineate that larger view.

This chapter will explore the title of prophet (*prophētēs*) as it was applied to Jesus and suggest how two other titles, rabbi (*rabbi*) and teacher (*didaskalos*), might be related to it. These common titles will begin to define the larger gestalt with which this study approaches the historical Jesus.

JESUS AS A PROPHET IN THE GOSPELS

It seems probable that Jesus was seen as a prophet and called a prophet.[2] Often, Jesus is called a prophet, or assumed to be a prophet, in materials seeking to make another, more christological point. During his entry into Jerusalem, the crowd identifies Jesus as "the prophet from Nazareth of Galilee" (Matt. 21:11). In what appears to be a formulaic fragment used by Luke in the Emmaus narrative, Jesus is called "a prophet mighty in word and deed" (Luke 24:19b). Members of Herod's court think Jesus is like "one of the prophets of old" (Mark 6:15; cf. Luke 9:8), and, in a reworking of what appears to be the same material, the disciples summarize current opinion about Jesus' activity by reporting that he is seen as "one of the prophets" (Mark 8:28; Matt. 16:14; Luke 9:19). In a Pharisee's house, Jesus is criticized for allowing a sinful woman to touch him when Simon, his host, notes simply, "If this man were a prophet, he would have known who and what sort of woman this is who is touching him, for she is a sinner" (Luke 7:39). Simon assumes that Jesus is recognized as a prophet and questions the appropriateness of the appellation. When Jesus is in Jerusalem, the authorities are forced to take precautions before arresting him because "they feared the multitudes [who] held him to be a prophet" (Matt. 21:46). The phrase is a Matthean addition to the tradition he has received from Mark, an addition not found in Luke and, therefore, probably not Q. John records an odd debate in which some Pharisees deny that any prophet can "arise from Galilee" (John 7:52), presumably because of its failure to observe Torah, but the denial assumes that Jesus has been called a prophet. The Samaritan woman perceives Jesus to be a prophet because he has recounted the story of her marital life (John 4:19) and, forced to make a confession by the Pharisees, the man born blind from birth first tries to get off the hook by saying, "he is a prophet" (John 9:17). All of the material just cited is either triple tradition, double tradition (Mark-Luke), special Matthean, or Johanine. The sole exception is the fragment quoted by Luke in the Emmaus account, which may reflect an earlier confession. Otherwise, it is special Lukan. The reason for citing these admittedly later materials is that they all assume Jesus was identified as a prophet; one case (John 7:52) questions his prophetic credentials because he is from Galilee. In none of these passages, except the one just mentioned, is the point that Jesus was a prophet; it is assumed as part of a larger narrative purpose. Therefore, even though the materials are later, they all take it for granted that Jesus was popularly acclaimed as a prophet or called a prophet by his opponents. This assessment of the Jesus tradition is also shared by N. T. Wright, who notes:

> the early church is highly unlikely to have invented many sayings . . . which call Jesus a prophet. It might have seemed risky theologically to refer to him in this way; it might have appeared that he was simply being put on a level with all the other prophets.[3]

If true, this would indicate why the materials that identify Jesus as a prophet are likely to be reliable.

It is possible to suggest how the association of Jesus with the prophets could have been developed christologically in at least two distinctive ways. In John 6:14, the miraculous feeding of the multitude leads the crowd to confess that "this is indeed the prophet who is to come into the world," an apparent reference to Jesus as the fulfillment of the prophet like unto Moses mentioned in Deuteronomy (18:15, 18; see 18:15–22). In Acts, the same identification is developed in Peter's sermon in Solomon's Portico (Acts 3:17–26). These texts suggest that the early church developed a Jesus–Moses typology, now clearly found in both Matthew and John, among other places. Similarly, Jesus is associated with Elijah. In the narrative that leads into Peter's confession (Mark 8:28; Matt 16:14; Luke 9:19) and, in similar materials set in the court of Herod Antipas (Mark 6:14–16; Matt. 14:1–2; Luke 9:7–9), Jesus is seen as Elijah returned from the dead. The raising of the widow's son at Nain leads the villagers to exclaim, "a great prophet has arisen among us," an apparent allusion to Elijah, who also performed similar mighty feats (Luke 7:11–17). Both the Moses and the Elijah typologies represent christological developments of Jesus the prophet, but the developments also assume the prior identification of Jesus as a prophet.

PROPHETS IN THE SAYINGS OF JESUS AND THE GOSPEL TRADITIONS

The title "prophet" is not without a certain ambivalence. When Jesus was rejected in his hometown, he responded by saying, "prophets are not without honor, except in their own hometown, and among their own kin, and in their own house" (Mark 6:4; cf. Matt. 13:57; Luke 4:24). Where prophets are concerned, familiarity breeds contempt, at least for the kind of prophet Jesus was. Prophets are ambiguous figures who will be evaluated in a variety of ways by their contemporaries. As Rebecca Gray has noted, Josephus himself recognized that prophetic signs functioning as "authenticating miracles" were usually "ambiguous and not self-authenticating."[4] They invited division and debate. Both the use of signs and their inevitable ambiguity created mixed responses to prophetic figures. The maxim cited by Jesus may, in part, reflect this experience. Prophets can also shift the balance of power in a given situation and, if they do, they will be evaluated according to the political position of the observer. This, too, adds to the ambiguity, even for prophets in their own country or hometown.

Jesus himself referred to a number of figures as prophets. The most obvious example is John the Baptist (Q: Luke 7:26 = Matt. 11:9), whom Jesus calls both "a prophet" and "more than a prophet."[5] The description of John associates his prophetic activity with "the wilderness," a location antithetically opposed to "royal palace or court" (Luke 7:25), thus implying an adversarial relationship between ruling powers and the prophet John, a feature not unfamiliar to the role of a prophet. Theissen has developed this thesis in considerable detail.[6] He takes the "shaken reed" as a popular characterization, even "a title of ridicule and recognition," of Antipas, who bent with the wind in order to maintain his rule (38). The central contrast of the saying is then between "the cleverly adaptive politician" and the "uncompromising prophet proclaiming his message" (41). Herod represents the "Hellenistic power elite" and John "the common people" who resent the intrusion of foreign customs into the Herodian court (41, 42). If Jesus sees John's prophetic role as typical of what a prophet does, then he is identifying with prophets who live on the edge or margins and yet address the rulers at the centers of power.

In Matthew's version of the sign of Jonah, Jesus speaks of "the prophet Jonah" (Matt. 12:39), an evident Matthean addition since it is found neither in his Markan source (Mark 8:11–12) nor in Q (Luke 11:29 = Matt. 12:39). However, the omission of the phrase "the prophet" in Q changes the import of the remark very little, since Jonah was widely viewed as a prophet. The difficulty with the tradition is in understanding what is meant by the phrase "the sign of Jonah." Morna Hooker surveys three options. The phrase can mean a sign given by Jonah or a sign given to Jonah, or it can mean that Jonah himself is the sign.[7] The problem with the first option is that Jonah performs no miraculous sign in the biblical account of his journey to Ninevah or his preaching in Ninevah. The difficulty with the second choice is that the sign given to Jonah concerns the prophet himself, not the Ninevahites he is called to visit. If one looks to the Q tradition for a clue (Luke 11:29–32 = Matt. 12:39, 41–42) and, for the purpose of this discussion, discounts the Matthean material comparing Jonah's sojourn in the belly of the whale with Jesus' burial in the tomb (Matt. 12:40), then the emphasis is on Jonah as a sign, especially his preaching to the Ninevahites. If the parallel saying about the "queen of the South" (Luke 11:31) is also removed, then Luke 11:29b–30, 32 contains a rejection of signs, except for the sign of Jonah the preacher, whose proclamation led to repentance by the Ninevahites. Their response is contrasted to the response of "this generation," who refused to repent when "something greater than Jonah" appeared. The "something greater" could have been the preaching of John the Baptist, in which case Jonah is being compared with John (both are preachers of a message of repentance), although the results of their common work yields different results (repentance vs. no repentance). Yet the Gospel accounts of John's preaching seemingly present a different picture (Mark 1:5; Matt. 3:5) in which all Jerusalem and Judea respond to his appeal for repentance. But, if the Q summary of John's preaching (Luke 3:7–9 = Matt. 3:7–10; cf. Luke 3:10–14) is accurate, it would not be difficult to surmise that his message met with a good deal of resistance and opposition. It is also possible that Jesus' reference may have been to John's preaching to the Herodian court, which did meet with lethal opposition and led directly to his death. Finally, the "something more" may be Jesus' wry comment on the surprising and unexpected contrast between Jonah's preaching to the hopelessly evil Ninevahites while he himself has failed to reach the hopelessly righteous of "this generation."

Jesus refers to other figures as prophets as well. In his sermon at Nazareth, Jesus speaks of Elisha the prophet (Luke 4:27) and refers to Elijah the prophet as well. Jesus is clearly using both figures to illustrate his aphorism about the fate of prophets (Luke 4:24). According to Matthew's version of the eschatological discourse, Jesus speaks of the "prophet Daniel" who spoke of the "desolating sacrilege standing in the holy place" (Matt. 24:15). The first example is taken from special Lukan material, and the second is quite likely a Matthean addition to the triple tradition (Matt. 24:15; Mark 13:14; Luke 21:20).

Other passages indicate that several figures were called prophets in the Gospel traditions. Some examples not already mentioned would be Isaiah (Matt. 4:14; 8:17; 12:17; Mark 1:2; Luke 4:17), Jeremiah (Matt. 2:17; 16:14; 27:9), and Joel (Acts 2:16). The persistence of prophetic figures in the Christian movement is confirmed by sayings such as Matthew 10:41, an apparent reference to extending hospitality to itinerant prophets, as well as Paul's inclusion of prophets and prophecy in his lists of the endowments of the Spirit (1 Cor. 12:28; 14:26–32; Rom. 12:6; Eph. 4:11). The *Didache* even lays down a rule limiting the stay of itinerants in the settled communities that provided their hospitality (*Didache* 11:8).[8]

All of these references to prophets and prophecy in the Gospels raise a more fundamental question. What does it mean to be called a "prophet?" What does it imply to identify a popular figure, like John or Jesus, with the prophets? These questions will be addressed in the rest of this chapter.

TYPES OF PROPHETS IN THE SECOND TEMPLE ERA AND TIME OF JESUS

It is clear that Jesus is associated with John the Baptist, and both are viewed as prophets (Matt. 14:5; see also Mark 11:32; Matt. 21:26; Luke 20:6). But what kinds of figures were included in the designation, and for what kinds of activity were they known? In his study of John the Baptist, Robert Webb has proposed a useful typology for understanding the variety of prophetic figures who appear in late Second Temple Judaism.[9] He identifies three types of prophets: clerical, sapiential, and popular.

Clerical Prophets

The clerical prophet is essentially a priest performing prophetic functions. The example par excellence, at least from Josephus's point of view, is John Hyrcanus I (135–104 B.C.E.), who combined in his person the roles of ruler, high priest, and prophet (*War* 1.68–69; *Ant.* 13.299–300). His prophetic gift manifested itself primarily in his ability to predict the future. Josephus tells us that Hyrcanus accurately foresaw, for example, that neither of his two elder sons would succeed him (*War,* 1.68–69; *Ant.* 13.299–300, 322), and on another occasion he predicted the military victory of his sons over Cyzicenus. At the time the battle was being fought, he himself was performing priestly functions in the temple, far from the battlefield (*Ant.* 13.282–283). In making the second prophecy, Hyrcanus had been prompted by a heavenly voice while he was burning incense in the temple, a fact implying that his ability to read the future grew out of the priestly role, which enabled him to interpret the purposes of God as they were revealed to him. To Josephus's descriptions of John Hyrcanus I, Webb adds the example of Josephus himself, who predicted Vespasian's rise to power (*War* 3.400–402) and recounted how he had received revelatory dreams through which God communicated this future to him (*War* 3.351–54). If Hyrcanus and Josephus are typical examples, then it can be inferred that clerical prophets come from the ruling class or priestly elites. Their prophetic gift entails the capacity to receive and interpret dreams, or to hear the divine voice through which God communicates with human beings. This, in turn, leads to the ability to predict future events or recognize the fulfillment of prophecies already recorded in scripture (317–22).

Sapiential Prophets

Sapiential prophets belong to groups who emphasize the need for purity as a precondition for the acquisition of wisdom, and they believe that wisdom is gained through the study of holy books and sacred texts. These prophets are classified by the groups to which they belong. Webb identifies two types of sapiential prophets: those who belong to the Essenes and those who are Pharisees. He finds three examples of Essene prophets. Judas the Essene predicted "the murder of Antigonus by his brother Aristobulus I" (323; *War* 1.78–80; *Ant.* 13.311–13), and an Essene named Menaham predicted "the rise of Herod (the Great) to kingship while Herod was still a boy" (324). Finally, by interpreting one of the king's dreams, Simon the Essene informed Archelaus that his rule was coming to an end (*Ant.* 17.345–47).

The Pharisees, also known for their foresight in reading God's plans, served as a retainer group deeply involved in court intrigues. When Herod was called to appear before the Sanhedrin to account for his execution of the social bandit Hezekias, he appeared with an armed guard to intimidate the formal body. Samaias (or Pollion), a member of the Sanhedrin, predicted Herod's rise to power and its disastrous consequences for the Sanhedrin. He was right on both counts (*Ant.* 14.172–76; 15.3–4). Josephus later recounts a failed court intrigue in which the Pharisees sought unsuccessfully to depose Herod and promote Pheroras as his successor (*Ant.* 17.41–45). In this instance, their prophecies proved bogus, and the court plot ended in their defeat. In the Pheroras episode, the Pharisees acted as client retainers attempting to pursue their political goals by attaching themselves to powerful patrons with standing in the court. They functioned as a political faction.

Whether Essene or Pharisee, sapiential prophets come from the retainer class, perhaps as intellectuals or sages whose counsel is valued because of their reputed ability to predict the future. The sole exception is Samaias (Pollion?), who appears as a member of the Sanhedrin and, therefore, most likely belongs to the ruling class. Essenes and Pharisees share a reputation for purity, wisdom, and expertise in the study of sacred books. Gray has speculated that the three virtues fit together to form a larger pattern of belief.

> Josephus . . . believed that God controlled history in a direct and comprehensive way and that events on earth unfolded in accordance with the divine plan. Predicting the future, then, depended on gaining insight into God's character, purposes and intentions. Scripture . . . had been written by God or . . . by prophets inspired by God and contained a record of God's actions in the past and his plans for the future. The practice of purifications brought one closer to God by eliminating the impurities that made contact between the human and the Divine impossible.[10]

What better way to learn God's seemingly inscrutable purposes than through purifications that prepared human beings to investigate the sacred books in which such mysteries were encoded, just waiting to be revealed to the inquirer who had "eyes to see." The political advantages accruing to any group who claimed to know the future are obvious.

Popular Prophets

Webb calls his third category of prophetic figures "popular prophets," which he divides into two subtypes, "leadership popular prophets" and "solitary popular prophets."[11] These same figures have been studied elsewhere under the rubric of "sign prophets" or "popular prophets."[12] Horsley and Hanson categorize the popular prophets into two different subtypes, "oracular prophets" and "action prophets."[13] Whatever their designation, the popular prophets had two traits in common. The leadership prophets all gathered groups of followers in preparation for some kind of dramatic action. During Pilate's procuratorship (26–36 C.E.), an unnamed Samaritan gathered a multitude and promised to lead them up Mount Gerizim, where he would show them "the sacred vessels" buried there "where Moses had deposited them" (*Ant.* 18.85–87). Pilate dispatched a military force of "cavalry and heavy-armed infantry," who routed the group after fighting "a pitched battle" and then summarily executed their leaders. Josephus's description implies that the group was heavily armed, the only group of such followers for whom this was the case. During the procuratorship of Fadus (44–46 C.E.), Theudas inspired a group to pack up their worldly possessions and follow him to the Jordan River, which he promised to part (*Ant.* 20.97–98). Once again, the group was brutally suppressed, its leader decapitated, and his head sent to Jerusalem as a trophy and a warning to others with similar aspirations. During the procuratorship of Felix (52–60 C.E.), an unnamed Egyptian was purported to have gathered a group of "thirty thousand" followers. Although there are discrepancies between the two accounts of the Egyptian's movement (*War* 2.261–63 and *Ant.* 20.169–72), it appears that he led his group into the wilderness and then out of the desert to congregate on the Mount of Olives, where he promised that he would command the walls of Jerusalem to crumble and fall. Thereafter, he planned to storm the unprotected city and establish himself as king. Josephus mentions two other instances of similar movements.

Under Felix, numerous such figures arose (*War* 2.258–69; *Ant.* 20.167–68) claiming prophetic inspiration and promising "signs of deliverance." Often, they led their followers into the wilderness in preparation for "revolutionary changes" or some mighty act of God that would deliver the people from the yoke of the Romans. Finally, under Festus (60–62 C.E.), another "imposter" arose promising "salvation and rest from troubles," but his movement ended as all the others, in the destruction and dispersal of the crowd.

The examples of solitary prophets are neither as numerous nor as notable, with the exception of "Jesus, son of Ananias, a rude peasant," who appeared in the temple and began to pronounce oracles of doom (*War* 6.300–309). His oracle is interesting because it contains an implicit claim to have heard the voice of God, the means by which Hyrcanus predicted the future.

> There came to the feast . . . one Jesus, son of Ananias, a rude peasant, who, standing in the temple, suddenly began to cry out, "A voice from the east, a voice from the west, a voice from the four winds; a voice against Jerusalem and the sanctuary, a voice against the bridegroom and the bride, a voice against all the people. (*War* 6.301)

For his impertinence, he was punished by local temple officials and flogged by the Romans, but he continued to prophesy until he was killed during the siege of Jerusalem. His actions are reminiscent of the oracular prophets, particularly Jeremiah, who also prophesied the downfall of Jerusalem.

Webb's other examples are neither as clear nor as convincing. During the fall of Jerusalem, a prophet bade his followers to gather on the Temple Mount and await "the signs of their deliverance," but they all perished when the Romans torched the portico in which they had gathered to wait (*War* 6.285). This example seems more like a leadership prophet who brought the same destruction on his followers as his predecessors had done. Instead of wandering the countryside, which they could no longer do in the besieged city, they journeyed to the temple, and instead of being slaughtered in the wilderness or by the Jordan River they perished on the Temple Mount. Likewise, the prophets who misled the inhabitants of Jerusalem during its final days by proclaiming that God would save the city look less like solitary prophets than prophets in search of a following, willing to curry favor with the masses, more like would-be leadership prophets than solitary oracles (*War* 6.286, 288). They may have been put to mean use by the leaders of the fratricidal factions, struggling with each other to maintain some semblance of control in a dying city, but they do not seem to have been solitary figures in the way Jesus, son of Ananias, was, pursuing his own proclamation of judgment without regard for its consequences. They seem less like Jeremiah and more like Hananiah (cf. Jeremiah 28), telling the people what they wanted to hear rather than telling the truth, the whole truth, and nothing but the truth, no matter how painful that truth might be. Josephus's invective against them is reminiscent of Ezekiel's prophecies "against the prophets of Israel who prophesy out of their imagination" and have brought ruin on Jerusalem. "They misled my people, saying 'peace,' when there is no peace" (Ezek. 13:2, 10; see the entire chapter). To prophesy out of one's imagination is not to prophesy out of the message delivered by Yahweh. Micah likewise prophesies against the false prophets who lead the people astray and promises that Yahweh will bring darkness to their vision (Micah 3:5–8).

The sign prophets share some critical commonalities, and these may shed more light on their role than the distinction between leadership prophets and solitary popular prophets. With the possible exceptions of the Samaritan and the Egyptian, they were all from the peasant class, but it seems probable, given the *modus operandi* they shared with the other sign prophets, that the Samaritan and the Egyptian were also peasant figures. Unlike the clerical and sapiential prophets, the popular sign prophets were not involved in issues of political succession, the fate of rulers, and court intrigues. Nor were they literate like the sapiential prophets, whose authority resided partly in their ability to interpret sacred books. They relied instead on popular memory and the appeal to signs. This may explain the confusing conglomeration of events described by Josephus. When they led their groups into the wilderness, were these popular prophets reliving the exodus led by Moses or reenacting the conquest led by Joshua? The answer is not clear. It is possible that the motifs of exodus and conquest had coalesced in the popular imagination into a general scenario of redemption. Or they may be reflecting the view of Hosea, who associated the time in the wilderness with the multiplication of prophetic visions (Hos. 12:9–10). In either case, the appeal to the past for help in solving a present dilemma is entirely in keeping with the time orientation of peasants in agrarian societies, and it suggests a word of caution in speaking about the beliefs of these prophets as "eschatological."[14] The popular prophets and their followers were looking for "signs of redemption" so close at hand that they were virtually part of the present, not the future. The Egyptian and his group evidently imagined that, when they reached the Mount of Olives, he would speak the word, and the walls of Jerusalem would come tumbling down. Their hope was so vivid that it seemed as much an accomplished fact as the story of Joshua before the walls of Jericho, and they made themselves characters in this enacted prophetic drama. Like Theudas, who promised to part the waters of the Jordan, these prophets were bringing the imagined past into present experience. They did not propose to do anything new or unprecedented.

Peasants in the Mediterranean area typically are oriented to the present rather than the past or the future, but not the present as Bultmann interpreted it, the existential moment detached from past and future. The present time orientation of the peasant included a time horizon shaped by the cycles of nature, tilling the land, and other rituals that marked the return of important events, such as Passover and the other pilgrimage festivals. This sense of the present, or what Malina calls "experienced time," took into account the antecedent processes being worked out in the present and the consequences that flowed from it.[15] It was a notion of time as cyclical and processual in nature, and it reflected the basic operations and conditions of peasant life. Beyond this present time frame, all past events and future possibilities existed in "imaginary time."[16] In other words, peasants had no sense of historical or linear time. They existed in an extended present beyond whose realm all past events and future possibilities blended together just beyond their time horizons. So Moses and Joshua were less inhabitants of a distant historical past than figures looming on the time horizon separating present from past. They were close at hand, as the periodic celebrations in the temple of God's mighty acts made clear. Since time is cyclical, what has happened is a clue to what is happening. This allowed the popular prophets to draw on the memory of God's great acts, located just beyond the time horizon of the present, in order to address the ever-pressing questions of survival.

Malina also observes that peasants act in the present to ensure their continued survival, often reflecting an integrated temporal perspective that views the proximate results being sought as "continuous with the present, yet with no personal control over the realization of outcomes."[17] This awareness of their political impotence may have led the prophets to repose their confidence in God alone. Gray notes quite accurately, "one thing, however, is reasonably certain: the sign prophets believed that the deliverance they expected and announced would be wrought miraculously by God."[18] Only God was powerful enough to deal with Roman colonial rule and the monopoly of power controlled by local elites. The peasant prophets were no fools; they knew that they were relatively powerless and politically vulnerable. It was enough for the sign prophets to lead their followers to sacred sites where God had acted, to the Jordan, to Mount Gerizim, the Mount of Olives, or the Temple Mount itself. They evidently believed that showing up at the site was adequate to inspire God to act again and trigger a repeat performance.

What motivated the popular prophets? The question is not an easy one to answer because Josephus, in his characterization of these figures, is unrelentingly critical. He accuses the anonymous group under Felix of "fostering revolutionary changes" (*neōterismous kai metabolas; War* 2.259), promising to perform "signs and wonders" (*terata kai sēmeia; Ant.* 20.168; see 20.167–68), or providing "signs of their deliverance" (*sēmeia eleutherias; War* 2.259; see also *ta sēmeia tēs sōterias; War* 6.285). Under Festus, an unnamed popular prophet who was designated an imposter by Josephus promised his followers "salvation and rest from their troubles" (*sōtērian autois epaggellomenou kai paulan kakon*).

Aside from the popular prophets who operated in Jerusalem during the siege and promised deliverance from the Roman army or, in the case of Jesus, son of Ananias, who prophesied the fall of Jerusalem and the destruction of the temple by the Romans, the popular prophets seemed to have tapped into a deep well of discontent. The promise of deliverance or redemption implies oppression and misery. The desire to uncover the "sacred vessels" hidden by Moses on Mount Gerizim implies discontent with the temple in Jerusalem and a critique of its profanation of sacred vessels. The effort to repeat the mighty acts attendant on the exodus and conquest implies a people held in bondage. In this framework, the story of the unnamed Egyptian is laden with irony. Now it is the Egyptian who leads the exodus from the burdensome oppression of the temple state and Roman colonial presence. As Webb notes of the movements of the popular prophets, "the entire orientation of the strategy and ideology of these prophetic movements indicates that their primary goal was deliverance," a factor that strongly implies a "widespread sense of oppression and dissatisfaction among the peasantry."[19] Horsley and Hanson note that Elijah and Elisha combined the activities of judge and prophet "in communicating Yahweh's redemptive action, his protection of his people against foreign invasion and domination."[20]

These concerns were shared by the sign prophets. In this political context and, operating out of a time orientation different from our own, the popular prophets and their movements make sense. They were acting to increase the possibility of their survival, a factor made increasingly difficult by the multiple layers of ruling classes (Roman, Herodian, and priestly) with which they had to contend. Their movements were symbolic appeals to the God who dwelt beyond the present time horizon of their lives to act to ensure their survival. They were not so much driven by a vision of a future as by confidence in the past, the past that had antecedently shaped their present and could continue to influence its forthcoming course.[21] All that was needed was a leader like Moses or Joshua and a people oppressed by their rulers.

To this list of prototypical heroes, Horsley and Hanson add the judges of ancient Israel, who combined a prophetic word with a call to action.[22] In times of crisis, the spirit of Yahweh would descend upon such leaders, calling them to respond by leading a military campaign or a reform movement. "Thus, combining both message and action, the *shophet* was not simply an individual messenger, but also the leader of a religiopolitical movement."[23] One of the characteristics of these figures portrayed in Josephus is that they seems to arise without warning, but this is characteristic of the period of the judges and the prophetic movements they led.

In her summary of the sign prophets, Gray identifies six characteristics of the group. (1) They led "sizable movements." Although Josephus's numbers are often suspect, especially his account of the Egyptian's "thirty thousand dupes" (*War* 2.261–62), he continually indicates that the movements were large enough to attract the attention of local elites and their colonial overlords, who took swift and brutal action against them. (2) The popular prophets recruited members out of the peasantry and common people. These were not elite movements. (3) The leaders "presented themselves as prophets" and appear to have modeled themselves after the great prophetic figures of the past, Moses and Joshua in particular. (4) The popular prophets led their followers on a journey, usually into the desert or wilderness, often with a goal in mind such as the Jordan River, the Temple Mount, or Mount Gerizim. (5) "The sign prophets announced to their followers that God himself was about to act in a dramatic way to deliver them," even though what they actually expected to happen is not spelled out with any precision or detail. (6) As a prelude to this divine act, the prophets promised to perform some sign.[24]

The very fact of these movements testifies to social unrest and political discontent. How significant and how extensive it was is not clear, although Josephus traces a spiraling escalation of social dis-ease in the years leading up to the First Jewish Revolt (66–73 C.E.). Aside from the animosity he harbored toward these figures because of his own elite and priestly status, Josephus evidently judged them harshly for another reason. Gray has argued that Josephus used "signs" (*sēmeia*) to refer to "authenticating miracles."[25] In his description of Moses, for example, Josephus speaks of Moses receiving three "signs" at the burning bush: "how to turn his staff into a serpent, how to cause his hand to turn white and then return to normal, and how to turn water into blood."[26] God's purpose in equipping Moses with these miraculous abilities was to authenticate his status as a prophet or magician in Pharaoh's court. If Josephus understood signs in this way, then the failure of the sign prophets to produce what they promised led him to conclude that they were charlatans and deceivers. Had they been authentic, they would have been able to produce what they promised. This judgment applies most fully to Theudas and the Egyptian who, alone among the sign prophets, not only announced that God would act but also proclaimed their own power to bring the promised liberation. Their actions would contribute to the coming deliverance. From Josephus's point of view, to those who claimed more is reserved the greater condemnation.

The sign prophets mentioned in Josephus all operated after the time of Jesus and John, although they are roughly contemporaneous figures. I have examined them in this chapter because their social and political conditions are much the same as those prevailing at the time of Jesus. While it is evident that Jesus was neither a clerical prophet nor a sapiential prophet, as Webb has defined them, he does seem, in some ways, to belong in the tradition of the popular prophets. There are obvious differences between them, however. The sign prophets gathered relatively large followings, whereas Jesus called a few disciples (Mark 1:16–20 // Matt. 4:18–22; Mark 2:13–17 // Matt. 9:9–13 and Luke 5:27–32) and may have been accompanied by an itinerant group including women (cf. Luke 8:1–3).[27] He attracted crowds in the villages and countryside of Galilee, but he did not attempt to lead a large multitude around with him. He was probably accompanied by a band of pilgrims on his journey to Jerusalem, but this is a far cry from the journeys of the sign prophets and their followers (Mark 11:8–10 // Matt. 21:8–9 and Luke 19:37–38). Clearly, Jesus was well received by the common people, villagers, peasants, rural artisans, and the more destitute as well. If he had not been popular with the masses (the crowd, *ochlos*), he would not have been tried and executed by Jerusalem elites and their Roman rulers. Like the popular prophets, Jesus does seem to have claimed to be a prophet, or at least he identified with prophets, at the time of his rejection at Nazareth

(Mark 6:1–6a; cf. Luke 4:16–30). Similarly, in his answer to John's inquiry, Jesus virtually identifies himself as a prophet (Q, Luke 7:18–23 = Matt. 11:2–6). Like the sign prophets, Jesus did announce God's impending action in the present, the coming of the reign of God, but he does not seem to have associated this coming kingdom with spectacular signs he promised to perform. However, in light of the actions of the sign prophets, it is possible to view the feeding in the wilderness as a sign (Mark 6:30–44; 8:1–10 and par.).[28] Jesus may also have viewed his exorcisms as signs of God's imminent rule (Q, Luke 11:20 = Matt. 12:28). Jesus was wiser than the sign prophets and more subtle. With the possible exceptions of the entry into Jerusalem and incident in the temple (Mark 11:1–10 // Matt. 21:1–9; Luke 19:28–40; Mark 11:15–17 // Matt. 21:12–13; Luke 19:45–46), he did not announce deadlines or concoct public events that challenged the hegemony of the temple or the power of Rome. Such frontal confrontations always ended in the death and destruction of those who encouraged them.

But it is a far cry from admitting this to asserting, with Gray, that "John and Jesus, I hope it will be agreed, were definitely apolitical by my definition."[29] Her definition of political is indebted to Sanders, "not involving a plan to liberate and restore Israel by defeating the Romans and establishing an autonomous government."[30] To limit the definition of political in this manner overlooks most of the means of political involvement available to non-elites.[31] It solves nothing to define the political in a manner inaccessible to Jesus and others of his peasant village class, and then to conclude on the basis of the definition that Jesus was apolitical. The only thing such a definition really proves is that Jesus was not an elite involved in the power games of the politically dominant ruling class and, therefore, was neither a clerical nor a sapiential prophet. Finally, it needs to be said that Sanders's definition assumes a modern Western view of linear time, future planning, and political action that one could not reasonably expect to find in the world of ancient Palestine. Its absence does not indicate that actors like Jesus were apolitical; it indicates that they acted politically in ways that we have not been trained to see.

The phenomenon of the sign prophets in their various manifestations raises the larger question of their relationship to the tradition of prophecy in Israel. To that matter, we now will turn.

ISRAEL'S PROPHETIC TRADITION IN HISTORICAL PERSPECTIVE

Any attempt to speak about the role of prophecy in the traditions of Israel must account for the perspectives of the Deuteronomic history (Deuteronomy through 2 Kings), which portrays Moses as the quintessential prophet and the model for all future prophets, since he assumed the mediating role between Yahweh and the people at Sinai.[32] Moses may have been, to use Webb's categories, the prototypical sapiential prophet. In large measure this means that "the chief function of the prophet is . . . to promulgate the law, preach its observance after the manner of Moses and transmit it to posterity."[33] The positive role of the prophet implies a negative counterpart, namely, warning the people of the consequences of their failure to observe the covenant expressed through the Torah. This responsibility was passed on from generation to generation, from Joshua and the judges through Samuel to the prophets of the monarchic period, culminating in Jeremiah, the last of the prophets in this great succession.[34] It is important to note that the prophet is not the one who speaks against the Torah but one who appeals to it and upholds its traditions of justice and judgment. The Torah functions then as one expression of the covenant between Yahweh and the people, and insofar as prophets appeal to the covenant, they are also appealing to the Torah.

The prophet is also a political figure, and prophets were visibly involved in the politics of the pre-monarchic era as well as the period of the Monarchy. Samuel's call involved a prophetic denunciation of the house of Eli, and the fact that his words did not "fall to the ground" but came to pass marked Samuel as a "trustworthy prophet" (1 Sam. 3:1–21). Twice, Nathan the prophet mediated the Word of the Lord to David. After David revealed his plans to build a temple for Yahweh, Nathan informed him that he would not be the one to do the job (2 Sam. 7:1–17), and the same Nathan confronted David with his sin after he had taken Bathsheba and ordered her husband, Uriah the Hittite, killed (2 Sam. 11–12). Gad, who is referred to as "the prophet Gad, David's seer" (2 Sam. 24:11), brings the word of Yahweh's judgment on David for conducting a census (2 Sam. 24:1–25). At a later time, Elijah and Elisha are similarly involved in the power politics of the Northern Kingdom. Elijah was a constant thorn in the side of Ahab and Jezebel (1 Kings 17–22). Elisha "anointed Jehu to be king in place of Ahab's son Jehoram (2 Kings 9:1–13).[35]

In their public role as political brokers, prophets could come into conflict with each other. For example, when Ahab consulted his court prophets, Zedekiah and his colleagues all predicted victory in battle against Ramoth-gilead, but Micaiah alone announced Ahab's defeat (1 Kings 22:1–40). Jeremiah locked horns with Hananiah over the fate of Jerusalem, Jeremiah prophesying its destruction and Hananiah its escape from capture (Jeremiah 28). Lester Grabbe has noted that the difference between true and false prophets may be in the eye of the beholder. Of Ahab's court prophets, including Micaiah, he notes that "all the prophets speak in the name of Yhwh," and it was "quite normal for omens to be tested against each other."[36] The same could be said of Jeremiah and Hananiah. Numerous passages bear witness to the presence of intraprophetic conflict in ancient Israel and Judah (Ezekiel 13; Hos. 4:4–6; 9:7–9; Micah 3:5–8; Zech. 7:7–14; 13:2–6).

In his study of the role of the prophets, Blenkinsopp has proposed a framework for understanding the development of prophecy.[37] Beginning in the eighth century, a new kind of intellectual leadership emerged in Israel. It was embodied in the work of Amos, Hosea, Isaiah, and Micah, all of whom came from a privileged class, yet managed to fashion a tradition of social protest and intellectual dissent that lasted for two hundred years. Their protest can be understood in the context of the emergence of the monarchic state and its effects on the peasantry and the clan or tribal systems already in place. As the state increasingly encroached on the rights, resources, and eventually the land of its peasant base, it co-opted the religion of Yahweh and its prophets to serve its purposes and legitimate the newly emerging state policies. The court prophets obeyed their rulers, but the four prophets mentioned here did not. They witnessed the collateral damage caused by the state system and denounced its abuses. They shared a common vision and advocacy:

> They spoke or wrote on behalf of the socially and economically disadvantaged, the victims of the gradual and inexorable undermining by the state of the cohesion and ethos of a more or less egalitarian system based on the kinship network.[38]

Though themselves insiders intellectually and socially, they were advocates for outsiders. Indeed, their genius was the way they used their social position as leverage. "What is clear is that all four belonged to the very small minority of the population that was literate and educated, and it was from that socially privileged position that their protest was launched."[39] The social, economic, and political conditions that the great prophets faced would have been familiar to Jesus.[40] In the first century C.E. as well as in the eighth century B.C.E., peasants were being alienated from their land, and ruling elites were redistributing wealth to an indigenous ruling class while creating bureaucracies to mediate their power and manage their control. Priests and prophets were collaborating with the emerging rulers, legitimating this juggernaut of change and justifying the ways it trampled and destroyed the traditional clan system and network of tribal loyalties.

The process of state control moved more smoothly in the Southern Kingdom of Judah than in the Northern Kingdom of Israel. The anti-monarchic tradition expressed so clearly in 1 Samuel 8:10–18 continued to influence the course of events in Israel. There, the conflict between "tribal ethos and state system" created "chronic political instability" and a tradition of "resistance . . . to the apparatus of state control."[41] The more unstable and uncertain the state's control, the more maneuvering room for the prophets. Many of the Elijah and Elisha traditions reflect this political situation, as does the story of Naboth's vineyard (1 Kings 21:1–29). It is helpful to remember that the Galilee of Jesus' day represented one portion of the former Northern Kingdom, a connection that Horsley notes carefully in his study of "the roots of Galilean independence."[42] Although the intervening history of rule by Hellenistic empires, Hasmonaean rulers, Herodian tyranny, and Roman hegemony must be factored into the history of Galilee, its roots remain entwined with the history of the Northern Kingdom and the aftermath of its fall.

It is tempting, albeit misguided, to place Jesus in the tradition of Amos, Hosea, Isaiah, and Micah and to view him as an extension of them, because he does share some commonalities with them. In spite of that fact, Jesus was not born into a socially or politically privileged elite. He may have known how to read Torah, but he was not an intellectual in the same way his illustrious prophetic ancestors were. Nor did he have their leverage either in the court of Herod Antipas or the temple courtyard in Jerusalem. He was more an outsider than an insider and, in this respect, he is closer to the popular prophets mentioned by Josephus. Jesus came from the margins of his society, not its centers of power, and recent efforts to turn Jesus into an urban sophisticate show how bankrupt such an approach can be.[43] Nowhere do the Gospel traditions depict a privileged Jesus using his social status and prominent position on behalf of the poor and the outcast. He emerges from the village life of Galilee, a representative of the little tradition, not an exponent of the great tradition. Like the great prophets, Jesus does argue Torah and appeal to the covenant traditions of Israel's past, as they reflect the interests of village life and peasant existence, and he brings not only good news of Yahweh's redemption but a word of judgment as well.[44]

JESUS AS PROPHET OF THE JUSTICE OF THE REIGN OF GOD

Two Scholarly Appraisals of Jesus the Prophet

In recent times, both R. David Kaylor and N. T. Wright have argued that Jesus should be seen as a prophet.[45] Kaylor understands Jesus as a prophet because he was a political figure with a political message. As he puts it,

> Jesus preached and taught a message that was thoroughly political, a message that demanded a social or political revolution. . . . To claim that Jesus was "political" is to say that Jesus promoted a restoration of the covenant community on the basis of the Torah and the prophets, both of which regarded the mundane aspects of life as "spiritual" issues.[46]

His crucifixion by the Romans for political crimes is in keeping with this interpretation of his public work. The Romans perceived Jesus as a political threat and determined to remove him. The heart of Kaylor's case focuses on the nonparabolic teachings of Jesus. Having surveyed the materials of the Gospel tradition, he draws the following conclusions about Jesus the prophet (= political figure):

1. Jesus' teaching focused on God.
2. Jesus' teachings appealed to the covenant and assumed knowledge of it.
3. Jesus taught "an ethic of repentance."
4. This repentance envisioned "a radical revisioning of society."
5. Jesus supplied neither rules nor wisdom but "taught his ethic by proclamation," an appeal to do "God's will" as "the basis for a just society."
6. Jesus based his ethic "on scripture."
7. Jesus' ethic was oriented toward living in this world; it was neither an "interim ethic" nor an otherworldly ethic.
8. Jesus taught his ethic parabolically, not by using casuistry.
9. The great commandments summarize Jesus' ethic.
10. "Jesus' ethic builds on the notion of grace, but grace is not cheap."
11. Jesus' ethic, to some degree, reveals Jesus' self-understanding. (114–19)

If Jesus was a prophet, he would appear to be a prophet in the "oracular" tradition of Israel's great prophets of the past. Although Kaylor works steadfastly and earnestly to make connections between Jesus' teachings and the social and economic conditions of the people, it is difficult to discern how the teacher of an ethic of love could come to such an end. That Jesus' ethic is engaged with the practical problems of everyday living is clear, but how that ethic became a political challenge to the powers that be is less obvious. In particular, there is a divide between his sketch of the political situation (1–91) and his summary of Jesus' teaching, which becomes increasingly theological and ethical in a way that seems to diminish, if not eclipse, the political (92–214). However, Kaylor has done a service to the third quest by making his case so clearly and demonstrating the presence of the political in the teachings and actions of Jesus.

Wright's argument is almost impossible to summarize in brief.[47] He believes that Jesus combines two prophetic traditions, that of the oracular prophet with that of the popular leadership prophet. In this role, Jesus brings good news and bad news. The good news is that the God of Israel is about to bring the exile to an end by restoring the people and coming to dwell with them once again.[48] Seen through these lenses, Jesus' healings and exorcisms were prophetic signs pointing to the return of God's mighty acts to liberate and make whole. But the renewed and restored Israel would not be like the old people of God; thus the bad news is that God's restoring work judges and condemns the abuses of temple and Torah alike. This is why Jesus eats at table with sinners, an enacted parable, and appeals to others to create this new community. Jesus announced the fulfillment of God's prophetic future for Israel, but as so often happens with prophecy, the fulfillment changes the original form of the promise. All of this is what Wright means by speaking of Jesus' proclamation as "eschatological." Eschatological does not refer to the end of the physical world, but to the end of one chapter of Israel's ongoing story and the opening of a new chapter of it. "We are not faced with a new story altogther, but with *a new moment in the same story.*"[49] The plot has taken an unexpected twist, but it is still the same story. This argument has affinities with the views advanced by Crossan in his study of the parables.[50] There, Crossan observed that

> Jesus was not proclaiming that God was about to end *this* world, but, seeing this as one view of world, he was announcing God as the One who shatters world, this one, and any other before or after it.[51]

Of course, Wright and Crossan are not making the same point. Wright is focusing on a new act in the same drama that is still being acted out today, whereas Crossan seems to be advocating a permanent eschatology that continually disturbs and disrupts. He makes this point quite clearly:

> The geographers tell us that we do not live on firm earth but on giant moving plates whose grinding passage and tortured depths give us earthquake and volcano. Jesus tells us that that we do not live in firm time but on giant shifting epochs whose transitions and changes are the eschatological advent of God.[52]

Wright emphasizes the continuity in the midst of discontinuity (it is a new chapter of the same story), whereas Crossan emphasizes a discontinuity that disrupts and even destroys continuity through its abrupt shifts and eruptions. But, in spite of their differing emphases, both share an understanding of eschatology as bringing a sociocultural world to an end rather than the physical world.[53] To use the language of Peter Berger and Thomas Luckmann, the world coming to an end is one "social construction of reality."[54]

Although Wright draws on Webb's categories and interprets Jesus as being, in part, a "leadership" prophet, both Wright and Kaylor see Jesus primarily as a prophet in the tradition of Israel's great oracular prophets. Jesus is involved in the struggle to reframe Israel's identity-giving narrative, or he is the giver of a new ethic capable of recreating community. Both Wright and Kaylor are keenly aware of the first-century setting but, after all is said and done, do not convincingly integrate the harsh political realities of colonial occupation and the remorseless oppression and exploitation of peasants inherent in the conditions of Roman, Herodian, and temple domination.[55] Jesus the prophet is still fundamentally Jesus the teacher, and it is not easy to move from theological and ethical concerns to the political context in which they were spoken or acted out. This will be the task of Parts 2 and 3 of this study.

Jesus as Prophet "Mighty in Word and Deed"

This study will propose that Jesus is an odd combination of prophetic types. First, he argues Torah, and he understands the role of Torah in the life of the common people as well as the purposes it has served for the ruling elites. Like a prophet cut out of the mold of the Deuteronomic history, Jesus continues the work of the prototypical prophet, Moses, because he uses Torah to disclose the will of God and to define the justice of God as well as to warn those who abuse the Torah as an instrument of oppression. Jesus neither opposes the Torah nor obliterates it, but attacks a reading of the Torah promulgated by the Jerusalem elites to justify their oppression of "the people of the land." His ability to argue Torah and apply it to the lives of his hearers may explain why, at least in part, Jesus was called "rabbi." This was not an official title but a mark of recognition and an honorific designation, that is, an honorable way to address one who "[taught] the way of God in accordance with truth" (Mark 11:14).

But Jesus does not simply argue Torah. He brings his own distinct message to his work, although this proclamation is neither discontinuous with the history of his people nor a denial of previous traditions. To use Malina's language, Jesus' teachings are the forthcoming result of antecedent tradition focused on the present questions of survival. In his study of cross-cultural parallels to prophecy in Israel, Grabbe identifies a key quality of Nuer prophets that made their work both memorable and durable. It resided, he suggested, in "their ability to enunciate a coherent set of ideas which helped the members of contemporary Nuer society comprehend their own time and situation."[56] This sounds as though the Nuer prophets were dealing with abstractions, but it can equally well mean that the prophets developed a critique of their society that illumined the larger processes affecting the lives of the people. This may be why Jesus was called "teacher" (*didaskalos*); critical analysis was part of the prophetic project. This is what I have already argued with regard to the parables. Put Jesus in the role of a peasant prophet, and he is a "pedagogue of the oppressed."[57] However, it is in this role that Jesus most resembles the oracular prophets of the great tradition. Like Amos, Hosea, Isaiah, and Micah, Jesus the prophet interpreted what was happening to the people of Galilee who were being increasingly squeezed by colonial domination and internal exploitation. He taught them to read their distressing situation not as God's will but as the consequence of the violation of God's covenant. Yet, as already noted, Jesus did not share the social privilege and political leverage of the great prophets of the past. He did not launch an advocacy campaign from a prominent position in court and society.

This is why Jesus must also be seen as a popular prophet who performed signs as part of his public work. Having little ascribed honor, Jesus had to contend for acquired honor in public debate (honor-shame ripostes) and to perform signs that evoked donations of honor from the crowds. These signs were primarily healings and exorcisms, but they were never done for mere effect; they were part of a larger conflictual context and political strategy. Healings and exorcisms are about power: who channels God's power, who mediates God's power, and on whose behalf it is exercised. Any claim to mediate God's redeeming power (healings) or liberating power (exorcisms) was inherently a challenge to those who, in their own estimation, held a monopoly on that power through temple and Torah. To call Jesus "a prophet mighty in word and deed" (Luke 24:19) is to claim for him a powerful role as the broker of God's patronal power. However, in his role as popular prophet, Jesus resembles Elijah and Elisha more than the sign prophets mentioned by Josephus, with the exception that, unlike Elijah and Elisha, he is not involved in the politics of the court and the shifting of dynasties. Jesus seems less overtly political than either of his predecessors but, like them, he is associated with mighty deeds. At this point, it would be tempting to use Scott Hill's portrayal of "local heroes" to build a bridge between Elijah and Elisha, on the one hand, and Jesus of Nazareth, on the other. Local heroes are, first of all, "holy" figures, that is, they are deemed to be holy "in conjunction with shifting balances in social forces," and in the midst of those shifting forces, they are seen "as having privileged access to power (generally meaning God) beyond the reach of other people."[58] They are venerated figures in their village and its surrounding environs, although they rarely attain national prominence. In their local domain, they are liminal, even numinous, figures.

> Beyond the realm defined by "conventional wisdom," however, there always lies an area of unrealized alliances, untapped power, unexpressed yearnings, and untold truth, and it is there that the prophets establish themselves. There are always flaws and oversights in the official explanations of where power and truth lie, and identifying these areas gives local heroes a following that separates them from leaders merely filling an established role. (45)

Needless to say, when such figures attract the attention of power brokers, they are labeled in negative ways, a tactic that actually serves to increase their power and expand their popular following. Still, it is in their relationship to their origins that their power resides. "By serving as a projection of a community's identity, local heroes allow that community to express power that has lain dormant" (48).

It may be useful to view Jesus as a type of "local hero," but it poses other problems. He was not venerated in his hometown and country, and he met stiff opposition when he did return to his own village (Mark 6:1–6a; Matt. 15:53–58; cf. Luke 4:16–30). Although, in one instance, Jesus was sought out to adjudicate conflicts (Luke 12:13ff.), he never became the focus of local shrines after his death, nor for that matter did Jesus gain ascribed honor through his family or kinship ties (48). Like local heroes, he was itinerant, but in the framework being proposed here, itinerancy actually enables local heroes to remain unentangled in the bickering and petty affairs of their village while providing the opportunity to expand their influence over a larger territory (51). This does not seem to reflect the reasons that Jesus became an itinerant. Jesus did expose the "tension between periphery and center, prophet and priest, popular and traditional, old and new" and, in his identification with Galilee, he stood, "consciously or unconsciously, at a key point of tension between the center and the periphery of power . . . where the fulcrum must be placed to achieve a new balance."[59] The figure of the local hero does provide useful insights for illuminating Jesus' role as a popular prophet, but it must be used with caution.

In his role as both a popular and an oracular prophet, Jesus exhibited the fundamental characteristic common to all prophets. Grabbe summarizes it succinctly: "the prophet is a mediator who claims to receive messages direct from a divinity, by various means, and communicates these messages to recipients."[60] The messages may be received by various means, "vision, audition, 'angel,' the 'spirit' or 'hand' of Yhwh, even a dream," and likewise the prophet can communicate that message through word or deed, including signs and bizarre symbolic actions (116). This is why prophets are associated with miracle workers.

> Many prophets have the reputation of an ability to call on God's power to accomplish supernatural deeds: to perform signs and wonders, to benefit friends or to harm enemies, to see into the spirit world and even into the future. (117)

In other words, Jesus' teachings and actions were all part of his prophetic identity. They need not, indeed they cannot, be separated.

This discussion of Jesus' prophetic role has studiously avoided the use of the words "charismatic" and "charisma," although Joseph Blenkinsopp does devote attention to Max Weber's discussion of charisma "as a way of encapsulating the irreducibly personal and nonascriptive element" in the prophet and the prophetic vocation.[61] To this extent, the notion of charisma may be helpful, but not much further. First-century Palestine was a dyadic society rooted in the values of honor and shame.[62] Leaders gained honor not by standing apart from the people but by embodying their values; a charismatic figure would most likely be viewed as a deviant unable to inspire others to follow. By contrast, Malina argues that Jesus was a "reputational" leader rather than a charismatic leader.[63] At the very heart of a reputational leader is his or her ability to dislodge the norms and values that have guided a particular society. So Malina notes,

> This authority derives from the successful criticism and disloca-
> tion of the higher-order norms which legitimate the authority
> prevailing in a given society. . . . This authority emerges from a
> person's effective ability to convince members of a given society
> to recognize no longer some higher-order norm as binding. (249)

This activity can get very pointed. An emerging reputational leader may convince large numbers of people that a high priest or government bureaucrat holds office not by a divine mandate but through "force, chicanery, collusion, conspiracy, or some other principle" equally unsavory (129).

Malina identifies a number of traits of such leaders.[64] For example, they do not claim a leadership position for themselves and are often associated with traditional institutions. Jesus emerges from traditional village life and is familiar with the synagogue and its traditions of interpreting Torah. He rejects the assertive claims of Gentile rulers in favor of a service-oriented leadership in which the leader does not stand out from the group (Mark 10:42–45 // Matt. 20:25–28; Luke 22:24–27 et passim). A reputational leader is at home with tradition and custom. He or she does not challenge familiar ways of doing things. Such a leader is "an incumbent in an accepted social role" and "administers power and justice according to accepted impersonal 'universalistic' standards" (130). In spite of a traditional and customary orientation, reputational leaders do contribute to the emergence of new structures. When they arise, such leaders show their virtue by "avoidance and relinquishment and/or sharing of power" (130).

Not all the characteristics fit Jesus with equal comfort. It would be hard to say that he oversaw the emergence of new institutional structures, and he was not in a position to act as a new judge of Israel, administering impartial justice according to some putative universalistic standard, like a first-century Samuel. While he was oriented to custom and tradition, he did not always draw on it in familiar and comfortable ways (cf. Luke 4:16–30; Matt. 5:21–48; but see Matt. 5:17–20). On what did Jesus' growing reputation depend? On his healings, his exorcisms, and his ability to best his enemies in honor-shame ripostes as well as on the enthusiastic reception granted his proclamation of the reign of heaven. He proclaimed "a forthcoming theocracy [that] was not so much an alternative to the political ideology prevailing in Israel as a hope for its radical realization" (130, 132). He embodied the values of Israel's past leaders, especially those figures in the Northern Kingdom like Elijah and Elisha, who advocated the values of the covenant in the midst of trying and changing times. Unlike Theudas or the Egyptian, he made no grandiose claims for himself nor did he persuade others to follow him in order to stake his claims. When he exercised power, it was on behalf of the very poor villagers from whom he came.

CONCLUSION

Jesus was a popular prophet whose roots were deeply embedded in Galilean village life. He most likely came from a peasant artisan family and shared the values of village life while being familiar with its customs and traditions.[65] Put differently, Jesus was a peasant prophet who interpreted the Torah not as a representative of the great tradition emanating from Jerusalem but as one who embodied the little tradition found in the villages and countryside of Galilee. At the same time, as a popular prophetic figure, he attracted crowds because he embodied the yearnings of the villagers of Galilee, who were increasingly separated from their land and traditions by an alien network of Roman domination, Herodian exploitation, and temple control. Insofar as he interpreted the Torah and argued its meaning, he was a prophet in the tradition of the Deuteronomist, a prophet who continued the paradigmatic work of Moses, the prototypical prophet. Insofar as he interpreted the social, economic, and political situation in the light of the covenant promises of Yahweh, he stood in the tradition of the great oracular prophets of Israel's past. Add to this mix Jesus' own distinctive voice, rooted in his reputation as a traditional teacher and healer, and the foundation is laid for understanding Jesus as prophet. The rest of this study will test this proposal.

PART 2

Jesus of Nazareth: A Contextual Approach

Part 2 addresses the question of context. Just as the church has learned that theology is contextual, so scholars have learned that the quest for the historical Jesus is contextual. To enter the quest for the historical Jesus requires that we pack our bags for time travel to a distant place and a time remote from our own. If we arrive, we will be surrounded by a strange world with political arrangements, social systems, economic patterns, and local customs alien to those of twentieth-century people. How will we make sense of the new context in which we find ourselves?

Chapter 4 is a survey of the kinds of tools that have been developed by biblical scholars during the span of the twentieth century in order to make sense of the Gospel materials. Each critical tool has defined context in a specific way, not all of which are particularly helpful for those interested in seeking the historical Jesus. Yet they all can be seen as responses to the fundamental necessity of any biblical interpretation, placing a text in its context.

Chapter 5 is a sketch of the kind of world in which Jesus lived and moved and had his being. It was a world of advanced agrarian societies, aristocratic empires, and colonial occupation. I also examine how these larger systems were at work in Galilee, where Herod Antipas ruled as a client ethnarch, and in Judea, where the high-priestly families formed a regime that collaborated with their Roman colonial masters.

Taken together, chapters 4 and 5 define the problem of determining context and then of sketching a context within which Jesus conducted his public work. The provisional results summarized in chapter 5 will be tested throughout the rest of the study. Can we make sense of Jesus as an inhabitant of this world?

4

The Search for a Usable Context:

Biblical Criticism and the Historical Jesus

The history of biblical criticism in the twentieth century has been, in part, a search for a usable context, since one essential task of biblical interpretation is the establishment of a context for understanding a biblical text. A text without a context is a pretext. The refusal to pay attention to the context of a biblical text creates a vacuum, and interpretation abhors a vacuum. This tempts interpreters to fill the vacuum with a contemporary context and then to read the biblical passage through its lenses. While this procedure may create the illusion of relevance, since the Bible appears to speak directly to present-day concerns, it fails to treat the biblical text on its own terms. To be understood properly, biblical texts need to be heard speaking a word for their time and place. When interpreters isolate biblical texts from their social and cultural worlds, therefore, they force the ancient text to speak a contemporary word through an act of theological ventriloquism.

THE PROBLEM OF DEFINING CONTEXT

However, the nature and character of context are not always self-evident, nor is it always clear what counts as context. Given the wealth of knowledge and information available about the ancient world, what counts as establishing the context of a biblical text? What information and theoretical models are applicable to a specific text? During the course of the twentieth century, biblical critics have given numerous answers to these basic questions. The rest of this chapter is devoted to a brief review of a few major proposals with an eye to their implications for the third quest of the historical Jesus. Finally, the chapter will indicate where the approach taken in this study fits into this larger picture.

FORM CRITICISM AND THE "SETTING IN LIFE"

Form criticism was based on the assumption that context was critical for understanding biblical texts and their oral antecedents.[1] The phrase used to describe context was the "setting in life" (*Sitz im Leben*). Essentially, form criticism attempted to reconstruct earlier forms of the tradition (both written and oral) by inferring backward from the Gospel texts. The purpose of such inferential work was to establish a history for the unit of tradition (pericope) in question. Critics believed that texts in the Synoptic Gospels consisted of layers of tradition laminated into a single text through the work of editors and storytellers. The form critic's task was to separate the layers contained in the text in order to construct a history of the saying or controversy or parable. For each stage of the tradition, the interpreter had to construct a context (setting in life) in which the saying made sense. Bultmann and Dibelius set the tone for much of the subsequent discussion by suggesting that the setting in life for many of the Gospel traditions could be found in the needs of the early church as it consolidated its own communal life, argued with its Jewish opponents, and conducted an apologia to justify its place in the Roman Empire.

Since form criticism was based on the assumption that biblical texts were composed of multiple layers of tradition, form critics looked for seams and inconsistences in Gospel texts that might reveal where disparate strands of tradition had been stitched together, causing shifts in the meaning of a pericope. The bias of the discipline was to look for disjunctures and to assume multiple origins for a given Gospel text. Hans Dieter Betz illustrates this tendency very well in his form-critical analysis of the healing of the ten lepers (Luke 17:11–19).[2] Betz identified two layers of tradition in the text, which can be shown as follows:

17:12–14   pre-Lukan apophthegm[3]
17:12–14, 15–16, 17–18 (19)   secondary expansion

The core miracle story (vv. 12–14) recounts a complete miracle. The supplicants approach Jesus (v. 12) and call out to him (v. 13). Jesus hears their plea and instructs them to go to the temple in Jerusalem to have their healing confirmed. Confident in the efficacy of the miracle worker, all ten depart and, presumably, because they all took Jesus at his word, they are healed on the way. Although none of them has "faith" in a distinctively Christian sense, all of them have confidence in Jesus as a miracle worker and healer. Indeed, the problem with the story is that it confuses the issue of faith by implying that confidence in a miracle worker is the equivalent to full-blown Christian faith. In order to prevent this misunderstanding, the church expanded the core miracle story by creating a second scene which combines the return of one of the former lepers (vv. 15–16) with Jesus' comments on his return (vv. 17–18, perhaps v. 19 as well). In the second scene, the nine fall away and the single figure of the Samaritan emerges as the model for the faithful. Unlike the nine, he "sees" that he has been healed (v. 15), so he returns to praise God and thank Jesus. The cultic acts of prostrating himself at Jesus feet and praising God indicate that the Samaritan has been "saved." He has experienced conversion, which is not the same thing as being healed by a "divine man." The identification of the one who returns as a Samaritan casts the nine others, now understood as Jews, in a negative light and may well indicate that the story received its present form after the breach had occurred between synagogue and house church, yet during a time when the Samaritan mission was experiencing some success.

All of this leads Betz to suggest that the original story of the healing of the ten lepers (17:12–14) served as a parody or satiric foil against which to tell the story of the one who returned. He notes that the absence of details in the original story contrasts with other healings (cf. Mark 1:40–45), but the absence of detail is a characteristic feature of parody. At the same time, the presence of ten supplicants introduces a satiric element into the story and exaggerates the magnitude of the healing. If this can be argued, then the writer or storyteller has selected an oral or a literary form, parody or satiric exaggeration, that is congruent with his message, for his point is that the "faith" of the nine lepers, namely, their naive confidence in the miracle worker, is a parody of the true faith that saves. The expansion of the story highlights this theme by converting the Samaritan into a positive role model of one who truly believes, then contrasting his behavior with that of the nine.

It is also possible to elaborate Betz's view by identifying three levels of tradition in the pericope and recontextualizing each layer of tradition. The three layers would be as follows:

17:12–14	core miracle story (focus on the ten)
17:15–16a, 17	first expansion (focus on the nine)
17:11, 16b, 18, 19	Lukan redaction (focus on the one)

The core miracle story treats all ten lepers alike. There seems to be little reason to introduce the distinction that Betz finds so compelling, namely, the pseudo-faith of the nine lepers set against the faith that truly saves the one who returns. Rather, in the original account, all ten lepers have faith in Jesus the master and depart to Jerusalem to have their healing confirmed by the priests in the temple, a practical expedient if they are to live in their society. As they journey on the way, they are healed. They have shown their faith by leaving for the temple before their leprosy is cured, because they believe Jesus has the power to make them clean. There is no need to minimize their faith or impute bad motives to them. They all show remarkable faith in Jesus to make them whole and return them to their communities. If this reading is arguable, then the story could have been told by the early church to illustrate Jesus' healing ministry, which they took as a model for their own, perhaps even to justify their efforts to heal lepers and other undesirables who seemed to be beyond the reach of any healing touch whatsoever. The continuing presence of healing rituals and actions in the early church is suggested by their presence in the list of the gifts of the Spirit in 1 Corinthians 12:9–10, the reference to a healing ritual in James 5:14–15, and the persistence of healing stories and exorcisms in Acts (e.g., 3:1–10; 5:14–16; 9:17–19, 32–35, 36–42; 14:8–18; 16:16–24; 19:11–20).

But at the second level of the account, the storytellers introduce a new theme that separates the nine from the one who "saw that he was healed" (v. 15). This one now returns to Jesus to give thanks (vv. 15b, 16a), a distinctively Christian act, and his act of worship and gratitude is contrasted, to their detriment, to the nine who did not return (v. 17). This refocusing of the healing may serve as a commentary on a dilemma the early church was experiencing. Why, in spite of the fact that the early church continued the practice of healing, did so few who were healed actually return to give thanks and remain part of the community? Why did they, like the nine, simply continue on their way as though nothing had happened? In spite of being "redeemed" from the hell of leprosy, the nine simply fade out of the scene and continue on their way, heedless of the source of their healing. This problem may have become the lens through which the early church retold and expanded the healing of the ten. At this level of the tradition, the emphasis shifted from the ten to the nine, as the parallel questions in verse 17 make clear. Since the questions in verse 17 are formulated in a fashion quite different from the longer question in verse 18, it is possible that they represent two distinct layers of tradition.

Finally, Luke redacted the story he had inherited from the early church and refocused it one more time. He provided a narrative context that stitched the pericope into his travel narrative (v. 11; see Luke 9:51–19:44), gave a Samaritan identity to the one who returned to give thanks (v. 16b), and then rephrased Jesus' question to focus on the faith of "this foreigner" (v. 18). The phrase "this foreigner" generalized the identity of the Samaritan. In this way, Luke turned the grateful Samaritan into a model for the Gentile readers in his own community who, like the Samaritan, were outsiders unlikely and unable to look to Jerusalem for confirmation of any faith concern. In other words, the third level of the tradition built directly on the contrast between the ten and the nine by focusing on the identity of the one.

Both readings reveal the strength of form criticism, which resides in its ability to separate seemingly contradictory strands of tradition and then to show how they might have been woven togther to produce the text as we see it. It also related each level of the composite text to some "setting in life," whether of the early church or the Gospel writer. At none of the levels is the historical Jesus a particular focus. The emphasis falls on the possible meaning of the text for the early church and its problems. Context means primarily the context of the early church or the evangelist. If Betz is correct, the original healing story is a literary creation, a parody of the healing materials in the Jesus traditions and, therefore, it has nothing at all to do with the historical Jesus.

In many ways, the most masterful use of form criticism is found in Joachim Jeremias's study, *The Parables of Jesus,* which applied the explanatory power of form criticism to the issue of the historical Jesus.[4] In the hands of Bultmann, Dibelius, and their followers, form criticism had become a tool for reading the Gospels as witnesses to the issues and concerns of the early church, much as Betz had done with the healing of the ten lepers. But Jeremias demonstrated that form criticism could clear a path to the historical Jesus by working through the concerns of the early church, a task that Bultmann had deemed impossible. The key methodological chapter in Jeremias's study was entitled "The Return to Jesus from the Primitive Church" (23–114). In that chapter, Jeremias identified ten factors affecting the transmission of the parables. Some were relatively minor, such as the "representational changes" that occurred when a parable of Jesus was removed from its Palestinian Jewish setting and retold in a Hellenistic environment, or the "embellishment" that arises in oral storytelling, or the unconscious shaping of the parables to reflect folkloric or Old Testament themes. Other alterations were more substantial, such as the "change of audience." Jeremias believed that Jesus had used the parables as weapons of controversy against his opponents to justify his announcement of the good news to the poor, the outcast, and other sinners. But the church had taken these parables, originally spoken to Jesus' foes, and transformed them into exhortations for the faithful. This "hortatory use of the parables" explained why it was necessary to reconstruct the parable of Jesus and distinguish it from the version of the parable retold by the church. Their purposes were as different from each other as their audiences and settings. Jeremias also calculated that "the influence of the church's situation" could be detected in how such matters as "the delay of the parousia," "the mission of the church," and "regulations for the leadership of the church" made their way into the parables of Jesus. These themes were anachronistic and, therefore, later than the conflicts that animated Jesus' ministry.

In the very title of this chapter, "The Return to Jesus from the Primitive Church," Jeremias outlined the project that Bultmann had argued could not be done. The discipline that, in Bultmann's hands, had denied access to the historical Jesus was used by Jeremias as the clue that solved the mystery of the historical Jesus. In part, this move was made possible because Jeremias had reconstructed a context for the historical Jesus that was both distinct from the settings of the Gospel writers yet contiguous with them and compatible with their concerns. Jeremias's Jesus was an eschatological prophet announcing the coming reign of God, demanding that his hearers prepare themselves for its imminent arrival. Strengthened by his confidence in God's coming action, Jesus proclaimed God's mercy to the most unlikely and incurred the wrath of the righteous guardians of the tradition. It was his reconstruction of this context for the historical Jesus that enabled Jeremias to organize the parables around a cluster of themes that both defined the moment and grew out of it. His list included familiar themes such as "Now Is the Day of Salvation," "God's Mercy for Sinners," "The Great Assurance," "The Imminence of Catastrophe," and "The Challenge of the Hour," to name just a few.[5]

One example may show how Jeremias applied form criticism to the parables in order to tease out a meaning substantially different from the meaning of the parable in its Gospel context. The familiar parable of the sower will serve as an example. Jeremias first studied the allegorical interpretation of the parable found in Mark 4:13–20 and concluded, on linguistic grounds, that it was the work of the early church. Its vocabulary was too foreign to the language of the parables and too redolent of the issues of the early church to be taken as the words of the historical Jesus. More importantly, the allegorical reading of the parable of the sower "misses the eschatological" message of Jesus contained in the parable and transforms the parable into a psychological exhortation. The four kinds of soil become four types of response to the Word, and the hearers are exhorted to "examine themselves and test the sincerity of their conversion" (77–79). By contrast, the parable of Jesus expresses the theme of "the great assurance." It has two scenes, sowing (vv. 3–7) and harvest (v. 8). The parable contasts the difficulties attendant on sowing seed with the vision of a bountiful harvest, a contrast that expresses Jesus' confidence in the eschatological work of God already begun in his ministry. The sowing may not seem promising, but God ensures a bountiful harvest (149–51). It is what Jeremias calls "a contrast parable." By comparing the early church's allegorical reading (psychological exhortation) with Jesus' parable (eschatological proclamation), Jeremias discovered a context in the ministry of Jesus that sustained his reading of the parable as a tale told by Jesus that became a twice-told tale of the church.

Although he did not pursue the issue further, Jeremias could have noted that his reading also restored the orality of the parable. Oral speech usually works by threes. The allegorical reading produced a fourfold typology: the path; the rocky ground; the thorny soil; and the good soil. But Jeremias's reading produced two sequences of three, one for each scene of the parable, as we see in the following outline (all verse references are to Mark 4:3–9).

scene 1	unpromising sowing	(vv. 4–7)
	the hard path	(v. 4)
	the rocky soil	(vv. 5–6)
	the thorny soil	(v. 7)
scene 2	the bountiful harvest	(v. 8)
	thirtyfold	(v. 8)
	sixtyfold	(v. 8)
	hundredfold	(v. 8)

The pattern of four has been replaced by two sequences of three. It is also possible to note a pattern in the verbs in scene 1 that would further nuance Jeremias's reading. In the case of the first and third seeds, the pattern of verbs is clear.[6]

Pattern	*First seed*	*Third seed*
sowing	seed fell	seed fell
predator introduced	birds came	thorns grew up
violent outcome	devoured	choked

After paring away the secondary expansions from the description of the second seed, a similar pattern emerges; "other seed fell on rocky ground, and the sun rose and scorched it."

Pattern	*Second seed*
sowing	seed fell
predator introduced	sun rose
violent outcome	scorched

The violent verbs create a dissonance with the seemingly ordinary agrarian scene of the parable and suggest deeper levels of opposition to the sowing of the seed of the reign of God. This is why "the great assurance" is needed, and perhaps this is why Jesus told the parable. The violent outcomes in the first scene of the parable reflect the growing opposition both to Jesus' public work (cf. Mark 3:6) and the reign of God he was proclaiming. This reconstructed context allowed Jeremias to read the parable of the sower through a set of lenses quite different from those provided by the Gospel writer. Owing to this discrepancy, Jeremias was quite certain that he had penetrated behind the kerygma of the early church and discovered the original voice of the parables' first proclaimer.

This result clashed sharply with the form-critical consensus that had served as the methodological counterpart to the period of the "no quest" for the historical Jesus.[7] The purpose of form criticism was to identify different layers of tradition with the hope of identifying the earliest layers of Palestinian Jewish material. But it was not seen, at first, as a tool that could aid the quest for the historical Jesus. Of course, by the 1930s, this assumption had been challenged by C. H. Dodd's study of the parables, and in both his introduction to form criticism and in his later commentary on Mark, Vincent Taylor both dissented from the skepticism of Bultmann and illustrated how form criticism could yield insights into the historical Jesus.[8] This tradition was continued in the work of William Manson and T. W. Manson to name just two figures who found in form criticism a tool to reconstruct the mission and message of Jesus.[9]

But the difference was more than methodological. Unlike Jeremias's quest for the historical Jesus, Bultmann's quest had produced a Jesus who was essentially a first-century Jewish existentialist philosopher, announcing the need to live authentically in the moment.[10] It was impossible to define any context for such a proclamation because the very nature of the proclamation itself denied the need for context. The only contexts left for Bultmann were the unfolding problems of the early church, with its moral problems and theological debates, which provided enough information to reconstruct a minimal historical reference.

In carrying out their program of interpretation, form critics did more than infer backward from Gospel texts. They also needed some external framework by which to judge what elements in the text were later accretions, that is, what elements derived from the primitive church as opposed to those that might be from the historical Jesus. To answer these questions, form critics developed a model to explain how the Jesus traditions had migrated from their rural Galilean roots and emigrated into the wider world of the Roman Empire. The journey had been made in three phases, each of which could leave characteristic imprints on the Jesus traditions. Those phases came to be known as the Palestinian Jewish, the Hellenistic (or diaspora) Jewish, and the Hellenistic Gentile, each of which was supposed to have clearly identifiable features and values that could, in turn, be identified in specific texts. For example, in discussing Mark 12:35–37a (the question about David's son), Bultmann concluded that the saying in its entirety was a community formulation, because Jesus initiates the saying, a certain sign of its "secondary formulation."[11] He also argued that the debate as framed in Mark could have no convincing setting in Jesus' ministry, since the Synoptic traditions contain neither references to a debate about Jesus' lineage nor exhibit any awareness of preexistence. These facts rule out a setting in the life of Jesus. The setting in the life of the early church could reflect one of two situations. Either the saying represents "the tension between faith in the Son of Man and hope in the Son of David" (a Palestinian Jewish concern) or it was "meant to prove that Jesus was more than the Son of David, viz., the Son of God" (a Hellenistic Gentile concern). Bultmann assumes that "Son of Man" is a Jewish title and "Son of God" a Gentile phrase, and on the basis of these identifications can assign the saying to one portion of the early church or another. Much as the dating of artifacts found on a tell depends on a stratigraphy that has been already established, so the dating of the sayings of Jesus depends on an intellectual stratigraphy established outside the text. In this stratigraphy, the three strata correspond roughly to a chronological framework in which the Palestinian Jewish is the earliest and the Hellenistic Gentile is the latest. The Hellenistic or diaspora Jewish layers of tradition fall between the other two. Once again, the fundamental issue is context. What believable and plausible framework can be found that will make sense of the sayings material or the debate contained in it? It is notable that for almost all of the form critics the debate about context was a matter of ideas and ideologies. Conflicts were understood as a war of words; the history of the primitive church was an intellectual history. Context meant a context of ideas, and the interpretation of a text consisted in identifying the ideas it proposed and placing them in an appropriate but previously determined framework. Did the early church use the question about David's son to argue that Jesus was Son of Man (a Jewish context) or Son of God (a Hellenistic context)? Once the chronology of ideas was established, the question could be answered.

REDACTION CRITICISM AND THE CONTEXT OF THE EVANGELIST

Form criticism dominated New Testament studies for more than thirty years, from 1919, when Dibelius published *From Tradition to Gospel,* to the 1950s, when a number of German scholars began to examine how the evangelists themselves had interpreted the Jesus traditions. Gunther Bornkamm launched this series of inquiries with his article "The Stilling of the Storm in Matthew" (1948), which was later combined with essays by two of his students and published as *Tradition and Interpretation in Matthew* (English translation 1963).[12] About the same time, Willi Marxsen published *Mark the Evangelist* (1956), a study of Mark less as a collector of traditions (the way he had been viewed by form critics) and more as a shaper of traditions, a genuine author willing to tailor and transform traditions to serve his vision of who Jesus was.[13] In 1954, Hans Conzelmann published his *Theology of St. Luke* (English translation 1960), an expansion of a major article he had first drafted in 1952.[14] Taken together, these studies launched what came to be known as "redaction criticism" (the phrase was first used by Marxsen).[15]

Redaction criticism was indebted to form criticism and used the results of previous form-critical study to identify how the evangelists had reworked and reshaped the traditions they had inherited in order to craft their own interpretations of Jesus. Since redaction critics assumed the "two-source hypothesis,"[16] they could readily observe how Matthew and Luke had used Mark as a source, but it proved to be much more difficult to infer how Mark had refashioned his hypothetically reconstructed sources[17] or how Matthew and Luke had worked with Q. Redaction critics assumed that the Gospels were written to address either urgent crises or ongoing concerns in their communities and, therefore, that they were occasional documents. Their distinctive contribution was found in the way the evangelists shaped the Jesus traditions to speak to the issues of their communities. These issues were often cast in terms of theological, christological, or moral disputes. What is the Christology of Mark's Gospel and how does it relate to his community?[18] Were the disciples ciphers for Mark's community?[19] How did Matthew's portrayal of Jesus as a new Moses shape the church's debate with the synagogue on the meaning of the Torah?[20] What was the attitude toward Jewish leaders, and how does this reflect the historical moment of the evangelist?[21] Clearly, redaction criticism was interested in the question of context, the context of the Gospel writers, and it was their context that had to be reconstructed in order to make sense of the Gospel texts.

In his introduction to the study of the parables in Matthew 13, Jack Dean Kingsbury cited the great gain of redaction criticism over form criticism.[22] Form criticism had to work with reconstructed and, therefore, hypothetical texts and contexts, a very risky and, at times, even arbitrary task, whereas the redaction critic dealt simply with the established text in the Gospel itself. Of course, what Kingsbury failed to note is that redaction critics had to reconstruct a context for the Gospel of Matthew within which the parables of Matthew 13 make sense and to which they are addressed. This is inescapably and inevitably a speculative project. Not surprisingly, when redaction critics attempted to reconstruct that context, they essentially followed the lead of the form critics. The Gospels were written to deal with a clash of ideas and a war of myths, and the texts were seen as addressing theological, ethical, and christological ideas, often in a polemical setting. Once again, context was less material than ideological. Conflicts were differences of opinion and conviction.

More importantly, as far as the quest of the historical Jesus is concerned, redaction criticism abandoned interest in the historical Jesus in favor of delineating Mark's Jesus, Matthew's Jesus, Luke's Jesus, and

John's Jesus.[23] It seemed a more manageable and controllable task, because the canonical texts were well established. The attempt to peer behind the Gospel texts seemed a less certain and more speculative enterprise. But, for all its innovation, redaction criticism still shared a conviction with form criticism. The establishment of the context of the evangelists was determinative to interpreting their work, and that context was external to the Gospels themselves. Insofar as the Gospels provided insight into the world in which they were created, they remained windows through which one could glimpse the life of the early church.

An example may illustrate the value and limits of the venture. The stilling of the storm passage attracted the attention of Bornkamm because Matthew had so obviously reworked his Markan source (Mark 4:35–41 // Matt. 8:23–27; see 8:18–27). In Mark, the stilling of the storm introduces a collection of four miracle stories (4:35–5:43), which follows directly upon the collection of parables in chapter 4 (4:1–34). The parables announce the mystery of the reign of God, and the miracles deepen the mystery. In Mark, Jesus enters the boat in order to leave the crowd, and the disciples "took him with them in the boat." Other boats follow them, presumably indicating that some of the crowd followed Jesus and the disciples onto the sea. As the boat is being swamped by water, the disciples awaken Jesus, addressing him as "teacher" and assailing him with the fear-filled and faithless question, "Do you not care if we perish?" Jesus rebukes the wind, using the same verb (be muzzled, or "shut up") he used to silence the demons in the synagogue (1:25) and then chides the disciples, "Why are you afraid? Have you no faith at all?" The rhetorical questions imply a clear answer. They are afraid precisely because they have no faith.

Matthew reinterprets the Markan pericope by changing nearly everything in it. First, he recontextualizes the pericope by framing it with sayings on discipleship (8:19–22). Next, Jesus leads the disciples into the boat, and they "follow" (*akoloutheō*) him. In Matthew, the verb is virtually a technical term for discipleship. When the great storm arises, the disciples reverently petition Jesus for help, "save, Lord, we are perishing." The dominical address, *kurie*, emphasizes Jesus' majesty. In turn, Jesus speaks to the disciples as men of little faith (*oligopistoi*), not as faithless men. Their little faith will grow; they are not hopelessly lost. Even the final question is nuanced differently. The disciples (now called simply "men") marvel and wonder, "Just what sort is this that even winds and sea obey him?" The question suggests its own answer, which can be found in passages like Psalms 65:8; 89:10; 107:23. Indeed, in his redaction-critical commentary on Matthew, Robert Gundry takes *potapos* to mean, "How wonderful that even the winds and sea obey him!"[24]

Gundry's reading of the passage differs from Bornkamm's reading in other ways (154–57). Bornkamm thinks that the description of Jesus in the boat with the disciples is a metaphor for the risen Lord in the church (symbolized by the boat), tossed about and threatened by tempestuous historical events. In short, Matthew has reshaped the stilling of the storm from a text of terror to a counsel of comfort. The disciples may fear, but their little faith will grow in the presence of the Lord who controls chaos and stills the storms of history before they can swamp and sink the boat. But Gundry believes that the text is more christological than ecclesiological; it is focused on the authority and majesty of Jesus. The key is found in the odd phrase used to describe the storm, *seismos megas,* which might better be used to describe an earthquake than a storm at sea. It means literally "a great shaking." *Seismos* is used elsewhere in Matthew, where it refers to the tribulations preceding the end of all things (24:7), the earthquake that occurs at the crucifixion (27:54) and, in 28:2, to describe the earthquake that rolls the stone away from Jesus' tomb so the angel can show the women where his body was laid. The verbal form (*seiō*) is used to depict Jesus' entry in Jerusalem (21:10). All of this indicates to Gundry that the storm "poses no threat to the disciples" but signals a Christophany modeled on the theophanies of the Old Testament (155). The great storm is a moment of revelation. When Jesus rebukes the disciples, he "implies that the disciples should have seen in the great shaking a sign of his majesty rather than a threat" (156).

Both Bornkamm and Gundry agree on one crucial point. The Jesus who appears in this text is less the historical Jesus and more the Lord of the church, and the story was retold and refashioned to speak to the needs of the community of faith, whether those needs required the reassurance that Jesus was in the boat with them during the disruptions of history or a christological reminder of the majesty of the Lord who has saved them. The context is the setting of the early church, not the world of the historical Jesus. The rise of redaction criticism paralleled the rise of the new quest for the historical Jesus, although it outlived the new quest by many years, and the primary goal of the new quest was the delineation of the relationship between Jesus and the kerygma of the early church. This is what Bornkamm and Gundry have done, each in his own way, with the pericope of the stilling of the storm.

LITERARY CRITICISMS AND NARRATIVE WORLDS

Redaction criticism was a major influence in New Testament studies for about thirty years, from 1950 to 1980, but by the 1970s it had begun to evolve in a new direction. The very name, redaction criticism, implied that the Gospel writers were still viewed predominantly as editors and shapers of preexisting traditions, whether oral or written. Although redaction critics held a higher view of the evangelists as authors than did form critics, they still did not regard them as creative writers. All of this was to change with the emergence of more literary approaches to biblical texts beginning in the late 1970s and flourishing in the 1980s.[25] The basic purpose of literary-critical approaches to the Gospel texts was to view each narrative as a complete world in itself and to analyze the components of that narrative world, such as the writer's rhetoric, plot, characters, settings, narrator, and the narrator's point of view.[26] This literary approach to the Gospels treated them more like novels or short stories and less like historical documents.[27] Any attempt to survey the results of these numerous approaches would divert this study too far afield from its focus, but it is important to note what the shift to literary approaches means for the question of context. The context of the Gospel increasingly becomes its own narrative world. The Pharisees and chief priests are viewed as characters in a story, not as historical opponents of Jesus; that is, they are seen as antagonists to the story's protagonist. In this setting, the question of the historical accuracy of the portrayal is less important than the delineation of their dramatic role.

Jesus himself is also interpreted as a character in the narrative, and to the degree that this occurs, the question of the historical Jesus becomes increasingly irrelevant. The story of the conflict with the Pharisees over what renders a person unclean (Mark 7:1–23) could be viewed as an episode in the larger theme of the conflict between Jesus and the authorities,[28] or it might be interpreted in light of the correlations between Mark 4 and 7,[29] including the repeated use of significant language (Look!), shifts of scenes, and the presence of parables, but in neither case is the interpreter concerned to use the episode to shed light on the conflict between the historical Jesus and his opponents. The point being made is not whether such approaches are valid and useful, for they clearly are; the point is that literary approaches to the Gospels minimize the question of the historical Jesus and recast Jesus as an actor in each of the four dramas called Gospels.

An example may illustrate the point more clearly. In her excellent study of Mark, Mary Ann Tolbert argues that the parable of the sower (4:1–9) and the later parable of the tenants (12:1–12) serve as plot summaries of the narrative.[30] As such, they are filled with clues to orient the reader or hearer to the story being told. The parables "reveal the fundamental typologies underlying the story" and organize the characters and events of the plot (128–29). This means that, for Mark, the parable is not about seeds but about the four types of earth or ground (149). More specifically, the hard-packed path represents "the scribes, the Pharisees, the Herodians and the Jerusalem Jews" who oppose Jesus from the moment he appears in the story until his death (153–54). The disciples are the "rocky ground," as Peter's own nickname, "Rocky," indicates. They follow Jesus but fall away at the critical time (154–56). Examples of the thorny ground are found in the rich ruler who turns away (10:17–22) and Herod Antipas, who executes John the Baptist (6:14–29) (156–58). Tolbert is less certain where examples of the good soil are to be found, although they may well be found in the incidental characters who arise and show faith in Jesus, as in the case of the Syrophoenician woman (7:24–30) or blind Bartimaeus (10:46–52). Mark has surrounded the parable with signs of its importance. The opening imperative, "Listen," sets the parable apart, and Jesus indicates that understanding this parable is the key to understanding all of the manifold riddles of the reign of God (4:13). Even the setting is important. Jesus is in a boat, sitting on the sea, but his hearers are "on the earth" or "on the ground." Jesus is the sower, and they are the kinds of earth receiving the Word (149–51). Throughout her discussion of the parable, Tolbert's attention is fixed on the parable's narrative role.

> By recalling these brief and highly mnemonic stories told by Jesus, the audience can interpret correctly the general point being illustrated in each episode or by each group of characters as the story progresses. The parables are meant to function, then, as sources of continual orientation for readers, and the narrative of the Gospel as a whole embodies and expands the typologies established by them. (128)

Of course, literary forms no less than cultural conventions are embedded in social and historical worlds, so, as many literary critics realize, it is not easy to treat narratives in a cultural and social vacuum (1–15). The question is rather how to relate the narrative world of the Gospel writer to his historical and social context. While literary critics may insist that a thorough analysis of the narrative is a logically prior exercise, they cannot reasonably exclude the effort to relate narrative world to historical reality or social construction of reality. All of this means that the question of context, though in changed form, remains at the center of the task of interpretation. Tolbert concludes her study by exploring where the Gospel might have been written and why (303–6). Her discussion is limited to Mark's context and does not focus on the historical Jesus, as one would expect.

Using literary approaches removes the question of context away from the historical Jesus and relocates it with the Gospel writer and even within the narrative being considered. Literary function takes priority over historical setting. This is why the very clue to the parable that Jeremias rejects as the creation of the early church, namely, the allegorical interpretation attached to it (4:14–20), becomes, for Tolbert, the key to reading the typology of soils contained in the parable. The differences between them trace to the fact that Jeremias is seeking the parable of the historical Jesus while Tolbert is seeking to understand the rhetorical function of the parable of the sower within the context of Mark's narrative.

THE USE OF THE SOCIAL SCIENCES
AND THE QUESTION OF CONTEXT

In 1979, Norman Gottwald published *The Tribes of Yahweh: Sociology of the Religion of Liberated Israel.*[31] Its appearance nearly coincided with the appearance of Gerd Theissen's *Sociology of Early Palestinian Christianity.*[32] Appearing, as they did, within a year of each other, these two works generated a heightened interest in the usefulness of the social sciences for interpreting biblical texts. By the beginning of the 1980s, numerous works were being published that advocated the same approach. In 1981, two key works appeared that demonstrated how the social sciences could be used to illumine New Testament texts. John H. Elliott published a major study of 1 Peter entitled *A Home for the Homeless: A Sociological Exegesis of 1 Peter, Its Situation and Strategy,* and Bruce Malina published *The New Testament World: Insights from Cultural Anthropology.*[33] The literature has proliferated throughout the 1980s and 1990s.[34]

Malina's study isolated five values central to understanding the world of the New Testament. They were: (1) honor and shame; (2) the first-century personality, especially the relationship between the individual and the group; (3) the meaning of a limited-goods society in which people tried to maintain their inherited status; (4) kinship and marriage patterns; and (5) the meaning of purity. Malina's work was built upon an earlier discussion among sociologists and anthropologists about the nature of the circum-Mediterranean region. Was it possible to identify a "Mediterranean sociology" or a distinctively "Mediterranean cultural anthropology"? Did the region around the Mediterranean display enough cultural continuity and similarity to enable researchers to speak of the region as a whole? In spite of local cultural variations, could one find the values of honor and shame exhibited in characteristically Mediterranean ways?[35]

If these questions could be answered in the affirmative (and many did so, although the issue remains a subject of debate), then the question arose whether it was possible to infer backward in time from current studies to the ancient Mediterranean world of the first century. The question has been raised in a number of forms. Kenneth Bailey posed the problem while developing his notion of an "Oriental exegesis" of the parables.[36] Essentially, Bailey argued that contemporary village life offered valuable insights into the biblical world because peasants "have changed their masters, their religions, their language, and their crops, but not their manner of life."[37] The isolation of villages, lack of easy access to the "outside" world, and the conservative nature of peasant culture lead Bailey to conclude that it is possible to gain insight into the biblical world by studying the contemporary village life of the Middle East. Malina would argue that occasional comparisons are not enough, because they are not placed within the framework of a larger model that enables us to catch and interpret the cultural cues coming from those removed from us in time and social experience. So Malina works with larger models and seeks to understand the details within the larger context provided by the model.[38]

For the purposes of this study, the answer to both clusters of questions is a guarded yes. The Mediterranean does supply enough cohesion to allow for the use of comparative studies and to permit guarded generalizations from them. For example, this study of the historical Jesus will work with the pivotal values identified by Malina and apply them to the world of first-century Palestine. This approach implies that it is possible to infer backward from current studies of the Mediterranean in order to illuminate the world of the ancient Mediterranean. Although the rest of this study will test the value of this approach by interpreting numerous texts from the Synoptic Gospels, it may be useful to illustrate how it works on a specific text. Mark 7:1–23 presents a conflict between Jesus and the Pharisees over the issue of purity. Form critics have long viewed the text as a composite creation, most likely constructed around a single authentic saying of Jesus in 7:15.[39] Many have noted that the question asked in 7:5 does not seem to be answered until 7:15. The text is broken down into a number of units of tradition, usually verses 1–5 (the question), verses 6–8 (the Isaiah unit), verses 9–13 (korban), verses 14–15 (the reply), verses 17–19 (the explanation of the reply), verses 20–23 (early church midrash). Most of the intervening material is judged to have come from the early church as a justification for setting aside food laws (7:19b). Jerome Neyrey reads the passage as part of Mark's portrayal of Jesus in conflict with the purity codes of the Pharisees.[40] Seen through this lens, the passage presents a coherent depiction of the clash between two modes of morality. The Pharisees emphasize the boundaries of the body and the need to keep impurity out. So they focus on the mouth, hands, pots, vessels, and food itself, because eating brings what is outside into the body. Their concern is with hands and lips. Jesus, by contrast, focuses on the heart. As the Pharisees proliferate their customs to cover all exigencies, Jesus shrinks his focus to the Decalogue itself. The list of vices in verses 20–23 covers much of the Decalogue (cf. 10:18–19) (120). The way Isaiah opposes lips to heart, therefore, fits the polemic of the passage and summarizes Jesus' critique of the Pharisaic "tradition of the elders." As Neyrey puts it, "Whereas the Pharisees' concern is with externals and surfaces (washings of hands, pot, cups and vessels, 7:2–4), Jesus' concern is with the interior and the heart" (113). All of this means, for Neyrey, that Jesus is not abolishing the purity rules but redefining them (116). His focus narrowed the concept of purity and concentrated it on the Ten Commandments, that is, keeping the "core law of God, not the traditional 'fences' of men" (113). Neyrey's reading brings much of the passage together, especially 7:1–8, 14–23, and the Corban passage (vv. 9–13) could be seen as related to Jesus' emphasis on the importance of the Decalogue over the tradition of the elders. What appears to form critics as a disparate collection of traditions, gathered together haphazardly by Mark, can be seen as a unified discourse contrasting conflicting views of purity.

The use of the social sciences has changed the question of context and what counts as context. Context now includes the material world and the political, social, and economic conditions of life, as well as the values and convictions (symbolic world) of the peoples of the biblical world. The structures of agrarian societies and aristocratic empires become part of the world of the New Testament, and the presence of Roman colonial rule is not an irrelevant detail but a central fact of life. The types of people who appear in the Gospels are also important. Where do peasant villagers fit in the scheme of things? With whom does Jesus spend his time? How does he interact with different groups? What is the role of temple and Torah? How are they viewed by Galilean peasants and rural artisans? The list of questions could be extended indefinitely. It is the task of the rest of this study to elaborate them and show their relevance for the study of the historical Jesus.

The use of the social sciences does not apply either exclusively or even primarily to the historical Jesus. Studies using these tools have been applied to all levels of New Testament literature. Neyrey's study of purity in Mark was concerned with purity as an issue for the Gospel writer, not the historical Jesus. But whenever these tools are applied, they do raise the question of context in distinctive ways, and that sense of context adds new dimensions to historical Jesus studies. In chapter 1, I argued that S. G. F. Brandon lacked the social models and detailed information of first-century life (such as we have it from limited sources) to complete the agenda he had set for his study of Jesus the Zealot.[41] One reason for his predicament was that the use of the social sciences to interpret biblical texts had not yet taken root and flourished. This study will draw heavily on the studies that have emerged from this approach to the Gospels and the historical Jesus.

The use of the social sciences has contributed greatly to the search for a usable context and, in so doing, has transformed what used to be called "the background of the New Testament" into the world of the New Testament itself.

CONCLUSION

Twentieth-century biblical scholarship has been preoccupied with the quest for a usable context. The century began with form critics' attempt to identify the "setting in life" not only of specific units of tradition (pericopes) but also of the multiple layers of tradition putatively found in each Gospel text. The setting in life was most frequently the setting in the life of the early church, not the setting in the life of the historical Jesus. Jeremias, however, demonstrated how form criticism could be used to explicate the parables and explore their setting in the work of the historical Jesus.

Redaction criticism refocused the question of context on the historical settings of the Gospels themselves. Redaction critics attempted to identify the composition and concerns of the communities for whom the Gospels were written. Their efforts led not to the identification of the historical Jesus but to the Jesus tailored to speak to the needs of each community addressed by the Gospel writers.

The emergence of literary criticisms refocused the question of context within the narrative itself. The narrative world created by each Gospel writer became the primary context in relation to which Jesus was to be understood. Of course, narrative worlds are related to larger social worlds, so the question of narrative structure did not totally eclipse the historical quest. Yet literary criticisms were relatively unconcerned with the historical Jesus.

The use of the social sciences has changed the question of context once again. Context now refers to the social, political, economic, and symbolic world of the biblical writers. The social sciences also provide tools for doing cross-cultural and systemic study of agrarian or ruralized societies and aristocratic empires. This enables interpreters to reconstruct and recreate the macro-world in which Jesus lived. Although the use of the social sciences is not limited to the quest for the historical Jesus, it does include it in a way that earlier forms of biblical criticism did not. This has opened up new possibilities, which this study will pursue.

5

The Quest for the Historical Jesus and the Quest for the Historical Galilee:

Jesus in the World of Agrarian Societies, Aristocratic Empires, and Colonized Peoples

The public activity of the historical Jesus occurred during the 20s and early 30s of the first century of the Common Era in Palestine. Scholars who intend to establish a context for the work of Jesus, therefore, need to investigate the character of the social, economic, and political life of Palestine during this period. That is the task of this chapter.

ADVANCED AGRARIAN SOCIETIES AND ARISTOCRATIC EMPIRES

The Ruler and Ruling Elites

The Palestine of Jesus' day could be described as an advanced agrarian society dominated by a traditional aristocratic empire (Rome) in whose image the Herods and temple high priests had molded themselves.[1] Wealth is based on land and the control of land. Typically composed of no more than 1 to 2 percent of the population, the ruling class controlled the vast majority of the resources of their society. They existed in a symbiotic, yet competitive, relationship with the ruler, or the representative of imperial control—the prefect of Judea, for example. In Galilee, the ruling class, probably called Herodians in the Synoptic Gospels, were those aristocratic families dependent on the rule of Herod Antipas and rewarded by him for their support. Such rewards included donations of land and the appointments to high government posts that allowed the ruling elites to enrich themselves through what Gerhard Lenski calls "honest graft."[2] The relationship between ruler and ruling class was that of patron to client, but even the ruling elites would, in turn, form patterns of patronage among themselves, the higher elites serving as patrons to those of less prestige and wealth. In the Roman world, alliances between elites are called patron-protégé relations, in order to avoid applying the demeaning label "client" to a member of the ruling class.[3] The language of "friendship" may have served a similar purpose in the world of Palestine. In Judea, the ruling class consisted of the high-priestly families and the lay aristocrats (called "the elders" in the Gospels) who supported them. When Herod the Great came to power, he was unable to occupy the office of high priest because, unlike the Hasmonaeans before him, he was not from a priestly family. Never at a loss for a way to exercise his power, Herod imported priestly families from the Diaspora and arrogated to himself the power to depose and appoint high priests. Pursuing his policy of limiting the power of the high-priestly office, Herod replaced its incumbents on a regular basis, thereby preventing any single officeholder from consolidating too much power and posing a threat. Over time, Herod's policy managed to strip the office of its legitimacy in the eyes of many Judeans and Galileans alike. However, the high-priestly families were not simply passive in the face of Herod's political maneuvering. Eventually, four high-priestly families did manage virtually to monopolize appointments to the office. Of the twenty-eight high priests who served during the Herodian and Roman eras, twenty-two came from four ruling houses, the house of Boethus, the house of Ananas, the house of Phiabi, and the house of Kamith.[4] It was something of a Pyrrhic victory, as Jeremias notes, for these high priests were widely viewed as illegitimate since they could not claim descent from the family of Zadok, a fact the sectarians at Qumran could not let them forget. While the arrangement worked well enough during the reign of Herod, its deleterious effects would become more evident during the Roman period. Nevertheless, the high-priestly families, with their lay collaborators, controlled the temple and its institutions, notably the Sanhedrin and the temple treasury.

Aristocratic empires were bureaucratic in nature, and a systemic tension was built into the relationship between the ruler and his or her bureaucrats.[5] The bureaucracies had to be invested with enough power to perform their two essential tasks, military control and economic exploitation—that is, enforcing the peace and collecting tribute and taxes. To ensure the smooth running of these bureaucracies, the ruler would often appoint members of the aristocracy to oversee key departments. The aristocrats attempted to use their position as a base of power, yet without threatening the ruler, and the ruler sought to minimize the power of his own ruling class. Wealth meant the control of land, and control of land entailed control of its usufruct, the ability to extract from peasants the so-called surplus produced by their labor. The surplus included everything except the barest subsistence that was left for the peasant laborers and their villages. Ownership was really not an issue in agrarian societies; it was control of land and those who tilled it that mattered most. The relationship between aristocrat and peasant was predatory, oppressive, and exploitative, a fact that required ideological concealment and restatement as a form of reciprocity (a false reciprocity). But the aristocrats needed the peasants because the wealth that made their lives of leisure possible began in the fields and the peasant villages of their domains.[6]

Whether in Herodian Galilee or the temple state of Judea, ruling elites showed solidarity to outsiders but contended with each other for power and prestige. In agrarian societies, ruling classes were locked in permanent struggles with each other for the increasing wealth needed to fuel their constant struggle for greater power and prestige.[7] There were also conflicts between the ruler and his ruling elites.[8] The ruler operated with a "proprietary theory of the state," that is, the ruler's entire domain was considered his personal estate, over which he had direct personal control.[9] This meant that an agrarian ruler could alienate his enemies from their estates through confiscation and redistribute the land to his allies and clients. When Herod came to power, for example, he executed numerous nobility loyal to the Hasmonaean Antigonus and imported his own aristocracy to replace them (*Ant.* 15.5–6; 17.304–7; *War* 1.358).[10] Naturally, the ruling elites attempted to institutionalize the rights they had gained, which meant, primarily, the right to pass their land to their heirs. As John Kautsky has noted, politics in aristocratic empires "consists of intraclass conflict."[11]

The Role of City and Village

In such societies, elites are concentrated in urban areas while the majority of the peasant population is dispersed into hamlets, villages, and market towns of various sizes. The Roman Empire was a patchwork quilt of cities controlling the hinterlands around them. The emergence of the city and the state are intimately related. The city is the correlate of the centralized state as well as the most visible expression of its power. Michelle Corbier describes the Roman Empire as a "checkerboard of cellular spaces of cities and their territories."[12] The primary reason for organizing the empire in this way was to ensure the efficient collection of tribute and taxes. Cities that collected their tribute in a timely manner were often rewarded with more territory over which to extend their control. The tribute took two forms, the *tributum soli,* a land tax, and the *tributum capitis,* or the poll tax. Taken together, the forms of tribute asserted and reinforced Rome's proprietary claim to the land and the bodies of those who worked the land. The purpose of collecting tribute was to support the ruling class and their retainers who devoted themselves to the maintenance of the empire. This arrangement implies a parasitic and exploitative relationship between city and countryside. "Yet, cities could only live by siphoning off the resources of the country, and this did not only take the form of rents. They derived profit from the collection of taxes and its inequalities."[13] According to most estimates, it took ten peasants to support one landed urban elite. Two historians have suggested that the extent and depth of exploitation during the period of the Principate "exceeded anything witnessed previously in the Mediterranean world."[14]

Since the placement of cities was a key element in any scheme for controlling land, archaeologists have attempted to find patterns linking urban centers with their rural hinterlands. Hopkins has advanced "the city region" proposal as a way to understand the distribution of cities in Roman Palestine.[15] An application of "central place theory," the proposal identifies four major cities (Joppa, Caesarea, Scythopolis, and Jerusalem) around each of which can be found a ring of smaller cities. In turn, these smaller urban centers are surrounded by a ring of market towns, which are connected with the villages of the countryside. There are difficulties with Hopkins's view, especially when applied to the time of Jesus. None of the cities mentioned is actually in Galilee; they are coastal cities (Joppa and Caesarea), an inland Ptolemaic foundation (Scythopolis), and a Judean city. Nor do they appear to be part of the administration of Galilee, which was centered in Tiberius and Sepphoris. The inclusion of Jerusalem further complicates the picture, because Jerusalem has a claim on Galilee even though it is not in Galilee but was part of the Roman province of Syria. In light of these problems, it could be said that Hopkins's article raises the larger question of whether Galilee fits the pattern of city and hinterland so obvious elsewhere in the empire. The pattern may not apply to Galilee, in part because, after the fall of the Northern Kingdom, Galilee had no native landed aristocracy, and without a landed aristocracy concentrated in cities, the conditions for control of the hinterland were not in place.[16] Whether or not Hopkins is correct in his attempt to apply central place theory to Galilee may be debated, but one fact is clear. After the building of Tiberius, "there was, within a day's walk of every village in Lower Galilee, a city in which lived their rulers and [tribute] collectors" (178). The purpose of Antipas's city building was control of the land, its villages and market towns, and their peasant inhabitants, for it was from this base that he extracted about two hundred talents of wealth per year (175). The villages of Galilee were far more independent of the local aristocracy than their counterparts in other areas of the empire, but they were still subject to Herod's intrusive rule.

A closer examination of Judea and Galilee will reveal that cities in these two areas served some of the essential functions outlined above even if they did not fit the more typical profile of the relationship between city and hinterland. In agrarian societies and aristocratic empires, cities serve one of two functions.[17] Either they serve an "orthogenetic function" of "codifying, conserving and constructing a society's traditions" or a "heterogenetic function" as centers of "technical, economic and cultural change." If this template were applied to Judea and Galilee, it would suggest that Jerusalem served primarily an orthogenetic function, whereas the cities of Tiberius and Sepphoris served a heterogenetic function.[18] Jerusalem was the central place where the Torah was copied and interpreted, and even though the oral Torah was, in fact, an innovative updating of the ancient text, it was presented as making explicit only what was already contained in the Torah, thereby upholding its ancient, sacred character. The pilgrimage festivals conserved traditions by rehearsing them in ritual fashion. But in Galilee, both Tiberius and Sepphoris became the places where "a new kind of Galilean Jew" could emerge, a Herodian Jew "who is at once a man of the Hellenistic world and a Jew."[19] This type of Jew, who "differed both from the older priestly aristocracy and the peasant people alike," was "a direct product of urbanization's effects on Palestinian Judaism" (133). Justus of Tiberius may be seen as an example of this new breed, because he was "at once sufficiently Jewish in his basic attitudes not to be able to identify with his pagan neighbors, yet so different that the uneducated rural Jew found him unacceptable also" (142). It would be just such figures who could be expected to gravitate toward a heterogenetic urban center like Tiberius. The aristocracy of Sepphoris clearly pursued a pro-Roman policy during the events leading up to the first revolt, and they acted with a deep suspicion and distrust toward their Galilean neighbors matched only by the hatred of the Galileans toward them. Sean Freyne speaks of "the Galileans' hatred of Sepphoris and their desire to destroy it."[20] Nor were peasant feelings toward Tiberius any more generous. Antipas not only built the new city over the site of a graveyard, in violation of a Torah taboo, but he also decorated his palace with animal representations in violation of the aniconic provisions of the Torah (*Life* 65, 68). Finally, Antipas organized the new city in the style of a Greek *polis*, with its magistrates (*archōn*), ten leading men (*prōtoi*), council of citizens (*boulē*), and popular assembly (*dēmos*) (*Life* 271, 278, 294; *War* 2.618, 639, 641).[21] Tiberius was a heterogenetic city, introducing political and cultural change.

Beyond their orthogenetic or heterogenetic orientations, cities can also be classified by their political, social, and religious roles. In his urban anthropology, Fox identifies several such roles, two of which apply to Jerusalem.[22] Jerusalem is both a "regal-ritual city" and an "administrative city." The primary function of a regal-ritual city is ideological, and although such cities are usually found in more segmented and decentralized societies, first-century Jerusalem retained some vestiges of its earlier regal-ritual functions. A regal-ritual city is a "theatre state," in which the "ideology, core values and symbols" of the ruling class are replicated and disseminated to the population. Such cities may normally have only a small population but are filled on the occasions of festivals and other significant public ceremonies. Jerusalem was not a small city, but it certainly experienced an expansion of its population during pilgrimage festivals. "The product of [a regal-ritual city] is an image of an ordered state rather than an industrial commodity."[23] Such cities would have a low tolerance for any movements or actions that disrupted the image they were seeking to portray and reinforce. But Jerusalem is equally an "administrative city" where the bureaucracies that maintain the political elite are located. This is why Jerusalem is more than a ritual center; it is a center of power. Such cities are associated with strong centralized and bureaucratized states and exist in symbiotic relationship with them. However, it is important to note that the city is a repository of the power of the state but not its source. The state creates the city; the city does not create the state. Fox argues that administrative cities do not carry on symbolic functions but focus on the extraction of wealth from the peasant base. Seen in this way, both Tiberius and Sepphoris more closely resemble Fox's notion of an "administrative city" than does Jerusalem. In fact, Horsley views Tiberius as a "royal administrative city," and Douglas Edwards notes that Sepphoris and Tiberius competed for the right "to maintain legal records" (read debt records), collect tribute and taxes, and "provide a judicial system."[24] In both cities, local elites altered traditional institutions "to bring Roman power within the context of their own symbolic world, thus giving them a modicum of control."[25] The presence of Herodian bureaucracies in each city and their role in collecting tribute and enforcing debt instruments laid the foundation for tense relations between urban center and peasant village. Freyne observes, quite correctly, "there can be no doubt that the rural animosities toward the cities were deep-seated and permanent."[26] The roots of the Galileans' hostility toward Sepphoris and Tiberius may also be tied to their loyalty to Jerusalem, whose orthogenetic role reinforced Jewish culture in Galilee and, thereby, alienated Galileans from their new heterogenetic urban centers.[27] Of course, this scenario would be operative only to the degree that Galileans recognized the authority of Jerusalem, and there is some debate about the degree to which Galileans supported the temple.

Retainers

Cities were also the place where those who served the elites gathered to do their work. The ruler and ruling elites were served by a class of people called retainers.[28] They staffed the bureaucracies required by a client kingdom, such as Antipas's Galilee, and by the temple state in Jerusalem. Retainers include such figures as ordinary priests, Levites and other temple officials, stewards, tax collectors and toll collectors, military personnel and body guards, clerks, and scribes. They formed about 5 percent of the population, but it was a crucial 5 percent. If 2 percent of a population attempts to control 98 percent, the control ratio is 1:49, a patently impossible situation, but if 7 percent of the population attempts to control 93 percent, the ratio changes to 1:14. Given the fact that the state has a virtual monopoly on the production, distribution, and use of weapons and military technology, the task becomes manageable. Most retainers were recruited from the peasant base of the population and, once they entered the retainer class, they too sought to maximize their rights, prerogatives, and perquisites. Like their elite patrons, retainers could use their bureaucratic positions to increase their wealth and consolidate their position. In this way, retainers identified with their patrons, not with the peasants from whom they had come but whom they were now exploiting. Imitating their patrons, retainers formed chains of patron-client relationships within their bureaucracies and among themselves. Scribes and clerks became increasingly important as the economy was monetized, making record keeping for debts and loans a central task. In carrying out the predatory policies of elites, retainers served as a barrier between the exploited and the rulers and, as such, they absorbed much of the hostility that would have otherwise been directed at the rulers. Retainers were indispensable to the task of extracting the so-called surplus from the peasant base and transferring it to the control of the ruler and political elites.

In the ancient world, bureaucracies typically had three levels of functionaries: (1) the lowest level of bureaucrats was composed of "illiterati" such as "porters and gaolers"; (2) the middle level consisted of the "literati," which included "scribes, lawyers, and accountants"; and (3) the highest level contained the "dignitates," the possessors of titles who held the high power positions and were often drawn from the aristocracy.[29] Holders of the highest positions in a bureaucracy would often be rewarded with grants of land in addition to what they could derive by way of "honest graft." An example of an upper-level bureaucrat and member of Herod the Great's inner circle would be Ptolemy of Rhodes, to whom Herod gave the village of Arus near Sebaste (Samaria) (*War* 1.473, 667; 2.14–16, 24, 64). The village was burned after Herod's death, an indication of the enmity between Herodian rulers and local villagers (*War* 2.69; *Ant.* 17.289–90). Herod Antipas's forcible relocation of the poor to Tiberius was, quite possibly, for the purpose of impressing them into service to staff the lowest levels of the bureaucracies in the city (*Ant.* 18.37).[30] The result was a city "divided primarily along class lines," as Horsley has noted. The division pitted "the respectable citizens" against the "riff-raff" or "party of the sailors and the poor" (*Life* 32–35, 64–67, 69, 296).[31] The bureaucracies of the urban centers were often segmented and in competition with each other. The political areas generating their own bureaucratic structures were ecclesiastical (temples and priests), military, economic (tribute, tax, and toll collection), judicial (codifying decrees and what few "laws" were operative), and administrative, which attempted, usually unsuccessfully, to coordinate the others. More often than not, bureaucrats exercised their power by blocking what others proposed. From top to bottom, bureaucracies were networks of patron-client alliances, and appointments to positions were the result of patronage and power struggles.

All the retainers staffing these bureaucracies required support from the peasant base, so the more elaborate the bureaucratic structures, the more resources were required to support them. Since both Sepphoris and Tiberius housed the essential bureaucracies of Herodian rule, the building of Tiberius only increased the burden on the peasant population. Add to this mix the fact that the aristocracies were not native to Galilee but imported from Idumea, and the tensions increase even more. Horsley has noted that Galilee had no native landowning aristocracy.[32] This situation led the Hasmonaeans to impose their own Judean-based aristocracy on Galilee, and later Herod would import his loyal ruling class from Idumea. The presence of two cities dominated by an alien aristocracy without ties to the land except through the extractive efforts of a bureaucratic apparatus was a recipe for increasing social tension and escalating political trouble.

In Judea, the Pharisees formed one of the retainer groups pressing its agenda on the temple leadership. They were opposed by the Sadduccees, some of whom were members of the retainer class while others were evidently members of the ruling elites. Both groups were involved in developing the ideological orientations that would ensure Jerusalem's dominance and perpetuate its claim to the loyalty of peasants in Judea and Galilee as well as other Judeans located throughout the empire. Eisenstadt notes that religious elites and their retainers seek to dominate their society through characteristic activities, such as:

> (1) the codification of sacred books; (2) the development of schools devoted to interpreting the texts; (3) the growth of special educational organizations to spread religious knowledge; and (4) the elaboration of total world-views and ideologies.[33]

The purpose of all of these activities is the creation and articulation of a great tradition that can accommodate and incorporate the little traditions of disparate places and different villages.

The question whether there was a Galilean halakah and the issue of the Galileans' loyalty to the temple define the arena of this struggle between Galilee and Jerusalem. The development of the oral Torah by the Pharisees and its elaboration by competitive schools, as well as the use of the synagogue as a place to teach the proper meaning of the Torah, indicate the presence of an effort to transform Torah into a "great tradition" binding on all. The far-reaching extent of the debates suggests that, by the first century, the Torah was providing a totalizing worldview and orientation. Seen in this context, Jesus' debates about the Torah are more than quibbles over details; they define a struggle over whose worldview will prevail.

Peasants, Artisans, and Village Life

By far the largest population group in agrarian societies is the peasant class, which comprises about 70 to 80 percent of the population.[34] Peasants live in villages, large and small, cultivating the land, raising livestock, and tending vines and olive trees. Peasants are closely related to the rural artisans who share village life with them and scrape out a subsistence existence along with the peasant villagers. Jesus' father, Joseph, was such a village artisan, a *tektōn,* which probably is better translated "handyman" or "jack-of-all-trades" rather than carpenter. Artisans were no better off than peasants and, if they lacked a patrimonial plot of land, they could be even worse off. Urban artisans lived on the very edge of destitution, and their country cousins fared little better. Artisans were generally not respected, except in the villages where they were essential to keeping tools mended and agricultural contraptions in working order.

Aristocrats tended to leave peasants alone and did not interfere in the politics of the villages, which were ruled by custom and a local group of elders or magistrates. But the peasant villages were dominated either by the ruler or the members of the aristocracy who controlled the use and usufruct of the land and could lay claim to the labor of the peasant villagers (through corvee or some other system of forced labor). For their part, peasants knew that the price of being left alone was the prompt payment of all exactions. There was no mutually beneficial reciprocity between the rulers and the ruled.

What distinguished Galilee from Judea was, in part, its distinctive history of domination and independence. Since the loss of the Northern Kingdom in 722 B.C.E., Galileans had lived under a succession of occupying powers, and even before the division of the united Monarchy under David and Solomon, the Galileans had treated the emergence of imperial rule with suspicion and mistrust. These reservations were summarized in Samuel's speech to the elders (1 Sam. 8:10–18). After the division of the kingdom, Israel lived under kings wielding more limited power than in the Southern Kingdom of Judah, and Israelite kings were subjected to the criticism of prophets, as the Elijah and Elisha cycle of stories testifies (1 Kings 17–2 Kings 13). From the return of the exiles to the coming of the Ptolemies and the Seleucids after the breakup of Alexander's vast empire, Galilee continued on a path distinct from Judea, remaining relatively untouched by the forced hellenization programs of the Seleucids. In contrast to Jerusalem with its codified Torah, Galileans expressed their culture and convictions in the "popular oral traditions" nurtured in their village life.[35] When the Hasmonaeans expanded their influence, they incorporated Galilee into their kingdom on the basis of "ancient allegiances," not forced conversion.[36] Owing to the absence of a native landed aristocracy, the Hasmonaeans imported their own ruling class, centered at Sepphoris. They would eventually be usurped and replaced by Herod's Idumean aristocrats. When the Romans recognized the Hasmonaean claim on Galilee by permitting them to impose "the laws and customs of the Judeans," they effectively subjected Galilee to the Jerusalem priesthood and temple, which were controlled by the Hasmonaeans and developed as their base of power.[37] The emergence of Herod the Great may have effectively ended Hasmonaean rule, but he perpetuated the pattern of his predecessors, laying claim to royal lands, confiscating and redistributing estates, and extracting as much from the peasant base, located in isolated villages, as he possibly could. The same struggle continued under new management. Josephus believed that Herod had, "in departing from native customs, and through foreign practices, gradually corrupted the ancient way of life" (*Ant.* 15.267), but his comments appear to underestimate the resilience of the peasant villagers. The villages remained bastions of the little tradition and its popular oral traditions, both of which were forms of resistance to the imposition of the great tradition backed by temple state, client kingship, and Roman rule. Living under a succession of dominating powers, both foreign and domestic, Galilean villagers cultivated their own "popular Israelite tradition" as a "way of maintaining their own identity over against the foreign culture of the imperial administrators."[38]

Another part of what is identified as Galilean independence is geographical. Even Lower Galilee, which is much more accessible than Upper Galilee, is divided by ridges and valleys that separate settlements from each other and encourage the development of village life in relative isolation from urban centers. This may be why the period of primary urbanization that witnessed the establishment of Hellenistic cities located around the edges of Galilee did not essentially change the natives or their lives, even though Ptolemaic tribute collecting was both thorough and ruthless. As Freyne notes, "the interior of Galilee was particularly suited to a peasant style of life with people living together in close ties of kinship in relatively small and isolated settlements."[39] The secondary urbanization represented by the rebuilding of Sepphoris and the building of Tiberius did little to alter this basic situation. If the construction of the two cities put the villages of Galilee within easy walking distance from them, the tale of those two cities indicates that they were unable and probably uninterested in bridging the social, cultural, and economic gap between the urban center and village periphery. City and village remained in different social and symbolic worlds.

In recent times, there has been an ongoing discussion about the relationship between urban centers and villages in Galilee.[40] One group of scholars portrays the relationship between city and village as reciprocal and mutually beneficial.[41] Archaeologists have discovered that pottery made at Kefer Hananiah was evidently sold throughout Galilee. The evidence reveals that pottery most likely manufactured at Kefer Hananiah has been found in the villages around Sepphoris and in the villages of the Golan and Upper Galilee as well.[42] The distribution seems widely dispersed. This situation convinced David Adan-Bayewitz and Douglas Edwards that a small village served as a center for pottery manufacturing, and the wide distribution of its pottery suggests "that a reciprocal market relationship between village and city existed even on the boundaries of the cities since Kefer Hananiah lies on the perimeter of several urban areas."[43] Indeed, Edwards imagines that historians have ignored "the varied, sophisticated market that addressed a large buying public" who sought the best consumer goods available to fulfill their needs.[44] Even more, cities offered a wide variety of services to peasants, including, as K. Hopkins supposes,

> law, protection, peace, rituals, ceremonies and medical advice, even surgery. Towns gave independent peasants and free tenants opportunity to buy extra food and services, necessities and luxuries (tools, pots, clothes, seeds, pastries).[45]

Finally, they argue that the political relationship between cities and towns appears to have been "administrative" but not exploitative. The services offered by cities included keeping "legal records," collecting taxes, and providing "a judicial system," although "the exact nature of the village's participation remains clouded."[46]

A few comments are in order as a response to this attempt to discover benign relations between city and country in Galilee. First, as Martin Millett noted, archaeological evidence consists of "the accidental byproduct of human activity," and "the information it communicates is latent, passive and static, so only articulated through interpretive models imposed by the observer, whether or not these are made explicit."[47] Too often, the evidence is interpreted as though it were "unbiased," although the covert interpretation offered under the guise of unbiased description may actually "echo our contemporary views of the world" in a manner "overlooked by those using archaeological data."[48] This is an apt description of what has happened in the current discussion of the relationship between cities and villages in Galilee. In the comments quoted above, Edwards and Hopkins have imported a capitalist view of a market economy and retrojected it onto the world of first-century Galilee.[49] The picture of a peasant—who lives at the subsistence level, barely able to survive from one planting season to next, in perpetual debt and near the razor's edge of destitution, at the point when the failure to pay off a loan could spell financial ruin—taking a trip to Sepphoris or Tiberius for elective surgery with a stop for pastries and tea borders on the ludicrous!

Even more importantly, Edwards has confused discovering the means of production with knowing the relations of production. From the time of the Ptolemies to the period of Herodian rule, elites have typically monopolized any lucrative agricultural or manufacturing scheme. If the peasants of Kefer Hananiah did engage in making pottery that was widely distributed, it is doubtful that they benefited from their labor. If their profits were significant, they would have attracted the attention of elites practiced in the business of stripping peasants of any profits they might enjoy while conducting a hostile takeover of the promising enterprise. It is much more likely that the peasants of Kefer Hananiah turned to pottery making because their agricultural subsistence was threatened. As Scott has noted, peasants turn to crafts and self-help trades when their subsistence is squeezed or threatened, perhaps due to circumstances caused by monetization. In situations of change caused by colonial rule, if the crafts succeed, they are taken over by elites and turned into industries. The mobilization of peasant labor implied by the manufacturing of pottery at Kefer Hananiah suggests just such a conversion.[50]

Finally, an "administrative relationship" is an exploitative political relationship; the two are not antonyms but synonyms. The distinction that Edwards proposes is a distinction without a difference. Kautsky is closer to the truth when he observes that the relationship between aristocrat and peasant is exploitative but concealed, and one way to provide ideological concealment to this exploitation is to attribute false reciprocity to it, such as the line that aristocrats provide protection to peasants.[51] From whom do peasants need protection? From the very aristocrats who are protecting them! This is why peasants avoid cities and turn their villages into self-sufficient units of consumption and production, or perhaps they extend their trade to other villages nearby or a market town. But the very "services" provided by administrative cities are, to peasants, threats to be avoided. What Edwards euphemistically calls maintaining "legal records" includes debt archives and contracts that could spell ruin to peasants. What is a "judicial system" in societies where laws are few, and the few that do exist are promulgated in the interests of the elites who formulate them?[52] The legal system is simply a tool of the ruler to move from "the rule of might" to the "rule of right," as Lenski describes it.[53] This process entails devising laws that appear to be impartial and just, while in fact they favor the ruling class and perpetuate its interests. "In short, laws may be written in such a way that they protect the interests of the elite while being couched in very general, universalistic terms."[54]

It is precisely because urban centers represent such a threat to peasant villagers that they avoided them whenever possible. Peasants turned their villages into self-sufficient enclaves, bartering with village artisans for needed implements and with other villagers for the necessities of life. As A. H. M. Jones noted long ago,

> The new cities served no useful economic function, for the larger villages supplied such manufactured goods as the villagers required, and the trade of the countryside was conducted at village markets. The only effect of the foundation of cities was the creation of a wealthy landlord class which gradually stamped out peasant proprietorship.[55]

The relationship between city and countryside could better be described by class struggle than by mutual benefits and reciprocity.

THE TWO FACES OF COLONIAL OCCUPATION: LOCAL ARISTOCRACIES AND CLIENT KINGSHIP

As Peter Garnsey and Richard Saller have observed, Rome never developed an imperial administrative bureaucracy that matched the scope and extent of the empire.[56] The colonial bureaucracies that did exist operated on the basis of patronage rather than rationalized criteria and suitability for service. The goals of Roman colonial rule were twofold: maintain order and collect tribute.[57] Since the empire did not have the structure to ensure these goals, Rome typically ruled through local elites whose interests were aligned with those of the empire. In Palestine, these forms of collaboration would take the form of client kingship in Galilee, and local rule through a priestly aristocracy in Judea.

The political arrangements in Galilee differed from those that obtained in Judea for historical reasons. Galilee was ruled by Herod Antipas, son of Herod the Great, and tetrarch of a portion of his father's kingdom, which included Galilee and Peraea. Antipas ruled from 3 B.C.E. to 39 C.E., when he was deposed by Rome. Judea fared differently, owing to the inability of Archelaus to govern Judea and Samaria. In his will, Herod the Great had actually petitioned Augustus to recognize Archelaus as his successor, but Augustus had reservations about Herod's choice and refused to honor the dead king's request; he did apportion the lion's share of Herod's former kingdom to Archelaus with the promise that, if he governed effectively, he would receive the title "king." As usual, Augustus turned out to be right. Archelaus governed for nine stormy years before he was deposed in 6 C.E., and Augustus converted Judea into a subprovince of the Roman province of Syria. Under the new arrangement, Judea would be overseen by a prefect of equestrian rank who was responsible to the Legate (or governor) of Syria. During Jesus' public life, Pilate was prefect of the province of Judea, which included Samaria (26–36 C.E.), but Pilate worked through the high-priestly houses that controlled the Temple in Jerusalem. Each of these arrangements contributed to defining the social, economic, and political context of Jesus' public activity. It will be helpful to sketch each one briefly.

Judea and the Failure of Roman Colonial Policy

Judea offers a case study in the weakness of Roman colonial policy. It was the custom of Rome to co-opt provincial aristocracies to maintain order and collect tribute. What they took for themselves beyond that basic requirement was left to the discretion of the collaborators. In other words, they were free to exploit the provinces, for which they were responsible, to whatever degree accorded with stability and maintenance of the status quo. It is normal for aristocratic empires to impose their rule on an area while leaving more local forms of rule intact so as not to disturb "hereditary interests." As Kautsky notes, "They simply added themselves at the top and made full use of the already existing administrative machinery, incorporating the local hereditary aristocracy" into their system of rule.[58] But, as Martin Goodman has argued at some length, this arrangement failed in Judea and eventually led to the first Jewish Revolt against Rome in 66 to 73 C.E.[59] After Archelaus was deposed, the Romans were confronted with the problem that there was no

> natural landed elite in Judaea but needing the cooperation of local rulers of some kind for their administration to work successfully, the Romans elected to entrust power to those Judaean landowners who did exist, regardless of whether such men could command any popular prestige. (40)

The class he is describing are the high-priestly families who were mistrusted, if not despised, by common Judeans because they came from illegitimate kinship roots. What small chance they had of ingratiating themselves with the populace had been destroyed by Herod when he reduced the high priests to puppets who could be appointed and deposed on a whim. To make matters worse, the people of Judea were not above setting the houses against each other, as they did when they called for the deposing of Joazar of the house of Boethus for his role in organizing the census in 6 C.E. The Roman governor turned to the house of Ananus, which proved little better, for the members of these four powerful families were "in a sense marginal within their own society" (46). This situation created a crisis of credibility, increasing the anxiety of the ruling houses and intensifying their sensitivity to any criticism of the temple or efforts to undermine its credibility.

The priestly houses anointed by Rome proved singularly ineffective in addressing the problems facing the province of Judea. The widening gap between rich and poor, typical of agrarian societies and aristocratic empires, led to unending enmity and hostility. The high-priestly families tended to focus on the health of the economy of Jerusalem to the detriment of the wider economy of Judea. Owing to the wealth accumulated in the temple, the aristocratic families of Jerusalem had money to lend to peasants so they could plant their crops, but the "only logical reason to lend was thus the hope of winning the peasant's land by foreclosing on it when the debt was not paid off."[60] The use of debt to ruin peasants only increased the level of hostility while it concentrated wealth in fewer and fewer hands. The priestly families were evidently unable to resist the temptation for immediate gain even when it worked against their longer term interests in maintaining social stability. Political elites can be notoriously shortsighted.

Their very base of power, the temple, posed its own quandary, because the temple was the symbolic center of a people who refused to assimilate into the Hellenistic culture and Roman world in the way that collaborationist elites in other areas of the empire had done quite gladly. The pilgrimage festivals symbolized the contradiction of colonial rule overseen by quisling priests. As Horsley puts it, "especially poignant at festival times was the conflict between Roman domination and the people's yearning for freedom under their true, divine 'king.'"[61] Yet these festivals of freedom and memories of liberation were presided over by high priests who were no better than "client-rulers beholden to Rome."[62] To maintain what little standing they had with the people, the priests had to maintain a temple system that marginalized them with their Roman overlords. The chief priests were also susceptible to the kind of critique leveled against them by the sectarians at Qumran. They were from illegitimate priestly families, and, that being the case, they could not offer legitimate sacrifices on the altar in the temple. All sacrifices were thereby judged to be tainted and ineffectual. Since God's favor depended upon the maintenance of proper sacrifices, their legitimation was in danger and their vulnerability great. Yet, as Horsley has argued convincingly, the high priests consistently sided with their Roman masters and faithfully carried out Roman colonial policy, even to the disadvantage and damage of the people they were supposed to rule.[63] In short, the high priests invariably "pursued their own political-economic interests, as collaborators with the Roman government." And when the Romans provoked or abused Jewish sensibilities, as in Gaius Caligula's attempt to place his statue in the holy of holies, they failed to represent the interests of their people. Abandoned by their supposed leaders, the populace organized their own mass protests. All of these factors left the province of Judea in a precarious position. It was a powder keg waiting to explode. Above all, it meant that any prophet, like Jesus, who criticized the temple could expect to receive prompt attention and a hostile response from a ruling class already stretched to the limit.

Galilee and Client Kingship

Nor was the situation in Galilee, where many of the same economic and political factors were at work, noticeably better, although the political framework was the client kingship of Herod Antipas. By Jesus' day, some of the trends initiated during the era of the Hellenistic monarchies (the Ptolemies during the fourth century B.C.E. and the Seleccids during the third and early second centuries B.C.E.) had changed peasant life in one fundamental way. This may be what Josephus was alluding to when he spoke of the deleterious effects of Herodian rule. During the Israelite period, peasants typically lived in what archaeologists call "the four room house."[64] These houses were located in the midst of the fields controlled by the clan or tribe to which the household belonged, and the family was composed of a multigenerational unit, the *beth av,* or patriarchal house. These small, isolated farms formed the backbone of peasant life, but with the upheavals and constant warfare brought by the Hellenistic monarchies and the Hasmonaeans after them, peasants began to move into villages for protection. The disintegration of the clan and tribal structure of Israel left the village as the only effective social unit larger than the peasant household. The rulers encouraged the movement to villages because it made the peasants easier to oversee and control.

In place of the four-room house that housed a multigenerational family, the village house was a courtyard house in which a nuclear family lived, sharing the common space of the courtyard with other nuclear families. By tracing "the rural settlement pattern in the Second Temple Period," Shimon Appelbaum has suggested that the extended family did not survive the Hellenistic age, but it is possible that the Hasmonaeans and the Herodians welcomed the change and exploited it to their political advantage.[65]

Eric Wolf has noted that there are four conditions under which the nuclear family tends to prevail over the extended family, two of which apply to the Galilee of Jesus' day.[66] They are, first, that land becomes so scarce that families can no longer use land as a base for consolidating a multi-generational household. Consequently, families break up in the search for alternative means for support. The scarcity of land in Galilee traces to a number of factors, including Herod's confiscations of land; the land already designated royal lands and handed down from one ruling dynasty to another, beginning with the Ptolemies and continuing through the Seleucids, Hasmonaeans, Herodians, and Romans; and the use of debt instruments to alienate peasants from their land. The second condition leading to the emergence of the nuclear family is the introduction of wage labor as part of the monetization of the economy. The lure of wage labor replaces the traditional emphasis on the extended family as a labor unit. A peasant household is both a producing and a consuming unit, and when the household becomes so large that its land base cannot support the number of its members, the family must be broken up. This usually means that younger sons (and perhaps daughters) are turned loose to seek employment wherever they can. In effect, they become day laborers or expendables.

The monetization of the economy also alters the basic relationship between peasant and landlord or landed aristocrat. As contracts are written in terms of monetary values and not as a portion or percentage of the crop, the social relationship between producer and consumer is further strained. As peasants lose traditional rights, social bandits emerge to protest the changes. While there is some disagreement about the prevalence of the phenomenon of social banditry in Galilee, it seems clear that it was present from 40 B.C.E., when Herod rooted out and killed Hezekias, until the time of the Jewish Revolt in 66 to 70 C.E., when it was epidemic throughout the countryside.[67] Social banditry represents a pre-political form of protest, oriented toward the past, not the future. Social bandits usually protest the loss of traditional rights and seek to get them reinstated.[68] From this brief description, it is clear that the weakness of social banditry lies in its inability to analyze why changes are happening and, therefore, what political steps should be taken. For present purposes, social bandits will be viewed as social indicators of the changes occurring in Galilee. Their presence allows us to infer, with a reasonable degree of probability, the presence of the economic forces and trends affecting peasant households and villages. In short, the families of the wealthy get richer and larger while peasant families get smaller and poorer.

Horsley has argued that Jesus aimed his public work at renewing village life in Galilee.[69] Knowing it was futile to appeal to the rulers, Jesus began to work among the ruled. One example may suffice to show the impact that Jesus' work could have had. Debt instruments were a major weapon in the hands of the elites. They used their power to lend money to peasants and then to control the prices of crops to increase the debt load on peasant families. When the peasant was finally unable to repay the debt, the lender foreclosed and confiscated the peasant's land. It was, of course, to prevent this cycle of poverty that the sabbatical provisions of the Torah had been given to Moses. Yet, although there is evidence that some of the sabbatical traditions were observed in Jesus' day, such as letting fields lie fallow during the seventh year, others were not. The sabbatical called for the forgiveness of debts during the seventh year, but the elites responded to this provision by refusing to make loans to peasants during the year or two leading up to the sabbatical year. This is why Hillel introduced the *prosbul*. Although it is not entirely clear just what the prosbul was, it nullified the sabbatical provision by one of two means. Martin Goodman has offered a clear summary of the rabbinic text:

> The prosbul was a public declaration before a court by a man seeking a loan, in which he stated that he would accept his legal duty to repay the money even after the advent of a Sabbatical Year rendered the debt automatically cancelled.[70]

The rabbinic text reads: " 'Whatever of yours that is with your brother your hand should release' (Dt 15:3)—but not he who gives his mortgage to the court."[71] The reason for the provision excluding forgiveness of debt is then given.

> Hillel ordained the prozbul on account of the order of the world. That he saw people, that they held back from lending to one another and transgressed what is written in the Torah.
> He arose and ordained the prozbul.
> And this is the formula of the prozbul: "I give to you, so-and-so and so-and-so, the judges in such-and-such place, every debt which I have, that I may collect it whenever I like," and the judges seal below, or the witnesses.[72]

Deuteronomy 15:9–10 had envisioned just such a situation and condemned it, but the prophetic voice of Deuteronomy was muted in favor of the more expedient solution. The prosbul meant that debt would be perpetual and unending. Appelbaum has suggested the economic context for the provision: "such a grave modification of a fundamental Jewish principle must have been the result of a situation in which the pressure for loans was extreme."[73] The intensity of that pressure was a direct consequence of the monetization of the economy and the severing of social ties between creditor and debtor.

The elites, therefore, used debt to press their advantages and to imperil the lives of others. They also used debt instruments ruthlessly among themselves. They saw debt as a weapon in their ceaseless struggle to grasp more power and prestige. Jesus saw debt differently. Rooted in the prophetic strands of the Torah, Jesus' view was that debt is an opportunity for forgiveness. It was such an important element in his teaching that he evidently taught a prayer that captured his prophetic vision. Although the Lord's Prayer is quite likely a composite of many of Jesus' prayer themes, it may contain the gist of what Jesus thought was important when addressing the Lord of the Universe. "Forgive us our debts as we forgive our debtors" resounds as a protest against the prevailing practices of his day. It was spoken to peasant villagers and disciples alike, because they were often tempted to shape themselves in the image of the ruling class and internalize their ideology.[74] So peasant villagers might use their opportunities to indebt others for the purpose of gaining social prestige. But Jesus taught that forgiveness of debt was a daily matter, not just a sabbatical provision. It was a petition that, if observed, would make the experience of the sabbatical a fact of life, not an exception to the rule. If this is a possible context for the Lord's Prayer, it fits the setting, being sketched in this chapter, of the historical Jesus and speaks directly to one critical area of his concern. The chapters in Part 3 will begin to turn this sketch into a more complete picture.

PART 3

Jesus the Prophet and the Praxis of the Justice of the Reign of God: Conflicts in Context

Part 3 contains four chapters that represent the heart of this study. It is an attempt to contextualize Jesus' public work and to interpret it in light of the dominant institutions and ideologies of his day. Throughout the analysis of the texts studied in these chapters, this quest has attempted to indicate the theological ramifications of political, kinship, economic, and social issues. Like most prophets, Jesus was a theologian as well as an acute observer of the political scene, and he understood how theology and politics needed to be seen in relation to each other.

In chapter 6, I focus on Jesus' relationship with the temple in Jerusalem, sketching the nature of Jesus' conflicts with the temple and its representatives and indicating how the conflict escalated to the point of irreconcilable differences. There were good reasons for the animosity and antipathy between temple authorities and Jesus. In chapter 7 attention shifts from the temple to its "constitution," the Torah. Jesus did not abrogate the Torah or supersede it in his own teaching. Rather, he interpreted the Torah in light of God's intent for it. The Torah was meant to be an expression of God's covenant with the people, a way of ensuring that God's land would be a haven of justice in an unjust world. This reading clashed with those who had co-opted the Torah for their own political interests.

Chapter 8 traces the escalating conflict generated by Jesus' public work. This includes debates about purity and controversies about Sabbath healings. Clearly, Jesus judged the symbolic order ordained by the temple to be inadequate, because it failed to pass the test of faithfulness to God's covenant justice. Chapter 9 explores the relationship between the land and the temple. The temple was part of a symbolic order meant to secure the blessings of the land for God's people, but it became a political power center that used its resources against the very people it was intended to serve. Jesus discerned this trend and addressed it in his teaching and healing. In brief, he argued that the temple was no longer needed, because God was approaching the people afresh. Jesus saw himself as brokering God's covenant love and mercy.

These four chapters define the central disputes that animated Jesus' teaching and healing. His public activity was a form of praxis, a combination of action and reflection for the sake of changing the world.

6

"Something Greater than the Temple Is Here":

Subverting the "Cave of Social Bandits"

In spite of the fact that the third quest for the historical Jesus has produced little consensus, one incident from Jesus' life has been widely viewed as an event tracing to the historical Jesus. That event is the incident in the temple, and it provides a place to begin exploring the public work of Jesus.

A READING OF THE TEMPLE INCIDENT

E. P. Sanders has argued that one important key to interpreting the ministry of Jesus is understanding the incident in the temple (Mark 11:15–18 and par.), an incident that he takes to be a substantiated fact of the Jesus tradition.[1] He summarizes his reading of this pivotal event in the following manner:

> Thus we conclude that Jesus publicly predicted or threatened the destruction of the temple, that the statement was shaped by his expectation of the arrival of the eschaton, that he probably also expected a new temple to be given by God from heaven, and that he made a demonstration which prophetically symbolized the coming event.[2]

Sanders thinks that this reading is preferable to the older notion that Jesus was somehow involved in "cleansing" the temple. Indeed, his reading of Jesus' actions sharpens the conflictual nature of the event and even suggests a reason for Jesus' crucifixion. His symbolic demonstration, announcing the destruction of the temple, captured the attention of the authorities in Jerusalem, who took a dim view of the action and determined thereafter that Jesus had to be executed.

At first glance, Sanders's reading appears to represent a clear gain over more traditional readings. It is probable that Jesus engaged in a prophetic demonstration symbolizing the destruction of the temple. He was not protesting the temple's lack of spirituality, nor was he merely criticizing the crass commercial activities associated with the sacrificial system, nor was he even protesting the exclusion of the Gentiles from the house of God, as others have suggested.[3] His protest was more fundamental than any of those alternatives supposes.

Up to this point, Sanders has followed a clear line of argument, but, having emphasized the conflictual nature of Jesus' actions, Sanders proceeds to take back what he has seemingly given away. If Jesus did indeed prophesy the destruction of the temple, he did so in the context of what Sanders calls "Jewish restoration eschatology," a form of Jewish expectation that envisioned a new temple as part of a promised new heaven and new earth. All of this means that the prediction of the destruction of the temple was not a protest against the temple as such but a preparation for a new temple. In effect, this transforms the so-called destruction of the temple into one more version of the cleansing of the temple, the very position he rejected at the beginning of his study. However, even though he has compromised the radical nature of his proposal, Sanders has brought the incident in the temple to center stage where it belongs, because Jesus did indeed conflict with the temple system, but his conflict was deeper than Sanders imagines. This study proposes that Jesus attacked the temple system itself. To understand why, it will be necessary to examine the function of temples in agrarian societies and aristocratic empires before examining some texts where Jesus' prophetic critique of the temple is visible.

THE ROLE OF THE TEMPLE IN AGRARIAN SOCIETIES AND ARISTOCRATIC EMPIRES: LEGITIMIZING THE POWERS THAT BE

In their study of human societies, Gerhard and Jean Lenski take note of the significant role played by temples in agrarian societies.[4] In Egypt and Mesopotamia alike, rulers were considered to be the living incarnation of deities, and the purpose of commoners was "to serve the gods by supplying them with food, drink and shelter so that they might have full leisure for their divine activities" (171). Advanced agrarian societies had replaced the hoe with the plow and augmented human energy with the use of draft animals. These advances in technology enabled peasants to produce a greater surplus than had previously been possible using the hoe and human energy alone. But this technological breakthrough also posed a problem for rulers and the ruling class. How were they to extract that attractive surplus from their peasant base? Ancient temples served a crucial function in making this form of economic exploitation possible. As the Lenskis warn:

> Technological advance creates the possibility of a surplus, but to transform that possibility into a reality requires an ideology that motivates farmers to produce more than they need to stay alive and productive, and persuades them to turn over that surplus to someone else. . . . [A] system of beliefs that defined people's obligations with reference to the supernatural was best suited to play this critical role. (173)

This means that the religion of the temple was always political religion with economic consequences, because the temple was an instrument of the policies of the ruler and the ruling class. In the ancient world, there was no separation of church and state. Temples reflected the interests of the rulers and articulated their ideologies. Indeed, temples were embedded in the political systems of which they were a part.[5] Their two most important functions were to legitimate a particular regime and to mystify its exploitation by re-presenting it in the form of obligation to God or the gods.[6]

The role of legitimating a particular regime was especially important because agrarian rulers often came to power by violent means. They were the fittest survivors of the internecine warfare among the members of the ruling class to achieve preeminence and power. Having survived this form of social selection, they were faced with the problem of legitimating their rule and converting their victory from a rule by might (raw power) to a rule by right (law).[7] But the ruler needed more than that. Rulers needed the legitimation that only religion could provide, the confirmation that they ruled by the mandate of heaven or the will of the gods or the election of Yahweh. This was the special role played by priests and temples. The veneer of legitimacy provided by the temple offset the inherent instability generated by the incessant intraclass struggle among aristocrats for supreme power. By contrast with the often recent pedigrees of rulers, the gods of the temples represented long-standing traditions and could mobilize loyalties across class lines.

It is, then, with good reason that John Lundquist has argued that the building of a temple is the culminating act in the formation of the state.[8] It could even be said that a state without a temple cannot fully have come into being. This explains why David wanted to build a temple in Jerusalem, and why David's kingdom did not become a full-fledged dynastic state until Solomon completed the temple. As Lundquist says pointedly, "the state . . . did not come into being, indeed could not have been perceived to have come into being in ancient Israel before and until the temple of Solomon was built and dedicated" (271). The temple was not the prime cause of state formation but served as the "integrative, legitimizing factor that symbolizes . . . the full implementation of what today we call 'the state' " (272). These themes are clearly displayed in 1 Kings 8, which includes Solomon's prayer of dedication, and 1 Kings 9. Standing before the altar, Solomon prayed:

> Therefore, O Lord, God of Israel, keep for your servant my father David that which you promised him, saying, "There shall never fail you a successor before me to sit on the throne of Israel, if only your children look to their way, to walk before me as you have walked before me." Therefore, O God of Israel, let your word be confirmed, which you have promised to your servant my father David. (8:25–26)

The same theme is repeated in 1 Kings 9, when Yahweh appears before Solomon after he has completed building the temple and his palace. The twin projects reflect the close ties between the house of God and the house of the king, for the temple is the house of the king of the gods, or in Israel's history, the king of the heavenly host. In 1 Kings 9, Yahweh declares,

> As for you, if you will walk before me, as David your father walked, with integrity of heart and uprightness [tell that to Uriah the Hittite!], doing according to all that I have commanded you, and keeping my statutes and ordinances, then I will establish your royal throne forever, as I promised your father, David, saying, "There shall not fail you a successor on the throne of Israel. (9:4–5)

In both passages, the confirmation of the emergence of the state, which began with the anointing of Saul and continued through the reign of David, has come to fruition and culminated in the building of the temple and palace. As an aside, one should note the power of the royal propaganda that surrounded Solomon. He taxed his people to ruination, used forced labor to build the temple, split his kingdom because of his exploitative and oppressive practices, and yet is remembered for his wisdom! However, as 1 Kings 11:1–43 reveals, the royal propaganda of Solomon was not accepted blindly, and Solomon was subjected to a retrospective critique. This is an important point to make because dissenting passages like 1 Kings 11 point to the presence of a prophetic judgment on the monarchy even after it had achieved its zenith of power and influence. The prophetic activity of Ahijah (11:26–40) seems to be more involved with the matter of succession than the question of justice, although, in his address to Jeroboam (11:37–38), he too repeats the conditional nature of the convenantal promise.

Indeed, the situation throughout 1 Kings 8–9 is more complex than it first appears. The Deuteronomistic historian has qualified the royal temple ideology expressed in the dedication of the temple and Solomon's prayer. If 1 Kings 9:4–5 expresses the dynastic hope, 1 Kings 9:6–9 renders the promise of divine support for the Davidic dynasty conditional.

> If you then turn aside from following me, you and your children, and do not keep my commandments and my statutes that I have set before you, but go and serve other gods and worship them, then I will cut Israel off from the land that I have given them; and the house that I have consecrated for my name I will cast out of my sight; and Israel will become a proverb and a taunt among all peoples. (9:6–7)

Since the temple is tied to the land, the failure to fulfill the covenant and do justice by keeping the commandments and statutes will lead to the loss of the land and the temple.

The building of the temple in Jerusalem fits a wider Near Eastern cultural pattern that can be summarized as follows:

> . . . the legitimizing decisions of the cosmic deities are transferred to earth and to the earthly monarch, the whole process symbolized by and centered in the building of a temple. . . . There is thus a tie between the temple as the abode of the king of the gods and the temple as a dynastic shrine of the earthly king, the adopted son of god. The temple and kingship are thus part of the "orders of creation," properly the eternal kingship of the god of order, the eternal dynasty of his earthly counterpart. (291)

As Solomon makes clear in his prayer before the assembly at the dedication of the temple, the temple will now be the abode of the God who had previously refused to settle down in any chosen city of any of the tribes (1 Kings 8:12–13). The royal hope is that the temple will capture and domesticate God as well as provide his abode, or the abode of his name on the earth. Equally clear is the fact that the dynastic promises are given cosmic sanction. Once again, however, those very dynastic claims are not unqualified. The Deuteronomic historian critiques the notion that the temple could be the abode of God. How could the creator of the heavens and earth be contained in a house constructed by human hands? (1 Kings 8:27–30). The critique is retrospective and may reflect the lessons learned from the destruction of the temple and the sojourn in exile, but it remains an important element in the recounting of these events. Dynastic presumption has been subjected to prophetic critique and covenantal qualification from the time of the nascent monarchy (1 Sam. 8:10–18) to the return from exile.

Just as the role of the temple is crucial, so is the manner in which the temple is built. If the state is, as Henri J. M. Claessen and Peter Skalnik suggest, "the organization for the regulation of social relations in a society that is divided into two emergent social classes, the rulers and the ruled,"[9] then the temple becomes a public confirmation that the state has the power to organize a massive public building project. In Solomon's case, this entails both massive taxation and the use of forced labor to build the temple. The Solomonic court historian attempts to mitigate this fact by noting that the king used only non-Israelites, "all the people who were left of the Amorites, the Hittites, the Perizzites, the Hivites, and the Jebusites" (9:20), in this role. The former enemies of Israel, currently occupying the land that has, at last, become a true state or kingdom, are reduced to servitude, providing yet another sign that the state has arrived in its full power. But the temple was not built without heavy cost. Solomon's debts to Hiram, king of Tyre, were so great that he ceded to him twenty cities in the land of Galilee (1 Kings 9:10–14), again illustrating the proprietary theory of the state. Solomon can cede his subjects to another ruler, treating them as chattel, in order to pay for the temple and palace complex.

The central importance of the temple in legitimating the state and establishing a dynastic claim may explain, in part, why, during his reign, Herod lavished such extravagance on rebuilding the temple in Jerusalem. Josephus's long description (*Ant.* 15.380–425) details the expansion of the temple grounds and the glory of the new temple building itself. Seen through the lens of Lundquist's study, the reasons for the typological characteristics of temple buildings seem clear.[10] The temple is usually built on a "cosmic mountain," the intersection of heaven and earth. On this matter, Herod had no need to change the site of Solomon's temple because it already resided on a mountain top. The space within the temple had to be "separate, sacral, set apart space." The second temple complex accomplished this through a series of increasingly inaccessible courtyards that separated Gentiles from Judeans, women from men, Levites and laity from priests, and the high priest from ordinary priests. Each courtyard was more exclusive and more sacred. This means that the movement from the outer courtyard, where Gentiles could congregate, to the court of the Israelites separated outsiders from insiders. Yet, within the temple precincts, the court of the women was lower than the court of the men, and the court of the laity was less sacred than the court of the priests where the altar of sacrifice was located. Every successive space separated the sacred from the profane and the unclean from the clean. The final distinction is that which separates the internal rooms of the temple building itself, the holy place and the Holy of Holies, from all external space. Only priests could enter the holy place, and only the high priest could enter the Holy of Holies, and then, only on the Day of Atonement.

In addition to the increasing seclusion of space and corresponding exclusion of people, the temple was constructed as a series of raised platforms expressing the idea of "successive ascension toward heaven" (275). The Temple Mount itself was elevated above the city of Jerusalem, especially the lower city. Within the enclosed Temple Mount, the outer courtyard was situated on the lowest platform. Anyone, even Gentiles and Roman soldiers, could enter the outer courtyard. The temple precincts were separated from the outer courtyard by a ballustrade, whose gates carried an inscription written in three languages announcing the death penalty for any person, except a ritually clean Judean, who attempted to enter the temple precincts. The temple precincts themselves were elevated above the courtyard of the Gentiles by "a few steps" (*Ant.* 15.417). Inside the temple precincts, the court of the women was lower than the court of the Israelite men, and the court of the Israelite men (laity) was separated from the court of the priests by a parapet. The temple building itself was elevated even higher than the court of the priests, in which the altar for sacrifices was located. The location of the altar in the court of the priests, in full view of the court of the laity, announced the centrality of sacrifice and the exclusive right of priests to offer sacrifices on the altar. Above all, the temple was the place of sacrifice, designed to imitate the cosmic mountain, the symbolic center of the cosmos, a feature tracing at least to the ziggurats found in Mesopotamia.

Nor was the architecture the only symbolic feature of the temple. The large menorah located in the holy place and the great golden vine ornamenting the door to the temple building may well have symbolized "the tree of life." The lavish decorations and ornaments were meant to associate the temple with "abundance and prosperity," implying that it was also the dispenser of these blessings (275). The temple was the protector of sacred law and promulgator of the laws that bound the people to the Torah. The standard scrolls of the Torah, from which all others were copied, were kept in the temple. The temple was thereby associated with the keeping of the law. The secluded quarters in which the priests ate their sacred meals and in which the sacrifices were conducted shrouded the temple's rituals in secrecy, especially when the rituals entailed entering the temple building itself. Sensitivity to this matter of shrouded mystery can be illustrated by the effort of Agrippa II, in the late 50s, to build a tower from which he could look down on the court of the priests to watch them making sacrifices (*Ant.* 20.189–96). The high priest Ishmael ben Phiabi ordered a wall built to block Agrippa's view, and he prevailed, even after the matter was referred to Caesar. The high priest's instincts were to protect sacred space from profane view.

The entire temple complex was a microcosm of the macrocosmic world. What Josephus says about the tapestries in the temple could be said about the entire structure: "Nor was the mixture of materials without its mystic meaning; it typified the universe" (*War*, 5.210–14). The temple, then, embodied in its very architecture and trappings a cosmology, a political theology, and an ideology. The ideology declared that Judeans were holier (and, therefore, purer or cleaner) than Gentiles and had to be separated from them. The barrier of purity thus created was so strong that it could be violated only with the severest consequences. The ballustrade around the temple precincts was, as the writer of Ephesians said, "a dividing wall of hostility" (Eph. 2:14). Nor did the hierarchy of holiness end with the separation of Judeans from Gentiles; it organized all of Israel as well. Men were purer than women; the court of the women was the lowest court in the temple precincts, separated from the court of the men by a twelve-step ascent that led to the Nicanor gate. The Levites would stand on these steps and sing the Hallel psalms or the psalms of ascent as pilgrims entered the temple. According to Sanders, the Levites took the sacrificial animals brought by women (usually two turtledoves) and conveyed them to the priests on their behalf, since women were not allowed to pass beyond the court of the women.[11] To continue the hierarchy, priests were holier than laity. While Israelite men could climb the stairs that elevated the court of the men above the court of the women and pass through the Nicanor gate, they could not trespass the parapet that separated the court of the men from the court of the priests, except during the Feast of Tabernacles for one ritual ceremony. The altar of sacrifice was located in the court of the priests in full view of the court of the Israelite laymen. In addition to offering sacrifices on the altar, the priests could ascend the steps to the temple building itself and offer the daily incense offering in the holy place, a task determined by lot each day. Finally, the high priest was holier and purer than all other priests; he was, in fact, the purest and holiest of all Judeans because he alone could enter the Holy of Holies on the Day of Atonement. In the temple's ideological depiction of the world, the priesthood was the model for humanity, and men were the model for laity. Judeans were likewise the model for God's people. Accepting this model for society, the sectarians at Qumran organized themselves into a community ruled by the sons of Zadok, the only true claimants to the office of high priest because they alone came from legitimate priestly families. Although they did not withdraw from society, the Pharisees set as the goal for their observance of Torah that they should eat each meal in a state of ritual purity equal to that of a priest eating a sacred meal in the temple. They were, in part, a table companionship sect, seeking to recreate the holiness of the temple and the priesthood at every meal.[12]

In addition to informing the political and purity agenda of the Essenes and Pharisees, the temple typified an approach to the world. As its own architecture symbolized, the world was organized into a hierarchy of holiness with clear and distinct boundaries separating groups from each other. This approach to the world led to the formulation of what are called "purity maps," which covered almost every aspect of life. For example, space can be ordered by its relative purity. In the Mishnah (*m. Kelim* 1:6–9), space is ordered as follows:

> There are ten degrees of holiness.
> The land of Israel is holier than any other land.
> The walled cities [of the land of Israel] are holier still . . .
> Within the walls of Jerusalem is still more holy . . .
> The Temple Mount is still more holy . . .
> The Rampart [surrounding the Temple precincts] still more holy . . .
> The Court of the Women is still more holy . . .
> The Court of the Israelites is still more holy . . .
> The Court of the Priests is still more holy . . .
> Between the Porch and the Altar is still more holy . . .
> The Sanctuary [the holy place] is still more holy . . .
> And The Holy of Holies is still more holy.[13]

In each case, the reasons for the increasing degree of purity are provided (605–6). Not only space but time could also be organized into a hierarchy of holiness. The entire Second Division of the Mishnah, Moed (Set Feasts), implies an order of sacred times, beginning with the most holy and listing other feasts in descending order. They are as follows:

1. Shabbath and Erubim (Sabbath)
2. Pesahim (Feast of Passover)
3. Yoma (Day of Atonement)
4. Sukkah (Feast of Tabernacles)
5. Yom Tob or Betzah (Festival Days)
6. Rosh Ha-Shanah (Feast of the New Year)
7. Taanith (Days of Fasting)
8. Megillah (Feast of Purim)
9. Moed Katan (Mid-Festival Days)

(99–216)

The purity maps did not stop with time and space but included human beings as well. Jerome Neyrey summarizes one such list from the Tosefta *Megillah*, beginning with the holiest and running down to the most unclean.[14]

1. Priests
2. Levites
3. Israelites
4. Converts (proselytes)
5. Freed slaves
6. Disqualified priests (illegitimate children of priests)
7. *Netin*s (temple slaves)
8. *Mamzer*s (bastards)
9. Eunuchs
10. Those with damaged testicles
11. Those without a penis

(*t. Meg.* 2:7)

Purity or holiness, as exemplified in this list, means, first of all, wholeness. The least pure are those with damaged bodies. Disfigurement indicates damaged goods. Close to them are those with disfigured bloodlines or family ties. The rest of the list is organized according "to one's standing vis-a-vis the Temple. . . . This *map of people,* then, replicates the *map of places* . . . just observed."[15] Jeremias provides a Synoptic comparison of three such lists of people as well as discussion of the rationale behind each list.[16]

What is important to note is that the temple, by its very structure and ideology, sanctions the ordering of life into a series of interlocking and mutually reinforcing hierarchies for the purpose of drawing boundaries and defining relative degrees of cleanness or purity. The temple embodied this approach to ordering society, and in so doing, legitimized the varying forms this structuring would take, whether at the hands of Roman colonial adminstrators, Herod Antipas, or the priestly aristocracy in Jerusalem. The power to define social relationships by including and excluding was as significant as the power to proscribe and prescribe behavior.

The temple was also the keeper of sacred law and order. This entailed justifying the rulers by declaring that their dominance was divinely ordained and blessed, and it included the task of codifying the criteria by means of which the classification and ordering of society would occur. The Sanhedrin met in the temple, although it was probably more of an informal advisory group than the ideal political institution depicted in the Mishnah.[17] Nevertheless, insofar as there was a judicial or legislative function, it was controlled by the temple. From the Hasmonaean period forward, the temple came increasingly to be seen as the dwelling place of God, the house of God, and the only place where God's relations with human beings could be mediated through the sacrificial system. The temple claimed a monopoly on sacrifice and forgiveness. This meant, in effect, that the traditions limiting the power of monarchy and subjecting the ruler to the justice of the Torah were minimized as were the prophetic critiques of the temple (see Deut. 17:14–20; 1 Sam. 12:19–25; Jer. 7: 1–34). Though latent, such strong strains of the Torah and prophets could not be totally repressed or ignored, as the public work of John the Baptist and Jesus would attest.

In an article focusing on the nature of the power available through temple and Torah in first-century Palestine, Sheldon Isenberg develops a sociological model for understanding the implications of a temple system for the lives of common people.[18] Every society conceives of itself as having been brought into existence by divine decree or election. The people of Israel were constituted by God's election, an action that indebted all members of the society or state to the God who brought their social and political world into being. This sense of indebtedness runs throughout the Torah whenever Yahweh reminds the people that he led them out of Egypt by his mighty acts, guided them through the wilderness, revealed the Torah at Sinai, and, finally, led them into the Promised Land. The purpose of the temple is to maintain proper relations with the constituting deity (or deities), and the primary way of maintaining those relations is the sacrificial system. Through sacrifice and covenant renewal ceremonies the people accept their debt to Yahweh and discharge their ongoing obligations to him. The temple and its sacrificial system and sacred rules are called the "redemptive media," because they provide the means by which a person or the people may discharge their indebtedness. All people feel obligated, because they have all passed through the same processes of socialization and, likewise, all members of the society know that their sense of debt can be discharged only through the temple.

In the case of first-century Palestine, the temple served just such a function. The Judean people believed that they had been the subject of Yahweh's election, and they were, consequently, indebted to Yahweh. The temple became the place where people could discharge their debt to the God who had elected them. All Judeans, wherever they lived in the ancient Near East, expressed this sense of indebtedness by paying the half-shekel tax to the temple, by making pilgrimage to the temple whenever feasible for one of the three great festivals, and by living in obedience to the Torah.

The Torah, which served as the constitution for the temple, was read in such a way that it spelled out the obligations and debts owed to the temple. These included the rendering of tithes and offerings, although the case of tithes was problematic because the Torah contained a number of statements regarding the tithe which could not easily be harmonized. The provision in Deuteronomy (14:22–29) describes the tithe as a meal shared at a central sanctuary between priests and peasants, whereas the provision in the Priestly Code (Lev. 27:30–33; Num. 18:21–32) envisions the tithes being distributed to the Levites, who in turn offer a tithe of what they have received to the priests. By the first century, the two codes, Deuteronomistic and Priestly, were believed to contain parallel systems of tithes that defined a double obligation. One tithe was owed to the temple, and the other was to be spent in Jerusalem, presumably while one was on pilgrimage. Sanders contests this reading and argues that the outlay was only eight tithes in every six-year cycle between sabbatical years.[19] This would yield an effective tribute rate of 13.33 percent rather than the 20 percent proposed by Horsley, Borg, and others. What Sanders fails to recognize is the oppressive burden of the entire system on peasants in Palestine, whether the temple's rate of extraction was 13.33 percent or 20 percent. When one adds Roman and Herodian tribute and tax collection on top of the temple's demand, peasants living at a subsistence level would be expected to yield between 28 percent and 40 percent (to take Sanders's low estimate and Horsley's high estimate) of their subsistence stores.[20]

What was at stake in tribute dodging? Why did it matter? The effect on peasants in Galilee was significant, for it meant that they were permanently and intractably in debt to the temple. They could never discharge their obligations because they could not afford to pay their tithes. The reasons were not far to find. A Galilean villager owed tribute to Herod Antipas to support his client kingdom; to the colonial power behind the throne, Rome; and to various landlords and local aristocrats who claimed their share through the imposition of rents, tolls, imposts, and other forms of direct and indirect taxation. Sanders has argued that the system in Jesus' time was no more oppressive than at any other time.[21] There was no triple level of tribute—Herodian, Roman, and temple—because Herod Antipas paid the tribute to Rome out of what he gathered for his taxes. So the demand was simply for a double level of tribute, Herodian and temple. His argument fails to note that Herod Antipas would adjust his tribute to accommodate the Roman demand, while maintaining his own level of tribute and taxation. What difference did it make that the third level of tributary demand, the Roman, was hidden in the demands of Herod Antipas? The result was the same. Add to these burdens the demand for a double tithe and other incidental offerings, and the peasant household was stretched to the breaking point and beyond. It was not possible to avoid either the Herodians or the Romans, who could enforce their tribute and tax collection with military sanctions, but the temple was reduced to the use of persuasion. So the peasants seem to have paid what they could and abandoned any efforts to pay their double tithe to the temple. The temple responded by labeling and condemning the peasants.

The threat posed to the peasants was not insignificant. They believed that the offering of sacrifices was the way to discharge their debt, and they believed that fulfilling their obligations to the temple, so that the temple could operate on their behalf, was essential to fruitful fields and orchards. The temple and the land were inextricably entwined. The sacrifices offered in the temple were meant to insure the fertility of the land by perpetuating the blessing implied in God's gift of the land. Without rains at the appropriate times, they would be ruined, for drought was the great enemy of the peasant smallholder. But without the intercession of the temple, they would be at risk. This dilemma left the peasants of Galilee permanently indebted and, therefore, permanently unclean and permanently vulnerable to farming their ancestral plots without benefit of temple protection.[22]

As the last comment suggests, debt was related to purity. If one were indebted to the temple and noncompliant with the Torah, then one was unclean. One's debt could not be discharged. It would not even be possible to seek a sin offering to restore one's purity, because one could not discharge his obligation to the temple. The sin offering provides an example for understanding how the sacrificial system worked. Whenever Judeans contracted uncleanness or impurity, physical or moral, they suffered an impairment. To be unclean was to suffer "an impairment of [one's] essential 'self,'" as T. H. Gaster puts it,[23] a condition that required the violator to offer a sin offering. The purpose of the sacrifice was twofold, to remove the contagion and to restore the cleanness of the supplicant. When offered, the sacrifice served as expiation for the loss of purity and resulted in forgiveness.[24] However, if a supplicant were permanently in "violation of cultic laws" or purity laws through an inability to pay the tithe, then he could not offer a sin offering and receive forgiveness. The temple system would be effectively closed and its benefits withdrawn.

When this occurred, the people so excluded could begin to question the appropriateness of the redemptive media, the interpretation of how debt is discharged, and the fitness of those who administer the redemptive media, as well as pursuing "strategies to unblock access to power."[25] Some of these strategies are found in the prophetic critique of the royal and priestly ideologies as well as the Deuteronomic perspective on the failed history of the monarchy. How actively these materials had become part of the little tradition in Jesus' day is an important issue.

With this sketch in place, it is time to turn to specific texts to explore Jesus' relationship to the temple.

JESUS AND THE TEMPLE

When we study conflict stories in the Gospels, two things are clear.[26] First, they are not verbatim reports. Public debate in the form of honor-shame ripostes took time. Second, it is possible that the conflict stories capture both the issues being contested and the dynamics of the public conflicts between Jesus and his adversaries, even though they do not record complete interactions on any given occasion. The question to ask is whether we can legitimately infer the larger issues from the highly shaped and refined pericopes of the Synoptic traditions. These studies intend to explore that possibility. In this sense, they are not far from the view of the materials proposed by Norman Perrin. They represent, he argued, "typical scenes" from Jesus' public work. One can say, "here are the elements that must have been a feature of that ministry," even though the evangelists clearly "used the tradition to serve their own purposes."[27]

The use of longer pericopes to explore the work of the historical Jesus cuts against the grain of current scholarship. Generally speaking, scholars believe that the shorter sayings and parables are earlier than the longer narrative passages.[28] The reason that longer narrations are suspect is that they are thought to show the hand of the evangelist in their framing and structure. The Gospel writers "invent narrative context," provide interpretive overlays, soften hard sayings, "attribute their own sayings to Jesus," and translate Jesus' words into "Christian" language (37–44). For all these reasons, the stories of the Gospel tradition have been given little weight in reconstructing the public work of Jesus. The assumption that these events and sayings have been recontextualized by the Gospel writers, so that they reveal the problems of the early church but not the historical setting of Jesus, needs to be questioned. In fact, taking one of Funk's criteria, what he calls "the plausibility test," provides a place to begin: "A plausible reading or interpretation for a historical context in Jesus' public life is required for sayings and parables that are to be correctly attributed to Jesus" (49). The same criterion can be applied to the narratives of the Gospels. If it can be shown that the conflict stories, for example, reflect a plausible "historical context in Jesus' public life," then they must at least be considered as shedding light on Jesus' work. To argue this point does not mean that the stories have not been shaped by subsequent hands and given literary form. It means that such reworking is not necessarily incompatible with preserving historical echoes of the conflicts and issues that surrounded Jesus. It is time to test this proposal.

Healing as a Challenge to the Temple (Mark 2:1–12)

The first text is the healing of the paralytic and accompanying debate in Mark 2:1–12. Form critics have long held that the pericope is composite, joining together an apophthegm, or pronouncement story, verses 5b–10a, with an earlier story of a healing miracle, verses 1–5a, 11–12. But Bultmann also knew that the pronouncement story in verses 5b–10 had not circulated as an independent unit because the debate contained

in it was inextricably related to the healing story.[29] It was more likely
that the debate was composed with the miracle story in mind as a setting
for the larger controversy. But whatever its history, "the insertion [of an
apophthegm] into an alien narrative is quite plain."[30] Agreeing with
Bultmann, Arland Hultgren thinks that the argument was composed to
augment the miracle.[31] Form-critically, "the dispute was prior," but,
from a literary-critical point of view, "the miracle was prior." In this assessment, most voices have agreed, including the likes of Vincent Taylor,
Jeremias, and Meier, although interpreters have differed in judging
whether the miracle traces to Jesus.[32] Taylor and Meier think it does,[33]
but Bultmann did not.[34] William Manson offered a variant version of the
original miracle, including verses 1–4, 5, 12.[35] In this way, he restored
the reference to forgiveness of sins found in verse 5 to the healing of the
paralytic. Bultmann assumed that the reference was secondary and reflected the concerns of the Hellenistic church in its debate with the synagogue. Moreover, Bultmann rigorously separated the miracle from the
controversy over the forgiveness of sins. Since "there is no other reference in the tradition (apart from Lk 7:47) to Jesus pronouncing forgiveness of sins," the references must reflect the later hand of the church,
attributing to Jesus what it had made part of its regular practice by the
end of the first century.[36] Jeremias, however, noted that Jesus spoke of
forgiveness in a number of guises. To be comprehensive, one had to
count more passages than the two in which the verb *aphiēmi* appears. In
fact, Jesus' whole message was, Jeremias argued, "one single summons
to accept the offer of salvation, one single appeal to trust in his word and
in God's grace; that is, it is a call to faith."[37]

Nevertheless, interpreters have been aware of the rough transitions in
the passage. The awkward insertion ("he said to the paralytic") in verse
10 and the awkward inclusion of "all" in verse 12b are two. The "all"
could not include the scribes, yet it seems to do so. In addition, the abrupt
introduction of the forgiveness of sins in verse 5, just when the hearers are
expecting to hear a word of healing, adds another awkward shift to the
story and raises questions about how the healing is related to the matter
of forgiveness. They seem to be separate issues, not two versions of the
same thing. As a result of the cumulative effect of all of these indicators,
interpreters concluded that the passage was composite in nature and revealed rough editing. Finally, the passage is complicated by the use of the
phrase "Son of Man," a problematic phrase when applied to the earthly
activity of Jesus. Bultmann was certain that the phrase here was simply a
circumlocution for "I," a self-referent used by Jesus, not a title.[38]

Theissen categorizes this episode as a "rule miracle," because its emphasis falls not upon the miracle but the rule the story is promulgating.
This explains why "the expositional argument dominates the whole

miracle story."[39] Rules were no small matter in the ancient world, since the ancients believed that breaking the rules established by God or the gods could have deleterious, even disastrous, consequences. "Every mistake, every failure involved sacred power, produced ominous consequences. Uncertainty in the area of rules took the form of numinous power." For this reason, rule miracles "seek to reinforce sacred prescriptions."[40] Reading the miracle from this point of view unites the miracle and the rule discussion in a more organic way. Therefore, Theissen reads some of the awkward changes differently. The sudden shift to forgiveness of sins in verse 5b, for example, may not be as unprepared for as it first seems because it is couched in "the normal form of an assurance" which is in itself "an anticipated healing" and could easily be part of the original miracle story. If that is true, then the argument about the forgiveness of sins is an integral part of the miracle story and verses 6–10 could also be seen as part of the original, since they develop the theme already introduced in verse 5b. The third abrupt change, the change of persons addressed between verses 10 and 11, "he said to the paralytic," is possibly a commentary in which the narrator emerges from the story and addresses the reader directly, as he does in Mark 13:14 ("let the reader understand") or Mark 7:3–4. If this perspective on the text is accepted, then Mark 2:1–12 can be read as a single unit and not as a composite text at all.

Whatever the status of the text, composite or unitary, the interpreter still has to determine whether it conveys information about the historical Jesus or merely reflects the concerns of the early church. Those who argue that the text conveys information about the early church assume that the argument about forgiveness is a mid- to late-first-century argument between the church and the synagogue, and that there is no reasonable context for it in Jesus' ministry. At first glance, the controversy may seem more at home in the early church than in the time of Jesus. Isn't forgiveness of sins a theological debate that presupposes the development of church doctrine? Doesn't the composite nature of the text really argue against its tracing back to an incident in Jesus' ministry?

Perhaps, but several commentators have noted the vivid details of the story. Meier speaks for many when he speculates that the digging through the roof suggests that "some event in the public ministry stuck in the corporate memory precisely because of its strange circumstances,"[41] and Theissen has already proposed a way of reading the text as a unitary composition. But can one find a conflict that reflects the setting in the life of Jesus (*Sitz im Leben Jesu*) and not just a setting in the life of the early church (*Sitz im Leben*)? To that matter we now turn.

At the center of the narrative is an anomaly. Jesus has just said, "my son, your sins are forgiven," or as Fernando Belo translates, "child, your debt is discharged."[42] As many commentators have noted, Jesus addresses the man using the divine passive, that is, he speaks about the activity of God by using a familiar circumlocution, a verb in the passive voice. This is what any pious Jew would do. Jesus does not say, "I forgive your sins"; rather, he announces that God has forgiven the man's sin and, if Taylor is right in his observation about the verb (punctiliar aoristic present), Jesus is saying that the man's sins "are this moment forgiven."[43] No sooner said than done! Whether this detail of the Markan text reflects Jesus' intent is impossible to discern, but it does indicate the intensity and immediacy of the conflict. Yet the scribes accuse Jesus of blasphemy: "Who can forgive sins but God alone (or the one God)?" (2:7). But that is just what Jesus has said. He has announced God as the One who forgives the man's sins and restores his identity as a child of God. Why then does Jesus' theologically correct remark draw the fire of the scribes?

The scribes are retainers, probably in some way representing the interests of the temple in Jerusalem. Whether they are village scribes, attached to their more illustrious counterparts in the temple and acting as their clients, or whether they are representatives from Jerusalem (see Mark 3:22) is not possible to determine. They do appear in this account as guardians of the great tradition and protectors of the temple's interests. From their point of view, the temple is the only place where sins can be forgiven and purity restored. This is the exclusive right of priests using the sacrificial system. To protect that monopoly is their likely intent in this clash. In their eyes, Jesus, who is not from a priestly family, has no right to place himself in the position of a priest announcing God's forgiveness. He is an interloper.

The matter can also be framed in terms of patron-client relations.[44] The social hierarchies of the ancient world were organized into an interlocking, often competing and conflictual, series of patron-client relationships. Patrons were wealthy aristocrats who provided economic benefits to the poor in return for the services they could render. The clients who received patronage (which was called *charis* in Greek) were expected to be at the beck and call of their patrons, performing services both menial and essential. But, in addition to the clientage of the poor, patron-client networks included everyone. The ruling class comprised a series of patron-client alliances (called patron-protégé relations in the ruling class) in which the wealthiest and strongest offered patronage to less wealthy aristocrats. The arrangement cascaded down the social scale. Retainers could mimic the actions of their social superiors by forming similar alliances.[45] Patronage was an outcome of what Kautsky calls a situation of "superstratification," in which a few who have almost everything dominate the many who have almost nothing. The poor seek patronage to ensure their survival, and the rich seek clients to enhance their social prestige and power.

For the purposes of this discussion, it is germane to note that the relations with the gods were also framed in terms of patrons and clients.[46] The gods were patrons, and their devotees were their clients. To put the matter in terms of the temple, Yahweh the Lord was the patron of the Judean people, and the people were his clients. But patronage does not come directly; it flows through an intermediary or intermediaries called brokers. In Jerusalem, the priests claimed to be the sole brokers of Yahweh's patronage. If one sought the benefits of Yahweh's patronage—fertile land, good crops, and timely rains—then one had to gain access to them by using the temple system brokered by the chief priests and ordinary priests. Without the access provided by the broker, people had no access to the *charis* of the patron God. When Jesus declares God's forgiveness of the paralytic's sins (debts), he steps into the role of a reliable broker of God's forgiveness, and by simply assuming this role, challenges the brokerage house in Jerusalem called the temple.

Isenberg asked a key question about the role of the temple and its priests in excluding people from the system of redemptive media:

> But what happens when the structure of society is such that a part of society feels itself so systematically excluded from participation in the redemptive media that it cannot "make it" within the present situation? At this point we may expect to find strategies to unblock access to power.[47]

But these strategies reflect a sense that something is wrong, that people are somehow (it is not always clear to people how or why) "prevented from attaining the goals dictated by society," and they may conclude that the system is flawed in some fundamental way: "the political structure is corrupt, the goals are wrong, the redemptive media are false or imperfectly managed or some combination of these factors."[48] The response of the authorities is invariably to adopt some form of "blaming the victim."[49] In fact, Crossan has seen quite clearly how the miracle addresses these dynamics.

> There is, first and above all, a terrible irony in that conjunction of sickness and sin, especially in first-century Palestine. Excessive taxation could leave poor people physically malnourished or hysterically disabled. But since the religiopolitical ascendency could not blame excessive taxation, it blamed sick people themselves by claiming that their sins had led to their illnesses. And the cure for sinful sickness was, ultimately, in the Temple. And that meant more fees, in a perfect circle of victimization.[50]

When he declares God's forgiveness, Jesus proposes a strategy of bypassing the temple and establishing another means of access to the forgiving Patron through his own brokering. This incenses the scribes.

The scribes have good reason, therefore, to find Jesus' theologically correct statement offensive, even blasphemous. They perceive the threat posed by his statement and seek to counter it. In order to understand the nature of the challenges in this conflict, it will be useful to view it through the lens of an honor-shame riposte. In Jesus' world, honor and shame were the most important social values, and honor could be acquired through public conflict and debate. First-century Palestine was an agonistic society in which public confrontations led to hostile encounters intended to increase the honor of some contestants at the expense of others. In a world of limited good and limited goods, every such confrontation was a zero sum game in which some won and others lost.

This controversy begins with scribes in Capernaum representing the honorable interests of the temple, its sacrifices and priesthood. In the same village is a man marked for shame. Lame or paralyzed, he cannot rise from his mat; he is a living embodiment of the judgment of God, suffering either for his own sins or those he inherited from his parents. He is permanently excluded from the redemptive media that are the temple and Torah, since he is unable to make pilgrimage to it, and even if he could, could not enter its precinct or offer sacrifices.

When the gossip network[51] gets the word out that Jesus is back in town in his familiar house, some friends show their loyalty to Jesus and trust in him (called faith, *pistis*) by bringing the man to Jesus, making a hole through the thatched roof of the humble house and lowering the man on ropes. This act of faith is also a positive honor challenge; the friends have announced to all gathered around the house their confidence in Jesus as a traditional healer, and Jesus must respond to their faith.

Anthropologists distinguish between illness and disease. Disease is a physical condition, but illness is a social condition in which "social networks have been disrupted and meaning lost."[52] Acting in the role of a traditional healer, Jesus first addresses the question of illness. This is why he first says to the man, "my son, your debt is discharged" (2:5). Not only does it not interrupt the flow of the story, it conveys what an ancient Mediterranean villager would expect to hear. Where modern eyes discern an abrupt discontinuity, the ancient eye sees continuity. But Jesus has made no innocent remark; he has hurled an honor challenge at the temple and its system of sacrifices. What the temple has failed to do, Jesus declares done. He has stepped into the role of broker of the forgiving Patron, Yahweh, the one Jesus calls "abba."

The scribes have heard the challenge, but they attempt to shame Jesus by speaking only among themselves. Mark no doubt intends to portray Jesus as reading the hearts of his opponents and discerning their inmost thoughts. Indeed, Taylor argues that Jesus demonstrates here "a spiritual discernment man [sic] shares with God which Jesus possesses to a preeminent degree."[53] In addition, Mark's phrase, "questioning in their hearts," reveals how profoundly opposed they are to Jesus' claim. But Matthew reads Mark a bit differently. When Matthew replaces Mark's phrase, "reasoned in their hearts," with "said among themselves," he changes the meaning of Mark's story (9:3; cf. Mark 2:6). In this case, the scribes would be talking to each other loudly enough to be heard by those gathered in the house, but without acknowledging Jesus' presence. It is an effort to shame Jesus that reflects the scribes' conviction that Jesus is too far below them socially to engage in a debate. Shaming by snubbing is their strategy.

They also use negative labeling to discredit and dismiss Jesus. He is a "blasphemer," a crime punishable by death. Bruce Malina and Richard Rohrbaugh think that Jesus' sensitive ears reflect the honorable man's "finely tuned sense of shame." He has "a keen awareness" of his honor standing and is sensitive to any challenge to it.[54] To this point in the controversy, the dynamics of the honor-shame riposte are clearly recognizable. Jesus hurls a challenge at the temple. The scribes do not respond to the accusation implicit in Jesus' claim to broker God's forgiveness. Instead, they escalate the challenge through name calling and snubbing. If the scribes began by questioning in their hearts, they finished by "discussing among themselves" the effrontery of Jesus, yet without including him in their conversation. Their purpose is to shame Jesus in order to discredit his challenge to the temple and preserve its honorable status.

How will Jesus respond to the snub? One thing is clear; he cannot defend himself against the charge of blasphemy. The honorable man never defends himself against a charge or answers directly a question posed by an enemy. Jesus must escalate the conflict further, which is exactly what he does. He ignores the label that the scribes tried to pin on him and returns to the focus of his challenge, his emergence as a broker of forgiveness. First, he confronts the scribes with a forced choice: "Which is easier to say to the paralytic, 'Your sins are forgiven' (or 'your debt is discharged') or 'Rise, pick up your mat and walk'" (v. 9). The scribes would find neither option particularly palatable, since both bypass the temple. They are silent, a continuation of their strategy of shaming by ignoring. It is quite possible that the conflict simply moved to the climax depicted in verses 11–12. Jesus would have said, "I say to you, rise, pick up your mat and walk." The phrase "I say to you" has long been recognized as a form-critical attachment formula, but it might function here as an intensifier of the conflict. It calls attention to Jesus as he acts out the role of broker. When they saw what Jesus had done, the crowd "glorified God," not Jesus. They understood that he was simply mediating God's healing and forgiving *charis*. If this story were a creation of the early church, it would seem likely that the ending would be more christological: "and they glorified Jesus."

Of course, the healing is utterly necessary if the conflict is to have any meaning. Without the healing, the conflict degenerates into a war of words, "I say, you say," and the man remains paralyzed on his mat. More to the point, the healing indicates that God's power is at work, confirming the identity and role of Jesus as a legitimate broker, and it completes the work of Jesus the traditional healer who, having addressed the more important question of illness, can now heal the disease. Joachim Gnilka has rightly indicated that a term like *paralutikos* might include a variety of maladies, including "every kind of serious disorder in motor functions," and Jeremias refers to the man's "lameness."[55] It is tempting to focus on the healing of disease and miss the significance of the healing of illness. Wright has picked up these resonances in his discussion of the healings.

> The effect of these cures, therefore, was not merely to bring physical healing; . . . but to reconstitute those healed as members of the people of Israel's God. . . . The vindication for which Israel looked to her god was being brought forward into the present, close up, in the case of these individuals.[56]

This was especially poignant because those healed had been banned from honorable status in the people of God by virtue of their deformity or disease. All of this means that the healing confirmed the forgiveness of sins by validating the words of Jesus, the truthful and faithful broker or mediator. But these events did not occur in a vacuum; they were challenges to the temple, subversive of its claims and corrosive of its power.

The discussion of the healing has, to this point, omitted verse 10, "But that you may know that the Son of Man has power on earth to forgive sins." The question of the Son of Man is too unmanageable and complicated to deal with in this context, but a comment or two may clarify its possible use in this setting. This reading will explore just two possibilities. First, the phrase is simply a circumlocution for "I," but not the christological "I."[57] Here, in emphasizing his role as broker, Jesus observes that he is a common human being (laity), not born into the priestly caste, whom God has chosen to use as a broker of forgiveness. In this case, verse 10 explains the basis for Jesus' initial announcement of forgiveness in verse 5 and provides the foundation for his subsequent declaration, "I say to you," in verse 11. The phrase "the human one" or "the Son of Man" refers to his role as broker and emphasizes what he has in common with the crowd. They are laity, not priestly figures. Insofar as God has chosen "a son of man" to declare forgiveness and mediate healing power, God has rejected the temple priesthood and opened an alternate way. The phrase also carries a prophetic resonance, since Ezekiel was addressed as "son of man." Second, the phrase *ho huios tou anthrōpou* can also mean "one like me," in which case Jesus would be claiming the role of broker not for himself alone but for his followers as well.[58] Jesus is forming a new brokerage house. Viewed in this light, the phrase claims a vocation for at least some of Jesus' followers. If this were arguable, then the scribes could only conclude that the contagion was spreading. Little wonder the crowd declares, "we never saw anything like this" (v. 12).

If this interpretation is arguable, then the conflict in Mark 2:1–12 can be placed in the context of the work of the historical Jesus. It depicts the conflict generated by Jesus' opposition to the temple and his claim to broker God's forgiveness outside of the official channels supplied by the priestly sacrificial system. In this context, the issue of forgiveness relates to the debt incurred by peasants who were unable to support the temple with the two tithes demanded by temple authorities. Their debt perpetually unforgiven, the peasants of Galilee received the "good news" proclaimed by Jesus as "tidings of great joy." Jesus had opened a new channel of God's forgiveness that could be appropriated without participating in the sacrificial system of the temple, and this forgiveness or cancellation of debt did not require new exactions of tribute.

Of course, behind Jesus' work of forgiveness is a different image of God from the one depicted by the temple. God was not a stickler for tithes who punished those unable to pay them and survive. Jesus' God addressed the paralytic as "my son" and offered him healing while he still remained on his mat. This was not a God who maintained debt records for the purpose of foreclosing on the poor but a God who canceled debt and restored life. The social conflict was also theological.

The Incident in the Temple (Mark 11:15–19)

Biblical scholars have proposed a number of interpretations of Jesus' action in the temple. It may be helpful to summarize some of the major proposals before exploring more recent disussion. (1) The most common explanation is that Jesus was offended by the presence of commercial activities in the outer courtyard of the temple because they interfered with the inward and spiritual nature of worship. Joseph Fitzmyer, for example, interprets the event as a prophetic act that purged the temple of "those who by their mercantile traffic were profaning its character as a house of prayer."[59] The difficulty with this reading, as Sanders has noted, is that it reflects a nineteenth-century view of what constitutes true religion.[60] The contrast between true religion, which is inwardly spiritual and ethical, and false religion, which focuses on external trappings, is a modern dichotomy unknown in the ancient world. The offering of sacrifices was at the heart of what the temple was supposed to be about, and that included all of the support services required to maintain the sacrificial system. In short, the so-called commercial enterprises were services offered to pilgrims to facilitate their participation in the temple system. Sanders says it clearly, "The business arrangements around the temple were necessary if the commandments were to be obeyed."[61]

(2) A variant of this interpretation holds that it was the abuse of these necessary arrangements that Jesus attacked. Taylor summarizes this view succinctly: "The action of Jesus is a spirited protest against injustice and the abuse of the temple system. There is no doubt that pilgrims were fleeced by the traders."[62] The problem with this view is that there is a great deal of doubt about the degree of abuse within the system. Rabbinic sources do not complain about the money changers, who performed an essential function for a nominal fee, or the sellers who provided the unblemished sacrificial victims and other ingredients (oil, wine, flour) required for offering a sacrifice.

(3) It is also possible that Jesus' demonstration was really aimed at purifying the temple cultus itself, not just the activities in the outer courtyard, as a way of preparing for the coming reign of God. Richard Hiers has made just such a proposal.[63] In this role, Jesus would have been fulfilling the prophecies of Zechariah 14:20 and Malachi 3:1–3. Jesus "was acting to prepare the Temple for the inauguration of the Messianic Age," perhaps fulfilling the expectation, found at Qumran, that a priestly messiah "would restore the Temple at the end."[64] This reformation or cleansing was a necessary step to prepare for "the blessings of the end time." This makes more sense than supposing that Jesus intended to abolish sacrifice since, as Sanders has shown, the early church in Jerusalem continued to show fast loyalty to the temple and its cultus.[65] The difficulty with this proposal is that it fails to account for the fact that the incident occurred in the outer courtyard and did not, in itself, criticize either the priests or the system of sacrifices.

(4) A variation on this theme suggests either that Jesus was claiming a place for the Gentiles in the temple, as currently configured, or that Jesus was acting out the eschatological promise that the mountain of the Lord would one day attract all peoples for the proper worship of God. This would explain why the action occurred in the outer courtyard, often called by scholars the court of the Gentiles, and why the quotation from Isaiah 56:7 was either spoken by Jesus or came to be associated with the event. So Gundry speculates that Jesus was "protesting the din of commerce that made difficult the praying of gentiles in the outer court."[66] However, it is not clear that the outer court was known as the court of the Gentiles in Jesus' time. Nor is there evidence that Gentiles came to the temple to pray, although they visited the temple to admire its grandeur. The focus on the Gentiles has given rise to a number of variations that show the clear interests of later Christian and churchly theology. So E. Schweizer reads the

event as "the abolition in principle of an institution which was restricted entirely to Jews,"[67] and by implication, making way for the church, which was open to both Jews and Gentiles. The clash at the heart of the incident, according to Schweizer, is the contrast between the exclusiveness of Israel over against the inclusiveness of God, whom anyone can approach in prayer.[68] Often interpretations that follow this path portray the temple as the dying insitution of an old order that was destined to be replaced by the spiritual temple erected by Jesus and his followers.[69] But such ways of construing the incident presuppose the development of the church as well as run the danger of becoming anti-Semitic or anti-Judaic. However, when placed in an eschatological context, the inclusion of the Gentiles may be read as an act of preparation for the coming reign of God and a fulfillment of prophecy (Isa. 2:1–5; Micah 4:1–5).

(5) Up to this point, the readings of the temple incident have been religious in nature. But, at least since Reimarus, interpreters have read Jesus' action as a political happening, an attempt at a hostle takeover of the temple inspired by the ideals of the Zealots. Brandon has argued this position most fully, noting that Jesus' political act was reinterpreted by the Gospel writers, who wanted to present his acts in a more innocuous light.[70] The political reading does highlight the violent and disruptive aspects of the temple action, a point emphasized by David Daube[71] but often submerged in the conviction that Jesus must have been nonviolent. However, the reconstruction of Jesus as a Zealot fails on a number of counts. It was built on what Horsley believes is a misconceived hypothesis, namely, the hypothesis that there had been a continuous nationalist liberation movement known as the Zealots from the death of Herod the Great to the end of the Jewish Revolt.[72] A more careful reading of Josephus has shown that not to be the case. In fact, the Zealots did not coalesce as a political faction until the First Jewish Revolt, sometime during the mid-60s, so it is simply anachronistic to project the situation of the 60s back onto the time of Jesus. Moreover, if Jesus had led a violent movement, he would have inspired some reprisal from either the temple police or Roman soldiers. Josephus makes it quite clear that royal claimants and messianic pretenders, like Simon the slave of Herod (*War* 2.56; *Ant.* 17.271–72) and Athronges (*Ant.* 17.278–85), or sign prophets like Theudas (*Ant.* 20.97–98) and the anonymous Samaritan (*Ant.* 18.85–87), were treated brutally and their movements crushed, even when they posed no immediate threat to Roman rule and temple hegemony. Yet, no such actions were taken against Jesus or his followers.

The political reading has produced two distinctive renderings of the Markan text. Situating the incident in Jesus' ministry, Cecil Roth has proposed that Jesus addressed the rebuke in verse 17b to his own followers because they had misconstrued his action. Jesus intended to preserve the sanctity of the temple "by the exclusion from it of mercantile operations of any sort," but his followers intended to purify the temple of all Gentiles and turn it into a "focus of nationalism," or "a den of nationalist rebels."[73] The misunderstanding traced to the two variant readings of one word in Zechariah 14:21, which could mean either "traffickers" or "Canaanites." Jesus saw himself fulfilling Zechariah 14:21, understood as banishing all traffickers from the temple, a move that set him at loggerheads with his followers who thought he was cleansing the temple of Gentiles. A second distinctive reading was proposed by George Buchanan, who believes that verse 17b is a gloss on the Zealot takeover of the temple during the First Revolt.[74] To say that God's house had become a *spēlaion lēstōn* (literally, a cave of social bandits) meant that it had become a "Zealot stronghold," and this could only be in the late 60s. On this political reading, the text does not relate to the time of Jesus at all but comments on the events occurring as Mark composes his narrative.

Mark 11:15–19 poses a number of problems. Bultmann proposed that verses 15a, 18–19 were editorial additions to the unitary apophthegm (pronouncement story) in verses 15b–17. But verse 17 poses another problem, because it does not seem to be spoken "to the retailers but much rather to the Jews at large."[75] It does not fit comfortably in its setting. It is equally clear, Bultmann argued, that the action (vv. 15b–16) and the saying were originally separate, because the emphasis in a pronouncement story always falls on the saying, yet the saying in verse 17 does not serve as the climax to the story but explains the previous action on which the emphasis falls. Since verse 17 was not original, it may have replaced an older saying now preserved in John 2:16, "destroy this temple, and in three days I will raise it up." What is clear to Bultmann is that the addition of the saying to the action had the effect of introducing a prophecy and creating an "ideal scene."[76]

Many commentators have assumed that the saying in verse 17 was not original to the event. Crossan takes a clue from the saying in the Gospel of Thomas 71, "Jesus said: I shall destroy this house, and no one will be able to build it again," and concludes that Jesus said something like, "I will destroy this house beyond repair."[77] This proposal gains some support from the fact that Jesus is twice accused of threatening to destroy the temple and rebuild it in three days (Mark 14:58; 15:29). In addition, Mark records the comment of Jesus in 13:2, that "not one stone will be left here upon another; all will be thrown down." Putting these pieces together, J. Duncan Derrett has concluded that Jesus treated the temple, the house of God, as a house contaminated with leprosy.[78] His actions on the Temple Mount repeated the three-step procedure, spelled out in Leviticus 14:34–53, for examining and condemning a leprous house. First, if a house was suspected of leprosy, the owner had to remove all the vessels that had been contaminated and prevent any "unstoppered" vessel from being introduced into the house, thereby protecting its contents from contamination. This is how Derrett reads the troubling and obscure verse 16, "he would not allow anyone to carry any vessel through the temple." Jesus either stopped the traffic of polluted vessels or prevented unstoppered vessels from being introduced to the temple. Second, a house with leprosy would also have its furniture removed, and if it were judged to be contaminated, it had to be destroyed, an act that Jesus symbolically reproduced by overturning tables and the chairs of the sellers. The verb *katestrepsen* can mean either to overturn or upset something or to ruin and destroy it. Just as the furniture of a leprous house was smashed and carted away, so Jesus destroyed the furniture of the house of God. Finally, if the leprosy were embedded in the walls of the house, the priest who inspected it had to have it dismantled stone by stone and then dispose of the leprous stones in a site devoted to unclean things (Lev. 14:34–53). This explains Jesus' saying that "not one stone is left upon another" (Mark 13:2). What underlies Jesus' attack is the belief that "crimes committed by occupants defile their space," a particular case of which is found in leprosy, which was, in Jesus' time, often considered to be "a penalty for concealed misconduct with assets."[79] If there is any merit to Derrett's ingeniously argued case, then the incident in the temple was indeed a prophetic protest and symbolic act expressing judgment on a temple too corrupted to warrant redemption or reformation.

The nature of the charge against the temple does need to be understood more fully, and to do so requires an understanding of the economic role played by the temple in Jerusalem and more generally by temples in the ancient world. Neill Hamilton raised the issue in an article published more than thirty years ago.[80] The temple cleansing cannot be divorced from the role of the temple as a bank. Owing to the annual half-shekel tax collected from every observant Jewish male, the temple rapidly accumulated large amounts of coins and currency and, as the local economies of small provinces like Judea and Galilee became monetized through Hellenistic and then Roman colonial expansion, the role of money became more important. The great wealth of the temple in Jerusalem can be inferred from the following events. In 4 B.C.E., Sabinus, the interim prefect of Judea who guarded Rome's interests until Herod's will could be adjudicated by Caesar, looted the temple treasury after suppressing a revolt. In addition to the looting done by the soldiers, Sabinus took four hundred talents for himself (*War,* 2.50; *Ant.* 17.50). About thirty years later, Pilate extracted money from the temple treasury to build an aqueduct, although Jerusalemites took offence more from the fact that he took the money from the portion of the treasury called *korbanas* than from the amount confiscated (*War* 2.175–77; *Ant.* 18.60–

62). Florus, the final procurator before the outbreak of the revolt, requisitioned seventeen talents from the temple treasury for the "imperial service," some of which lined his own pockets. He may have been partly motivated to expropriate funds in order to bring the tardy payment of tribute up to date (*War* 2.293). What is evident in each of these instances is the large amount of money stored in the temple. When the temple became the primary political institution, after the deposing of Archaelaus, its treasury served as the "state exchequer" and bank for the aristocracy of Jerusalem. It is quite possible that, under the pressure of this increasingly wealthy elite, the temple began to make loans on their behalf or to hold their capital so that they could proffer such loans to the poor. Martin Goodman has speculated that the practice of making loans to rural peasants, urban craftsmen, and plebs led to a predictable result. The poor "fell heavily into debt as much because the rich landowners needed to invest surplus income profitably as because the poor needed loans to survive."[81] This division between the haves and the have-nots was the result of the wealth that flowed into Jerusalem. While Goodman, at first, portrayed this process in innocent terms, he did add a more sinister note to his later description of the increasing debt load in Judea and Galilee. The introduction of the *prosbul* testified to the breakdown in social ties between debtor and creditor, the reason for which may be found in the predatory behavior of the rich, for "the only logical reason to lend was thus the hope of winning the peasant's land by foreclosing on it when the debt was not paid off as agreed."[82] The temple was, therefore, at the very heart of the system of economic exploitation made possible by monetizing the economy and the concentration of wealth made possible by investing the temple and its leaders with the powers and rewards of a collaborating aristocracy. It was no accident that one of the first acts of the First Jewish Revolt in 66 C.E. was the burning of the debt records in the archives in Jerusalem (*War* 2.426–27).

At the very apex of this system of exploitation stood the families of the high priests and the lay aristocrats who supported them (perhaps Sadducees were included in this group). The high priests controlled the temple and its functions, in the process converting the temple into a tribute-collecting machine, much like any ruling class trying to perpetuate its aristocratic empire. That the temple state was a client dependent on Rome for its right to rule does not alter the economic behavior of these urban elites. Recent excavations in Jerusalem near the Temple Mount have revealed the great luxury in which the rich lived.[83] The temple was not only a religious and political institution; it was a major economic force, controlling massive amounts of money while continuing to accumulate more. All of the functionaries mentioned in the incident in the temple were part of this system and served it. Its bureaucrats oversaw the temple's many functions, including its staggering payroll, and they oversaw the temple contracts for goods and services that defined the economy of Judea.

When Jesus took action against the temple, therefore, he touched a raw nerve. As Meier has put it, "if one accepts the historicity of the entry and cleansing, we have the match set to the barrel of gasoline."[84] It is an understanding of the economic role of the temple that provides the framework for understanding how the action and the saying fit together. Since Bultmann, many scholars have found the saying in the pericope unrelated to the action and have, as a result, concluded that the saying was not originally tied to the event itself but was attached to it for later theological purposes, such as justifying the inclusion of Gentiles in the church. Usually, interpreters reach this conclusion by following a common method. First, they posit some statement about the meaning of the incident in the temple based on a religious reading of Jesus' actions and then observe that the saying does not fit the preconceived formulation. Therefore, they conclude, it must be a secondary addition.

In its current form, the quotation in verse 17 is a composite of Isaiah 56:7 and Jeremiah 7:11. It is obviously an edited compilation of two key texts. The question to be answered is whether the prophetic critique contained in these texts fits Jesus' prophetic action in the temple. Jeremiah preached "the temple sermon" shortly after the death of Josiah and before the ascension of his son Jehoiakim to the throne. Jehoiakim, a vassel king propped up by Pharaoh Neco II, was neither careful to maintain the reforms of his father nor solicitous of his own people. He constructed a new palace for himself using conscripted labor (Jer. 22:13–17) and did nothing to prevent the oppression and exploitation of the people of Judah.[85] "The word that came to Jeremiah from the Lord," which he was to stand in the temple gate to preach, addressed these conditions:

> if you truly amend your ways and your doings, if you act justly one with another, and if *you* do not oppress the alien, the orphan and the widow, or shed innocent blood in this place . . . then I will dwell with you. (7:5–7, italics added)

Critics who would deny the Jeremiah quote to Jesus remark that Jesus addressed the temple functionaries but Jeremiah the worshipers who came to the temple. But Jeremiah's denunciation was not spoken to everybody in Judah; it was addressed to the "you" who were oppressing the alien, the orphan, and the widow, a trilogy of terms identifying the vulnerable poor living at the mercy of a predatory elite, who assumed they could do injustice, violate the covenant, and then come to the temple and offer sacrifices to insure the perpetuation of their reign. This becomes especially clear in Jeremiah 7:9: "Will you steal, murder, commit adultery, swear falsely, make offerings to Baal, and go after other gods that you have not known, and then stand before me in this house?" John Bright notes quite rightly that "the crimes listed are violations of the eighth, sixth, seventh, ninth, first, and second commandments," that is, they "constitute an almost total breach of the covenant stipulations."[86] The focus in the temple sermon is not on the increasingly unsettled international situation but on internal oppression and violence. As an advocate for the dispossessed, the prophet addresses King Jehoiakim and his ruling class. Just as the collaborationist elites of the Judea of Jesus' day were involved in reducing the people of the land to servitude and destitution, so the client king Jehoiakim and his cronies were exploiting the common people of their day. In both situations, the temple played a key role in legitimating oppression (Jeremiah) or in actively extracting all but a subsistence from the poor (Jesus). The difference in the roles played by the temple reflects the fact that the institution of kingship still existed in Jeremiah's day but had been replaced by a temple state in Jesus' time. As Jeremiah's sermon foretells destruction for the temple by recalling the fate of Shiloh (7:12–15), so Jesus symbolically acts out the destruction of the Second Temple.

The parallels between the situation of Jeremiah and the setting of Jesus' action, while not identical, show a strong enough resemblance to permit the possibility that Jesus could have used some citation from Jeremiah's temple sermon. Given the ancients' habit of quoting a portion of scripture to invoke a larger whole, it is possible that Jesus deliberately evoked the incident from Jeremiah to provoke his hearers.

But why select the portion of the sermon that refers to "this house which is called by my name" as "a robber's hide out," as Bright translates it (52)? The reference to the cave of robbers harkens back to the previous verse, in which the ruling class is condemned for violating the commandments and then seeking refuge in the temple, saying "we are safe." The people addressed commit all sorts of crimes, according to Bright, "and then flee to the temple for safety . . . just as bandits lie low until pursuit dies down, and then go out to commit fresh depradations" (56). It is worth noting that the image of the robber suggests their role in taking what belongs to others, often by force. The very wealth they bring to support the temple and to buy sacrifices has been taken from the poor. If Jesus cited Jeremiah, he may well have intended to invoke the parallel between then and now.

In its current form, however, the saying of Jesus hints at another meaning. "You have made it a cave of social bandits." The phrase *spelaion lestōn* is striking, especially when one considers the role of social bandits. Social bandits were guerrilla bands of peasants who had taken to the hills or the wilderness. They may have been peasants who were conscripted for military purposes and then released when their services were no longer needed. Since they had no villages and families to return to, they were forced to work as day laborers, beg, or take to the caves. Social banditry is an indicator of economic and political stress. Usually, social bandits arise when peasants are losing ground economically and being squeezed into increasing forms of dependency. They represent a "pre-political" form of protest, oriented to the past rather than the future; they want the restoration of things as they were before changes began to deprive peasants of their subsistence safety net. Throughout his *Jewish War* and *Jewish Antiquities,* Josephus treats social bandits as deviant and violent outlaws whose rash actions eventually contributed to the ill-fated revolt against Rome. They are accused of plundering, pillage, and other forms of outrage against peasant and ruler alike.[87]

If the saying uttered in the temple carried any resonance of social banditry, then Jesus was reversing the judgment about who was deviant and who prominent. The prominent members of the ruling class viewed the social bandits as deviant outlaws and deplored their acts, but Jesus wryly suggests that the real social bandits are not to be found hiding in the caves of the Judean wilderness or Arbela. No, the chief priests, the very paradigms of rectitude, are the social bandits creating havoc in the land. They are the true deviants! While this reading cannot be attributed to Jesus with certainty, it does highlight one possible dimension of Jesus' polemic against the temple priesthood.

The situation of Isaiah 56, the beginning of the oracles of the prophet known as Third Isaiah, presents a different set of problems. Isaiah 56 was composed in Jerusalem in the aftermath of the return of the exiles, when two groups with widely divergent agendas were locked in conflict. Frederick Gaiser reconstructs the situation as follows:

> On the one hand, the community of outcasts responsible for Third Isaiah is broad and universalistic in outlook, "welcoming all faithful people to the temple, which will become a 'house of prayer for all peoples' (56:7). On the other hand, the priestly establishment contends that the Babylonian captivity resulted from contamination by foreign ways and influences.[88]

Led by Ezra (9:1–2; 10:11) and Nehemiah (9:1–2; 10:28–31; 13:1–3), the establishment's "restoration program will be narrow and isolationist." Against this isolationism, Isaiah (56:1–8) speaks a prophetic word with a sharp edge. According to the Torah, any male with damaged testicles or penis, that is, a eunuch, was blemished and, therefore, banned from "the assembly of the Lord" (Lev. 21:16–23; Deut. 23:1). But Isaiah's oracle expressly includes eunuchs in its vision of Yahweh gathering the outcasts of Israel together with the foreigners "who join themselves to the Lord" by accepting the demands of the covenant. In spite of the inclusive vision of "Isaiah" and the exiles, however, the context of the promise to the eunuchs posed a significant theological dilemma since the Torah is clear about those who bear such a blemish. How could the community resolve the conundrum? Gaiser captures the dramatic irony of the moment:

> The situation drips with poignant irony. God (through God's law) becomes the barrier to God's deliverance (in the promise). Such a radical situation demands a radical response . . . God's word will prevail *even if that entails abrogating a previous divine word.*[89]

So God overturns a provision of the law in order to fulfill the promise. As Myers has seen clearly, Isaiah 56:7 stands as the "climax to an oracle that is perhaps the fullest Old Testament vision of an inclusive Israel."[90] It also fits the shape and themes of Jesus' ministry to the outcasts and the marginal, those who because of their uncleanness and cultic impurity were either banned from the community of Israel or pushed to its very edge. By citing prophet against cult in his oracle of judgment against the temple, Jesus has also continued the tradition of the God who abrogates and creates anew. In short, the oracle of Isaiah 56:1–8 is eminently applicable to Jesus' action in the temple and congruent with it.

Why then does Jesus restrict his activities to the outer court and low-level functionaries? Why does he not confront the priests themselves? One answer to these questions is practical. Jesus was unclean and could not have passed through the gates leading into the temple precincts themselves, and, since he exhibited no inclination to ritually purify himself for this purpose, he was restricted to the outer court. Another answer is more substantive. In attacking money changers and sellers of doves, Jesus was attacking "not things peripheral to the system but integral parts of it."[91] The money changers were, in Myers's apt phrase, the "streetlevel representatives of banking interests of considerable power."[92] But more importantly, they were essential operatives in the collection of the temple tribute. According to the Mishnah's tractate *Sheqalim* 1:3, the money changers set up their tables throughout the provinces on the fifteenth Adar, and on the twenty-fifth Adar set them up in the temple. Their purpose was to collect the half-shekel tribute in proper coinage and deliver it to the temple. The money so collected was for the purpose of providing "the public daily whole offerings."[93] By supporting the public daily offerings from the treasury, the priests intended to show that the offerings served "all Israelites, individually and collectively, as atonement for sin" (289). Neusner is convinced that only someone who "rejected the Torah's explicit teaching concerning the daily whole offering could have overturned the tables." Since the disruption of the activity of the money changers struck at the very heart of the sacrificial system itself, it was a "rejection of the most important rite of the Israelite cult" (289–90). Jesus' actions in the outer court reverberated all the way to the altar in the court of the priests. It was, as Neusner has rightly observed, a rejection of the cultus itself. In light of the discussion of the healing of the paralytic, the action in the temple makes sense. If Jesus has assumed the role of a broker of God's forgiveness by reincorporating the outcasts into the people of God, he also believed that the temple was no longer necessary. His symbolic destruction of the temple, therefore, fits with the prophetic orientation of his public work.

Jesus' rejection of the temple may well have derived from his analysis of the economic situation created by it. As the temple amassed wealth, the people of the land were getting poorer and poorer. In a society governed by the notion of limited good, Jesus drew the logical conclusion that the temple was getting rich at the expense of the peasants, villagers, and urban artisans. If everything is limited, from food to honor, then one can gain only at the expense of another. To be rich, then, meant to be able to extract from the poor what belonged to them—whether through extortion, fraud, or oppressive foreclosure was irrelevant. The rich were those who could take from the poor and make it stick. The poor, then, were the vulnerable, those unable to protect their goods or their honor, the victims of the voracious greed of the rich. As the rich pressed their claims in order to fuel their competition for power and privilege, they expropriated more and more from the poor, forcing them into more debased forms of dependency. The poor lost their land, their family, and their honor. They could not maintain even what little they had. Jesus made the temple a symbol of these economic forces by identifying it as the "cave of bandits," the place they stored "their ill gotten gain."[94] All of this meant that "large numbers of persons were simultaneously becoming poor and unable to maintain their honor as 'sons of Israel.' "[95]

This situation also provides a context for understanding Jesus' remark, "for you always have the poor with you, and you can show kindness to them whenever you wish" (Mark 14:7). Why are there always the poor? Because there are always ruling class oppressors fleecing the people of the land. Far from being a saying about the prevalence of the poor, it is a wry saying about the omnipresence of oppression and exploitation. It does not mean that there will always be the poor because there will always be lazy, unemployed workers. The saying is Jesus' midrash on Deuteronomy 15:4–6: "there will, however, be no poor among you, because the Lord is sure to bless you in the land that the Lord your God is giving you as a possession to occupy, if only you will obey the Lord your God by diligently observing this entire commandment that I command you today." The poor continue in the land because the entire commandment has been ignored and distorted to justify the presence of the poor in the land and then to blame them for their poverty. Jesus' comment is not a concession to the fact of poverty but a prophetic critique of its continuing presence.

CONCLUSION

Jesus' action in the temple, then, was not a cleansing of the temple but an enacted parable or prophetic sign of God's judgment on it and, therefore, of its impending destruction. For all the reasons developed here, it seems that Sanders is only half right. Jesus did predict the destruction of the temple but not to prepare for a new version of the old evil. Jesus did believe that the end of the old temple would lead to something new, but not a new temple. The destruction of the oppressive institution that the temple had become was one step toward the coming justice of the reign of God, who gathers the outcasts and foreigners and invites them to build a community where, in the words of Isaiah,

> in righteousness you shall be established;
> you shall be far from oppression;
> for you shall not fear;
> and from terror, for it shall not come near you.
> Maintain justice, and do what is right;
> for soon my salvation will come
> and my deliverance shall be revealed.

The symbolic destruction of the temple was a prelude to the coming justice of a different kind of reign, the reign of God.

7

"What Is Written? How Do You Read?"

The Torah: Debt, Purity, and Social Control

Not too long ago, studies of the historical Jesus had reached a consensus about some aspects of Jesus' ministry. Jesus worked in the synagogues of the towns and villages in Galilee large enough to have a synagogue, and, when he entered those synagogues, he argued Torah with the Pharisees or the scribal Pharisees. The Gospels seemed clear on this much: Jesus debated Torah in the synagogues with the Pharisees. Now, in more recent studies, much of that synthesis has been called into question.

THE QUEST FOR THE HISTORICAL SYNAGOGUE

Based largely on what has come to be known as the Theodotus inscription, unearthed in Jerusalem just before World War I, scholars built a consensus description of the Judaism in which Jesus was raised. It was a Judaism that had its own distinctive leaders (rabbis), its own places of meeting (synagogues), and a clearly formed way of interpreting its scriptures (halakah). But more recent work on the Theodotus inscription, based on epigraphical evidence and a critical reevaluation of where it was found and how it was dated, now places it in the second century sometime during the reign of Hadrian (117–138 C.E.) or Antoninus Pius (138–161 C.E.).[1] Nor have archaeological excavations sustained the earlier synthesis. After a considerable number of excavations of ancient synagogues, archaeologists have found no synagogue buildings in Galilee from the first century. All synagogues excavated thus far, including the well-known synagogue at Capernaum, are second century or later, often a good deal later (third to fifth centuries C.E.). Attempts to demonstrate that the assembly hall structures at Masada and Herodium served as synagogues have proven unconvincing. The evidence is simply too ambiguous to permit any such conclusion. Joseph Gutmann notes that there is no evidence for the presence of a synagogue at either site except for the excavators' "wishful thinking,"[2] and S. B. Honig, who has reached the same conclusion for the supposed synagogue on the Temple Mount, summarizes the current state of the problem as follows:

> even recent archaeological findings have not revealed any syna-gogue buildings in Judaea; [the] Herodium and Masada excava-tions do not definitely indicate a place of formal worship; they may be merely assembly areas. Those synagogue edifices that have been discovered are in the Galilean area and even these are not of the [Second] Temple period but belong to the latter period of the Second Century. There is no evidence too that there existed a synagogue (a place of formal Prayer) within the Temple proper. No Tannaitic or even non-rabbinic sources substantiate such a contention.[3]

There is currently no reason to suppose that Jesus ever saw a synagogue building in Galilee, much less argued Torah with Pharisees in such a structure. If this is the case, then the Greek word *synagōgē*, as it appears in the Gospels (with the sole exception of Luke 7:5), must refer to a meet-ing rather than a meeting place, to a gathered community rather than to a building that housed the gathering. Still, a community must gather someplace. Where, then, did the synagogue congregate?

At least two possibilities exist. First, the community could have met in a home designated for such a purpose. If so, then Gutmann is probably correct when he observes that the synagogues mentioned in the Gospels were "probably indistinguishable from domestic architecture."[4] It ap-pears that the early house churches owed more to the synagogue than previously imagined, and the situation may shed light on passages such as Mark 2:1–12, where Jesus is in a household teaching. Howard Clark Kee thinks this situation may explain the use of the phrase "their syna-gogues" in the Gospels.[5] The phrase distinguishes one house gathering from another. Perhaps, by the late first century, Matthew's community had begun to use the word *ekklēsia* to distinguish the house church from the house synagogue. Kee sums up the situation in the following way:

> What seems most plausible, therefore, is the conclusion indicated by a convergence of archaeological and literary studies of both Jewish and Christian materials: Jews and Christians in the Galilee in the pre-70 period met in homes or small public halls for study of Scriptures, worship, and instruction.[6]

The primary difficulty with this hypothesis is that the transformation of domestic property into public space cannot be traced earlier than the An-tonine period (mid to late second century), which may indicate that this option is not as secure as it seems to be at first glance. Therefore, a second possibility should be considered, namely, that the gathering referred to by the word *synagōgē* occurred in an open space, such as a city square or village gate. Honig has argued this possibility at some length.[7] This would mean that the synagogue began not as a religious gathering at all but rather as a community gathering to deal with the issues and concerns of the village or town. It was a political and social gathering as much as a religious assembly. Given the character of ancient life, the religious and political were not as separate as they seem to us today, so the proposal makes sense. Evidence for this use of public space can be traced as far back as Ezra (10:9) and Nehemiah (8:1ff.), both of whom gathered the people in a prominent open square. In a similar vein, Josephus (*Life* 272–82) describes a meeting in the *proseuchē* (prayer hall) at Tiberius at which Jonathan and his faction attempted to dislodge Josephus from his position of leadership. Josephus describes this *proseuchē* as "a huge building, capable of accommodating a large crowd" (*Life* 277). It does not appear to be a building anything like the forerunner of a synagogue, nor does Josephus use the word *synagōgē* to describe it. It was rather a community meeting hall for large assemblies of citizens, perhaps an urban version of the city square now changed into a public building.

Honig suggests that the city square or village plaza (*r'hov* or *plateia*) may have been the marketplace of the town or, in a smaller village, the place by the gate where the elders were accustomed to meet. He identifies three types of functions carried out in the city-square: public mourning; public revenue collection; and public worship. The rabbinic materials provide glimpses into the adversarial relationship between temple and city square, reiterated in the ideological conflict between the "Sadduccean priestly aristocratic" view of the domination of the temple and the "Pharisaic lay-democratic" emphasis on participation in the life of Israel. The lessening of this tension is reflected in the development of the *ma'amadot,* "the stations for the laity to assemble in the city square to read the pertinent sections of the Torah while the sacrifice was being conducted by the corresponding *mishmar,* priestly watch in the Temple" (450). If this is plausible, then the city square may have been a place of worship before there were synagogue buildings. In the villages of Galilee where the peasants belonged to the same tradition, this would make sense. There was no need for a private meeting space.

Honig documents the use of the city square for mourning the dead and offering appropriate funerary observances, as well as collecting "local levies and excises for various needs and welfare," perhaps taken from what was known as the second tithe (461). It is even possible that visitors to local villages were assessed for their use of the city square and the monies so collected used by the village. Some aspects of worship were also acted out in the city square. Honig identifies the blowing of the shofar on *rosh hashanah* as one such activity, except when the day of blowing the shofar fell on a Sabbath. Then the shofar could only be blown at the temple. In addition, the "recital of the priestly benediction" accompanied by "the raising of the hands," was performed "in the city square on occasion of fast days or *ma'amadot*." In each case, the activities in the city square paralleled those occurring in the temple. In Honig's words, "the city square was the locale parallel to the temple service" (468). The parallels did recognize the difference in sanctity between the village and the temple but provided a way for villagers to participate in the rituals of the temple even though they were geographically removed from it.

In similar fashion, Horsley reconstructs early synagogues as "village assemblies."[8] The synagogue was a form of local assembly for governance, fostering social cohesion in the village. Beyond the household, the synagogue was the primary form of village social life. These gatherings were probably held twice a week in market towns to coincide with market days (probably on Mondays and Thursdays).[9] Smaller villages without local markets may have met on a different schedule. Since Roman and Herodian rulers left the villages to their own devices as long as they paid their tribute and taxes, the synagogue probably was the primary form of village governance. At such gatherings, the Torah may well have been read and perhaps even discussed. Horsley, therefore, views the synagogue gatherings as one primary means by which the villages organized themselves to preserve their customs and traditions. In his words, the synagogue was the instrument that allowed "semi-autonomous villages apparently" to preserve "indigenous social structures and customs inside a democratic framework."[10]

WHO WERE THE PHARISEES?

The major difference between Honig's and Horsley's reconstruction of the synagogue as village gathering is the absence of Pharisees from Horsley's view. The synagogues, according to Horsley, were overseen by a council of village elders. The size of the council and its responsibilities depended on the size of the village and its distinctive customs, but the pattern is plain enough.

> Governance and cohesion of village and town communities were provided by local assemblies (and courts) operating more or less democratically with certain officials such as the *archisynagōgos* and *hypērētes* mentioned in the synoptic Gospel tradition responsible for supervising communal finances, aid to the poor, public works and religious matters.[11]

The problem with this view is that it leaves no place for the Pharisees. The Pharisees were, according to Josephus, located in Jerusalem, not

Galilee, although they could be sent to Galilee as part of a deputation to communicate or implement Jerusalem's interests, as illustrated by the embassy sent from Jerusalem to depose Josephus (*Life* 195–98). This embassy included two members "from the lower ranks and adherents of the Pharisees," a priest of Pharisaic leaning, and a descendant of high priests. But this embassy did not travel to Galilee to defend the temple's reading of the Torah or to investigate an itinerant rabbi and charismatic healer, as the Gospels depict them doing. Nor does the picture sketched by Horsley support the notion that the Pharisees controlled the synagogue as a base of support over against the Jerusalem Sadduccees, as Honig suggests. Indeed, the rabbis seem to show a reluctance to associate with the *amme ha-aretz,* the peasants who were not scrupulous about keeping the Torah according to the oral Torah of the Pharisees.[12] References like those in Mark 12:38–39 and Luke 11:43 indicate little more than that "the scribes or Pharisees expected deference in the *agorai* and seats of honor at assemblies and feasts when they visited towns and villages, as we might expect from 'retainers' of the Temple-based rulers in Jerusalem." But they neither conducted the customary courts nor governed the local assemblies.[13]

Who then were the Pharisees? Neusner argues that, by the first century, the Pharisees had become a table-fellowship sect that "required keeping everywhere the laws of ritual purity that normally apply only in the Jerusalem Temple, so Pharisees ate their private meals in the same condition of ritual purity as did the priests of the holy cult."[14] It was their way of fulfilling the promise in Leviticus that all Israel should be a kingdom of priests and a holy people. This meant, therefore, that "one must eat secular food (ordinary, everyday meals) in a state of purity *as if one were a Temple priest*" (83). The daily fulfillment of this project involved a meticulous keeping of the laws of purity as well as the scrupulous tithing of all food. The extension of the complicated purity laws to every Jew in his or her household meant that "the Temple altar in Jerusalem would be replicated at the tables of all Israel" (146). As the title of his study indicated, Neusner saw the evolution of the Pharisees from an active political party during the Hasmonaean era, in and out of favor with monarchs from John Hyrcanus to Alexandra Salome, to a withdrawn purity sect, less interested in politics than in the purification of the Judean people. Anthony Saldarini has proposed a modification to Neusner's scheme, for he thinks that the Pharisees remained actively involved in public life and political issues.[15] In Saldarini's view, the Pharisees are essentially a political interest group that comprises not members of the ruling class but members of the retainer class, who depend on the patronage of the powerful to promote their political agenda. They can gain power only through the agency of their powerful patrons. The problem with Neusner's portrayal is that it presents the Pharisees as an introversionist sect (to use Bryan Wilson's typology of sect types[16]), when they were much more a reformist sect seeking gradual changes in public life inspired by their vision of Torah purity. Throughout Jesus' lifetime, they remained a power group lobbying for their interests against the interests of other similar groups. It is precisely because they were a retainer class group that they fell in and out of power. When they were patronized by an Alexandra Salome, they could wield significant power, but when the ruler changed and shifted loyalties to another retainer faction of clients, such as the Sadduccees, then they lost their position, power, and prestige, since they were dependent on the favor of powerful rulers.

Neusner was convinced that the three main issues over which Jesus and the Pharisees argued, as presented in the Gospels, were historically accurate.[17] They were "Sabbath observance, ritual purity, and tithing," all of which are congruent with the portrait of the Pharisees found in rabbinic traditions.[18] One could add the issue of divorce to the list, as Saldarini does.[19] If Jesus did conflict with the Pharisees in Galilee, then at least the Gospel writers have got the issues right. But did Jesus and the Pharisees lock horns in the synagogues of the villages, or is Horsley right in asserting that the Pharisees are a figment of the Gospel writers' imaginations and never did spend much time in Galilee?

THE GREAT TRADITION AND THE LITTLE TRADITION

Before answering that question, it might be helpful to sketch the conflict between the center and the periphery, or between the Jerusalem temple and the villages of Galilee, since the Pharisees appear to be go-between figures. The temple was, among other things, the guardian of the great tradition. The great tradition is the definition of the world propogated by the rulers through their literate retainers; it is their "social construction of reality."[20] Through the media of inspired texts and sacred scriptures, the great tradition defines what is real and identifies that reality with the current social, political, and economic order. Clearly, the carrier of the great tradition in first-century Palestine was the Torah, and the group that could control the interpretation of the Torah could define "world," that social and political construction of reality that could specify the meaning of purity, demand tithes, and control behavior. The great tradition is usually grounded in an urban center and, in Jesus' time, that center was Jerusalem.

In this context, the Pharisees are one literate group among others (Sadduccees, for example) contending for the right to interpret the great tradition, and the "oral torah" of the Pharisees represents their reading of reality as spelled out in the great tradition called Torah. It is important to remember that this struggle for control of the great tradition was a political struggle with economic and social consequences. Although the issues might look religious to our eyes and sound religious to our ears, they are fundamentally about wealth and power. Those who control the great tradition reap its benefits, and this is why the struggle for control of the Torah engaged the ruling class and its retainers. More specifically, these groups included the high-priestly families of Jerusalem and the lay aristocrats or "the elders" and perhaps some Sadduccees who supported their rule. The retainer groups involved in the struggle included the Pharisees, some of the Sadduccees, the Essenes, and groups like the ordinary priests and Levites. In other words, the conflict between the great tradition and the little tradition reproduces the larger antagonism between ruling elites and the dominated masses. The ideological imposition of a particular reading of the Torah would serve the interests of the ruling elites insofar as it could be used to prescribe and proscribe behavior, and compel tithes and tribute. This is what Isenberg believes the Pharisees and Essenes share: "control of redemptive media based on a monopoly of exegetical authority."[21]

By contrast, the little tradition was rooted in the villages and towns of the rural countryside where the peasants lived. Needless to say, peasants take a dim view of the great tradition, although they do not have enough power to oppose it directly. This leads to the formation of what James Scott has called "a shadow society," that is, "a pattern of structural, stylistic and normative opposition to the politico-religious tradition of ruling elites."[22] The ideological task of the rulers is to transfer their view of the great tradition to their peasant masses and implant it in their villages. The peasants' task is to resist the domination implied in the project. Quite clearly, the tension between great and little traditions derives, in no small part, from the fact that they are associated with classes whose interests are antithetical.

The degree to which the ruling class is able to impose the great tradition on the rural hinterland depends on several factors. First, the more unitary the great tradition is, the more powerful will be its influence. In the case of first-century Judea, the control of the great tradition was a subject of dispute, and competing political interest groups were vying for the right to interpret it. Any such power struggle weakened the unity of the ruling class and served peasant interests. Second, the great tradition was centered in Jerusalem, but Galilee was under the client ruler Herod Antipas. The power of the great tradition emanating from Jerusalem, therefore, would encounter further hindrance from Herod Antipas, whose political interests had to balance his acknowledgment of the temple against his own interests in exploiting his peasant base to support his own rule and reward his loyal ruling class (Herodians) who supported his reign because they benefited from it. Rather than concede the role of Jerusalem as the sole urban center to whom his subjects owed loyalty, he reconstituted Sepphoris after its destruction by Varus in 4 B.C.E. and, in 15 C.E., began construction of Tiberius. These two cities represented the center and power base of his rule. If Freyne is right, the Herodians represented a new type of Jew: "a new kind of Galilean Jew emerges, who is at once a man of the hellenistic world and a Jew."[23] While Antipas regularly journeyed to Jerusalem for the major festivals, he steered Galilee along a course that was politically independent of the temple. The effect of this policy on the villagers of Galilee was to weaken the force of the great tradition over their lives. Of course, the weakening of ties to Jerusalem did not necessarily lead to increased loyalty to Antipas. In the case of Galilee, "colonial conquest produced, if anything, a much sharper cleavage between the little tradition and elite culture."[24] The peasants of Galilee probably had less in common with the Herodian ruling class than with their priestly rulers in Jerusalem, and were, therefore, less inclined to support it. A major reason was that Antipas had to embrace Roman power and Hellenistic culture in order to please his colonial masters, but neither inclination endeared him to his subjects. To the contrary, his decisions isolated him from his own peasant population. The Galileans' hatred of Sepphoris and Tiberius is well-known and surfaced both at the death of Herod the Great and during the Galilean phase of the First Jewish Revolt. Freyne sums it up well: "there was likely to have been little sympathy or understanding between the country peasants and Tiberius' upper class."[25]

A final factor to take into account in evaluating the relative strength and unitary nature of the great tradition is that, in the case of the Torah, it contained its own critique. The prophetic and Deuteronomistic strains coexisted with the priestly strain within the Torah and in the collection of "the Torah and the prophets." This allowed villagers some latitude in dealing with the great tradition. If the Torah as read by the scribes called for a double tithe, or some version of double tithes in two out of each six years, it also called for the sabbatical year cancellation of debt and the redistribution of wealth and land during the jubilee year, provisions more overlooked than honored. Yahweh had promised Moses that there would be no more poor in the land if only the people would listen to the voice of the Lord and keep all the commandments (Deut. 15:4–5). Insofar as the Torah represented the great tradition, it represented a version of the great tradition that did not serve merely the interests of the rulers, even when the rulers were the high priests of the temple itself.

If the outcome of the imposition of the great tradition depends, in no small part, on the unity of the great tradition and the cohesiveness of the class that is propogating it, the struggle will also be influenced by the character of the little tradition and the nature of the villages where it is honored. The stronger the traditions and customs of village life, and the more coherent their social ties, the better the villagers will be able to counter the persuasive power of the great tradition. This resistence is built into the very structure of agrarian societies. Scott says it well: "as one would expect, when we move down the stratification ladder we encounter growing scepticism,"[26] or to put it a bit differently, the farther away from the center and the closer to the periphery one gets, the more elusive and elastic the great tradition will become. The very character of Galilee itself would tend to strengthen the peasants' hand in this regard. As many have noted, Galilee was not like other areas of the Roman Empire, in which cities controlled a clearly definable hinterland. The two major cities of Galilee, Sepphoris and Tiberius, enjoyed no such relationship with the villages around them. Both cities were more like foreign bodies in the tissue of Galilee than integral parts of it. So there was no pattern of city and hinterland that justified the elites' claim on the villages. Freyne noted this fact in his chapter on the geography of Galilee and the distribution of cities around it. "Urbanization was never likely to take over the control of life in central Galilee, and in fact never did."[27] Positively stated, this means that "the interior of Galilee was particularly suited to a peasant style of life with people living together in close ties of kinship in relatively small and isolated settlements," the very environment in which the little tradition could flourish.[28]

It is in this environment that what Scott calls "the shadow society" can emerge. The shadow society develops and lives out a set of values in contradiction with the great tradition. Hegemony engenders its opposite, and "every great tradition institution may find its 'counterpoint' or 'shadow' institution within the folk culture."[29] Often these values are expressed in millennial dreams that mirror "existing social inequalities and privations" or the emergence of various deviant actors and festivals, "popular theatre, folktales, folksayings, myths, poetry, jokes and songs" (20–21). It may well be that the apocalyptic visions and parables of Jesus need to be placed in this context. The development of the little tradition as a shadow of the great tradition permits peasants to disguise their defiance while absorbing the orthodoxy of the great tradition. "Folk religion is inherently syncretistic" (26), and this syncretism allows the village to absorb an inherited great tradition but to accommodate it to older deities, a process that preserves the identity of the village and its values even as the village feigns loyalty to the great tradition. In the case of Galilee, villagers could draw on traditions involving Elijah and Elisha, and the God of those prophets who called the powerful to account and judged their apostasy.

The most important response to the imposition of a great tradition lies in what Scott calls profanations, which include "rituals of reversal . . . popular sacrilege" and other "moments of madness" (29–33). Rulers permit these profanations, knowing that such ritualized and symbolic forms of protest may serve as an outlet for deeper tensions. These rituals often assume the guise of excess, ecstatic cults, drinking and feasting, or sexual hedonism. One example from the life of Jesus may illustrate how he encouraged the shadow society of peasant life. The Gospels record Jesus sitting at table with toll collectors and sinners (Mark 2:15–16). The Pharisees were a table companionship sect that attempted to transform every meal into a ritual of purity equal to that of the priests consuming a meal in the temple. The implications of the project were wide ranging. Neusner summarizes the greater implications.

> The setting for law observance was the field and the kitchen, the bed and the street. The occasion for observance occurred every time a person picked up a common nail, which might be unclean, or purchased a seah of wheat, which had to be tithed—by himself, without priests to bless his deeds or sages to instruct him. So keeping the Pharisaic rule required neither an occasional exceptional rite at, but external to, the meal. . . . It imposed perpetual ritualization of daily life, and constant inner awareness of the communal order of being.[30]

The social behavior of the Pharisees constituted an interpretation of the Torah (the great tradition), and every time they reclined at table, they were fulfilling the commands of the Torah as they read it.

> [The] part of the Torah which originally pertained to the priests in the Temple, and now was meant to sanctify all Israel and transform each man into a priest and the whole nation into a holy people, had to do with eating: the sanctification of the body and of the body of believers.[31]

Set against this background, Jesus' table companionship with toll collectors and sinners was a profanation of the Pharisees' version of the great tradition, and therefore, an offense to Moses. Jesus reclined with the impure and the unclean, without apology or hesitation. He turned the meal into a ceremony of a different kind of community, but it had an edge.

Scott says simply, "popular sacrilege is at the core of these 'moments of madness.'"[32] This sense of outrage and offense may lie behind Jesus' defense of his behavior. In the Q tradition (Luke 7:33–35 = Matt. 11:18–19), Jesus says,

> For John the Baptizer has come eating no bread and drinking no wine, and you say, "he has a demon." The Son of Man has come eating and drinking, and you say, "Look! A glutton and a drunkard, a friend of toll collectors and sinners." Yet wisdom is justified by all her children.

The wisdom of the little tradition, that is. The strategy of the Pharisees is clear. They use negative labeling to shame Jesus and discredit his activity. Calling Jesus names has been a staple of his opponents' attacks.[33] Notice that the labeling concerns Jesus' eating and drinking and the companions with whom he reclines at table. He is accused of excess and bad company. When he does recline at table, Jesus is acting out a different vision for Israel. He rejects the priestly model for purity and the table at the temple as the paradigm for the table in the village. He also rejects the barriers of purity and stigmas of impurity that would render his table companions unclean, indebted, and outside the fellowship of the true Israel. The Pharisees have got it all wrong. If what Jesus is doing is honorable, then the table-purity sect is shameful and misdirected. Jesus' profanation of the Pharisees' project amounts to a challenge to their reading of the great tradition.

What has this discussion of the relationship between the great tradition and the little tradition to do with the problem of whether there were Pharisees in Galilee? Owing to the cultural distance between the center and the periphery, those at the center of power and prestige had to monitor the periphery for evidence of compliance and signs of unrest. Typically, rulers sent their retainers to fulfill this role. The high priests needed to retain the loyalty of Galilean villagers to the temple, and they attempted to keep the ties strong by encouraging pilgrimage, those ritual contacts with the center meant to cement ties and build loyalty, and by sending agents to the villages and towns of Galilee. This is the role played by the scribal Pharisees in the Gospels. The Pharisees were most likely based in Jerusalem, as Josephus depicts them, because, as a retainer group, they needed to stay close to the center of power in order to curry favor and promote their agenda. But it is certainly possible that scribal Pharisees traveled to Galilee to perpetuate their reading of the Torah in the service of the temple. To use Horsley's apt phrase, "The Pharisees and other scribes/sages served a mediating political-economic-religious function in that Judaean temple state."[34]

Antipas could have permitted such contacts as long as they posed no threat to his rule, and he may well have seen such activity as contributing to the pacification of the villages. Without such contact, it is hard to see how the Galileans could have maintained any loyalty to the temple at all. Of course, there is some dispute at this very point. Building on his belief that peasant life was inherently conservative and isolated, Freyne finds evidence for Galilean support of the temple.[35] There is, first of all, no evidence that any alternative cult center was established in Galilee, while there is evidence that Galileans took pilgrimage obligations seriously. Galileans did not seem to be meticulous about paying the half-shekel temple tax, and they were lax in paying their tithes, but, in spite of it all, they remained loyal to the temple, because the temple was connected to the land and the productivity of the land. The source of blessing was Yahweh, and when Yahweh was worshiped in the temple and appropriate sacrifices were offered to him, the land would prosper. The temple represented, according to Freyne, part of the safety net that supported peasant subsistence life.[36]

Horsley thinks the structural conflict built into the claims of the Jerusalem rulers would have undermined peasant loyalty to the temple.[37] It was the source of "a tributary economy centered in the house of God" (131), and, as such, it was no different from any other tribute-collecting machine. Even if Galileans did undertake pilgrimages, they did so far less frequently than Judeans, and when they arrived in Jerusalem, they discovered that the festivals focused their deep ambiguity about the temple. The high priests who presided came from families that had been installed by Herod the Great and were now serving as puppets of the Romans. The festivals celebrated the mighty acts of God in liberating the people from slavery in Egypt and giving them the Torah at Sinai. This may explain the level of conflict that often attended the pilgrimage festivals (*War* 2.4–7; *Ant.* 17.206–7). The contradiction between the current situation of the people and the focus of festivity was simply too great. At most, Horsley believes, "the level of the Galileans' devotion to the Temple remains unclear" (147). The same could be argued for the Galileans' reading of the Torah.

Whether one accepts the more optimistic position advocated by Freyne or the more minimalist position of Horsley, it is clear that the temple hierarchy had to cultivate its relationship with Galilee. To do this necessitated contacts initiated by the temple, as well as the journeys of pilgrims to the temple. What was at stake was control of the great tradition. It is in this context that Jesus' interpretation of the Torah becomes an important factor for understanding his public activity in Galilee and Judea. The Pharisees who appear in the Gospels as Jesus' opponents probably came from Jerusalem to monitor compliance and control interpretation of the Torah. They have, no doubt, local sympathizers who report to them. Their task is to maintain balance between the demands of the center and the wanderings of the periphery. It appears as though Jesus was exploiting this tension as he carried his reading of the Torah to the villages of Galilee and issued his challenge to the legitimacy of the temple.

JESUS AND THE TORAH

When a scribe learned in the Torah approached Jesus to ask how to inherit eternal life, Jesus responded by asking two questions, "What is written in the Torah? How do you read?" The two questions are not the same. It is one thing to know what is in the law and quite another to know what it means. The first question seeks to establish textual common ground on which both interlocutors can agree. The second question asks for an interpretation of that common text. As we have seen, in Galilee, the Torah was in dispute. The interpretation of the great tradition conflicted with more local readings. How did Jesus read the Torah and what was at stake in his reading?

Purity and Debt: The Two Codes of the Torah

In a lucid chapter from a book that can be quite obscure, Fernando Belo offers a framework for understanding two systems of legislation in the Torah.[38] He calls these the debt codes and the purity codes. The debt codes are found mostly in the Jahwist (J) and Elohist (E) strands of the Torah, while the purity codes are found primarily in the priestly (P) strand of the Torah. Deuteronomy restates the two on its own terms. Each of the codes generates rulings that apply to the table, the household, and the sanctuary.

The purity code is rooted in the creation story and the command, "You shall be holy, for I am holy," says the Lord God. The purpose of the purity codes is to separate incompatible pairs, much as God separated the light from the darkness in creation. For example, Deuteronomy 22:9–11 forbids planting two kinds of seed in the same ground, wearing clothes made from two kinds of cloth, and ploughing with two kinds of animals. The principle could be extended far more broadly. A menstruating and a nonmenstruating woman are an incompatible pair. Since the woman's normal state is nonmenstruating, she must be unclean when menstruating. Some animals are clean for eating, and others (with cloven hoofs, for instance) are not. Some animals can be offered as sacrificial victims, firstborn and unblemished, but others cannot. Some people are clean (Israelites) but others are not (Gentiles). Within Israel, some are clean (those who obey the Torah) and others are not (the *amme ha-aretz,* those who fail to follow the halakah). Once begun, the system can be extended indefinitely until it comes to include every aspect of life, as the purity maps introduced earlier can testify. The purity codes will govern what food is consumed at table, who will marry whom in the household, and what will be offered at the altar in the temple. L. William Countryman sums up the theological impulse of the purity codes:

> Israelite attention to "wholeness" demands two things: first, that every individual should be a complete and self-contained specimen of its kind (hence the limitations placed on the "blemished"), and second, that there should be no mixing of kinds.[39]

The community follows the demands of purity in order to avoid the threat of pollution or contagion, and to know that one has avoided contagion requires drawing clear lines of demarcation or boundaries. "Pollution means confusion and dissolution of the elements involved; it is a curse. . . . It brings death."[40] To countenance impurity is to accept a dissolution of creation into chaos. This is the curse that the purity codes are constructed to avoid.

The debt codes begin with the exodus from Egypt and the gift of the land. Yahweh gave the land to be a blessing, and the land belongs to Yahweh alone. Leviticus 25:23 states the principle well: "The land shall not be sold in perpetuity, for the land is mine; with me, you are but aliens and tenants." The debt codes are built on the principle of extension, extending the blessing by sharing the yield of the land. This is why the people tithe every third year "to the Levites, the aliens, the orphans, and the widows, so that they eat their fill within your towns" (Deut. 26:12). The same principle underlies the sabbatical year (Deut. 15:12–18) and the jubilee year provisions when debts are canceled, slaves freed, and the land redistributed to its original families (Lev. 25:23–55).

The purpose of the debt codes was to avoid the violence that arises when a ruling class exploits a peasant base. Belo believes this to be

> the locus of the violence that must be exorcised: the desire that is brought to bear on the other's source of subsistence, the desire that is the origin of aggressive violence. . . . This violence . . . is the source of the class system, the enrichment of some at the expense of others, and the formation of large scale ownership. (44)

The problem with the debt codes of the Torah is that they generated a hidden contradiction. As the land yielded abundantly, fulfilling the principle of extension, it was no longer regarded as a gift but as a source of wealth, and those who benefited no longer distributed their surplus but hoarded it for the sake of status display and conspicuous consumption, like other ruling classes in the ancient world. Belo summarizes the process clearly and well:

> the debt system has within it a contradiction much like the one we found in the pollution system. It consists in this, that blessing and abundance engender the covetous desire to have more; this means that the blessing may well develop under its aegis the violence that is the curse. (54)

This is quite likely what happened in first-century Galilee.

These two systems do not coexist on equal terms. One is usually read in terms of the other; one is focal and the other subsidiary and mediated through it. This has enormous consequences for understanding every aspect of life. For example, take the matter of poverty. Interpreted from the point of view of the purity codes, poverty is the result of uncleanness. If one were to respect the quest for purity, one would experience blessing and life. This is why the temple authorities whose legitimation rested squarely on the purity codes devoted their efforts to blaming the victims of their exploitation by portraying them as unclean *amme ha-aretz*. The dirt-poor peasants were that way for a reason. But from the point of view of the debt codes, poverty is the result of covetous greed, which violates the will of Yahweh and compromises the justice of the reign of God. In the parable of the rich fool (Luke 12:16–20), Jesus portrays the very attitude that sabotaged the debt codes. Having received abundantly from the land, the rich fool does not ask how he can participate in the principle of extension by giving what he does not need, but hoards his abundance for his own use. He embodies the covetous greed that destroys the Torah's view that the land is Yahweh's alone. To give is to live becomes to have is to hold.

The Dialogue and the Decalogue (Mark 10:17–22 and Parallels)

It is rare that the Gospels portray Jesus interacting with a member of the ruling class. This makes his encounter with the rich man of more than passing interest. Since the dialogue so clearly invokes the Decalogue, it may be useful to compare the two lists of commandments in order to notice what has been included and what omitted.

The Decalogue (Exodus 20:1–17)	The Dialogue (Mark 10:17–22)
1. No other gods before me.	1.
2. No idols.	2.
3. No wrongful use of God's name.	3.
4. Keep the sabbath holy.	4.
5. Honor your father and mother.	5. Honor your father and mother.
6. You shall not murder.	6. Do not kill.
7. You shall not commit adultery.	7. Do not commit adultery.
8. You shall not steal.	8. Do not steal.
9. You shall not bear false witness.	9. Do not bear false witness. [Do not defraud?]
10. You shall not covet your neighbor's house, wife, slaves, ox, donkey, or anything else that belongs to your neighbor.	10. [Do not defraud?]

From a comparison of the lists, it is clear that Jesus recites either five or six commandments and omits either five or four. He cites the fifth through the ninth commandments (or the fifth through the tenth commandments) but omits the first four and, possibly, the last or tenth commandment. Matthew (19:18–19a) follows the Markan order but adds in 19:19b, "and you shall love your neighbor as yourself." Luke changes the order of commandments cited in Mark, reversing the first two commandments cited by Mark, so that his list begins with the prohibition of adultery. Kenneth Bailey thinks the change is made to create a concentric structure:[41]

do not commit adultery	7 (loyalty to family)
do not kill	6
do not steal	8 (property)
do not bear false witness	9
honor father and mother	5 (loyalty to family)

Bailey's designation of the three central commandments as reflecting concerns with property seems more applicable to the tenth commandment, against covetousness. The concern with murder, stealing, and false witness seems more related to maintaining the fabric of a stable social and communal life. If so, then the three central commandments, in Luke, relate to village life while the framing commandments relate to the integrity of the household and family. Whether right or wrong in details, Bailey has made the point that Luke has rearranged the Markan material in the interest of his own thematic concerns, and Matthew has added the commandment about love of neighbor to bolster his own ethical concerns. This leaves us with the Markan order as the basis for discussing Jesus' interaction with a ruling class elite.

In its current form, the exchange is in the form of an honor-shame riposte. The man approaches Jesus with a positive challenge. By labeling him a "good rabbi," he may be showing respect, and by asking him about a matter like inheriting eternal life, he acknowledges his status to answer the question. Most commentators think that the man is attempting to flatter Jesus. So Bailey speculates that the ruler has addressed Jesus with a term of respect expecting to receive a similar honorific, such as "Noble Ruler," in return. "In the Oriental world, one compliment requires a second."[42] Taylor rejects Gustav Dalman's suggestion that is is "mere insolent flattery" because the course of the story, especially 10:21, indicates otherwise.[43] By contrast, Malina and Rohrbaugh detect a hostile challenge in the address.

> In a limited good society, compliments indicate aggression; they implicitly accuse a person of rising above the rest of one's fellows at their expense. Compliments conceal envy, not unlike the evil eye.[44]

Jesus fends off the implied aggression by denying that he has any special portion of goodness that would injure others and deflects the question of goodness by referring the matter to God. In this way, Jesus "pushes away the challenge and diffuses any accusation that might fuel the position of his opponents."[45]

Having defused the hostile approach, Jesus can focus on the commandments. The Markan text contains one odd phrase, "do not defraud," which is omitted by both Matthew and Luke, either because they did not see how it related to the Decalogue or they thought it was a gloss on the ninth commandment, prohibiting false witness. The verb (*apostereō*) carries a wide range of meanings, including appropriating "property held on deposit," presumably as collateral against a loan or debt obligation, acquiring wealth illegally through embezzlement, and stealing or withholding wages owed to workers.[46] In this context, the phrase may echo the concerns of Leviticus 6:2–5:

> When any of you sin and commit a trespass by deceiving a neighbor in the matter of a deposit, or a pledge, or by robbery, or if you have defrauded a neighbor, or have found something lost and lied about it—if you swear falsely regarding any of the various things [then make restitution by repaying the original amount plus one-fifth].

The text clearly identifies swearing falsely with defrauding, so the phrase "do not defraud" may be a midrashic expansion of the commandment "do not bear false witness." A similar cluster of concerns is found in Malachi 3:5 (cf. James 5:4–6):

> Then I will draw near you for judgment; I will be swift to bear witness against the sorcerers, against the adulterers; against those who swear falsely, against those who oppress the hired workers in their wages, the widow and the orphan, against those who thrust aside the alien, and do not fear me, says the Lord of hosts.

If understood within this semantic field, the command "do not defraud" could be seen as a loose reference to the tenth commandment, prohibiting covetousness, the implication being that coveting leads to defrauding others of their possessions. The more natural reading would see the phrase "do not defraud" as an expansion of the ninth commandment, which specifies the economic implications of bearing false witness. A final answer to this puzzle will have to await further discussion of the dialogue.

The partial list of the commandments is but the first phase of the encounter that leads to a more drastic statement of the import and implications of the commandments in 10:21. To understand the relationship between those two statements it is necessary to follow the dynamics of the honor-shame riposte, which can be outlined as follows:

10:17	The rich man: Statement (address; hostile compliment) Question /challenge (positive honor challenge)
10:18–19	Jesus: Counter-question (rejects hostile compliment) Counter statement/riposte (A reading of the Decalogue)
10:20	The rich man: Second challenge: Been there; done that!
10:21	Jesus: Second counter-statement/riposte (A second reading of the Decalogue)
10:22	The outcome: rich man leaves stunned

It may be helpful to follow the dynamics in more detail.

The conflict begins with a positive honor challenge. Malina and Rohrbaugh are right in reading the initial address as a hostile compliment.[47] It also discloses the rich man's view of life. He accuses Jesus of doing what he has done all his life, gaining at the expense of others. In a society dominated by the notion of limited good, one can only gain at the expense of others, so the initial address is an accusation that reflects the man's mindset.[48] He can only conceive of gaining by dispossessing others. That is what it means to live in a limited-good society where everything is a zero sum game. Jesus deflects the compliment but accepts the honor challenge contained in the question. Typically for a man of his class, the rich man has put the question in terms of inheritance. How can I position myself so that I am in line to inherit the life of the age to come? Inheritance is an important way of transferring wealth and property from generation to generation, of keeping the wealth in the family and passing along the name and the household. Inheritance implies family ties, and he no doubt views the life of the age to come as his rightful inheritance according to the covenant to Abraham, but he does remember that the covenant came with stipulations, so he is assessing his standing in the family.

This explains why Jesus responds by citing a portion of the Decalogue. Five commandments cited with one gloss; five omitted. It is probably this partial list of the commandments that permits the rich man to respond as he does. He has never murdered another person. He has not committed adultery, and he honors his mother and father because that is the safest way to ensure the inheritance of wealth from one generation to the next. Being exceedingly wealthy, he has no need to steal, and as an honorable member of the community, his word or testimony is accepted in public forums, whether in court or in the city-market and, if Luke is right in describing him as a ruler (*archōn*), in the councils of government as well. According to the standards of his class, he is Torah obedient. He is the living embodiment of the Deuteronomic view of life: the wicked perish but the righteous prosper. But the list of commandments that spell out the obligations of the covenant is partial. The rich man is moral but selectively moral; he is observant but selectively observant. The omission of the first four commandments and the tenth requires a closer look.

The first four commandments reflect directly on the honor of God. The first and great commandment forbids Israel from having any other gods before Yahweh. The reason is stated in terms of Yahweh's great act of liberation, "I am the Lord your God, who brought you out of the land of Egypt, out of the house of slavery" (Ex. 20:2). The second commandment, which forbids fashioning idols, carries both a threat and a promise. The threat comes from the judgment of God, which carries to the third and fourth generations, and the promise is the persistence of God's "steadfast love to the thousandth generation for those who love me and keep my commandments" (Ex. 20:5–6). The third commandment prohibits lifting up God's name to emptiness, or as the NRSV states it more prosaically, "You shall not make wrongful use of the name of the LORD your God," an offense for which there is no acquittal. The importance of preserving an *honorable* name is paramount in the ancient world, and misuse of the Lord's name brings God's reprisal. The fourth commandment relates to keeping the Sabbath day holy. If the first commandment was rooted in God's liberation through the exodus, the fourth commandment was grounded in God's act of creation (Ex. 20:11). Most importantly, keeping the Sabbath entails rest, respite from work, and not just for the members of one's family but for slaves, alien residents, and animals as well.

How do these absent commandments apply to a member of the ruling class of Judea or a member of the Herodian aristocracy? The Q tradition (Luke 16:13 = Matt. 6:24) contains a saying in which Jesus speaks of the impossibility of serving two masters. "You cannot serve God and Mammon." *Mamōnas* (from the Hebrew *mamona'*; Aramaic *Mamon*) probably comes from a root meaning "to place one's trust in."[49] But the word acquired a distinctively negative meaning, refering not just to possessions or wealth, but to the unjust ways they were acquired, through cheating, "spoiling a neighbor's property," bribes, and other forms of gain through the oppression and exploitation of others. "It denotes the dishonest profit which a man makes in a matter or transaction by selfishly exploiting the situation of another."[50] Taken in this sense, Jesus' remark about "the Mammon of injustice" (Luke 16:9, *mamōnas tēs adikias;* 16:11, *adikō mamōna*) is redundant. The evolution of "mammon" from a term describing possessions to a pejorative term indicating exploitation reflects the deteriorating social fabric of Judea and Galilee. Malina and Rohrbaugh[51] have noted that the rich are those strong enough to deprive others of their property and livelihood, leaving only enough to maintain a subsistence existence. The only way to become rich was to exploit others, so wealth was not an expression of blessing but the mark of a social predator. At one level, Jesus' omission of the first two commandments is a commentary on the rich man's political faith. He has set a god before Yahweh; that god is his acquisitive drive for wealth and power. And, in time, he has turned Mammon into an idol. The Q saying personifies Mammon, indicating its idolatrous status.

To have no other gods before Yahweh means to keep Yahweh's covenant by respecting Yahweh's gift. If the land is Yahweh's gift, then it belongs to all of Yahweh's people, and the bounty of the land was meant to be extended to include especially those in need, the widow, the orphan, and the poor. The debt codes of the Torah, found mainly in Deuteronomy, were fashioned to express that basic impulse behind the covenant and to warn against losing covenant perspective.

> Take care that you do not forget the Lord your God, by failing to keep his commandments . . . which I am commanding you today. When you have eaten your fill and have built fine houses and live in them, and when your herds and flocks have multiplied, and your silver and gold is multiplied, and all that you have is multiplied, then do not exalt yourself, forgetting the LORD your God. . . . Do not say to yourself, "My power and the might of my own hand have gotten me this wealth. (Deut. 8:11–14, 17, NRSV)

But that is what did happen when the ruling class, to which the rich man belonged, came to power and used their power to exploit the peasant and the poor. They abrogated the sabbatical year provision for cancellation of debts (Deut. 15:1–11), abolished even the thought of keeping jubilee (Lev. 23:18–55), and abandoned the vision of a land from which poverty had been banished (Deut. 15:4–5). The principle of extension, "the more you get, the more you give," was replaced with the principle of hoarding and accumulating at the expense of the peasant smallholder and rural poor. But to kill the principle of extension enshrined in the debt codes was to dethrone Yahweh and replace him with the gods of the colonial occupiers. The gods of the Romans had no such scruples or concerns about distributive justice. When the rich ruler pursued his path of accumulation in violation of the covenant, he was placing other gods before Yahweh and serving an idol called Mammon. In short, his very life was a violation of the first two commandments.

What made his idolatry worse was that his class disguised its apostasy by invoking the name of the Lord to sanction the whole enterprise. When the rich man attributed his wealth to Yahweh's blessing, he was lifting up the name of the Lord to nothingness, turning the God of liberation into a god of oppression, transforming the God of the covenant into a god of convenience. This was a violation of the third commandment, for it made wrongful use of the Lord's name. Wright sums up the attitude in the following way:

> Some Jews assumed, perhaps on the basis of a facile reading of Deuteronomy and certain psalms, that wealth was a sign of YHWH's favour. It signalled, apparently, that one was already in receipt of covenant blessings.[52]

In fact, it signaled the very opposite, namely, that their abrogation of the covenant had unleashed their covetous greed. They had made a mockery of the covenant provision against taking interest on loans (Deut. 23:19–20) and expropriating the pledges on loans made by the poor (Deut. 24:10–13). They had demonstrated a callous disregard for the covenant each time they withheld the wages of a day laborer (Deut. 24:14–15). They had defamed the name of the Lord their God and defrauded the Decalogue. They had exchanged the justice of the reign of God for the injustice of the Pax Romana. It is likely that, while the rich ruler, his house, and their class kept the Sabbath, they purchased that leisure at the expense of their peasants, artisans, and villagers whose life was one of endless toil just to maintain a subsistence existence. What good was the Sabbath when it did not apply to all? Of what good was the Sabbath to a day laborer whose wages had been withheld? Of what good was the Sabbath to a peasant villager whose coerced labor for his master forced him to work his own plots on Sabbath? Of what good was Sabbath to a peasant at harvest time when the demands of the master to complete his harvest took precedence over the peasant's crop that had to be harvested at other times? How could Sabbath be kept when the leisure of the few was constructed on the endless labor of the many? The ruler may have kept Sabbath, but he did not keep it holy as long as a single peasant on any of his estates was forced to labor on the Sabbath day.

Finally, Jesus omitted the tenth commandment, the commandment against covetousness. The reasons are obvious and hardly need to be enumerated. The rich man has devoted his life to coveting what others have and gaining it for himself. Whether he uses the instrumentality of high-interest loans followed by oppressive foreclosure or heavy extractions from his villages is not the point. The violation of the covenant is. Every time he or others of his class ruin a peasant family and alienate them from their plot of land, they are violating the covenant by seizing for themselves what belongs to Yahweh alone, and every time they dispossess a peasant family, they are arrogating to themselves what is the prerogative of Yahweh alone. But once the heart has been infected by covetous desire, it cannot be satisfied. When the gift of the land is violated, Yahweh is violated. To deny the covenant is to deny Yahweh. It is to put other gods before Yahweh, to construct idols, thereby shaming and misusing God's name.

Yet none of this appears on the surface of the conversation, especially the first exchange between Jesus and the rich man. This explains the man's confident response, "all these I have observed from my youth." Bailey thinks this response is a bit brazen, since according to the Talmud, only "Abraham, Moses and Aaron are reported to have kept the whole law. The rich ruler seems to calmly to put himself in rather exalted company."[53] But the ruler's confidence is rooted in more than mere presumption. He believes that he has kept all the commandments cited, because he belongs to a faction that interprets the commandments through the demands of purity, and he holds fast to those stipulations. Seen through the lenses of the purity codes, the problems of keeping the covenant are quite different. It means that he keeps a kosher table, eating only acceptable animals properly slaughtered so that he never consumes blood, and perhaps that he tithes all that he purchases. He has married a woman from a house with pure bloodlines, and he has abstained from adultery. He participates in the temple, offers appropriate sacrifices, supports it with his tithes, and cleanses himself after contracting impurity. He takes his wealth to be a sign of God's blessing, and the poverty of others to be a sign of God's judgment. He has honored his father and mother through his prominence and status.

Perhaps it has not occurred to the rich ruler that, while he has never killed a man face to face, he has most likely degraded peasant farmers to the status of day laborers, and from the time a peasant becomes a day laborer, devoid of the safety net of the village and with nothing left to sell but his animal energy, to the time he dies of malnutrition is a matter of a few years at most. Every time he alienates a peasant family from their land, he has pronounced a death sentence upon them. He has destroyed a family and killed its members. It may never have occurred to the rich man that, while he has not borne false witness in a court, he has defrauded the people of the land. Every time he has blamed his victims for the plight that he and his class have visited upon them, he is bearing false witness against them. It probably has not occurred to the rich man that, while he has never mugged anyone on the street and taken their money, he has used the system to rob the poor blind. He could not achieve his prominence and wealth except at the expense of others, but he does not see this as stealing. It is called getting ahead and climbing the ladder of power and prestige.

Quite clearly, the rich man has a robust conscience bolstered by his reading of the Torah and supported by his daily effort to root out impurity and so avoid the contagion of pollution. This is why Jesus must restate the import of the Decalogue in a startling way. All ten commandments can be viewed as an expression of the debt system. They provide different points of entry into the world of the covenant and its demands for justice in the land. But the rich ruler has read them through the demand for purity, and as a result he can no longer perceive the great injustice at the heart of the purity codes. So Jesus lays it out for him. No sooner has he declared his full compliance than Jesus stops him dead in his tracks—"Just one thing you lack":

> *go*
> *sell* what you have
> *give* it to the destitute
>   (and you will have treasure in heaven)
>
> *follow me*
>   (coming along!)

The four commandments, go, sell (dispossess), give (distribute), and follow me, summarize Jesus' reading of the Decalogue as seen through its debt codes. His four commandments are neither a transcending of the Torah nor a replacing of the Torah with a "Christian" ethic, as many have wrongly suggested. Jesus, rather, reads the Torah as a demand for the justice of the reign of God, a reign that has been subverted by the colonial rule of Rome and its client rulers as well as the hegemonic domination of the ruling class of Judea, especially the high-priestly families of Jerusalem. But Jesus' commands do not articulate a new Torah and a higher righteousness, as Matthew might have assumed; Jesus reads the Torah as God intended the Torah to be. Just as Jesus is bold enough to interpret the creation intent of God in the argument over divorce (Mark 10:2–9, culminating in the citation of Gen. 2:24), so here Jesus is audacious enough to interpret the intent of Yahweh in giving the Decalogue. The Torah is about the distributive justice of God, who gave the land as a gift to be received and shared, not hoarded at the expense of ruining others. So Jesus challenges the rich man to practice the principle of extension by dispossessing and redistributing his wealth to the utterly destitute. It is a challenge steeped in the tradition of the jubilee but not a challenge likely to be well received. The man turns away, stunned. Only at the end does the narrator explain the reason for the rejection of Jesus' challenge. The man owned many properties; that is, he had great estates. He belonged to the elites who had almost everything. "Treasure in heaven" was poor collateral compared to the wealth he already possessed.

What will likely puzzle any reader is why a member of the ruling class should approach Jesus with such a question. Perhaps the encounter is the product of the imagination of the early church or of Mark. If so, it was a unitary composition, as Bultmann noted long ago, although he attributed it to the Palestinian church, even allowing that it might trace to an early oral tradition that existed before it was committed to writing.[54] The story's early provenance and themes make it possible to read it as an encounter that traces to the historical Jesus, and the challenge it issues is in keeping with the themes of Jesus' public work. It was most likely remembered because it posed an either / or that was foundational to Jesus' ministry. Horsley sums it up well in the following way:

> "unrighteous mammon" would have meant, in effect, trust in unrighteous dealings. In biblical terms this was exactly the way one would acquire wealth. That is . . . the principal ways one could gain wealth would have been at the expense of the peasant producers, either through fraud in collecting taxes and tithes, or through lending to peasants having trouble meeting their obligations and then foreclosing or calling in the loans. What God required in the covenantal commandments was just nonexploitive social relations.[55]

And the purpose of those relations was to embody the justice of the reign of God, a justice already encoded in the Torah and awaiting the decoding of a prophet of God. It is not surprising that Jesus was called "prophet" and "rabbi."

167

8

Resistance and Conflict:

Jesus' Healings and Debates

The previous two chapters have sketched a case for historical conflict. If Jesus subverted the temple and proposed readings of the Torah different from those advocated by the authorities in Jerusalem, then he would have entered into conflict with powerful opponents, provided that he had attracted a following large enough to be considered dangerous or destabilizing. In this chapter I will explore this possibility in more detail and will also propose that Jesus spoke of the "reign of God" as an alternative reality to the world of temple dominance and the rule of Torah.

"THE WEIGHTIER MATTERS OF THE TORAH" (MATT. 23:23)

In his polemic against the scribes and Pharisees in Matthew 23, Jesus criticizes them for tithing "mint, dill, and cummin," herbs not covered by tithing requirements, while neglecting "the weightier matters of the law: justice and mercy and faith" (Matt. 23:23a). This is, he argued, like straining out "a gnat" but swallowing "a camel" (23:24). The issue in these remarks is not abolishing Torah but interpreting it. Jesus judges the Pharisees for being overscrupulous about tithing provisions while ignoring the greater demands of justice, mercy, and faith, a first-century version of majoring in the minors. The issue joined in the debate is how Torah is to be construed. What provisions of the Torah are focal and what provisions are subsidiary? If this reading of Jesus' comments is accurate, then the sayings in Matthew 23 are in keeping with Jesus' remark in Matthew 5:17, "do not think that I have come to abolish the law or the prophets; I have come not to abolish but to fulfill." The law and the prophets are not set against each other but related to each other. Jesus implies that his reading of the Torah is compatible with the prophets, not opposed to them. In other words, any reading that truly fulfills the Torah must be congruent with the vision of the prophets. One single hermeneutic will govern Jesus' reading of the Torah and the prophets alike. The two will inform each other and, therefore, fulfill both. In staking out this position, Jesus locates himself in the line of the prophets envisioned by the Deuteronomist, prophets whose function is to honor and interpret the Torah while warning of the consequences of disobedience.[1] Jesus sees this task as compatible with his sense of the prophetic vocation.

But Jesus is also a popular prophet who emerged from the village life of Galilee, not a prophet born into either the privileged or the retainer class.[2] Add to this the fact that he most likely received his training in Torah at the synagogue in Nazareth, and perhaps from his father as well, and one would suspect that Jesus' reading of the Torah will be influenced by the little traditions as they were nurtured and developed in the village life of Galilee. This scenario, of course, assumes that Jesus was literate, at least to the degree that he could read the sacred scrolls, if not fully literate like a scribe who could read and write. The presumption of Jesus' literacy is rooted, in part, in the situation of the Judean people in the first century. As Meier has observed,

> For all the differences among various groups of Jews, the narratives, laws, and prophecies of their sacred texts gave them a corporate memory and a common ethos. The very identity and continued existence of the people Israel were tied to a corpus of written and regularly read works in a way that simply was not true of other peoples in the Mediterranean world of the 1st century.[3]

If Jesus were to stake a claim to honor and authority, he had to know how to argue Torah. That his efforts were viewed as destroying Torah and dangerous to the interpretive traditions sanctioned by Jerusalem is implicit in his solemn pronouncement about fulfilling the law and the prophets (Matt. 5:17). His affirmation is couched to mask a denial.

Naturally, any argument about the Torah is simultaneously a debate about the character of God, since the Torah reveals the nature of the God who gave it. So Jesus' debates with his opponents may appear to focus simply and solely on issues of purity, but behind them lurks the deeper question of the nature of God.

The Controversy over Purity and Defilement (Mark 7:1–23)

The passage on defilement (Mark 7:1–23; Matt. 15:1–20) provides an opportunity to test this proposal. Since the advent of form criticism, the passage has been viewed as a composite construction, including the following units (all references are to the Markan text unless otherwise noted):

Verses 1–5	initial charge and background information
Verses 6–8	Isaiah unit
Verses 9–13	korban unit
Verses 14–15	saying on defilement
Verses 17–19	private explanation to disciples
Verses 20–23	generalizing conclusion with vice catalogue

Evidence of Markan redaction has been found extensively in the pass-sage (vv. 2b, 3–4, 9a, 11c, 13c, 14a or 14, 17, 18ab, 19c, 20a, 23, and 21–22, if the catalogue of vices comes from Mark's hand).[4] Two issues seem to have been conflated in the composition of the narrative, namely, the status of tradition ("the tradition of the elders") and the question of defilement (common hands). This situation gives the appearance of two controversies rolled into one, with verses 1–13 addressing the matter of tradition and verses 14–23 the issue of defilement.[5] The passage also ex-hibits abrupt breaks, as though material has been edited in a clumsy fash-ion. The question posed in 7:5, for example, is not answered until 7:15, most likely an indicator that the material in between was added to ad-dress other matters. So Bultmann concluded that "the artificiality of the composition is clear as day."[6] In addition, the quote from Isaiah 29:13 reflects the LXX translation, which differs significantly from the Hebrew text. The key phrase, found in verse 7, is set in parallel columns below:

Isaiah 29:13 (MT)	Isaiah 29:13 (LXX) (= Mark)
and their worship of me	in vain do they worship me
is a human commandment	teaching as doctrines
learned by rote	the precepts of men

Insofar as the meaning of Jesus' reply in verse 7 is dependent on the LXX, the text must reflect the redacting work of the early church. Hultgren concludes that this must have been done in the Hellenistic church, and Booth, following Dodd's earlier argument, views the prophetic quotation as part of a group of testimonies used against the synagogue.[7]

With these formidable barriers in place, it would seem to be folly even to attempt a more unified reading of the passage, but it may prove worth-while to interpret the text as reflecting an ongoing conflict and revealing the dynamics of that conflict in the public work of Jesus. Put in this con-text, the text presents an honor-shame riposte or a "challenge riposte form."[8] Identifying the social form found in a text is important, because interpretation of texts is partially based on constructing social scenarios. So Malina notes:

> literary forms as well as literary genres derive from social sys-tems. . . . Consequently, the place to look for both the structure

of a literary form as well as the meanings mediated by that structure is in some social system. Here in Mark 7 the literary form is a challenge-riposte form.[9]

Without doubt, the current form of the text reflects Mark's editing as well as other redacting influences. But to acknowledge that Mark has shaped verses 1–5, for example, is not to deny that they describe a conflictual situation prevalent in Jesus' time. The two are not mutually exclusive conditions. An important question is whether the scenes and conflicts found in Gospel texts antedate the time of their editing and reshaping. This study proposes that they do, provided that the interpreter can convincingly place them in a setting in the ministry of Jesus.

The language of Mark 7:1 is confusing, since it mentions scribes and Pharisees but does not define the relationship between them. The distinction is important because not all scribes would be Pharisees. Scribes refer to a profession based on literacy, the phenomenon that Freyne calls "scribism."[10] But Pharisees are bound together by their common commitment to a way of life and a political agenda. So, in speaking of Luke, Freyne is correct to make a "distinction between scribism as a profession (Luke 11:46–52; 20:46) and Pharisaism as a way of life (Luke 11:39–42, 44)."[11] Moreover, the scribes are identified with Jerusalem, but the Pharisees are not. Their geographical location is less obvious. While there is no need to repeat in detail the arguments advanced in an earlier chapter, a few comments may be in order. The scenario described in chapter 7 of this study fits the situation described in Mark 7. Either the representatives of the center, the "scribes who had come from Jerusalem," combine forces with their local operatives, denoted here as "Pharisees," or both the Pharisees and some of their scribal members came down from Jerusalem as a group to monitor compliance with the great tradition's version of the Torah, the Torah as interpreted by "the tradition of the elders." Sanders has dismissed this possibility out of hand: "The extraordinarily unrealistic settings of many of the conflict stories should be realized . . . nor is it credible that scribes and Pharisees made a special trip to Galilee from Jerusalem to inspect Jesus' disciples' hands."[12] Sanders attempts to see the incident as an end in itself, rather than understand its larger symbolic and political significance. Noncompliance with the political directives of the great tradition posed a threat wherever it was found, since the authority of the whole system supported the implementation of each part. For this reason, Wright need not be so squeamish about denying the role of the Pharisees as a first-century version of "thought police." The analogy may not be flattering, but it does suggest the potentially threatening role that the scribes and Pharisees played in Galilee. However, it may be more accurate to view them as moral entrepreneurs and rule enforcers, a direction that Wright himself seems to prefer.[13] Whatever their role, figures associated with the center of power are depicted as visiting the periphery to reinforce their influence over the lives of Galilean villagers. The villagers, in turn, probably viewed these outsiders with suspicion, not only because they were associated with Jerusalem, but because they might be seen as innovators. As surprising as it may seem, in those few instances where Galilean and Judean attitudes toward Torah can be contrasted, "the Galileans were more stringent in regard to the law than their Judean coreligionists."[14] The Galileans were, for example, stricter in protecting a widow's rights than their Judean neighbors, a fact indicating that their "strictness" was focused and particular.[15] It is also possible that Galileans had noticed a pattern in the innovative interpretations of the oral Torah found in the tradition of the elders. The rules so promulgated, such as the prosbul or further refinements on the meaning of purity, nearly always worked against their interests and, for this reason, they were suspicious of the Pharisaic readings of the great tradition. Yet, in spite of these differences, the scribes and Pharisees would bring with them the power of Jerusalem and the presumption of honor.

With an eye for deviant behavior, they observe members of Jesus' faction eating without ritually purifying their hands. The issue is purity, not hygiene. The Galileans have not followed the ritual ablutions that would render them clean, so their hands remain "common." Mark probably adds the phrase, "that is, unwashed" (v. 2b). When representatives of the center are circulating in an area, eating with "common" hands is both a defiant act and a challenge to their reading of the Torah. It is an affront, therefore, to their authority to control behavior. So, predictably, the scribes and Pharisees lodge a grievance or complaint. The grievance is also an attack aimed at Jesus. They ask him, "Why do your disciples not live according to the tradition of the elders but eat with common hands?" Like most questions in a challenge-riposte, this one is meant to indict and to shame. A question is a weapon of controversy, not a disinterested inquiry, because a good deal is at stake in the disciples' seemingly innocent behavior. By rejecting ritual ablutions for hands, according to Malina, Jesus and the disciples "in effect reject the Pharisaic conception of the social order and the values that order mediates. The argument about purity rules is always one about adequate social structures for the realization of core values."[16]

A much larger issue than inspecting hands is at stake, but this is what Sanders does not seem to see. The status of hands is a threshold issue, a portal to the much larger question of whose vision will govern the people of the land. The scribes and the Pharisees, therefore, accuse the disciples of shameful behavior, because they are abandoning the honorable "tradition of the elders." This stigmatizes them as deviant and dangerous. By undermining the role of Torah, they are separating the people of Galilee from the God who requires compliance. It is also the case that the two issues, the role of "tradition" and "common hands," are so interlocked as to be one. They belong together in the debate, the first as a blanket accusation (you do not live according to the tradition of the elders), and the second as a specification of charges (you eat with common hands).

The challenge contained in the disciples' behavior and the grievance it elicits are summarized in verses 1–2a, 5. By invoking the tradition of the elders, the scribes and Pharisees portray themselves as defenders of what is publicly acknowledged as honorable. It is also the basis for the boundary drawing that determines who is an insider and who is outside the group. But why such an emphasis on hands? The Pharisees are a table companionship sect or political faction that seeks to eat every meal in a state of ritual purity equal to that of the priests eating a sacred meal in the temple.[17] The temple and the priestly caste provide the model for purity. For the body of Israel to replicate that level of purity or holiness in their everyday lives, all of Israel must achieve the kind of purity embodied in the temple and modeled by the priests. This goal can be achieved only when each member of the community is scrupulous in observing the tradition of the elders. In the case of meals, this means tithing all food purchased, preparing it in pure vessels, serving it in clean dishes, and eating it with pure hands. The editorial insertion in verses 3–4 tries to depict the larger patterns of behavior from which the ritual hand washing takes its meaning. Even if food is properly tithed and prepared, and if all the vessels used to serve and consume the meal are properly cleansed, but the hands are not ritually clean, then they will contaminate whatever they touch and render the entire exercise futile.

The Pharisees are operating with the view that the human body can serve as a symbol for the social body. What happens at one level symbolizes what is happening at the other. Every member of the community is a microcosm of the macrocosmic community. If the community is viewed as pure, then sources of impurity are external to the group; contagion comes from the outside into the group. This is why the Pharisees are so concerned about eating, for meals are one of the most important and regularly occurring times when what is outside the body (food) is taken into the body. The threat of defilement is great, so the measures taken to ensure the maintenance of purity must be commensurate with the threat. To maintain purity at table is an essential task if the table companionship faction is to retain its identity and standing.[18] Clearly, Jesus' disciples do not follow the tradition of the elders. Perhaps their meals are intended to be a profanation of the great tradition's emphasis on purity and meals.[19] Seen through the eyes of the great tradition, every meal consumed by Jesus and his disciples is nothing more than table companionship with toll collectors and sinners (cf. Mark 2:13–17; Matt. 9:9–13;

Luke 5:27–32). Their behavior is provocative and, for this reason, elicits a grievance.

Once the grievance has been spoken (v. 5), the conflict is enjoined. The scribes and Pharisees attack Jesus by slandering the behavior of his disciples. It may be an indirect attack, but it would be clearly perceived by all. If Jesus is to retain his honor as a respected "rabbi," he must respond but, in doing so, he can neither defend himself nor his disciples. To defend their behavior would be to concede ground to his opponents. He must counterattack, and this is exactly what he does (vv. 6–8).

The appeal to Isaiah invokes a long tradition of prophetic protest against the abuses of the Torah, and with a few swift strokes it defines two approaches to the problem of purity. Jesus sets the "heart" over against the "lips," thereby defining two approaches to morality. The contrast between heart and lips is central to the sustained argument. It sets a prophetic "heart ethic" against the Pharisees' "orifice ethics." This also seems to be the point of the saying in 7:15, in which Jesus contrasts what goes into a person with what comes out. Contagion is not ingested as the system of orifice ethics has it; contagion flows from the heart outward, and that is why "the things which come out" are what defile. The early church devised a vice list, now found in 7:21–23, to explain and elaborate this parable (riddle), but it is unlikely that it was part of the original conflict.

Looking beyond the LXX version of Isaiah 29:13 to the Hebrew text enriches the debate. Speaking through Isaiah, the Lord says to the people of Judah, "their worship of me is a human commandment learned by rote." In the context of this debate, the countercharge fits. Jesus degrades the tradition of the elders by comparing it to human directives (contrasted implicitly with the divine commandment) that are learned by rote. The rituals of purity illustrate such "rote" behavior by which the community supposes it is worshiping God by obeying the purity codes. In the following verse, Isaiah 29:14, the Lord mocks such "wisdom of the wise" and "discernment of the discerning," the very discerning wisdom that the scribes and Pharisees presumed they had in abundance. Yet, according to Isaiah, this is the wisdom that "shall perish," and it is precisely this discernment that "shall be hidden." The prophetic judgment is clear, even as Jesus applies it to a new situation. By his response, Jesus has deprived his adversaries of the high ground, for they have appealed to the tradition of the elders, a particular reading of the Torah, whereas Jesus has appealed directly to the prophetic critique of the Torah. Since it is also true that Isaiah 29:11–12 fits Jesus' prophetic critique, this raises the question whether Jesus quoted Isaiah 29:13 in order to evoke the arguments in the sections surrounding the text cited (cf. 29:11–14). Dodd has proposed that, when the ancients cited specific texts, they often intended to invoke a larger section of related materials.[20] Whether or not this is the case, the passage from the Hebrew Bible version of Isaiah 29:13 is congruent with Jesus' argument. It does not depend on the Septuagint (LXX) text.

It is one thing to level a charge against opponents but another to make it stick. The purpose of mentioning the practice of korban is to illustrate the judgment of Isaiah. More is known about the effect of korban than its mechanism; what happened because of it is clearer than how it was done. Some pieces of the picture are clear. Korban is a vow "by which a person pledges personal wealth to God upon death while retaining the use of it during life."[21] While this may have seemed a pious act, it evidently could interfere with a son's providing for his parents, thereby establishing a conflict between kinship obligations and temple devotion. The effects of the korban were clear:

> Two things are certain: the effect of the *qorban* behavior pattern deprives parents of support deserved from a son; the word *qorban* definitely belongs to the temple semantic network and draws its primary meaning therefrom.[22]

The korban provision, then, offered an illustration of the conflict between divine commandment and human tradition. Jesus shifts his scriptural ground from Isaiah's denunciation to the Decalogue, where the fifth commandment held children honor-bound to assist their parents (Ex. 20:12; Deut. 5:16). The commandment was so important that its fulfillment ensured the blessings of long life and peaceful days in the land. In addition, the Torah specifically prohibited any behavior that "cursed" parents (Ex. 21:17; Lev. 20:9). The latter two texts refer most obviously to the language of cursing, but Jesus has enlarged their meaning to include any behavior that effectively curses parents by subjecting them to abandonment and destitution in their old age. Taken together, the passage from the Decalogue (v. 10a; cf. Ex. 20:12; Deut. 5:16) and the other Torah texts (10b; cf. Ex. 21:17; Lev. 20:9) present a familiar covenantal theology of blessing for fulfilling the commandments and curse for failing to observe them. It is as though Jesus were solemnly invoking the Shechem covenant ceremony (Deut. 27:1–26; see esp. 27:16) in order to remind the people that they have neglected their responsibilities to their kin. If Jesus began his riposte with an appeal to the prophets, he has gone for the jugular with the appeal to the Torah and the Decalogue, which is the heart of the Torah. The theme of blessing and woe is not unique to this passage but can also be found in Luke 6:20–26.

At first glance, the use of korban seems an odd choice. Even now, it is little known and much debated, but it serves the purpose of revealing a hidden contradiction and focusing the conflict. Pilch has noted clearly that the conflict is between society's two "formal social institutions, kinship and politics" (38). The conflict can be outlined in the following way:

> When a secondary rule like *qorban,* which was intended to support the political institution of the Temple, appears at the same time to threaten the kinship institution of the family by subverting observance of the commandment of "honoring," i.e., providing old age security and care for father and mother, Jesus does not hesitate to attack it for it not only threatens actual kinship groups but society as a whole as well. (37)

In an unexpected way, korban was also symbolic of a conflict rooted deep in peasant life. Although peasants would not have enough resources to take a solemn korban vow, they did know what it was like to live with a conflict between temple and kinship obligations. Peasants could either support the temple with their tithes and offerings or provide for their parents in their old age. They could either do their duty to God or to family and kin who depended on every seah of barley they could conserve. The life of peasants was one endless conflict between the demands of the temple and the need to ensure their family's survival. So the hidden contradiction, unearthed by Jesus' appeal to korban, would have struck a sensitive chord in the crowd watching the challenge-riposte, even if they would have had no occasion to declare their own resources "korban." By publicly demeaning the provision of korban, Jesus was breaking down a barrier that excluded many peasants from participating in the covenant people. He was laying the foundation for a new fictive kinship group that would take its identity from Jesus' reading of the Torah.

The appeal to korban escalates the attack on the scribes and Pharisees, who are representatives of the temple system. Jesus exposes their vulnerability. Far from instructing the people of the land in how to fulfill the Torah in their lives, they actually render the Decalogue void, and thereby they threaten to bring a curse on the land because of their lopsided and misguided emphasis on the temple and its needs. Jesus is specific in identifying where the problem lies. It is with "your tradition," that is, the tradition of the elders, "which you hand on" (v. 13). The responsibility is in their hands, and the curse is on their heads. Jesus' riposte has transformed "the tradition of the elders" from an honorable way to live the Torah into a shameful way to debase parents, from a source of blessing into a source of curse.

But the issue is not the value or the validity of the Torah, both of which are assumed. What is at stake is the interpretation of the Torah. Jesus will read the Torah through the eyes of the prophets and the concerns of the Deuteronomist. His opponents will read the Torah through the priestly eyes of the purity codes with their concern for the temple, even when its support comes at the expense of the kinship obligations of the villagers. Along with his group, Jesus is redrawing the boundary lines to include those who cannot meet their obligations to the temple and maintain their families, a boundary drawing that includes those excluded by the temple. In effect, Jesus is redefining the people of God by removing the obstacles that hinder the outsiders from believing that they belong. Insofar as the movement is rooted in his prophetic reading of the Torah, Jesus could be said to be forming a group around himself as God's reliable broker. But the conflict is deeper than a social disagreement about who is an insider and who an outsider. It is a clash of core values that defines the character of God.

The Pharisees' core value is purity, because they wish to replicate in their social life the holiness of God by maintaining the holiness to which God has called the people. "You shall be holy, for I the Lord your God am holy" (Lev. 19:2). As Neyrey, following Douglas, has noted, "God's holiness [is] God's power to bless and to curse, that is, to classify the world," and the withdrawal of God's blessing leads to "confusion, along with barrenness and pestilence."[23] Jesus' core value is forgiveness, because he views God as a God of mercy: "be merciful, as your heavenly Father is merciful" (Luke 6:36).[24] Neyrey has conveniently outlined the profiles of the two groups, the Pharisees and the Jesus movement, by identifying the key features where they remain in conflict:[25]

	Pharisees	*Jesus and Followers*
Core Value	God's Holiness (Lev. 11:44)	God's Compassion (Ex. 33:19)
Symbolized In	Creation-as-Ordering	Election and Grace
Structural Implications	Strong Purity System, Exclusivist Tendency	Weaker Purity System, Inclusivist Tendency
Strategy	Defense	Mission, Hospitality
Legitimation in Scripture	Exodus, Leviticus, Numbers, Deuteronomy	Genesis and Prophets

The legitimation-in-scripture issue is more complex than the chart makes it appear. In the debate in Mark 7, Jesus has shown that he is adept at drawing from both Exodus and Deuteronomy. But the debate is more than a battle of proof-texts. The deeper question is how the Torah is to be interpreted, through the lens of Jesus' prophetic hermeneutic or through the lens of the "tradition of the elders." Each reading is rooted in an understanding of God, the God who defines and orders or the God who liberates and provides, the God who demands purity and holiness or the God who shows mercy and forgives, the God who draws boundaries or the God who redefines the rules, the God of the temple or the God of the prophets. Of course, these alternatives are, in some measure, false, but debates have a way of overstating alternatives in order to disclose what is at stake in the disagreement.

Sabbath Controversies and Healings

The Synoptic Gospels contain six Sabbath controversies, four of which include either healings or an exorcism.

Sabbath Controversies with Healing or Exorcism

Texts	Incident/Setting
Mark 1:21–28; Luke 4:31–37	Exorcism in synagogue
Mark 3:1–6; Matt. 12:9–14; Luke 6:6–11	Healing withered hand in synagogue
Luke 13:10–17	Healing bent woman in synagogue
Luke 14:1–6	Healing man with dropsy on road

Sabbath Controversies without Healing or Exorcism

Texts	Incident/Setting
Mark 2:23–28; Matt. 12:1–8; Luke 6:1–5	Plucking grain in fields
Mark 6:1–6; Luke 4:16–30	Rejection at synagogue in Nazareth

It seems evident that the tradition has wedded healings and exorcisms with Sabbath controversies. Since three of the four healings occur in a "synagogue," it will be useful to remember that in Galilee during the time of Jesus, "synagogue" most likely referred to a household converted for public use or an open space where the business of the village was conducted, a marketplace or village square (see chap. 7). This means that the apparent change of scene in Luke 14:1–6 may not be as great as first appears. Although the village is specified only in the case of the rejection at Nazareth, it is also likely that the other Sabbath controversies occurred in the context of Galilean village life. Once again, it may be helpful to examine three passages to determine whether they contribute to an understanding of the dynamics of conflict in Jesus' public work.

Few would deny that the pericope of the healing of the man with the withered hand in its present state (Mark 3:1–6 // Matt. 12:9–14; Luke

6:6–1) reveals the editorial influences of the Gospel writers and, perhaps, of the hand that originally worked Mark 2:1–3:6 into its present concentric form.[26] Meier and Hultgren have both argued against the unity of the passage.[27] Meier says that the position of the healing at the close of a tightly edited cycle of stories (2:1–3:6) argues against its historicity, while Borg says that its association with pre-Markan tradition weighs for its authenticity.[28] Meier further believes that the controversy (3:4) is loosely connected to the healing (3:1–3, 5) and appears to be formulated with christological concerns in mind. Finally, Jesus "performs no actions" in curing the withered hand and, therefore, cannot have broken the Sabbath. All of this leads Meier to conclude that, "shorn of the Sabbath controversy, the brief and bland miracle story we are left with lacks those signs of concreteness, peculiarity, or singularity" that distinguishes material tracing to Jesus.[29] Sanders has said clearly that the controversy lacks any basis at all. "The matter is quite simple: no work was performed."[30] Therefore, there can be no controversy. This may be so, but a closer look is warranted.

The conflict in the synagogue can be viewed as a challenge-riposte. Viewed through this lens, Matthew's version may portray the dynamics more fully than Mark. In Mark, Jesus acts and speaks without any verbal opposition, and the rhetorical question he poses (3:4) really does not do justice to the Torah debates about the Sabbath.[31] This reading will follow the Matthean version of the challenge-riposte exchange and healing. The introductory framing clearly reflects Matthew's hand, especially his use of "their synagogue" (v. 9). The conflict begins in earnest with a loaded question, "Is it lawful to heal on the sabbath?" (v. 10a). Matthew implies that the presence of the man with a withered hand may have triggered the question, in which case the question is also an honor challenge. They are daring Jesus to act, perhaps in an effort at entrapment, "so that they might accuse him" (v. 10b). But the question also contains an implied grievance, indicating their awareness that, on other occasions, Jesus has healed on the Sabbath. The Markan passage depicts the onlookers standing aloof, not interacting with Jesus. As indicated in an earlier discussion, this stategy attempts to assert superior honor status by snubbing and ignoring, but Matthew pictures an attempt to shame by means of a more active engagement.

Jesus' riposte begins with a parable (v. 11), draws an inference (v. 12a), and concludes with an escalation of the original question (v. 12b). At first glance, Jesus seems to be arguing Torah, seeking a precedent from which to argue from the lesser to the greater. However, it is unclear just what precedent he is invoking. At least two possibilities can be found, but neither is promising. Exodus 21:33–34 refers to an animal falling into an open pit, but the concern of the passage is that the owner of the pit compensate his neighbor for the death of the ox or donkey that occurs, and

Deuteronomy 22:1–4 deals with returning to its owner an animal that has wandered away or lifting up an animal that has fallen on the road. Neither text really offers a precedent for Jesus' argument. So the saying in verse 11 appears to be a parable, in the original sense of *mashal*, a riddle to be puzzled out. In fact, Gundry has argued that Matthew composed the parable based on Luke 14:1–6 and 15:1–7.[32] However, the saying may be Q (Luke 14:5 = Matt. 12:11), in spite of significant differences between the two versions of the saying. Variations aside, both versions do point to a similar argument. If the Torah does not have an exact precedent, it does speak a great deal about oxen, donkeys, and sheep, because of their value in an agrarian society. Sheep and oxen were valued so much that, if they were threatened by falling into a well (Luke 14:5) or a pit (Matt. 12:11), villagers would, without hesitation, rescue them. Nor would the rescuer be accused of violating the Sabbath. If this is the case, then why should anyone object to restoring a human being to wholeness? Why are beasts of burden visible while the deformed man invisible?

The issue is less about how the Sabbath is to be kept than it is about why the Sabbath is to be kept and for whom it is to be kept. How is it that the Torah can be read to render a man with a withered hand invisible while focusing on oxen and sheep? So the parable sets up the hearer by focusing on the lesser and posing a scenario that everyone will hear in essentially the same way. The next step seems equally reasonable, a familiar argument from the lesser to the greater, "of how much more value is a man than a sheep!" (v. 12a). But this seemingly innocuous inference raises the specter that Jesus might heal the man with the withered hand, the very person whose presence originally triggered the conflict. But the healing cannot occur until its justification is clear. This is why Jesus reformulates the question that began the debate: "so it is lawful (= consistent with Torah) to do good on the sabbath" (v. 12b). The conclusion is sweeping, far exceeding the boundaries drawn by the initial question, "Is it lawful to heal on the sabbath?" (v. 10b). In his riposte, Jesus has redrawn the boundaries for Sabbath observance, which now includes "doing good" to others. The Sabbath is not so much about avoiding scribal definitions of work as it is about showing mercy to others.

In the prophets, the Sabbath is often linked with the covenant, so that the violation of one entails the abnegation of the other. Isaiah links keeping the covenant with not profaning the Sabbath (56:2, 6), and he identifies trampling the Sabbath with pursuing one's own affairs (58:13–14). Similarly, Jeremiah associates keeping the Sabbath with refraining from doing business in Jerusalem on that day (17:24–25), and Ezekiel, in his debunking history of the people, defines Sabbath violation as ignoring the covenant (20:14–16). In the period of the restoration, Nehemiah ordered the gates of Jerusalem closed on the Sabbath to prevent trafficking in the city (13:15–22). His assumption also seems to be that profaning the Sabbath is violating the covenant. Any change in defining the Sabbath, therefore, carried covenant implications. By redefining the question asked of him (v. 10b), Jesus is restating the meaning of the covenant (v. 12b). The covenant based on mercy includes doing good to others, not just avoiding the violation of purity stipulations. Jesus' restatement carries an implicit claim that he can broker such a reinterpreted covenant. When he assumes this role, he places himself in direct conflict with his interlocutors, who assume that priests alone can claim that role. Like his opponents, Jesus is propogating an "oral Torah" of his own that, like its Pharisaic counterpart, has the power to explain how the covenant promise is meant to be lived.

Why not end the challenge-riposte here? What more is needed? Unearthing the political nature of the conflict may help to answer those questions. The group who challenged Jesus by asking the initial question is composed either of local operatives with ties to Jerusalem or of representatives from Jerusalem who have traveled to Galilee to ensure compliance with their reading of the Torah. They are the moral entrepreneurs and rule-enforcing intermediaries who protect the role of the priests as brokers of the covenant by means of offering sacrifices and keeping the festivals. Jesus has challenged their authority to claim that role. How will the impasse be resolved? The healing serves this purpose by confirming Jesus as a reliable and empowered broker of God's covenant mercy. The issue really is neither Sabbath keeping nor the abolition of the Sabbath, a stance that would be unthinkable to any Galilean peasant. Rather, the issue is whose claim to broker God's covenant will receive a grant of honor from the crowd of onlookers. An honor-shame riposte is meant to be a public activity and, if the "synagogue" is a marketplace or other public space, the conflict occurs in the right setting. In front of these adversaries, the healing itself is not without irony. The healing restores the man's hand, "whole like the other" and, therefore, renders him clean, since holiness entails wholeness. Any blemish or physical deformity renders one perpetually unclean. The power of the scribes and Pharisees is to classify and define who is pure, who is not, and who cannot be. The power of the covenantal God, for whom Jesus serves as broker, restores and recreates.

In his study of Jesus' miracles, Meier noted an interesting outcome:

> the historical fact that Jesus performed extraordinary deeds deemed by himself and others to be miracles is supported most impressively by the criterion of multiple attestation of sources and forms and the criterion of coherence. . . . The curious upshot of our investigation is that, viewed globally, the tradition of Jesus' miracles is more firmly supported by the criteria of historicity

than are a number of other well-known and often readily accepted traditions about his life and ministry.[33]

Yet the discussion of any particular miracle may provide grounds for regarding it as a creation of the early church, as Meier's subsequent work illustrates.[34] This study assumes that Jesus did heal and exorcise but does not attempt to determine how he did it or what such healings might entail. It is enough to observe the role that a healing or exorcism serves in the larger conflictual context of which it is a part. As the earlier chart of Sabbath controversies shows, healings and exorcisms are often embedded within larger debates and serve the interests of those clashes, rather than standing on their own. This means that reconstructing the context of the conflict is a necessary prerequisite to understanding the role of the healing or exorcism. Combining healings and controversies within a single pericope is also a reminder that Jesus was more than a debater and a wordsmith. He was a figure whose actions, no less than his teaching, mediated the power of the covenant God. In the case of the man with the withered hand, Jesus' pattern of reflection (debate) and action (healing) provides a glimpse of the way these two components of his public work came together. In what he said and did, Jesus remained a prophetic pedagogue of the oppressed engaged in the praxis of the justice of the reign of God. If praxis is, as Freire defined it, "reflection and action upon the world in order to transform it," then Jesus was certainly engaged in transforming the world of Palestine.[35]

The conclusion to the controversy raises another set of questions (v. 14). Sanders is convinced that, in this conflict, nothing could have happened to warrant such an extreme reaction. At their most extreme, the Pharisees would have concluded that Jesus stretched the "save life" rule more than they would have done.[36] Malina and Rohrbaugh conclude that the Pharisees "are understandably infuriated and determine to kill him to get satisfaction for their besmirched honor."[37] The latter emphasize the high stakes involved in the honor-shame riposte as well as the consequences of losing honor and, therefore, losing face. If the insult was considered great enough and the threat posed by Jesus menacing enough, then they could well have considered a violent solution to their problem. Sanders does not think the debate could have lethal consequences because he does not consider the political character of the conflict. It is more than a clash of ideas; it is a power struggle. If the conclusion cited in verse 14 were historically accurate, it is impossible to know where it fits in a chronology of Jesus' public work. The closer to the end of his public activity, the more likely it is to be accurate. Still, it is improbable that a single incident would have triggered such a reaction unless it was the straw that broke the camel's back. Even under these circumstances, the reaction would have been in response to a pattern of such encounters, not as the result of a single one.

The pericope of the healing of the bent woman (Luke 13:10–17) reinforces many of the themes introduced in the healing of the man with the withered hand. It is cast in the form of a challenge-riposte but, in this case, Jesus initiates the challenge by healing the woman (vv. 12–13). The healing consists of a solemn declaration followed by the laying on of hands. The declaration is appropriately in the passive voice, indicating that Jesus is announcing what God is doing (v. 12b). He does not claim healing power for himself but acts as a broker, a claim signified by the laying on of hands. Nevertheless, his action may have raised the question whether Jesus violated the Sabbath prohibition against work. The woman recognizes Jesus as the broker of God's healing power, so "she praised God," not Jesus (v. 13b). This opening exchange between Jesus and the woman contains a complete miracle story (vv. 10–13). Nothing more is needed, and if it had circulated by itself, it would have shown Jesus responding to the needs of an individual. But the incident is more complicated, for the healing, conducted as it was on the Sabbath, hurls an honor challenge at the synagogue leadership, and "the ruler of the synagogue," knowing that his honor is on the line, responds.

The identity of the "ruler of the synagogue" cannot be known precisely. He is most likely a local figure, prominent in his village. It is probable that he has Pharisaic leanings, but there is no certain way to tell. His concern to preserve the Sabbath from encroachments was shared by a wide variety of Judeans, including Sadduccees and Essenes. He appeals directly to the creation account in Genesis 1:1–2:3 and draws a seemingly obvious inference from the story. It is shameful to heal on the Sabbath, for healing is work, and work on the Sabbath violates the Sabbath. The woman's condition was not life threatening and, therefore, it could have been treated on any other day of the week (v. 14). By appealing to the creation account, the ruler invokes what is widely recognized as honorable and, by grounding his objection in that portion of the Torah, he hopes to clothe it in the righteous and honorable garment of unassailable authority.

Although he may seem callous, the ruler of the synagogue knows how important the Sabbath has been as a focus of identity for the people of Israel and Judah. In 586 B.C.E., when the temple was destroyed and Jerusalem sacked, the people of God lost access to sacred space. The place of sacrifice was no longer standing. But their conquerors could not deprive them of sacred time, and so the people centered their continuing identity in keeping the Sabbath, most likely in the emerging institution that would become the synagogue. To assault the Sabbath, then, was no small matter. It constituted an attack on the very heart of Judean identity and, as such, it threatened to impair creation and return the people to the chaos from which they had emerged. This is why the appeal to the creation account is so powerful in this context. The ruler implies that Jesus is a chaotic and disorganizing force, undermining the order of creation and subverting the rituals that preserve its order. Even a healing, when out of place, is not a cause for rejoicing but a cause for concern, and the healing of the woman is a healing out of place and, therefore, deviant.

Of course, the strong response of the ruler of the synagogue puts Jesus on the spot. In typical fashion, Jesus responds by labeling the ruler and his loyalists in the synagogue. They are "hypocrites" (*hypokritai*). The meaning of this label is not immediately clear, because the ruler of the synagogue is not a hypocrite in the modern sense of the word, namely, one who says one thing and does another. The Pharisees were dedicated and lived by their rules. The basic meaning of the word *hypokritēs* is "a stage actor," and by extension it came to mean a "pretender" or "dissembler."[38] In the context of this hostile encounter, Jesus may be calling the ruler of the synagogue an imposter who plays the role of brokering the "instruction" (this is the basic meaning of Torah) of the covenant God but actually acts as a functionary of a corrupt temple system that oppresses the very people of the land it was ordained to serve. Seen in this light, the ruler is not a hypocrite because he says one thing and does another but because he portrays himself as honorable defender of God's Torah and broker of its meaning when he is actually dissembling in order to obstruct the unexpected healing power of the covenant God brokered by Jesus.

Having attacked his accuser, Jesus must find a way to demonstrate the honorable nature of his healing, and he does so in two ways. First, he appeals to common practice, "loosing" an animal "bound" to a manger to lead it to water. For the appeal to work rhetorically it must refer to what everyone would agree to; it is a noncontroversial example that is about to become a highly controversial precedent. The purpose of this reference to common practice is to indicate that the prohibition against work is not absolute. Many forms of activity are countenanced on the Sabbath and not regarded as work. If ordinary practices, like loosing an animal from the manger and leading it to water, are acceptable, then where does one draw the line, or in Jesus' case, where will he redraw the line? Second, Jesus argues from the lesser to the greater by comparing the animal's tether to the woman's bondage (v. 16). The significance of the woman is captured in the way Jesus speaks of her, as "a daughter of Abraham" (v. 16a). As Malina and Rohrbaugh note,

> Illness in antiquity was a social as well as a physical phenomenon. A person with a disease or deformity was socially as well as physically abnormal. Healing therefore required reestablishing relationships as well as restoring physical health.[39]

The woman was "bound" by Satan, but loosed on the Sabbath. What better day to be released from Satan's bondage and restored to the community of Abraham's kin than the Sabbath?

The language of "binding" and "loosing" carries other overtones. The task of the perpetuators of the oral Torah was either to bind the people to a reading of Torah or to loose them from a particular reading. So the language in which the debate is cast echoes the social function of people like the "ruler of the synagogue." By his exorcism (or healing) and his portrayal of it, Jesus is essentially loosing the people in the synagogue from a particular reading of the Sabbath provisions. As he has broken Satan's control over the woman's body, so he is breaking the ruler's control over the members of the synagogue. The two acts, one physical and one political, parallel each other. The healing was not as innocent and good-hearted as it seemed. It was indeed a challenge to the control of the synagogue over people's lives, and it intended to undermine the authority and position of the ruler of the synagogue.

If the Lukan conclusion (v. 17) reflects any historical echoes at all, it recalls the outcome of the challenge-riposte. Jesus received a grant of public honor while his adversaries were shamed. In the zero sum game that was the riposte, this means that Jesus won and the ruler of the synagogue lost. By means of such encounters, Jesus acquired a status not supplied by the circumstances of his birth and family ties (the traditional sources of ascribed honor).

The Sabbath controversies in the synagogue are important because they are part of Jesus' larger strategy. They prepare the way for understanding the action in the temple. Every Sabbath controversy in a "synagogue" setting is a preparation and a practice run for the attack on the temple itself. It is as though Jesus practiced his tactics in the synagogue debates before shifting his strategy to confront the priestly rulers in Jerusalem.

Sabbath Controversy and the Little Tradition

The pericope of Jesus and the disciples plucking grain on the Sabbath (Mark 2:23–28; Matt. 12:1–8; Luke 6:1–5) is, like all the texts examined in this chapter, considered to be a creation of the early church. Sanders ridicules the setting of the incident to expose its implausibility.

> Jesus' disciples are picking grain, when suddenly Pharisees appear. But what were they doing in the midst of a grain field on the sabbath? Waiting on the off-chance that someone might pick grain? We have here, again, retrojection.[40]

Sanders has not been alone in puzzling about the setting of the pericope. Eduard Schweizer asked, "Where do these Pharisees come from, since one is permitted to go only about half a mile on the Sabbath?"[41]

The narrative integrity of the passage has been questioned as well. Hultgren supposes that the original controversy story was contained in verses 23, 24, and 27. But, he judges, not even this original controversy story was unitary, since verse 27 did not need the framing provided by verses 23–24, but could stand on its own. The materials concerning David (vv. 25–26) were added later, as was the christological conclusion in verse 28.[42] Schweizer speculates that the pericope was assembled in three stages. First came the saying of Jesus in verse 27 (perhaps elucidated by v. 28). The Davidic material (vv. 25–27) was added to explain the new state of affairs implied by the original saying. These materials probably reflect the debate between "the church and Judaism." Finally, the grain field setting was provided (vv. 23–24).[43] On both historical and literary grounds, then, the passage would appear to be surrounded with "more than a slight air of artificiality."[44]

The question of the setting must be addressed. If the pericope presents the reader with an impossible situation, then it will necessarily be judged an artificial construct, or what Bultmann called "an imaginary scene."[45] The relationship between fields and villages varied in Samaria and Galilee. Shimon Dar has conducted an extensive survey of Samaria, and shorter studies have been conducted on the settlements in the mountains of Lower Galilee and the patterns of agriculture utilized in the fields and hills of that region.[46] The larger features of Galilean regionalism have been discussed extensively by Eric Meyers.[47] Villages not built on the slopes or ridges of valleys were often built in the midst of the fields, orchards, and vineyards under their purview. If a village were sizable and its fields extensive, then villagers would construct paths connecting the village to its fields. Since each village constructed its own system of roads and paths, without attempting to connect them to neighboring villages, it is possible to estimate the limits of land associated with each village. Where the paths end, the village land ends. The villages themselves were connected by a network of rural roads. In the interest of using every bit of land, fields were often planted right up to the edge of the village. Or a village might plant an orchard of olive trees or a vineyard close to the buildings of the village, depending on the character of the land and its prudent usage.[48] The land surrounding villages was likely to be a patchwork quilt of fields, orchards, and vineyards, most of whose produce would go to Herod and the Herodians who controlled as much of the production of the towns and villages as they could.

Depending on the location of paths and crops, it would be quite possible for villagers, keeping Sabbath in the village square or near a "village gate," to observe what was happening in their fields, even if, owing to their scruples about keeping the Sabbath, they would not leave the village to investigate or protest. It is, therefore, at least possible to construct a setting for the pericope. Jesus and the disciples are traveling between villages, perhaps cutting through the fields, trying to find a way from the end of one set of field paths to another as they move from the domain of one village to its neighbor. This is why they must begin "to make their way" (*autou ērxanto hodon poiein*) through the fields of wheat. Mark notes that they are "bypassing" (as J. Duncan Derrett translates *paraporeuesthai*), a verb that can connote a certain furtiveness (cf. Mark 9:30). Derrett assumes that they are bypassing to avoid the "quadrilateral Sabbath limits" that defined how far one could walk on the Sabbath.[49] They could equally well be keeping to off-road paths in order to avoid contacts with a growing number of enemies. In Samaria, at least, forts were placed at strategic points along rural roads to provide "protection" to travelers and probably to collect tolls and imposts as well. In the process of moving from field to field, Jesus and the disciples trample some of the wheat, and, rather than waste it, they glean it as they go. From the village, the peasants watch them approach, and since it is Sabbath, either visiting Pharisees or local rulers of the synagogue are present, perhaps leading a village "synagogue" gathering in the open square. As Jesus and the disciples enter the village, the Pharisees challenge them. The point of this reconstruction is not to assert that this is the way it happened, but to suggest that it is possible to create a plausible scenario for understanding verses 23–24. At the very least, it should give pause to those contented with ridiculing the opening scene of the pericope.

Jesus and the disciples walk straight into a challenge-riposte. The problem is to determine exactly what they had done that was a Sabbath violation (v. 24). Is it the fact that they traveled beyond the limits prescribed for the Sabbath? Or the fact that they have trampled grain stalks? Or that they have stripped the ears of grain? With regard to the last alternative, Deuteronomy 23:25 would seem to permit such activity, although it does not specifically mention the Sabbath. Whatever the charge, the Pharisees, representatives of the great tradition, shame Jesus by exposing the behavior of his disciples. They accuse them of violating the Sabbath. The challenge has been issued, and the grievance filed. Jesus must respond, and when he does, his reply is surprising. It begins with a dig, or as Myers says, "a wry poke," at his opponents:[50] "Have you never read . . . ?" One might reasonably expect a reference to Torah or the prophets, but Jesus selects an unusual text on which to make his case. He draws on the example of David (1 Sam. 21:1–6). The passage seems only minimally related to the situation of Jesus and his disciples and, as Robert Banks notes, "the point of the analogy is contested."[51] Some find the point to be the conflict between ritual observance and moral law, while others think the reference to David is a veiled christological claim (Jesus as son of David). Derrett sees the situation of Jesus as analogous to that of David. Both were real but unacknowledged kings on a campaign. This permitted each to "commandeer" what was needed.[52] This is why Jesus can claim food for his disciples as David claimed the shew-bread of the altar for his men.

A closer look at the passage from 1 Samuel 21:1–6 is warranted. Saul has decided to kill David, and Jonathan has helped David to escape (1 Sam. 20:1–42). When David arrives at Nob to speak with the priest Ahimelech, he is alone and on his own. This is what most commentators seem to overlook. David has no men, and the mission he describes to Ahimelech is pure prevarication. David is a coyote figure spinning a fictitious tale in order to get the "bread of the presence," which he should not be able to eat. He will shortly repeat his story in order to procure Goliath's sword from the priest (1 Sam. 21:8–9). Then, armed and provisioned, he continues his journey as a fugitive from Saul's mad intent. Only much later will he gather a group around him (1 Sam 22:2). But, at the moment he comes to the priest Ahimelech, he is alone and but a step ahead of the posse. Ahimelech and the priests at Nob will pay for their support of David. They are slaughtered; only Abiathar, Ahimelech's son, will escape (1 Sam. 22:11–23).

When Jesus responds to his challengers, he assumes the role of David and repeats David's deceptions as though they were true, and his Pharisaic interlocutors fail to catch him in his ploy. If Jesus identifies with David, it is not with David the king but David the fugitive, the coyote figure who lives by his wits while others are seeking to destroy him. This is a David figure who would be appreciated in the villages, a little tradition David, rather than the David of the royal court. Jesus has also stiffed his adversaries. By arguing, in effect, "what's good for David is good enough for me," Jesus indicates that he will follow David's lead and employ David's survival tactics. These Davidic traditions are similar to what Walter Brueggemann called "the trustful truth of the tribe,"[53] except that the peasants of Galilee had few illusions about royal figures. They were decidedly not naive. But the reference to "tribe" is appropriate in this context, since, for Brueggmann, tribe means

> a unit of society standing apart from and over against the regimentation and legitimation of the state. I do not mean simply rustic, ethnic prestate communities, but units of the marginal who are cast into the marginal role by social necessity and social coercion, who do not have access to the wealth and power of the state and who tend to be irreverent to the civilities of the state.[54]

The remnants of the tribes of Yahweh lived on in the villages of Galilee.[55] It is to these elements in the village that Jesus appealed by invoking David. As David evaded Saul, so Jesus is evading his enemies.

At this point in the Matthean parallel (12:5–7), Matthew introduces three sayings to clarify the conflict. Although it is unlikely that they were part of the debate, their introduction does enhance and clarify the kind of argument Jesus engaged in. The first saying (v. 5) focuses on the privileges of priests. They are allowed to perform sacrifices in the temple on the Sabbath (that is, they work) and yet are considered guiltless of breaking any Sabbath provision. The second, related saying claims that "something greater than the temple is here." The presence of similarly structured sayings in the tradition (Q: Luke 11:31–32 = Matt. 12:41–42) suggests that this was a familiar form of teaching, whether from Jesus or the early church. The temple saying need not be read christologically. But what is the "something greater than the temple" that has come? One answer is that it is the covenant God's forgiveness of debt and call to merciful living being brokered by Jesus.

The related saying (v. 7) combines a citation from Hosea (6:6) with a polemical attack. The Hosea citation raises an important question, because it sets sacrifice and mercy in opposition to each other. How can sacrifice be construed as merciless? The answer may be clearer if "sacrifice," by the principle of synecdoche, is intended as a reference to the whole temple system whose demands have become oppressive and exploitative. It demands sacrifice on more than one level. Not only does it demand sacrifices for its altar, but it demands that peasants sacrifice family obligations to support the central sanctuary, and it even demands that peasants sacrifice their survival needs to maintain their support of the sacrificial system and its priestly operatives. When these matters are on the line, the behavior of the hungry disciples in stripping the heads of grain is unimportant. To attack the disciples' behavior while ignoring the greater injustice which they perpetrate is like trying to take a sliver out of their neighbor's eye while ignoring the log in their own (cf. Matt. 7:4–5). This amounts to nothing less than condemning the guiltless (12:7b). In Mark 12:38–44, Jesus identifies the same pattern of injustice, when he warns against the scribes who "devour widows' houses" while maintaining a facade of piety by uttering "long prayers." The temple, which was supposed to support widows and orphans, is depicted as the institution that extracts their last copper coins.

The closing sayings (vv. 27–28) may well have circulated independently, but they fit this challenge-riposte as well. Jesus claims that his enemies have got it all wrong. They have forgotten that the Sabbath was God's provision for restoring human life and renewing human community. But they have turned the Sabbath into an endless series of tasks required to maintain purity. This system turns people into the objects of their system, rather than making them the subjects of God's creative caring. But the saying also implies that human beings can restore the Sabbath to suit the creative purposes of the covenant God. This is why Jesus and his disciples are changing the rules of the game, as their Sabbath stroll through the wheat fields indicates. They live as though they are not bound by their opponents' rules about the Sabbath. In this context, the "Son of Man" reference in 2:28 fits a familiar pattern. If it is simply a reference to an ordinary person ("mortal"), then Jesus is claiming that an ordinary lay person can create and change the rules that govern the observance of the Sabbath, if that person is brokering God's covenant mercy and love. This implies that peasants and Pharisees are on the same footing and can claim the same prerogatives. More importantly, the villagers need not take their cues from the Jerusalem priests but can work things out in their own context. If "Son of Man" is a veiled self-reference, Jesus is identifying his role as God's broker of this new way of doing things, and if the phrase refers to "one like me," then Jesus is claiming the same role for his disciples and others who follow him. The "Son of Man" reference can be interpreted so that it fits the context of the dispute remarkably well.

CONCLUSION

This chapter has examined a variety of challenge-riposte texts to indicate how they might have communicated the dynamics of the conflicts that animated Jesus' public work and preserved in compact form the types of issues debated. This chapter does not assume that these pericopes contain verbatim reports. The effort has been to discover whether they retain echoes of longer and more complicated differences. The commentary wrapped around them has been an attempt to enflesh the dry bones found in these encounters. This is especially important because, for so many years, interpreters have held that the issues found in these texts reflect the debates and christological concerns of the early church. The interpretations in this chapter have proposed that the topics found in these texts can be contextualized so that they reflect the situation of the historical Jesus. If these readings are arguable, one can ask no more. Certainty is not possible in this kind of historical reconstruction and reimagining. Hopefully, the readings are persuasive enough to encourage engagement and conversation.

9

The Temple, the Land, and the Reign of God

The previous three chapters have sketched a course for Jesus' public ministry that would bring him into conflict with the temple authorities and their representatives. There is little evidence to suggest that Jesus engaged the Roman colonial overlords, although, as Horsley has argued persuasively, Jesus conducted his work in a context of imperial domination and colonial occupation.[1] Rather, he focused his attention on the temple and its claim to the loyalties of the Galilean peasants, and he devoted some attention to Herodian client rule.

This chapter proposes that Jesus' strategy was to separate the temple from the land and to critique the domination systems found throughout his world. He did this, in part, by hearkening back to a time when Yahweh was thought to be the only ruler worthy of the people's loyalties. This was what Jesus called "the reign of God," and it was a critique of all ruling classes and rulers.

THE LAND AND THE TEMPLE: AN INDISSOLUBLE BOND?

Seen through peasant eyes, the land was, first and foremost, a gift of Yahweh. Yahweh had promised the land to the patriarchs, as the earliest descriptions of the covenant reveal (Gen. 12:1–3; 15:1–21). If the land belonged to Yahweh alone, then it was his to apportion as he willed.[2] Leviticus expresses this conviction quite clearly: "The land shall not be sold in perpetuity, for the land is mine; with me, you are but aliens and tenants" (25:23). Yahweh's effective control and disposition of the land is indicated by the fact that he distributed the land to the tribes according to their size (Num. 26:52–56). The principles of equity and justice guide the division of the land. Because the land is a gift, the people must leave their gleanings for the sojourner and the poor (Lev. 19:9–10; 23:22; Deut.

23:25; 24:19–22), and because "the land is mine," the people must bring their tithes to the Lord, as a sign of their gratitude, their recognition of Yahweh's generosity (Lev. 27:30–33; Deut. 14:28–29; 26:1–15).

The same fundamental conviction underlies the practice of the sabbatical year, when the land was to lie fallow, debts were to be canceled, and slaves were to be freed (Ex. 21:2–6; 23:10–11; Lev. 25:1–7; Deut. 15:1–11). But, while the land may have lain fallow, debts were not canceled, nor were the victims of debt servitude always released (Lev. 26:34–35; Jer. 34:8–22). Nehemiah exhorted the people to keep the Sabbath because he saw the violation of the Sabbath as a step that would lead to the abandonment of the sabbatical year (10:28–31). The entire cycle of Sabbath and sabbatical was supposed to culminate in the celebration of jubilee (Lev. 25:8–38; cf. also Isa. 61:1–4; Luke 4:16–30, possible references to jubilee). If the Sabbath was kept imperfectly, there is little evidence to suggest that the jubilee was ever observed at all, except to use as a means for reckoning time. The reason for the nonobservance of sabbatical and jubilee traditions appears to coincide with the attenuation of the theology of the land that lay behind them.

In the first century, the traditional view of the land was being eclipsed by another perspective, shared by Roman conquerors, Herodian client rulers and even the temple elite, all of whom saw the land as a commodity to be exploited for economic gain. The conflict was not new. The prophets had long denounced a ruling class who alienated peasants from the land in order to pursue the enhancements of life made possible by the monarchy (Micah 2:2; Isa. 5:8; Neh. 5:1–10), and the Torah itself had recognized the possibility that its provisions might not be heeded (Deut. 15:1–11). The story of Naboth's vineyard (1 Kings 21:1–19) indicated how fragile a peasant's claim to the land could be when faced with a powerful enemy, but Naboth's attachment to the land was clear and deeply rooted (21:3–4). It was his "ancestral inheritance." This was a view most likely shared by the peasants of Galilee, who believed that their ancestral plot was a visible embodiment of their covenant with Yahweh. H. G. Kippenberg summarizes the clash of views as follows:

> The sources describing the social history (of Palestine) in the Roman period testify to the oppression . . . of free peasants under the system of the appropriation of surplus. The important institutions of the older era which arose as resistance against class formation . . . are no longer in force. . . . The erection of an economy of profit was a contradiction to the egalitarian religious traditions.[3]

Since peasants lived literally one harvest removed from ruin, the fruitfulness of the land was an important matter, and this need to ensure the fertility of the land may explain their attachment to the temple in Jerusalem. In peasant life, there was little margin for error.

In his survey of Galileans' attitude toward the temple, Freyne notes that the Galileans were not scrupulous about paying their tithes, although they did try to maintain their offerings, and they were lax in paying their half-shekel temple tax, but, in spite of it all, they did remain loyal to the temple in Jerusalem.[4] Why?

> Their attachment was based on the belief that the God of the temple in Jerusalem was the one who provided them with the necessities of life from the land, and faithful worship of him was therefore of paramount importance. . . . for the Galilean peasants the Jerusalem temple was not the center of messianic hope but the source of their confidence in the ongoing struggle for the necessities of life.[5]

It was a pattern of perceived dependence and loyalty that could be exploited to the advantage of the priestly caste and their aristocratic cohorts. This structural situation produced the system of perpetual indebtedness described earlier in this study (see chap. 6). The temple allied itself with an internal ruling class who collaborated with their Roman masters, producing an arrangement of convenience and necessity, since the Roman prefect controlled the high-priestly appointments. As the priestly elites curried favor with Rome in order to cement their own standing, they increasingly shifted the interests of the temple from serving the people of the land to exploiting them for the resources they needed to consolidate and maintain their position. This development placed the peasants in a dilemma. If they were perpetually indebted to the temple, by virtue of not paying their tithes, then they were barred from effective participation in the benefits of the sacrificial system. Yet, the fertility of their land and the timeliness of the rains depended on God's favor. What were they to do?

Violence and the Land: The Parable of the Sower (Mark 4:3–9)

Viewed as a parable of Jesus, the sower is told in two scenes, the unpromising sowing (vv. 4–7) and the unexpected harvest (v. 8). Each of the scenes presents a sequence of three. The first scene describes three sowings that promise little, whereas the second scene describes a triply bountiful harvest, yielding thirtyfold, sixtyfold and a hundredfold. In chapter 4 of this study I suggested that the verbs in scene one form a pattern that can be charted as follows:

Pattern	first seed	second seed	third seed
sowing	seed fell	seed fell	seed fell
predator introduced	birds came	sun rose	thorns grew
violent outcome	devoured	scorched	choked

The repetition of violent outcomes creates dissonance with the apparently ordinary, everyday scene of the parable, a peasant broadcasting seed on the fields. What is going on in the parable?

In an earlier study of the parables, I compared them to what Paulo Freire called "codifications." Codifications are pictures of the world that become the focus for peasant reflections on the way that "world," as a social and political construction of reality, functions. As groups of peasants decode the codifications placed before them, they discover how systems of oppression and exploitation work, as well as how they can respond to them.[6] Freire used visual codifications, because he lived in a culture that lived by its eyes, but in an illiterate oral culture peasants live by their ears. This makes it likely that Jesus would have used aural codifications, such as parables. The parable of the sower can be read in this framework, but, if it is, what is the parable codifying? The most striking feature of the parable is the discrepancy between the seed sown and the seed harvested, a discrepancy that traces to the presence of the predators in the first, most lengthy, scene of the parable. The opening scene may reflect the peasants' habit of dissembling by displacing and, therefore, provides access to what James Scott calls the "hidden transcript" of the oppressed. When peasants live in a setting in which their rulers control the vast majority of the population through force and intimidation, they develop two ways of speaking and acting. When they are "on stage," that is, in public, they act and speak as loyal and obedient subjects who consent to the rule of the elites. But when they are "off stage," that is, in their own village with trusted neighbors, they speak the hidden transcript of their opposition and resistance to the exploitation that dehumanizes them, and they analyze their situation more truthfully. Rather than speak about a concern in a clear and straightforward manner, the peasant, when on stage, will speak indirectly and in code. Scott calls this kind of public speech "a hidden transcript."[7]

Read in this way, the violent verbs provide a clue for reading the parable. The work of the sower seems routine, but every broadcast of seed attracts a predator. Of course, the predators appear as coded symbols: the birds, the sun, and the thorns. But their presence raises questions for the hearers to ponder. Who swoops down on the seed sown by the peasant villagers and devours their work? Whose scorched-earth economic policy burns up the crops year after year? Who aggressively chokes the growth of the peasants' seed so that it yields a subsistence crop and nothing more? When the harvest is gathered in, the representatives of the Herodian aristocrats who exploit the villages and the servants of Antipas himself actually appear on the threshing floor to claim their tribute, rents, and taxes. They devour and choke the peasants' harvest, leaving barely enough for subsistence and survival, a scorched-earth policy pursued year after year, driving the peasants into increasingly degrading forms of dependency.

By placing the coded symbols of the elites in the first scene of the parable, Jesus can address the more fundamental question of the land in the second scene. But "other seed fell onto the good land (*eis tēn gēn tēn kalēn*) and brought forth grain . . . thirtyfold, sixtyfold and a hundredfold." The reference to the land should not be missed. The land is still God's "good" gift, and it remains fruitful, abundantly fruitful; the land is still "a land flowing with milk and honey" (Ex. 3:8, 17), still the Promised Land (Ex. 6:8). It produces thirty, sixty and a hundred times more than the peasants need to survive. How, then, can the peasants of the land be living in poverty, near destitution, when the land produces so abundantly? The problem is not with the land; it lies elsewhere, the elsewhere already portrayed in coded and ambiguous form in the opening scene of the parable. The scarcity with which the peasants live is not the result of an unproductive land, no longer blessed by Yahweh because the villagers cannot pay their tithes. To the contrary, even without peasant tithes to support the temple, the land produces abundantly, a situation that implies that the temple may not be the key that unlocks the abundance of the good land. The problem is not with the production of the land but with the distribution of what is produced.

It is possible that the parable of the sower encodes a hidden transcript that analyzes the problem of scarcity in an abundant land. The forces that destroy the seed in the parable—the birds, the sun, and the thorns—are portrayed in violent terms. They represent the forces that attempt to devour, scorch, and choke the fruitful land. The problem, then, is neither the lack of compliance in fulfilling the purity codes nor the refusal to pay tithes. The problem is with the rapacious and greedy who devour the peasants' crops and choke their efforts to make ends meet. To blame the scarcity on their inability to fulfill the Torah is to distract the peasants from the true source of their poverty, the ruling elites who take almost everything and leave almost nothing.

Although 4:9 is an independent saying of Jesus, it certainly fits the context, because it is a call to "hear" the hidden transcript contained in the parable. Listen to the parable but hear the hidden transcript it conveys through its dark signs and obscure symbols. The saying is reminiscent of Jesus' comments in the Sermon on the Mount, "so have no fear of them; for nothing is covered that will not be revealed, or hidden that will not be known" (Matt. 10:26; Mark 4:22; Luke 8:17). The time will come when what is uttered in secret will be proclaimed plainly, "What I say to you in the dark, tell in the light, and what you hear whispered, proclaim from the housetops" (Matt. 10:27). The day will come when hidden transcripts will become public transcripts, but for the moment, they remain underground as surreptitious messages for those with "ears to hear."

The Land without the Temple (Mark 4:26–29): Thy Kingdom Come, Thy Sabbatical Be Done

The parable of the seed growing secretly (Mark 4:26–29), found only in Mark, has puzzled interpreters. Dodd noted that the meaning of the parable depended on where the interpreter placed the emphasis: if on the seed, then the reign of God is within; if on the process of inevitable growth, then the reign of God is akin to progress in history; and, if on the harvest, then the reign of God is an eschatological event confined to the future.[8] Jeremias read the parable as counseling patient waiting upon the purposes of God. The man in the parable "followed [his] ordered round of sleeping and waking, night and day: without his taking anxious thought . . . or any active steps, the seed grows from stalk to ear, and from ear to ripened corn."[9] The parable was, then, a contrast parable proclaiming "the great assurance." Crossan took his cue from the version of the parable in the *Gospel of Thomas* 85:15–19, where the emphasis is on the activity of the farmer. This most likely means that the earliest version of the parable contained only verses 26–27, 29. It was a "parable of action," indicating that the reaper knew just the right moment to begin his activity.[10] Bultmann was certain that the meaning of the parable was contained in the word we translate as "by itself" (*automatē*) but was uncertain as to its meaning: "What does 'by itself' mean? That the kingdom of God comes without your agency with the same certainty as the seed grows and produces fruit?"[11] To make matters more confusing, Bultmann thought that the "kingdom of God" introduction was secondary, thus obscuring the parable's original meaning.[12]

The parable does focus, at least in passing, on "the land," which produces "by itself." The word is odd, but it does appear in the Greek translation of the Old Testament in Lev. 25:5, where it translates the Hebrew *sapiyah*, a reference to "the free growth of the sabbatical year,"[13] and in 25:11 it contains the same reference in the context of jubilee (see Lev. 25:1–17). The difficulty with this reading is that the parable seems to picture, not the unsown growth of the sabbatical year, but the sown crop of the man who scattered seed. The emphasis is on the productivity of the land as a force in itself; the land is not dependent on its inhabitants worrying the crop from sowing to weeding to harvest. The land brings the crop to fruition; all the sower needs to do is harvest it when the time is ripe. The word *automatē* captures this process as "something that happens without visible cause."[14] If Jesus is focusing on the land, then he may well be telling a story that emphasizes the disjuncture between land

and temple. The land does not require the sacrificial system and elaborate purity injunctions to ensure its fertility. The land produces seemingly by itself, reflecting the invisible generative power that derives from the blessing of the covenant God, a blessing unrelated to the machinations of the temple and the manipulations of the priests. The allusion to the sabbatical policy of letting the land lie fallow fits this picture. The land blessed by God's creative hand is so fertile that it produces even during the sabbatical year when it has not been sown (Ex. 23:10–11; Lev. 25:2–7). But this blessing is rooted in God's covenant with the people, not the fulfillment of the purity codes and the maintenance of the sacrificial system.

The closing line of the parable alludes to Joel 3:13, an oracle of judgment (Joel 3:9–21). The connection to the reading of the parable proposed here is not entirely clear. However, the linking of harvest with judgment does resonate with the situation in the Palestine of Jesus' day, where every harvest that deprived the people of the land of all but a bare subsistence was a moment calling for judgment and vindication—judgment on the exploiters, who no longer regard the land as an embodiment of the covenant with the people, and vindication of the exploited, who suffer the deprivations caused by such neglect (cf. Deut. 9:4–7; 11:8–21). It is possible that the coming reign of God was just the moment when the hoped-for vindication would appear. Linking the parable with the reign of God (4:26a) may be awkward but accurate. For Jesus, the renewal of the covenant is found in the coming kingdom, and the linkage of the kingdom with the judgment depicted by Joel suggests the theme of an eschatological reversal leading to justice in the land.

Whatever the outcome of the interpretation of the allusion to Joel, the central theme of the parable remains the strength of the land, even when it is not maintained by the temple system. Jesus saw the fertility of the land as a symbol of the continuing covenant of God with the people of the land, a covenant to which all had access through the brokering role that Jesus had assumed. If his assumption of this role created conflict, that was to be expected. Violence attends the sowing of the reign of God. However stiff the opposition, it could not prevent God from completing his work, as the parable of the secretly growing seed hints.

If the sabbatical image is integral to the parable, the parable may be relating the justice denied, by the abrogation of the sabbatical year, to the coming reign of God, which will restore the practice of sabbatical to the land. The meaning of the parable would then be, to paraphrase the Lord's Prayer, "thy kingdon come, thy sabbatical be done on the land as it is in the reign of heaven."

One of Jesus' shortest parables makes essentially the same point. The treasure hidden in the field (Matt. 13:44) seems deceptively simple, even though commentators have read it in many ways. Crossan found this parable to be a "meta-parable" revealing the structure of the corpus of Jesus' parables. That structure was found in the parable's three central verbs: found, sells, buys. Taken together, they define the pattern of advent (found), reversal (sells), and action (buys). The parable depicts "a man whose normalcy of past-present-future is rudely but happily shattered."[15] At the close of the parable, he stands called to an undefined future "as absolute in its call as it is unspecified in its detail."[16] For Jeremias, the point of the parable is the overwhelming joy occasioned by the unexpected discovery. This is a metaphor for the joy found in the inbreaking of the reign of God.[17] Bernard Scott attempts to untangle the legality of the treasure finder's actions in reburying the treasure and buying the field, and after an extensive survey of options and opinions he concludes that the parable is about a treasure that "comes before our deeds" which is "not only grace but potential corruption."[18] Gundry believes that the parable is a Matthean composition stressing "the necessity of economic self-deprivation to true membership in the kingdom."[19]

The reading proposed here begins with the assumption that the association of field and treasure would not be lost on Jesus' peasant audience. In an agrarian society, land is both the guarantor of subsistence and the source of wealth. Every field (*agros*) is a source of treasure, and every field harbors a secret treasure, since almost every field produces more than enough for subsistence and survival. The land is the "good land" that the Lord has given to the people, a land filled with the treasure of streams, springs, fertile crops, and minerals (Deut. 8:1–20). Yet those who work the fields receive very little of the yield, because the ruling class controls the land and its usufruct. They are the ones who alienate peasants from their land in order to turn the land to more productive purposes in a monetizing economy.

The surprise of the parable is that a peasant, or a day laborer, reverses the process. In the parable, it is the peasant who purchases the land from a (presumably) rich landowner in order to secure the treasure for himself. The ethics of the parable are more of a concern to modern readers than to ancient auditors. The peasants would enjoy the coyotelike character who reburies the treasure and buys the field, cheating the owner of his treasure. But the scene is completely unrealistic; few peasants, and no day laborers, could afford to buy a field from those who controlled the land. It was just not feasible.

But the parable is not about economics from below but the reign of heaven from above. The land does indeed contain hidden treasures, but they are controlled by the current powers that be. The coming of the reign of heaven would reverse this control, so that peasants, even day laborers, who discover and discern the hidden treasure of the land, will one day possess the treasure hidden in the land. When they do, how will they act? Will they hoard the treasure for themselves (see Luke 12:16–21) or return the treasure of the land to the people for whom it was intended? In the present, the hidden treasure may carry a more prosaic meaning, since peasant villagers regularly hide and stow away whatever they can to preserve as much of the treasure of the land as possible before the tribute collectors and tax enforcers lay claim to the fruit of their labors. When the reign of heaven arrives, the treasure of the land will return to the hands of the people of the land who are now deprived of it. The parable then provides a glimpse of another reality when the dispossessed who work the land will one day reclaim the treasure of the land. "Blessed are the humble, for they shall inherit the land" (Matt. 5:5). The land is wealth, and the land is treasure, but it is a gift with a provision. To keep the land, the people must keep the covenant, especially its provisions for caring for the poor (Deut. 15:1–18).

Summary

This section has examined some of Jesus' parables dealing with the land. In the case of the parables of the sower and the secretly growing seed, Jesus emphasized the fruitfulness of the land, independent of the temple system in Jerusalem. In telling these parables, Jesus was driving a wedge between the temple and the land. If the temple and its sacrifices were not needed to ensure the fertility of the land, then the peasants had no reason to pay their tithes to the temple or to conform their lives to the purity standards and practices of the Pharisees. Both were irrelevant. After all, God sends "the rain on the just and the unjust," and he "makes his sun rise on the evil and on the good" (Matt. 5:45). If this is the character of God, then the rains will nourish the land because God wills it.

Why then were the peasants so desperately poor? Not because their land was not producing abundantly, but because they were being ruthlessly exploited and oppressed by internal elites and colonial overlords, all of whom took their tribute, tithes, and taxes from the peasant base. The treasure hidden in the fields they worked would remain hidden until that day when they could reclaim the land and its resources. If Jesus pursued this policy, then he ran afoul of local Herodian elites and Jerusalem rulers. His argument about the land affected the Romans only indirectly but affected them nevertheless, because any agrarian reformer posed a potential threat to the collection of tribute in a timely manner.

The Kingdom of God at the Close of the Century

At the close of the nineteenth century, Johannes Weiss published his study of Jesus' proclamation of the kingdom of God. His work called into

question the then regnant theological synthesis shaped by the leading figures of Protestant liberalism.[20] According to Weiss, the kingdom that
Jesus proclaimed looked nothing like the reign of God in the human heart
so treasured by liberal Protestants (Herrmann and Harnack), nor could it
be described as a social ideal to be realized in human history (Ritschl). It
was rather a proclamation of what God was about to do, without human
aid or assistance. On Jesus' lips, references to the kingdom of God were
thoroughly eschatological. Weiss, therefore, posed what Schweitzer called
the third alternative in the quest of the historical Jesus, "either eschatological or non-eschatological."[21] Following the work of Weiss, which was
confirmed and expanded by Schweitzer, New Testament scholars would
simply assume that Jesus' proclamation of the kingdom of heaven was eschatological, a view that would dominate the studies of Jesus' teaching
and ministry for most of the century. The problem to be addressed was
how to interpret this eschatological proclamation.

It is ironic that, as the century comes to a close, members of the Jesus
Seminar led by Marcus Borg have challenged this settled synthesis, much
as Weiss did a century earlier.[22] As noted in chapter 1 of the current
study, Borg first drafted his ideas in an essay in a memorial volume dedicated to his mentor, G. B. Caird. It was called, "An Orthodoxy Reconsidered: The End-of-the-World Jesus." Published in 1986, the essay led
to a more programmatic statement, "A Temperate Case for a Non-
Eschatological Jesus," which appeared in *Forum*, the journal of the Jesus
Seminar, in September 1986. In both essays, Borg argues that scholars
viewed the kingdom announced by Jesus as imminent because his kingdom sayings were wedded to the "coming Son of Man" sayings (e.g.,
Mark 8:38 // Luke 9:26; Mark 13:24–30; Matt. 16:27; Luke 12:8).
Taken by themselves, the kingdom of heaven sayings neither communicate nor connote any eschatological urgency at all. More importantly,
the kingdom sayings fail to include references to the Son of Man. The
Son of Man sayings and the kingdom sayings represent two discrete bodies of material. Since New Testament scholars have, by and large, dis-
counted the coming Son of Man sayings as authentic historical Jesus
material, they have effectively removed the foundation on which the eschatological edifice was built. As Borg puts it, "without the coming Son
of man sayings, there is no reason to think of the Kingdom of God as the
imminent end of the world" (54).

If not an evocation of apocalyptic eschatology, to what, then, does the
"kingdom of God" refer, and what does it mean? Borg has a ready answer. In the context of first-century Jewish life, the "kingdom of heaven"
was a symbol meant to invoke and evoke "the primordial tradition." The
primordial tradition is a view of life, shared by many cultures, which contrasts the world of everyday life with a world of spirit and numinous

power. Not only do the two worlds coexist, but inhabitants of the ordinary world can mediate and channel the power of the spiritual realm to this world. Such figures are usually shamans, healers, exorcists, prophets, and the like. This leads Borg to infer that Jesus used the phrase "kingdom of heaven" as

> a symbol pointing to the kingship of God—the divine power and sovereignty, compassion and justice. The reality of God as king could be known, and the power of the Spirit (God acting as king) could flow into this world. (57)

Since these two realms continually coexist, there is no reason to interpret the kingdom of God sayings as eschatological, that is, as statements about the end of the world.

Plowing similar terrain with different tools, Crossan argues that Jesus proclaimed a kingdom present in the here and now, a "sapiential kingdom of God," rather than an apocalyptic kingdom of God.[23] This sapiential kingdom is "the kingdom of Wisdom eternally present, available, on the one hand, to anyone who heeds her call and, on the other, punitively transcendent to all the evil rulers of the world."[24] This kingdom of "nuisances and nobodies" does not look to the future but solely to the present and centers its activities on "magic and meal," free healings and open commensality.[25]

Even when scholars speak of Jesus' proclamation as eschatological in some sense, they do not necessarily think of the coming kingdom as apocalyptic conflagration. Sanders believes that Jesus announced a form of "restoration eschatology," but this is not to be confused with traditional forms of apocalyptic thought.[26]

> There is other evidence which points to the expectation of an other-worldly kingdom in a different sense: one on an earth renewed by God's hand. . . . The idea of a new temple points toward an expectation of a kingdom on earth in which there are analogies to present life.[27]

So eschatology, even for a figure like Sanders, can be simultaneously otherworldly and worldly. The "otherworldly" component is necessary, since the renewal of the world can only be accomplished by an act of God, and yet the focus of the renewal is the world. So eschatology leads to the reconstitution of the world, not its dissolution. Ben Meyer argues a very similar position in which he focuses Jesus' eschatological message on the renewal of Israel.[28]

Wright believes that the meaning of the kingdom sayings can only be understood when they are placed within the larger narrative of Israel's history. Symbol takes its meaning from the story of which it is a part.

The same holds for the meaning of "eschatology," which Wright defines in the following way:

> Eschatology is the climax of Israel's history, involving events for which end-of-the-world language is the only set of metaphors adequate to express the significance of what will happen, but resulting in a new and quite different phase *within* space-time history.[29]

So eschatological language is a way of speaking about events that bring a phase of Israel's history to a close, ending one chapter of the story while opening a new one. But it is the same story, not the end of one narrative and the beginning of an entirely different story, or it is a way of taking the same story to an entirely new phase. In this way, Wright finds in eschatological language a way to express the discontinuity found in the continuity of history.

Following more overtly political agendas, both Horsley and Kaylor minimize the traditional eschatological understandings of the kingdom to pursue more earthly interpretations. Horsley defines the meaning of the kingdom in clearly political terms, while indicating why such an approach is in order:

> Jesus' overall perspective was that God was bringing an end to the demonic and political powers dominating his society so that a renewal of individual and social life would be possible. . . . Ironic as it might seem, the understanding of Jesus' preaching of the kingdom in terms of cosmic catastrophe led to apolitical quietism.[30]

Horsley then defines eschatology in terms similar to those advanced by Wright. This means that Jesus' language about the kingdom signals that God is about to do a new thing in the life of the people, "that God's new (expected) liberative action is at hand, is happening in and through the experience and actions of those very leaders and followers."[31] Although he does not appeal to the language of narrative and story, as does Wright, Horsley nevertheless spins a plot of "renewal, vindication and judgment" and fills it with scenes of banqueting, healing, renewal of village life, exorcisms, and forgiveness.

The discussion of eschatology has indeed taken a turn from the post-Schweitzer debates fueled by Bultmann (existential reinterpretation of eschatology), Dodd (realized eschatology), Jeremias (imminent yet future eschatology), and Cullmann (already but not yet eschatology), to name just a few. In spite of the considerable diversity of approaches, current scholars seem to have found some common ground, even if they have not achieved a large synthesis. With this background in mind, it is time to turn to the materials of the Synoptic tradition.

The Reign of God Is Like . . .

Both Mark and Matthew summarize Jesus' proclamation as announcing the imminent coming of the kingdom of heaven. Mark summarizes the typical message of Jesus as, "The time is fulfilled, and the kingdom of God is at hand; repent and believe" (1:15). The phrase "in the good news" is either a Markan addition or a restatement of the first part of the announcement. Matthew provides a shorter summary: "Repent, for the kingdom of heaven is at hand" (4:17). The imagery of the proclamation is political, and it does not require much imagination to understand how profoundly unsettling such an announcement could be in a world dominated by Roman imperial rule, Herodian client kingship, and the vestiges of a temple state in the Roman subprovince of Judea. By implication, none of those arrangements is "the reign of heaven," and therefore all are found wanting. The verb *kērussō* is poorly translated as "preaching." It refers to the announcement of a herald.[32] From the Homeric era forward, heralds were courtiers who represented a prince or other high royal figure. Their authority derived from this fact. "The essential point about the report which they gave is that it does not originate with them. Behind it stands a higher power. The herald does not express his own views. He is the spokesman for his master."[33] By extension, the role of herald was applied to prophets and philosophers, who were viewed as "heralds of the gods" (692–94). Although the verb *kērussō* is not often applied to prophetic speech, there are notable exceptions such as Isaiah 61:1 (700–702). In this well-known passage from Isaiah, the role of the herald is clear. "His word is efficacious because he is sent by God and the Spirit of God rests on him" (701). The same dynamic is present in the portrayal of Jesus' inaugural proclamation at Nazareth (Luke 4:16–30). All of this means that Jesus was not a lone voice crying in the wilderness of Herodian oppression, but a herald of God speaking with authority and not as one of the scribes (cf. Mark 1:22).

In an expansion of his basic formula, Matthew will include a triad of activities associated with Jesus' appearance as herald of the reign of heaven. He taught in the synagogues, proclaimed the good news of the kingdom, and healed diseases and infirmities (4:23). The role of this herald was more than announcing; he articulated the meaning of the coming reign of God, and he mediated its power. This is, in part, what is implied in his remark, "but if it is by the finger of God that I cast out demons, then the kingdom of God has come upon you" (Q: Luke 11:20 = Matt. 12:28). The disagreement in language between the two sayings is not as great as has been supposed. Whether Jesus accomplishes his exorcisms by the "finger" of God (Luke) or the "Spirit" of God (Matthew), he acts as a broker of God's power. The "finger of God" phrase echoes the struggle between

Moses and Pharaoh's magicians (Ex. 8:19). After Moses has produced the plague of gnats that Pharaoh's court magicians cannot reproduce, they conclude that "this is the finger of God," but Pharaoh ignores their insight and refuses to listen to them. The second reference to the finger of God relates to the giving of the Decalogue, "the two tablets of the covenant, tablets of stone, written with the finger of God" (Ex. 31:18; cf. Deut. 9:10). In both instances, the image of the finger of God refers to God's agency. The same thing could be said of the "spirit" of God in creation (Gen. 1:2) and in the anointing of people for appointed tasks (Gen. 41:37–45; Ex. 31:1–5; 35:30–35; Num. 24:1–9; 27:18–19; Judg. 3:10; 6:34; 11:29; 13:25; 14:6; 14:19; 15:14; 1 Sam. 10:6–7; 16:13, to cite just a few passages). In Ezra's speech to the people gathered for public confession of sins, he associates the spirit of the Lord with the prophets: "Many years you were patient with them and warned them by your spirit through the prophets; yet they would not listen" (Neh. 9:30). Both images, therefore, evoke a long history. If the finger of God inscribed the covenant with the people on tablets of stone, Jesus is renewing the covenant by re-inscribing it in the lives of people freed from demonic possession and other forms of bondage. They become the material on which the renewed covenant is inscribed. Their shattered lives made whole speak of the covenant-renewing power of the finger of God. As the "spirit" of God descended on the judges, called to lead the people through moments of threat and crisis, the same spirit now rests on Jesus to lead the people through another time of crisis and transition. In neither case is the implied role innocuous or apolitical. The association of the finger or spirit of God with God's redeeming activity in the world implies that the guardians of the land are doing their job in a manner that neither pleases God nor fulfills the conditions of the covenant.

Jesus' announcement of the advent or the imminence of the reign of God contained a prophetic judgment against the principalities and powers in Rome, Sepphoris, Tiberius, and Jerusalem. It, therefore, stands in a venerable tradition of anti-monarchic sentiment. Unlike the nations, Israel never conceded absolute and unchecked power to its kings. They were always subject to Yahweh's covenant and ruled with God's favor only so long as they obeyed the covenant and only insofar as they implemented it in the life of the people. The classical text in Deuteronomy 17:14–20 expresses this point of view powerfully and well.

> When he has taken the throne of his kingdom, he shall have a copy of this law written for him in the presence of the levitical priests. It shall remain with him, and he shall read in it all the days of his life, so that he may learn to fear the Lord his God, diligently observing all the words of this law and these statutes. (17:18–19)

Clearly, the covenant encoded in the Torah was to rule the people, the king being the agent of its just and equitable reign. Only to the degree that he fulfilled his Deuteronomic role was the king legitimate. The history of Israel is replete with reminders that, "in those days, there was no king in the land; all the people did what was right in their own eyes," although the chaos to which this period subjected the tribes of Yahweh was no argument against the monarchy (Judg. 17:6; 18:1; 19:1; 21:25). The suspicion of the institution of kingship in the land was nowhere better expressed than in Samuel's address to the elders of Israel who came to him seeking a king. Samuel reminded the elders that kingship entailed the establishment of a ruling class, forced exactions, conscription, and endless wars, exploitation, and maldistribution of wealth. He described perfectly the "proprietary theory of the state" so dear to agrarian rulers, as well as the abuses characteristic of monarchic rule (1 Sam. 8:4–22). Samuel would have occasion to remind the people that kingship was conditional (1 Sam. 12:12–25), and he would even have occasion to withdraw God's anointing from Saul (1 Sam. 15:23–31). Not even King David was immune from the prophetic correction of Nathan (2 Sam. 12:7–15). Yet, in spite of the prophetic critique, the lure of power was simply too great, and the abuses of monarchy triumphed over the restraint imposed by Torah and prophet alike, as the story of Naboth's vineyard makes so clear (1 Kings 21). The only remedy for the evils of Herodian rule and the ills of priestly aristocracies was the coming of a different kind of reign from the only power capable of ruling justly, the reign of God.

But just what was this reign of God to be like, and what were the hallmarks of this unexpected reign? Several of Jesus' parables speak to the character of the reign of God. The parable of the mustard seed (Mark 4:30–32; Matt. 13:31–32; Luke 13:18–19) has often been seen as revealing the reign of God announced by Jesus. Wright, for example, reads the parable as a "redefinition of the kingdom" that appears inconspicuously but will one day appear in "its full splendour" so that the Gentiles can reside in its branches. The parable describes simultaneously the kingdom of God and the ministry of Jesus which represents the kingdom's "strange beginning."[34] For the purposes of this reading, the Lukan version of the parable will be taken as the version closest to the parable told by Jesus, although the triple tradition may simply contain different performances of an originating structure.[35] The decision not to use the Markan version of the parable indicates that the contrast between smallest and greatest is a secondary interpretation of the parable, perhaps tracing to Mark. However, the Lukan version will require two changes, both of which are borrowed from Mark. Rather than sowing the seed "in his garden," this study proposes that the Markan phrase "on the land" suits the reading better, and in place of "a tree" (13:19), I propose to keep the Markan phrase, "the greatest of all shrubs." The reasons will, I hope, become clear. In more recent discussion of the parable, two trends have dominated. Funk and the early Crossan saw the parable as a lampooning of triumphalist expectations regarding the kingdom. As Funk notes, "the parable of the mustard seed parodies the mighty cedar of Lebanon as the symbol of Israel's Davidic hopes," and it thereby achieves its purpose by "comic inversion."[36] The image of birds nesting in the branches of a great tree evoked the portrayal of the kingdom as a great cedar of Lebanon whose limbs provided shelter and protection for smaller client kingdoms (Dan. 4:20–21). Ezekiel applied the same image to Pharaoh (Ezek. 31:3, 6) and to the messiah (Ezek. 17:23). The parable was an ironic retelling of the story of the great cedar to indicate that the kingdom Jesus proclaimed was not to be found in an apocalyptic advent but in its miraculous "gift-like nature, the graciousness and the surprise of the ordinary."[37] More recently, Crossan has argued that the mustard shrub is known for its ubiquity. It spreads like a weed and is not always welcomed where it takes root and spreads, because it can destroy the garden in which it has been planted. The mustard shrub becomes a fit image, therefore, for his kingdom of "nuisances and nobodies," the unwanted weeds and shrubs of their society.[38]

The parable would seem to admit elements of current readings and a hint of the more traditional meaning attributed to it. The seed is sown "on the land," a reference to the Promised Land, the land that is the embodiment of the covenant with Yahweh. Although this image is preferable to the "garden" image in Luke, it is possible to read the reference to the garden as an image of the land as a new Eden, in which case the two variants are not so far apart as they seem. The seed sown on the land, or in the land, then became a great shrub, not a tree, but a shrub capable of providing a nesting place for the birds of the air. The shrub remains a shrub, an image of the movement Jesus has planted in the land, and it is a nuisance to those who are attempting to cultivate another kind of garden on the land and, perhaps, even a threat. Crossan notes that the mustard plant is "as domesticated in the garden, dangerous, and, as wild in the grain fields, deadly."[39] Once sown, it spreads like a weed, causing havoc on the ordered garden of the land. It also throws purity boundaries into confusion precisely because it spreads indiscriminately, thereby violating the prohibition against planting two kinds of seed in the same field (Lev. 19:19; Deut. 22:9). The mustard shrub becomes an agent of confusion and source of uncleanness. The goal of sowing it is not to turn it into something it isn't (a tree) but to maximize what it is (a ubiquitous shrub), a force to be reckoned with. Like the land itself, the purpose of the shrub is to provide for others, the birds of the air. If the parable is about the pesky spread of Jesus' kingdom movement, then the image may reflect the hospitality offered wherever the weeds are flourishing.

The parable of the leaven (Q: Luke 13:20–21 = Matt 13:33) discloses another dimension of the reign of heaven announced by Jesus. Its introduction, "the kingdom of heaven is like leaven," is disorienting, since leaven is considered a symbol of uncleanness.[40] For this reason, the people of Israel are admonished to prepare for Passover by removing leaven from their houses or risk being cut off from the people of Israel (Ex. 12:14–20; cf. Deut. 16:1–8). Even Jesus uses leaven as a negative symbol when he warns the disciples to beware the leaven of Herod and the Pharisees (Mark 8:15; cf. Matt. 16:6–12; Luke 12:1). In these settings, the leaven probably refers to the corrupting teaching of the Pharisees and Sadduccees (Matthew) or the hypocrisy of the Pharisees (Luke). So the parable of the leaven is odd indeed, not only because of the mention of leaven, but also because of the amount of meal. The woman hid leaven in "three measures" of meal. Jeremias calculated that three measures equalled about fifty pounds of flour, enough to make cakes for about one hundred people.[41] The reference to "three measures" of meal may be an allusion to Genesis 18, where the Lord appeared to Abram and Sarah at the oaks of Mamre (Gen. 18:1–15). When the three figures appeared, Abram and Sarah prepared a meal for them using three measures of meal, thus extending hospitality to strangers. Their act of kindness gave rise to a proverb about entertaining angels unawares (Heb. 13:2). More importantly, the outcome of their hospitality was a renewal of the promise that Sarah would bear a child.

The parable contains yet another oddity, for the woman is described as "hiding" the leaven in the meal. Her action is surreptitious and covert, although Wright thinks its meaning is clear:

> what Israel's God was doing in the ministry of Jesus was veiled and cryptic. The leaven of Jesus' message is hidden within Israel, so that it may work its way through the whole people. The parable is a warning not to look (yet) for sudden dramatic events; it is an invitation to see Israel's God at work in the secret workings of Jesus' paradoxical activity.[42]

Once again, Jesus has described his work in bringing the reign of God to an unreceptive client kingdom and a threatened temple whose leaders can only view his work as corrupting and unclean. The parable hints that the announcing of the reign of heaven is no less a revelation of God's covenantal purpose than was the appearance of the divine messengers under the oaks at Mamre. How will people know when the reign of heaven has come? When everything is unclean! As Jesus' work succeeds in quiet ways, the contagion is spreading. Disguised as mustard shrubs and leaven, the reign of God reoccupies the land and leavens the whole lump. The purpose of the hiddenness may be practical as well. If he is beginning to attract powerful opponents and vindictive enemies, he may have good reason to conceal his activity, rather than operating naively in the public sphere, as many of the sign prophets did. By comparing the spreading reign of God to leaven, Jesus uses a technique of ironic reversal. He describes his movement as seen through the eyes of its enemies (it is corrupting leaven!) in order to intimate the power of its mysterious working. Once leaven is introduced into the meal, it is impossible to separate. It will accomplish its work through its leavening influence.

The Praxis of the Reign of God

Paulo Freire defined praxis as "reflection and action upon the world in order to transform it."[43] How did the hidden, outlaw Jesus movement make a difference in the world of first-century Palestine? Its first impact was to loose peasants from the grip of the temple. If peasants were no longer bound to the temple system with its incessant demands for tithes and offerings, then they were better able to maintain the kinship networks on which their survival depended. This, in itself, could contribute to the renewal of village life. What was important, for Jesus, was the covenant, and the covenant antedated the temple as surely as it had preceded the emergence of the monarchy. Both temple and kingship were subject to the authority of the covenant and the covenant God. In these emphases, Jesus was a prophet in the Deuteronomic tradition, a prophet who stood in a long line of prophets stretching back to the eighth century, blending his voice with those of Amos, Hosea, Micah, and Isaiah, even though he shared neither their status nor their access to the institutions of power.

However, Jesus assumed a role beyond that of prophet. He stepped into the role of broker of Yahweh's justice and covenant favor. In this role, Jesus claimed that he was the mediator of God's healing and saving power, evidenced by his own healings and exorcisms. These "mighty acts" reminded the people of the God of the exodus who brought a people out of slavery "with great power and a mighty hand" (Ex. 32:11). Only Yahweh had dared to "take a nation for himself from the midst of another nation, by trials, by signs and wonders, by a mighty hand and an outstretched arm" (Deut. 4:33–34). Yahweh became the *go'el*, the redeemer who rescued the people from slavery, and now, once again, a new redeemer, acting on Yahweh's behalf, had done the same thing, using only the "finger of God" instead of the mighty hand and outstretched arm. Wherever God's people were in bondage to Satan (Luke 13:10–17) or his demonic minions (Mark 1:21–28; 5:1–20), Jesus searched them out to liberate them. The Beelzebul controversy makes sense only if Jesus was performing exorcisms (Mark 3:19b–27; Matt. 12:22–30; Luke 11:14–15, 17–23). In the controversy, it is implied that the Pharisees themselves also conducted exorcisms: "By whom do your sons cast them out?" If so, why then did they object to Jesus' activity? One answer may be found in the disciples' objections to the unknown exorcist (Mark 9:38–40). In that passage, the disciples protest the activity of the unauthorized exorcist because he uses Jesus' name but does not belong to the band of disciples. Yet Jesus shows no apparent concern about the incident and assumes that, in time, the exorcist shall align himself with the disciples or at least that he will not oppose their work. The Pharisees, then, may be objecting to Jesus on similar grounds. He conducts exorcisms, much as the Pharisees do, but he neither belongs to their political faction nor shares their goals. Unlike Jesus, however, the Pharisees have good reasons for wanting to retain control over exorcising activity. But why? Paul Hollenbach has written an article that may provide a tentative answer.[44] Demon possession and madness are two forms of accommodation found in colonized populations where the imperial occupier has attempted to strip away the identity of the local populace and sought to impose an alien identity on them. This is a process that had assumed a variety of forms in ancient Palestine, the most virulent being the reform instigated by Antiochus IV Epiphanes, the more lenient being the pressures applied by Hasmonaean rule and Roman colonial occupation. In these circumstances, demonic possession becomes a form of "oblique protest" against the colonial overlord because, if he is viewed as possessed, a demoniac can express what others feel but repress. Hollenbach reads the Gerasene demoniac in just this way (Mark 5:1–20):

> It is likely that the tension between his hatred for his oppressors and the necessity to repress this hatred in order to avoid dire recrimination drove him mad. But his very madness permitted him to do in a socially acceptable manner what he could not do as sane, namely, express his total hostility to the Romans; he did this by identifying the Roman legions with demons. His possession was thus at once both the result of oppression and an expression of his resistence to it. He retreated to an inner world where he could symbolically resist Roman domination. (581)

This situation placed local collaborators in a difficult situation. They knew that they had to control the potential disruption caused by these forms of possession and protest, so they labeled those affected as mad or demon-possessed. It was a form of social control. In effect, this labeling degrades the possessed "by destroying their selfhood" and denying what they have experienced and expressed in their fits of possession (579). Necessarily, collaborators will attempt to gain control of the phenomenon by stepping into the role of authorized or official exorcists. In this way, they will try to manage the shaky accommodation achieved between exorcist and colonized population. When unauthorized exorcists arise to address the problem, collaborators will stigmatize them by using witchcraft accusations or branding them as sorcerers. Demon possession, then, is a threatening phenomenon because it symbolizes the situation of the people in whom it occurs. They are occupied by a colonial power, just as the possessed is occupied by demons. More to the point, the possessed speak the truth in madness as part of their "oblique aggressive strategy" to protest their loss of cultural and personal identity.

Once the social significance of possession is noted, the role of the Pharisees becomes more obvious. They are trying to manage the phenomenon by controlling access to rituals of exorcisms and determining who has been cured. This allows them to process deviants, classify the status of these figures, and control this potentially explosive form of "political leprosy." Possession becomes another form of impurity and uncleanness. Jesus disrupted their efforts at social control and classification by interpreting possession differently and practicing other forms of exorcism. The Pharisees, and perhaps Herod as well (Luke 13:31–33), wanted to destroy Jesus because he was invading dangerous territory and offering an alternative vision of its meaning. The Pharisees saw the possessed as dangerous deviants requiring social ostracism or cure because they were a threat to the social order; Jesus saw the possessed as God's people in need of liberation from alien oppression and redemption from evil control. In exorcising the possessed, Jesus was also disrupting the forms of social accommodation being acted out in their behavior. The exorcised could no longer utter their protest as a form of displaced insanity; they were now accountable for what they had seen and responsible for what they said. This made them politically dangerous and socially disruptive, but it also placed them outside the bounds of Pharisaic definitions. For the Pharisees, exorcism was eliminating another social problem, and those who failed to respond were labeled and condemned. For Jesus, exorcism was yet another strategy for reconstituting the people of God under God's covenant love (*chesed*). Every time Jesus exorcised a possessed demoniac, he was descending into hell to redeem another imprisoned spirit and declaring liberty to those who had been held captive. It was a tactic in his larger strategy for establishing the justice of the reign of God.

If peasants were no longer obligated to send their tithes to the temple, then how were they to keep the covenant? Jesus' summary of the Torah provides one way to answer this question (Mark 12:28–34; Matt. 22:34–40; Luke 10:25–28). A scribe (*grammateus*) or a lawyer (*nomikos*) challenges Jesus to define the heart of the Decalogue: "Which commandment is first of all?" (12:28b). Jesus responds by citing the *shema* (Deut. 6:4) and a passage from the Holiness Code (Lev. 19:18). Once again, the prophet is interpreting the Torah for the people. Matthew 22:40 makes the connection between Torah and prophets clearer than Mark: "On these two commandments depend all the law and the prophets." Jesus' summary is not as innocuous as it sounds to our ears. In the debate about what renders a person unclean, Jesus had argued that, when the demands of the temple (showing love for God) clash with the need to provide support for parents (loving your neighbor), the love of neighbor trumps the demands of the temple. In his own vision of the demands of the Decalogue, Jesus believes that the love of God and love of neighbor are mutually supportive and reinforcing. They are not in competition. This interpretation implies that any demands regarding the love of God (as expressed through the temple) that do, in fact, conflict with the needs of neighbors are bogus. The love of God and love of neighbor are mutually reciprocal obligations.

How then is the love of neighbor to be shown? In offering forgiveness and cancellation of debt. The chief danger caused by Herodian control was that villagers would be tempted to mimic the behavior of their rulers. This meant using debt to gain control over others and, in pursuing this course of action, breaking down the kinship ties of the village and the commitment of neighbors to each other. Since the village had, in effect, replaced the clan and extended family, whatever eroded village life undermined the fragile fabric of what kinship remained. I have already argued that the Lord's Prayer can be understood in this context.[45]

The importance of forgiving appears in another scene from village life found in Luke (7:36–50).[46] A village Pharisee has extended hospitality to Jesus by inviting him to dine in his home.[47] Bailey speculates that Jesus, the itinerant rabbi, might have been invited to teach in the synagogue on the Sabbath and was invited to the Pharisee's house for a meal after the meeting. The house was open for the village to attend, although the villagers would not be invited to share the meal, only to hear the rabbi converse about Torah. When Jesus arrived, his host, Simon, denied him the basic rituals of hospitality which would have included, at the very least, foot washing and a kiss of peace. If he judged Jesus to be a distinguished guest, he might have anointed his head as well. According to Bailey, the snub would "electrify" the assembled crowd. Jesus would be expected to "offer a few tight-lipped remarks about not being welcome and withdraw."[48] By denying Jesus the basic social courtesies, Simon has confronted him with a negative honor challenge, but Jesus does not go away quietly. He responds by reclining at table. Of course, he has not ritually washed his hands, and so he contaminates whatever he touches. Every time he breaks off a piece of bread and dips it in a common dish, Jesus challenges Simon and his other guests, who presumably share Simon's concerns for purity. If the snub at the door was intended to scare Jesus away, it failed to achieve its purpose. His reclining at table may be Jesus' riposte to Simon's challenge. But before Simon can respond, the woman intervenes in such a way that she brings the host's enmity to the surface. By wiping Jesus' feet, kissing them, and anointing him with ointment, she compensates for each of the rituals of hospitality denied to him. The narrator says simply that she was a sinner, a designation that means that she was not Torah obedient, as the Pharisees defined that. There is no hint that she is a prostitute.

The woman has changed the nature of the challenge-riposte between Simon and Jesus. Her actions now provide the arena in which they will contest with each other. Simon reproaches Jesus for not being particular about who touches him, but does so in a subdued tone of voice. He thus reflects his Pharisaic concern about impurity. Jesus accepts the challenge by telling the parable of the two debtors (vv. 41–42). By doing so, he sets the concern for purity against the necessity for forgiveness. It is a restatement of the familiar conflict between the purity codes of the Torah and its debt codes. The parable communicates the most basic meaning of forgiveness, forgiveness of debt. It also poses a problem for Simon to solve, but no sooner has he resolved it than Jesus presents him with a more complicated one. The parable justifies the woman's actions while condemning Simon. Now Jesus offers the "tight-lipped" comments expected of him earlier, but they are not so much for the purpose of condemning Simon as they are for the purpose of justifying the woman's actions. Taken by themselves, the woman's actions are shocking and shameful. She has touched a strange man and abased herself in public. But after Jesus' recital of her actions, set against the insults of Simon, she becomes a sinner who has loved much. This recital then provides Jesus with a platform from which to announce God's forgiveness: "I tell you, although her sins are many, they are forgiven" (7:47). Ever quick to jump on an issue, the table companions and neighbors of Simon ask sarcastically, "Who is this, who even forgives sins?" (7:49). Who presumes to speak for God with such confidence? Jesus does not even bother to respond but turns to the woman in order to honor her publicly: "Your faith has saved you; go in peace" (7:50).

At one level, the most surprising outcome is Jesus' statement that her sins are forgiven because she loved much (7:47). Love evokes forgiveness, not the other way around. In this context, love refers to her attentiveness to the rituals of hospitality that honor guests. Love is shown in socially specific ways. The economy of the reign of God suggests that those who need little forgiveness will love little but, in most villages, very few will be in Simon's position. This is literally good news for the sinners of the villages in which Jesus moves. But the scene has deeper resonances. Forgiveness is associated with covenant renewal in Exodus (34:1–35, see esp. 34:6–7; cf. Num. 14:18), where God's "steadfast (= covenant) love" is identified with "forgiving iniquity and transgression and sin." The same combination of covenant love and forgiveness is found in Psalm 86:5, and God is associated with forgiveness elsewhere in the Psalms (cf. 99:8; 130:4). All of this implies that Jesus was acting as the broker of the covenant God's forgiving love, and in that role, acting as an agent of covenant renewal, reconstituting the people of God by embracing those on the margins and shepherding them back into the fold (cf. Matt. 10:5–6).

If village life were to reflect the justice of the reign of God, then villagers had to abandon their scorekeeping, their unceasing efforts to indebt others and exercise control over them in the interests of serving each other (Mark 10:42–45; Matt. 20:25–28; Luke 22:25–27; Mark 9:35–37). If villages organized around this principle, their social relations would assume some form of generalized reciprocity, that is, "open sharing based on generosity or need."[49] These types of social interaction are found in kinship groups, or fictive kinship groups, where members regard each other as family. If Jesus were interested in the renewal of village life, he may have advocated just such sharing. The village would replace the clan and extended family, both of which had disappeared from the scene of Israel's life. For this to happen, however, peasants had to forge new ties and regard each other in a new light. Jesus models this possibility when he redefines the meaning of kinship in his own family (Mark 3:31–35; Matt. 12:46–50; Luke 8:19–21): "Whoever does the will of God is my brother and sister and mother" (Mark 3:35). His disciples will benefit from the formation of a fictive kinship network in the villages because it will provide hospitality and support for the movement (Mark 10:28–30).

The maintenance of the justice of the reign of God in the villages of Galilee required the end of feuding and social conflict. The spiral of violence only raised the stakes involved in conflicts and shredded the fabric of fictive kinship ties. This impulse may lie behind Jesus' concern for nonretaliation (Matt. 5:38–42). The problem with "an eye for an eye" is that it escalates conflict in the name of limiting it. To turn the other cheek offers an opportunity to break the cycle of mutual retaliation and bring the feud to a halt. Village life was filled with grudges, grievances, small feuds, and efforts to indebt others, perhaps involving appeals to local courts. Jesus' concern is to interrupt the cycle at its start. Crossan once argued that, in these three injunctions (5:38–41), Jesus was parodying the case-law approach to life. "Jesus' set of three situations represents case parody, a deliberate comic subversion of the wise and prudent necessity of case law."[50] He came to this conclusion because Jesus was advising his hearers to join in their own despoiling.[51] This ludicrous outcome signaled to Crossan that Jesus was subverting the case-law approach to life by suggesting a larger morality.

On one point, Crossan is certainly on target. The passage does seem to call for extreme behavior. The sayings in Matthew 5:38–42 can be organized as follows:

prophetic covenant principle	38–39a
case 1: physical attack	39b
case 2: lawsuit	40
case 3: forced conscription	41
case 4: redistribution of resources	42

The antithesis formula (Matt. 5:43a, 44a) is congruent with everything this study has proposed. Jesus is contrasting a prophetic hermeneutic against the reading of the Torah proposed by the power brokers in Jerusalem. Here, Jesus puts it to the test. In the first case, Jesus contemplates an incident of violent assault and public shaming. A man has been hit on the right cheek. Assuming the assailant is right-handed, the blow was a back-handed slap, a demeaning blow delivered by a social superior to a social inferior. No doubt, peasants had received such blows from overseers, stewards, and other retainers representing the interests of the ruling elites. When this behavior was replicated in the village, it was most likely learned behavior by which one peasant attempted to shame another who may have been indebted to him. He was making a display of his superiority. Jesus recommended that the victim not accept the insult but offer the other cheek, which would force the assailant to strike him with the palm of his hand, a gesture asserting his basic humanity and social standing. He, too, is a member of the village; the dispute is between two people in socially similar situations.

In the case of a lawsuit adjudicated in a local Torah court or, perhaps, in a traditional court in a market town, the peasant losing the case is to surrender not only the tunic or garment worn next to the skin (*chitōn*) but the outer garment as well (*himation*). (Luke reverses the order, suggesting that the person has lost clothing in a robbery.) The situation echoes the Torah's concern for the way neighbors treat each other when making loans (Ex. 22:25–27; Deut. 24:10–17). The point is that neighbors should not exploit the occasion to make a loan by extracting necessities from those in need. The dramatic gesture of surrendering both inner tunic and outer cloak would leave the villager naked, and his nakedness would shame his creditor, who has violated the Torah. Let the elites throw the Torah to the winds in their desire to exploit and destroy, but let not villagers behave toward each other as their social superiors would. In the village, let forgiveness of debt replace repayment on demand and taking of pledges. This reference to the Torah may be the reason why 5:42 is attached to the three cases. It is an ethical exhortation to give to the destitute and lend to the neighbor.

The final case is not parallel to the other two, because it involves out-siders. The situation envisioned by 5:41 reflects the prerogative of an oc-cupying force to command civilians to carry their gear for a specified distance. Usually, such service was performed grudgingly. Jesus counsels an unexpected twist. Do what is required and more. The surprising re-sponse may lessen the hostility and enmity between occupier and occupied.

The prophetic word against adultery and divorce (Matt. 5:27–32) ad-dresses another area of disruption in village life. But this admonition is not about sexual ethics as much as it is about property rights. It is an application of the tenth commandment (Ex. 20:17; Deut. 5:21). Jesus' words have a practical meaning in a world where all goods, including women, are limited, and there is intense competition for them. Mediter-ranean honor and shame is a gender-based system of sexual ethics and manners. As Schneider notes rather pointedly, "women are contested re-sources, much like sheep . . . like pastures and water, so much so that kidnappings, abductions, elopements, and the capture of concubines ap-pear to have been frequent occurrences."[52] The conflict of expectations between men who aggresively seek honor and women who cautiously guard against shame sets the stage for endless village conflicts.[53] In this social setting, to stare at a woman lustfully was a socially explosive act. From the point of view of the woman's family, it was like casting an "evil eye," threatening to bring shame on the family by despoiling one of its women. Similarly, divorce created havoc and often led to conflicts over contested resources. Both predatory male behavior and divorce could threaten the values of village life. The saying focusing on consequences (vv. 29–30) does take a surprising turn. Men were socialized into the role of aggressor; looking boldly at women could be seen as part of their nor-mal behavior. Yet Jesus turns the acceptable aggressor into the sinner who needs to repent from his sin. The consequences are drastic: mutila-tion rather than aggression against a woman and her family. Rather than place the responsibility upon the woman to avoid shame, Jesus puts the onus on the male's shoulders. In similar fashion, Jesus limits the grounds for divorce to "screwing around" (*porneias* usually refers to indiscrimi-nate sexual behavior, not some vague sense of unchastity). Such flagrant and repeated behavior creates chaos and animosity in small communi-ties. It would be foolhardy to recognize such a marriage long after its sta-tus had been degraded and the family shamed in the village. Jesus' concern about divorce is well attested in the tradition (Mark 10:2–12; Matt. 19:3–12; Luke 16:18). In no small measure, the reasons lay in the concern for the integrity of what was left of family life as part of the vil-lage. In this instance, too, Jesus was arguing Torah. The bill of divorce passage (Deut. 24:1–4) was a subject of dispute. Jesus read the passage in a more restrictive sense than did Hillel. In a case where *porneia* was not the issue, the protection of the woman's rights would be the reason for the strict view. Jesus looked to protect the weak and vulnerable and, in normal divorce cases, the woman was at risk. Jesus' appeal to the creation story (Mark 10:6–8; Matt. 19:4–6) places the Torah in the broader context of God's creative purposes and proposes to align the two.

A similar hermeneutic could equally well be applied to the passage about anger and murder (Matt. 5:21–26). In a society filled with honor-shame ripostes, angry challenges, and snide ripostes, it was easy for anger to escalate into name calling ("you fool") with hellish consequences. In the village, within the fictive kinship group, reconciliation was more important than escalation. Its importance is implied by the two imagined settings, temple and law court. The need to reconcile takes precedence over sacrifice and adjudication; the informal means of conflict resolution found in the village leaves the matter in the villagers' own hands rather than turning over their disputes to priests or judges. The occasion provides yet another opportunity to forgive debts and debtors, thereby living out the covenant in the context of village life.

CONCLUSION

In each of the cases examined, the antithesis has afforded the opportunity to create and experience the justice of God's reign in a local setting. This involves redistributing resources, including honor and shame, in order to fashion a village more aligned with the values and practices of the reign of God. True, they may look corrupting and unclean when seen through the eyes of temple authorities and Herodian elites, but they are spreading and will continue to grow in the villages of the land. In order to realize this hidden reign of God, the villages needed neither the sacrificial system of the temple nor the aid of Herod. They needed to nurture their own "little tradition" reading of the Torah and its covenantal provisions. To encourage this movement, Jesus traveled throughout the villages of Galilee and Judea and kept sowing the mustard shrub of the kingdom.

PART 4

O Jerusalem, Jerusalem:
The "Show Trial" and Resurrection

Part 4 contains two chapters, both covering the final events in Jesus' life, with a postscript on the resurrection and the beginnings of Christology.

Chapter 10 proposes that three charges were leveled against Jesus. They are: (1) that he forbade the payment of tribute; (2) that he threatened to destroy the temple; (3) that he claimed to be a messianic king. Although he was executed as an enemy of the state, based on the third charge, it was probably the only one that was not true. The other two were.

Jesus' arrest led to a "show trial" in Jerusalem. A show trial is not a trial, as we understand it. It is a political event, an example of political theater designed to shame and discredit a political menace before executing him. Jesus' guilt had been determined before his show trial and, I would argue, with good reason. He was a threat to the temple and, therefore, indirectly to the Romans.

Chapter 11 argues that the resurrection was God's way of honoring Jesus, declaring that all he taught and did was right while the quislings who executed him were wrong. It was a bit like Yahweh speaking to Job out of the whirlwind. Job got it right, Yahweh said, and the friends got it wrong. So here: Jesus got it right, and the collaborators and their colonial masters got it wrong. This carries implications for us and suggests why the study of the historical Jesus remains a vital quest in the church today.

10

The "Show Trial" in Jerusalem:

"Why? What Evil Has He Done?"

Aside from a few details, very little can be known about the chronology of Jesus' public work. It is likely that John the Baptist mentored him, and after John's imprisonment and death Jesus began his prophetic work in Galilee. He traveled to Gentile areas contiguous with Galilee, and perhaps he worked in Samaria or journeyed through Samaria on pilgrimage to Jerusalem, although it is more likely that he traveled down the Jordan rift to Jericho and then went up to Jerusalem. At some point, he made a fateful decision to journey to Jerusalem for Passover. Whether he traveled to Jerusalem more than once, as the Gospel of John has it, or whether he made one journey, as the Synoptic Gospels portray, can no longer be determined. What is important is that his only or final trip to Jerusalem ended in his arrest, show trial, and execution.

This chapter will discuss the charges pressed against Jesus, the basis for them, and a brief examination of the show trial itself.

THE RAP SHEET ON JESUS

Insofar as the Synoptic Gospels provide accurate information, it appears that Jesus was accused of three crimes. First, he was accused of blocking the payment of tribute. The kangaroo court (which was not the Sanhedrin) that determined Jesus' guilt is reported to have said, "We found this man perverting our nation, foridding us to pay tribute to Caesar" (Luke 23:2ab). The second charge was that Jesus threatened to destroy the temple (Mark 14:58 // Matt. 26:60; Mark 15:29 // Matt. 27:40). This charge would include the charge of blasphemy. The third charge is closely linked to the first two. He claimed "that he himself is the Messiah, a king" (Luke 23:2c). Of course, the crowd of clients loyal to the Jerusalem elites was programmed to respond by shouting some shibboleth like

"We have no king but Caesar" (John 19:15). It was more a show of political expediency than political loyalty. As will become evident, there was reason enough to press each charge, and at least two of the charges were true. The charge on which Jesus was executed was the only one of the three that was false. In other words, the Jerusalem elites had reasons enough to collaborate with their Roman overlords to execute the troublesome prophet from Nazareth. It was in their political self-interest.

But this must be said at the outset of the investigation: the chief priests, their scribal retainers, and the elders acted as agrarian elites would be expected to act under these or similar circumstances. They were not acting as "Jews," nor were their actions particularly "Jewish." Their actions and reactions were mostly determined by their social location and ruling class values. They were first-century Judean rulers and retainers with a great deal at stake in maintaining internal order to please their colonial masters. But to treat them as though they were "Jews" persecuting a "Christian" is anti-Semitic, anti-Judaic, historically anachronistic, and horribly misguided. No one holds twentieth-century Italians responsible for what first-century Romans did. This chapter will examine the show trial of Jesus in Jerusalem as the final act of hostility, guided by urban elites against an agrarian disturber of the people of the land, but in no way should this study aid or abet those who would use history to justify contemporary hatred and bigotry.

It is time to examine each of the three charges pressed against Jesus.

Forbidding the Payment of Tribute

The most obvious place to look in order to determine the accuracy of this charge against Jesus is the debate with the Pharisees and Herodians over whether the people should pay tribute to Caesar (Mark 12:13–17; Matt. 22:15–22; Luke 20:20–26). Before examining that incident, it will be helpful to inspect a peculiar passage relating to the temple tribute (Matt. 17:24–27) and the general comments about Jesus' association with toll collectors and sinners as a way of setting the context for the debate about tribute to Caesar.

The pericope on the payment of the temple tax is found solely in Matthew (17:24–27). It is usually dismissed because of the legendary ending (v. 27) attached to the conversation between Jesus and Peter. Bultmann considered it an "imaginary scene" crafted by the early church. Peter is first questioned by the collectors of the temple tax and then turns to Jesus, a metaphor for the church turning to the Risen Lord for counsel.[1] Whatever doubts he had about the text, Bultmann was surely right to see the point of the passage in the "brief dialogue of vv. 25f., which in the manner of argumentation . . . gives an impression of age."[2] Meier has argued that, in "structure, vocabulary and theology," the passage reflects Matthean concerns, a viewpoint shared by Gundry.[3] In addition to its internal features, Meier has shown how the incident fits into the narrative structure of Matthew and showcases his characteristic theological themes.[4] It is important to ask, however, whether these characteristically Matthean attributes point to Matthean creation or Matthean adaptation of traditional materials. The topic itself, for instance, suggests an early provenance. If Matthew was written after the destruction of the temple, why would he create a story about paying the temple tax? It is more reasonable to suppose that he adapted a traditional story to suit his purposes.[5] If one removes the legendary story about the coin in the fish's mouth (v. 27), what remains is an issue very pertinent to Jesus' time and public work. The pericope depicts the collectors of the didrachma (= half-shekel) tribute for the temple circulating through the villages of Galilee. The half-shekel tribute was a poll tax or head tax, like the Roman *tributum capitis*. In both cases, paying the tribute was an acknowledgment that the body of the person being assessed was under the command and control of another.[6] In the case of the temple tribute, the message was supposed to be that those paying the tribute were showing their loyalty and indebtedness to Yahweh, but in fact the half-shekel poll tax became a way of asserting the dominance of the high-priestly ruling class over the people of the land. This is the point of the question that Jesus asks Peter. His use of "the rulers of the earth" (or "the rulers on the land") draws a parallel between temple demands and more monarchic forms of extraction (e.g., Herodian or Roman). Both types of tribute lay claim to the labor of the peasants by asserting their control over their bodies in the form of a poll tax. In spite of this, it is true that the temple half-shekel tax "did not rest upon any requirement of the Mosaic law" but had been established by precedent and continued by custom.[7] Even though it was a custom that "became a symbol of national and religious unity," it rested on moral suasion, not coercion.[8]

Apparently economic or political issues often provide a front for theological concerns, and the same can be said for this conversation between Peter and Jesus. Masked behind the collection of tribute is the picture of Yahweh as king, a portrait in stark contrast to the characteristic way Jesus spoke about God as "abba," or father. The kingly God, like his earthly counterparts, demanded and collected tribute, whether or not the people of the land could afford to pay it. The paternal and patronal God proclaimed by Jesus treats the people like his own kin. If God really is as Jesus proclaimed, then "the sons [and daughters] are free" (v. 26b). The meaning is clear and unambiguous. Neither Jesus nor his disciples are bound to pay the half-shekel tribute to the temple. Would Jesus have acquiesced and paid the tribute "not to give offense" (v. 27a)? In light of Jesus' campaign to separate the temple from the land, and in light of his claim to broker God's forgiveness apart from the temple, it is improbable that Jesus would have paid the tribute. It was too late to consider not giving offense. His declaration of independence is neither surprising nor anachronistic. It may be, as Meier has argued, that "some sort of scholastic dispute about whether Jewish Christians should pay the temple tax lies behind Matthew's composition,"[9] but it is not necessary, though it may be useful, to identify the nature of that dispute when the issue can be so clearly contextualized in the setting of Jesus' work.

The nonpayment of the half-shekel was a matter of simple justice. The temple tribute implied a form of reciprocity, most likely unbalanced reciprocity. If peasants pay their half-shekel tribute, they will receive the blessings of timely rains and bountiful harvests, the utter necessities ensuring survival and subsistence. Of course, the demand to pay the half-shekel tribute was only the beginning of obligation. Beyond the poll tax loomed the claim for tithes and offerings. It is interesting to note that the temple system of tribute taking paralleled the pattern of Roman exactions: the land tax (= tithes and offerings) paralleled the *tributum soli,* and the head or poll tax (= half-shekel tax) paralleled the *tributum capitis.* As long as the temple could make the pretense of a claim to offer reciprocal benefits in return for its exactions, then the tribute collectors could persuade peasants like Peter to participate. In the passage, Peter is shamed into saying yes (v. 25a), because he cannot say no to the honorable demand of the temple and the God of the temple. But if God is like a father with his kin, not like a king over his subjects, then the situation has been fundamentally altered. If "the sons [and daughters] are free," they are loosed from their bondage to temple demands. By declaring the peasants free of the temple's head tax, Jesus is liberating them from the bondage imposed by a false theology, fashioned in the interests of the rulers at the expense of the people of the land. God as abba, or father, regathers the kinship group and, in so doing, redefines who are children of Abraham and Sarah.

The test case of this ingathering was the toll collectors and sinners. Toll collectors seem to have been almost universally despised, although tax collectors, who carried with them the imprimatur of the state or prestige of the temple, were not.[10] Jesus himself could use the expression "Gentile and toll collector" in a negative way (Matt. 18:17), and he himself was stigmatized as "a friend of toll collectors and sinners" (Q: Luke 7:34 = Matt. 11:19). Jesus returned the favor in a particularly polemical indictment of the Jerusalem leaders, when he declared that "toll collectors and prostitutes are going into the reign of God before you" (Matt. 21:31), a charge he further justified by refering to John the Baptist. The toll collectors and prostitutes believed John because he came in "the way of justice" (*hodō dikaiosunēs*). Paralleling the "reign of God" with the "way of justice" suggests that it was the justice of the reign of God that appealed to the toll collectors and prostitutes. The reason is not far to find, for both groups had been forced to "prostitute" themselves in order to survive in the unjust systems that dominated Palestine. As the victims of exploitation, they will go into the reign of heaven ahead of the defenders of the status quo, who stigmatized the poor and the degraded rather than seeking justice for them. It is in this context that Jesus' call of a toll collector to be part of his band of disciples (Mark 2:14; Matt. 9:9; Luke 5:27–28; cf. Matt. 10:3) and his table companionship with toll collectors and sinners makes sense (Mark 2:15–17; Matt. 9:10–13; Luke 5:29–32). This study has already proposed that Jesus' table companionship was intended as a profanation of the Pharisaic project of eating meals in a state of ritual purity. This is why his practice elicited the scornful question, "Why do you eat and drink with toll collectors and sinners?" (Luke 5:30).

Jesus told the parable of the children in the marketplace to justify his table companionship with "toll collectors and sinners" (Q: Luke 7:31–35 = Matt. 11:16–19). The charge in the Q tradition is excess; Jesus is labeled a "glutton and a drunkard." Some members of the Jesus Seminar have taken this to mean that Jesus was a bon vivant and a party animal. He did it for the hell of it, to show that living in the present is all that mattered,[11] but it hardly needs to be said that this view trivializes the social significance and theological import of Jesus' actions. Crossan thinks that this "open commensality' modeled the egalitarian tendencies of Jesus.

> Open commensality profoundly negates distinctions and hierarchies between female and male, poor and rich, Gentile and Jew. It does so, indeed, at a level that would offend the ritual laws of any civilized society. That was precisely its challenge.[12]

The difficulty with the way Crossan interprets open commensality is that egalitarianism is a modern notion unlikely to be found in the ancient world, nor would it have been valued if it had been found. The issue is not equality, but reciprocity and mutuality. In return for brokering God's forgiveness, toll collectors and sinners offer Jesus table companionship. Their hospitality is their expression of gratitude, their reciprocity. The reference to Jesus being "a friend of toll collectors and sinners" should not be missed. The language of friendship is often used in patron-client settings, the patron or client being refered to as the "friend," and friendship the shorthand for patronage. This may mean that outsiders viewed Jesus as the "patron saint" of toll collectors and sinners, their defender and advocate. In reality, Jesus simply brokered God's friendship for toll collectors and sinners, even if his opponents saw matters differently. Their common meals expressed this mutual and reciprocal bond of hospitality and acceptance. Every time he reclined at table with outcasts and peasants, Jesus lived out of a symbolic universe different from the one perpetuated by the temple and its functionaries. Crossan is certainly right to observe:

> The popular religion and culture of peasants in a complex society is not only a syncretized, domesticated, and localized variant of larger systems of thought and doctrine. They contain almost inevitably the seeds of an alternative symbolic universe.[13]

The table companionship with toll collectors and sinners was a scene in that new drama of the coming reign of God being acted out by Jesus.

Jesus' efforts to associate with sinners and broker God's forgiveness to them served as a social tactic in his larger strategy to disrupt the regnant forms of hieratic control and imperial exploitation. If he could include toll collectors and sinners as table companions, then they were no longer enemies of the common people but their allies. This appears to be the tactic adopted by John the Baptist, who demanded that they "collect no more than the amount prescribed" for them (Luke 3:12–13). John realized that the poor could not avoid participating in the system of toll collection, but they could work as toll collectors in as nonexploitative a way as possible, refusing to line their pockets by defrauding peasants, artisans, and merchants. Jesus followed this tactic as a way to interrupt the cycle of exploitation by working with the lowest level functionaries of the system.

In what may well be an idealized scene, the story of Zacchaeus illustrates what is at stake in Jesus' strategy. When Jesus calls upon Zacchaeus, the chief toll collector (*architelōnēs*), to host him, Zacchaeus responds with a generosity befitting repentance by promising to distribute half of his goods to the poor and to restore fourfold to any he has defrauded. In his zeal, he has exceeded the requirements of the Torah, which requires that, "when you have sinned and realize your guilt, and would restore what you took by robbery or by fraud . . . you shall repay the principal amount and shall add one-fifth to it" (Lev. 6:4–5; cf. 6:1–7; Num. 5:6–7; Ex. 22:1). In response to this confession of faith, Jesus proclaims, "Today salvation has come to this house; because he too is a son of Abraham" (19:9). The repentance of a chief toll collector leads to a redistributive form of justice in which those defrauded by an exploitative system are repaid fourfold. Of course, this is no easy task for a chief toll collector whose street-level operatives have been defrauding travelers for months or years. The restoration of kinship status involves repentance, and repentance involves redistributing what has been taken falsely. Zacchaeus's confession indicates an understanding of the debt codes of the

Torah. Although he remains condemned by the purity codes, he can accept God's forgiveness of his debt as a call to justice. In his case, this means justly redistributing his wealth to the poor as well as recompensing the victims of his toll collecting.

Whether the Zacchaeus story is historical or literary (and the two terms are not necessarily antithetical), it reveals why Jesus might have devoted time to toll collectors and sinners. Not only were they a limiting case of God's forgiveness, but they were functionaries in an oppressive system, whether low-level functionaries (toll collectors) or wealthier exploiters (chief toll collectors). If they could experience God's forgiveness with its demand for the justice of the reign of God, then they could become allies, not enemies, of the peasant villagers, artisans, and merchants, agents of redistribution rather than agents of exploitation. This means that Jesus' table companionship with toll collectors and sinners was an integral part of Jesus' economic concerns for the people of the land and expressed his interest in redirecting the redistributive economies that dominated Herod's client kingdom, the temple's collaborationist hegemony and Rome's imperial control.

After all this has been duly noted, the primary passage that addresses most directly the charge leveled against Jesus is the conflict on the Temple Mount over the question of tribute (Mark 12:13–17; Matt. 22:15–22; Luke 20:20–26). This discussion will focus on the Markan version of the incident, and all references are to the Markan version, unless otherwise noted. Form critically, Mark 12:13–17 has been viewed as an integral unit. Bultmann was certain that the saying in verse 17 had never circulated independently, nor did he think the passage a community creation.[14] In this judgment, Taylor concurred: "of its genuineness there can be no question."[15] It is equally clear that Mark has placed the incident on the Temple Mount. There is nothing in the pericope itself to suggest that it belongs there, and the presence of Herodians may indicate a Galilean context. In the absence of compelling reasons for relocating the conflict, this reading will accept the Markan setting, but the temple setting is not essential to the interpretation suggested here, for the charge of obstructing payment could have stemmed from the memory of a challenge-riposte in Galilee or on the Temple Mount.

To contextualize this conflict, it will be useful to delineate the larger setting in which it occurs. When power relations are asymmetrical, it is probable that the political speech of the weak will dissemble, that is, it will feign loyalty and obedience to the ruling class while pursuing its own hidden agenda. James C. Scott has devoted a study to situations in which an oppressive elite dominates a suppressed population.[16] In a situation of "superstratification,"[17] there will be a "public transcript" of events controlled by the rulers and "hidden transcripts" of the same events produced surreptitiously by the oppressed. The public transcript is a "shorthand way of describing the open interaction between subordinates and those who dominate," whereas the "hidden transcript" is what characterizes the "discourse that takes place 'offstage,' beyond the direct observation of the powerholders."[18] In other words, the hidden transcript contains what the oppressed say to each other and think about their rulers, while the public transcript is "the self-portrait of dominant elites as they would have themselves be seen" (18). Needless to say, there will be a significant discrepancy between the public transcript of the dominant elites and the hidden transcript of the dominated.

Of course, each group will have both a public and a hidden transcript. The public transcript of the oppressed, for example, will appear to conform to the world created by their rulers and will contribute to "the flattering self-image of elites" (18). It is simply a matter of survival for the powerless to appear compliant and obedient. This is the communication that occurs "on stage," where the controlling elites conceive the plot, write the script, and choreograph the political play. The variance between this safe form of public discourse and the hidden transcript would appear to create an impassable gulf. How can one ever get from one to the other? The task would be impossible were it not for a third form of political discourse found among oppressed classes. Scott describes it as "a politics of disguise and anonymity that takes place in public view but is designed to have a double meaning or to shield the identity of the actors" (18–19). The consequence of this situation is that "a partly sanitized, ambiguous and coded version of the hidden transcript is always present in the public discourse of subordinate groups" (19).

This study of the debate about the tribute to Caesar argues that Jesus' response is an example of just such a hidden transcript. In an earlier study entitled *Weapons of the Weak* (1985), Scott disclosed the forms of "symbolic compliance" and described the "rituals of deference" of the weak, what he called "everyday forms of peasant resistance—the prosaic but constant struggle between the peasantry and those who seek to extract labor, food, taxes, rents and interest from them." The weapons in this struggle are "foot dragging, dissimulation, false compliance, pilfering, feigned ignorance, slander, arson, sabotage and so forth."[19] To this list, I would add "dissembling." If it is simply too dangerous for the oppressed to disclose their hidden transcripts on stage, they will dissemble when they are entrapped or when their rulers threaten to unveil their hidden transcript. When forced by Herodians and Pharisees to disclose the hidden transcript of resistance to Roman colonial rule, Jesus dissembles. It is no accident that the topic chosen to force the issue is tribute, a primary focal point for everyday resistance. Scott has made it clear that everyday forms of peasant resistance tend to form around "the material nexus of the class struggle—the appropriation of land, labor, rent, taxes, rents, and so forth."[20] With these theoretical materials from Scott as a context, it is possible to read the dispute on the Temple Mount in such a way that it supports the charge eventually brought against Jesus.

Whatever the original setting might have been, the text clearly depicts a conflictual encounter. Mark is as clear about this (v. 13) as Jesus is (v. 15b). Every element in the account points in this direction: the nature of a challenge-riposte debate; the flattery of the Pharisees and Herodians; the explosive question about tribute; the use of the denarius; and the rapid-fire exchange culminating in Jesus' aphorism. It will be useful to examine each element.

Basing his comments on the Lukan version (20:20–26), J. Duncan Derrett has argued that the verb appearing in 20:26, *apocrisei,* is "a technical term for a *rescript:* it is what we lawyers call a *responsum,* a technical answer to a technical question, particularly in the field of behavior."[21] This position is further supported by the opponents' comment about Jesus teaching "the way of God" (20:21). The reference indicates that Jesus is being asked to render a formal opinion about whether the payment of tribute is congruent with Torah obedience. Put more precisely, their question could be paraphrased, "What does the Torah say about payment of tribute to Caesar?" On these slender threads of evidence, Derrett builds his case that Luke is depicting Jesus as God's appointed emissary who, in the tradition of Moses, declares God's will before a gathering of the people. Therefore, Jesus' response is decidedly "not merely a piece of evasion," but an update on the meaning of the Torah for the age of Tiberius.[22]

Derrett's clever and informative interpretation overlooks the obvious elements of entrapment that inform the account and animate its conflict. The setting is neither a courtroom nor a public reading of the law but a plot filled with political intrigue. The Herodians and Pharisees are trying to tease out the hidden transcript of Jewish resistance to Roman rule as that resistance was focused on the issue of tribute. In Mark and Matthew, the issue is very clearly the *kēnsos* or the *tributum capitis,* the tribute assessed on every male between the ages of fourteen and sixty-five, and on every woman between the ages of twelve and sixty-five.[23] The tax carried a special meaning for the poor.

> For the well-to-do the *tributum capitis* was a tax on movable property. . . . For the poor, however, who possessed little or nothing of any value in movable property the tax was on his (*sōma*), his body. Just as all land was considered as belonging ultimately to the Roman Empire, and thus, subject to taxation as a kind of rent, so also did one's body belong to Rome.[24]

This fact lent the question a symbolic value that might otherwise be missing.

Malina and Rohrbaugh are, therefore, closer to the ethos of the encounter when they describe the interaction as "a challenge-riposte encounter."[25] In first-century Palestine, opponents clashed in public debates in order to defend or acquire honor and avoid shame. All ripostes were zero sum games; somebody won and somebody lost. The winner gained at the expense of the loser, and the crowd determined who won. This conflict begins as just such an exchange, except that the Pharisees and Herodians disguise their hostility beneath flattery, but, instead of responding to their flattery, Jesus "answers with an insulting counterquestion." When challenged, "the honorable person . . . pushes away the challenge and diffuses any advantage his opponents might believe they have."[26] This is also why Jesus neither quotes nor debates the Torah in response to his enemies' question (contra Derrett). He knows that their intent is not disinterested inquiry but challenge and entrapment.

The initial flattery is not intended to deceive Jesus at all, but to put him on the spot. The flatterers are preparing the crowd, while setting up Jesus to disavow the tribute. By calling him a "true" teacher who neither judges people by their social station nor curries favor with the powerful, the Herodians and Pharisees are "daring Jesus to commit himself in this loaded political situation."[27] Every ostensible compliment raises the stakes, forcing Jesus to save face with the crowd by opposing the payment of tribute. In its current Markan form, the opening salvo is in chiastic form:

A   you are a true teacher
  B   and do not concern yourself with public opinion
  B′   you do not regard human status
A′   but truly teach the way of God[28]

Each half reinforces the other, and each theme interprets the other. In order to be a true prophet who truly teaches the way of God, Jesus must disregard human opinions and speak the truth without regard for consequences. If Jesus fails this test, he loses his stature as a truthful teacher. The flattery throws down the gauntlet.

The question posed by the Herodians and Pharisees is not a general question about the tax rate or a complaint about creeping tax brackets. It is a specific question about paying tribute. Tribute had been a volatile issue since Pompey laid Jerusalem and Judea under tribute in 63 B.C.E., because it was a sign of subjection to Rome. When Augustus converted Archelaus's failed kingdom into a Roman province in 6 C.E., he conducted a census in order to develop a basis for computing the tribute. The census was a tool of imperial policy, a way of implementing the ideology of domination and financing the cost of control. It served as a practical basis for calculating the extent of exploitation possible in any given area controlled by Rome. As Paul Finney noted, "the census constituted the numerical basis (computed in hectares and human heads) from which the Romans levied their so-called poll (or head) tax," which all non-elites were expected to pay in "imperial specie."[29] The census conducted in 6 C.E. triggered the revolt of Judas of Gamala, who evidently argued that "the payment of tribute to the Romans was incompatible with Israel's theocratic ideals"[30] (*War*, 2.118; *Ant.* 18.23). From the inception of Judas's "fourth philosophy" and what F. F. Bruce judges to be its unprecedented position with regard to paying tribute to pagan rulers, the issue of tribute became a permanent bone of contention.[31] Ched Myers thinks that the topic presented "a test of loyalty that divided collaborators from subversives against the backdrop of revolt."[32]

When the tribute was collected in Roman coinage, it was part and parcel of Roman political propaganda. The denarius was the stable and durable coinage of Tiberius's reign, and wherever Rome subjugated local populations, the denarius was certain to follow. Minted at Lugdunam in Gaul, the denarius was introduced as a step toward monetizing local economies. The tribute was usually collected in denarii.[33] The obverse of the denarius contained a profile of Tiberius's head, "adorned with the laurel wreath, the sign of his divinity,"[34] and it was inscribed with the epigram (abbreviations removed), *Tiberius Caesar Divi Augusti Filius Augustus* (Tiberius Caesar, Augustus, son of the divine Augustus). The reverse depicted the emperor's mother, Livia, "sitting on the throne of the gods, in her right hand the Olympian sceptre, in her left the olive branch" (125) to symbolize her incarnation as the heavenly *pax*, the divine counterpart of the Pax Romana. This side of the coin was inscribed with the phrase *pontifex maximus* (high priest). In sum, the coin was "a symbol both of power and the cult. It is a symbol of power, for it is the instrument of Roman imperial policy, of Roman currency policy [and] of Roman fiscal policy" (125). The durability of the denarius and its ubiquity made it a staple of Caesar's power and presence. It was no ordinary coin.

To deflect his opponents' momentum and to defuse their question, Jesus combines a counterquestion with a demand for a denarius. In doing so, he captures the initiative from his aggressive interlocutors and takes control of the terms of the discussion. This is why the coin is so critical. While numerous commentators have recognized the centrality of the denarius, few have pursued the reasons why.[35] Finney is correct when he observes that the request for the coin interrupts and redirects the flow of the dialogue.[36] By directing attention to the coin, Jesus shifts the terms of the controversy away from the Torah. He does not intend to debate the Torah because he knows that his opponents' interest in his pronouncement about the application of Torah to the question of tribute is a ruse. Better to establish other ground.

The denarius also distinguishes Jesus from his adversaries. They had asked the initial question in such a way that they seemed to be aligning themselves with Jesus: "Is it Torah observant to pay tribute to Caesar or not? Should *we* pay them, or should *we* not?" When Jesus asks them to produce a denarius, neither Pharisees nor Herodians have one in hand and they have to scurry about to find one, according to some interpretations.[37] It is equally possible that the Herodians have a coin ready to hand, since they harbor no scruples against using Roman coinage. Whether they have to procure a denarius from a money changer or can produce one on the spot, they separate themselves from Jesus when they produce it. They are now associated with the coin, but Jesus is not, since he had to ask for it. As Belo noted, the coin symbolizes "the uncleanness inflicted on the country by the occupying power,"[38] and it embodies the economic exploitation and political suppression accompanying the so-called Pax Romana. In terms of the symbolic significance of their actions, the Pharisees and Herodians have become identified with the coin, even though they have handed it over to Jesus. They are the source of the denarius.

As soon as Jesus takes the coin, he escalates the conflict by asking a nasty question: "Whose image (*eikōn*) and inscription (*epigraphē*) is this?" The question has a sharp edge. If the act of producing the coin did not shame his opponents, the question skewered them. The question was superfluous, since everyone in the crowd knew what was on the coin, and most of them hated its flagrant violation of the commandments. That violation was a statement of blasphemous idolatry, and his opponents knew it. They seek the most innocuous answer possible, vainly seeking to invoke the honorable name of their colonial master by muttering, "Caesar's." But the jig is up, for they have answered the question, thereby conceding ground to Jesus.

The very act of holding up the coin for everyone to see and playing dumb borders on the sarcastic, as J. S. Kennard noted long ago.[39] Imagine a rabbi lifting up a denarius containing the profile of the best-known figure in the Mediterranean world, Tiberius Caesar, and asking, almost innocently, "Who is this guy? What does he say about himself here? I can't figure it out." Both image and epigram condemn the denarius as a violation of the second commandment, which forbids making graven images of things on earth, below the earth, or in heaven (Ex. 20:4–6; Deut. 8:5). More importantly, it identifies Jesus' adversaries as idolators, since they produced the denarius. Ironically, even though he is holding the coin, Jesus has distanced himself from it. His opponents have been shamed in the exchange, but Jesus is still on the spot, for he has not responded to the original "friendly" challenge, and the crowd, no doubt, still expects a response.

Fulfilling that expectation is the purpose of the closing aphorism, "Pay back to Casear what is Caesar's, and to God what is God's" (v. 17). Until more recent times, the majority opinion has been that Jesus condoned paying tribute to Rome. Bruce compared Jesus' "counsel of non-resistance to Rome" with Jeremiah's "counsel of submission to Babylon."[40] As Jeremiah advised Judah not to resist the Babylonian empire, Jesus counsels Judea to cooperate with the Roman Empire by paying tribute. Throughout his discussion, Bruce assumes that Jesus would more likely be aligned with the prophetic tradition of cooperation with international superpowers than the recently emerged "fourth philosophy" that considered any payment of tribute a betrayal of Israel's theocratic ideal. Stauffer shares this basic conviction, but goes beyond Bruce by suggesting that the statement supports payment of temple tribute as well.[41] Jesus' aphorism is in the form of two parallel halves, one of which counsels paying tribute to Caesar (to Caesar what is Caesar's), the other of which condones paying tribute to the temple (to God what is God's).

Pursuing a different path, Kennard believes that Jesus limited his advice to those who asked the question—"the upper-class quislings" and aristocrats who collaborated with Rome and benefited from its rule.[42] Since they already possessed the denarii, Jesus advised them to repay Caesar, whose policies had brought them so much prosperity. I. Abrahams was convinced that this counsel would have been in keeping with rabbinic thought and prophetic tradition, both of which advocated support for foreign monarchs unless they forced the Jewish community to compromise on matters of Torah.[43]

But the issue may not be so easily resolved, precisely because the Roman denarius did involve a Torah issue as well as a political one. The very form of Jesus' aphorism implies a conflict. Robert Tannehill entertained the notion that Jesus' statement was in the form of an "antithetical aphorism," but after further reflection he qualified his judgment in light of his conviction that Jesus was staking out a position in the middle of the political spectrum. It is permissable to pay the tribute, but it is even more important to contemplate what things are owed to God.[44] In effect, Jesus answered the question while minimizing its importance by introducing the more momentous question of debts owed to God. The difficulty with Tannehill's position is that it appears to be unduly influenced by his prior assumption regarding Jesus' political stance, and in light of that, he seems willing to abandon his careful analysis of the antithetical nature of Jesus' aphorism. Having made his case, he then abandons it.

Belo disagrees with all of the approaches summarized above. Each one is, from his point of view, "a nonreading of the narrative, an act of ideological blindness imposed by the interests of those who make it."[45] Of course, the same charge could be pressed against his own work.

Whether or not one accepts Belo's harsh judgment, there are good reasons for questioning the readings that attribute to Jesus support for paying the tribute. Developing Tannehill's thesis more consistently, Ched Myers argues that the final saying is an antithetical aphorism that sharply contrasts opposing loyalties. The tribute laid a heavy load on the backs of the peasantry who bore the burden of paying it. Since Jesus devoted so much of his public work to the very people who would be most adversely affected by tributary demands, he would not easily have accepted their validity. Horsley agrees with this conclusion and supports his contention by noting the shift of verbs from challenge to riposte.[46] Should we "give" (*dounai*) tribute to Caesar? "Pay back" (*apodote*) to Caesar what is his. The latter verb (*apodidōnai*) refers to repaying a debt. It is "the standard term used where people are obligated to recognize the rightful claims of others." In short, the verb invokes "the imperial situation of domination and subjugation."[47]

This situation is entirely in keeping with what Gerhard Lenski calls "the proprietary theory of the state," so common among agrarian rulers.[48] The conquered domains of agrarian empires belong to the rulers who can dispose of them as they choose. The payment of tribute is the basic recognition of this right. Since aristocratic rulers require vast amounts of wealth in order to pursue their political goals, and since they can generate revenue from only two sources, internal tribute through exploitation or external booty through conquest, they rely on the payment of tribute to sustain them in power. This is why such empires are "tribute-collecting machines."[49] All of this means that the question of tribute struck at the heart of the legitimacy of the Roman Empire's most essential function. The question of tribute was a clandestine referendum on Rome's right to occupy Judea.

For this reason, Horsley is convinced that Jesus escalated the question of tribute into the question of lordship.[50] What "things" do not belong to God? The use of "things" can equally well refer to "rights" and "claims" as well as to material things. Kennard also realized that all things belong to God: the land, the earth and the fullness thereof, the heavens, and the richness of the firmament.[51] What then can belong to Caesar? One thing only: the coin that he minted in his own image and likeness. That can be given back to Caesar, because it came from Caesar. Indeed, it is imperative that the denarius be paid back, for it is idolatrous and polluting. As such, according to Belo, it signifies "the uncleanness inflicted on the country by the occupying power; what Jesus is rejecting is the occupation."[52] The issue is the more poignant since it is the head tax form of tribute under discussion. The payment of this form of tribute was an acknowledgment that one's body belonged to Caesar.

But the creation story (Genesis 1–2) told a different tale in which women and men were minted in God's image and belonged to God. The reference to returning to God the things that are God's (*ta tou theou tō theō*) alludes to the creation stories and sets the terms of the conflict. The implications of Jesus' argument for the payment of *tributum soli* (the soil tax or land tax) are also reasonably clear. Yahweh had said, "the land is mine" (Lev. 25:23), and if the land belongs to Yahweh, then Caesar can have no valid claim to tribute from the land. The coin alone belongs to Caesar and can be returned (paid back) to him.

What then is Jesus saying in his famous dictum? He is saying in a disguised, ambiguous and coded way, "Return the coins to Caesar. He minted them in his image, and they should be returned to the one in whose image they were made." This would have the salutary effect of ridding the land of the idolatrous and blasphemous denarii. But this is not a call to pay tribute; it is a call to expel the coins from the land, to rid the land of their presence, masked as an ambiguous and indeterminate aphorism. Tannehill's initial instinct was right; Jesus' declaration is an antithetical aphorism. But it is uttered, like all hidden transcripts, in coded and ambiguous speech, not because Jesus wants to confuse his hearers, but because he has to exercise caution in a situation of entrapment. He certainly spoke clearly enough for "those who have ears to hear."

What good did Jesus do by using his clever aphorism? He did not change the fact of paying tribute. Even if the peasants of the land thought of themselves as returning the coins to Caesar, they still had to pay the poll tax. Were they not acknowledging Caesar's claim over their bodies after all? The answer is not easy, especially for those of us who have never lived in conditions of domination and subordination, but it is one thing to pay inevitable and unavoidable tribute to Caesar as a subject, but quite another to pay the tribute as an act of resistance. The attitude of the one paying the denarius was important.

In summary, Jesus dissembled to avoid entrapment, and the history of the interpretation of this pericope bears eloquent testimony to the success of his strategy. If this reading has anything to commend it, it means that the passage speaks a word about resistance, not accommodation, about refusing Caesar, not catering to him. Jesus' opponents were "astonished" at his answer precisely because they knew what he was doing and were helpless to expose it. His dissembling left them powerless to arrest him while permitting him to speak the coded "hidden transcript" of resistance in a way that could be understood by the crowd. Yet, his public transcript was in no way actionable. The message of opposition to the tribute did get through, and eventually it led to one charge in the indictment against him, namely, that he forbade the payment of tribute. Those who later pressed this charge had evidently heard the message of resistance hidden in Jesus' aphorism.

We Heard Him Say, "I Will Destroy This Temple."

The second charge was that Jesus threatened to destroy the temple (Mark 14:58 // Matt. 26:61; Mark 15:29 // Matt. 27:40; cf. Mark 13:1–2; Matt. 24:1–2; Luke 21:5–6). Earlier chapters of this study have already suggested grounds on which this charge could credibly be pressed.[53] To examine the case against Jesus, it will be helpful to study briefly one other controversy dialogue, in part because it raises questions about Jesus' relationship with John the Baptist. This is the debate about authority (Mark 11:27–33; Matt. 21:23–27; Luke 20:1–8).

Although Hultgren classifies the pericope as a "unitary" conflict story, he is convinced that its "earliest recoverable form" includes verses 27b, 28, 29a, 30.[54] The other materials were added either by Mark or by other pre-Markan editors. Bultmann was puzzled by the lack of antecedent for the expression "these things," and he believed that the counterquestion in verse 30 marked the end of the debate. The scribes' internal debate in verse 31 betrays Christian language ("believe in him"). This means that the original account included verses 27b–30, while the verses that follow "derive from an Hellenist."[55] Of course, the verb "believe" does not have to carry the Christian freight that would later be loaded onto it. In this context, it can mean that the scribes did not accept John's version of things; they did not "trust" him but treated him with the suspicion with which all insiders treat outsiders. Nor does Hultgren's reconstruction seem convincing. It simply poses a question, "Who gave you authority?" against a counterquestion, "Was the baptism of John from heaven or men?" Within this limited framework, the larger public dimensions of the debate are lost. However, the reconstructed original does focus attention on Jesus in a christological way, as Hultgren makes clear:

> Rather, it is apparent that in the formulation and preservation of this conflict story the interest was from the beginning centered upon Jesus as an agent of God's eschatological authority. That is to say, the interest was Christological.[56]

Working with this perspective, Hultgren trims the story to its essentials so that it carries the christological message he attributes to it. This reading does excise the political nature of the conflict.

The debate is set on the Temple Mount in the outer courtyard, where even Gentiles were permitted. If Jesus' opponents are "the chief priests, and the scribes and the elders of the people," then the Temple Mount is a reasonable setting. However, it seems questionable that the chief priests themselves would have engaged Jesus in a public challenge-riposte. They would have viewed their social status as being too far above that of Jesus to deign to confront him. People usually engage their social equals or near equals in an honor-shame contest. If the elders were the nonpriestly members of the ruling class in Jerusalem, the same could be said of them. They would be more likely to send their retainers to engage Jesus in debate. Setting their scruples aside, the chief priests and elders could have sent their proxies to represent their interests in the encounter. Since the scribes were familiar figures, the crowd would have known whom they represented and, consequently, they would have known that the conflict was, in truth, between Jesus and the priestly ruling caste as well as their nonpriestly cronies, even though the actual public interaction was between Jesus and some scribes. The relationship between high priests and scribes was that of rule creator to rule enforcer. As Malina and Neyrey have seen quite clearly:

> Interest groups serve both as rule creators and ultimately, as rule enforcers, for even if interest group members do not directly enforce rules, they surely control those who do enforce them. Interest group members function as moral entrepreneurs who indicate to their society that certain actions by some alleged miscreant are deviant in a system to which they are all committed.[57]

Two other factors argue for a Temple Mount setting. Form critics suggest that, in his narrative, Mark augmented a primitive sequence of events that included the triumphal entry (11:1–11), the cleansing of the temple (11:15–18), and the question of authority (11:27–33) by inserting the cursing of the fig tree (11:12–14, 20–24) and some related sayings (11:25–26).[58] If the reconstruction of this primitive sequence is accurate, it explains the meaning of "doing these things" (*tauta poieis*). The phrase refers to the cleansing of the temple, a connection still evident in Luke (19:45–20:8) and John (2:13–22). Without that connection, the phrase does not have a clear antecedent. If the argument about authority contains an allusion to the temple cleansing, then it probably belongs on the Temple Mount. Both primitive sequence and the referent to the phrase "doing these things" indicate a setting on the Temple Mount.

This interpretation will portray the challenge-riposte as a conflict between temple scribes, acting as proxies for the powers that be, and Jesus, and it assumes a setting in the outer courtyard of the temple. However, the reference to "doing these things" may have a wider resonance than the incident in the temple. The scribes may be accusing Jesus of arrogating to himself the role of broker of God's forgiveness, in competition with the sacrificial system of the temple, and thereby acting in an unauthorized capacity. He lacks the authority to assume the role. The scribes may also be alluding to Jesus' teachings that the temple is not essential to ensure the fruitfulness of the land. If this is true, then the symbolic destruction of the temple (or temple cleansing) is simply the latest in a long line of provocations, all of which could be caught up in the phrase "doing these things."

The scribes, acting on behalf of their high-priestly patrons and the ruling class of Jerusalem, who depend indirectly on the temple for their wealth, challenge Jesus in the public courtyard of the temple. They have the power to initiate the challenge, since Jesus is in their space, and their challenge reflects their privileged status. In essence, they accuse Jesus of acting beyond his appropriate and authorized role. He is out of place and, therefore, impure. Malina and Rohrbaugh note that "actions out of keeping with one's social standing required some form of legitimation if they were not to be thought inspired by evil."[59] By contrast to Jesus, the high priests and elders have ascribed honor, owing to their noble birth, and the scribes have acquired honor, owing to their literacy, their achievements in interpreting the Torah, and their association with the temple authorities. If Jesus were to achieve any public credibility, he could have earned it primarily through honor-shame contests; the path of acquired honor was as open to him as the avenue of ascribed honor was closed. So Jesus would have been impelled to take on the scribes, since "whatever its source, a social standing commensurate with what one did and said in public would have been required for public credibility."[60] The scribes' challenge contains a backhanded compliment, since the very fact of their public challenge indicates that they consider Jesus socially equivalent and worthy of engaging in a public contest. They enter the challenge-riposte with the presumption of honor on their side; they are the heavy favorites to prevail against a rural rabbi from Galilee.

The opening questions set the tone for the debate. The two questions are roughly parallel, although Hultgren judges the second question more original than the first one.[61]

> By what authority are you doing these things?
> Who gave you this authority to do them?

It is possible that the second question does reflect a more primitive outlook because it personalizes the issue in a manner typical of Mediterranean societies and contains a Semiticism, which also implies an early provenance. But the two questions can be seen as posing two intimately related and finally inseparable issues. The first question challenges Jesus' role as interpreter of the Torah. The phrase "by what authority" can be read as a question about the sacred adjudicator of Judean life, the Torah. The book of Leviticus addresses such matters as the consecration of priests (chaps. 8–10), and the specifications for the day of atonement (chap. 16). Similarly, Exodus contains sections on the priestly vestments (chap. 28) and the ordination of priests (chap. 29) and two chapters devoted to matters related to the priesthood (chaps. 30–31). In short, the Torah seemed to validate the role and authority of priests, the bringing of tithes and offerings (Lev. 27:30–33; Num. 18:21–32; Deut. 12:15–28; 14:22–29; 26:12–15), and the offering of sacrifices (Leviticus 1–7). If this authority, given by Yahweh through Moses, defined the life of the people, on what basis was Jesus doing things that undermined the honorable authority of the Torah? The implication of the first question could be understood as claiming that Jesus was shamefully destroying the role of Torah in the life of the people.

The second question reflects the scribes' view that their patrons have all authority on earth and distribute it as they see fit. "Who gave you this authority to do them?" Typically, in agrarian societies, authority is personally controlled and distributed. In a limited-goods society, authority, like all other goods, is limited, and access to it is carefully controlled. The assumption behind the question is that, if the high priests, elders, or their functionaries did not authorize Jesus, then his claim to authority is illegitimate. The very fact that the scribes are asking this question indicates that they have not authorized Jesus. Their question is an attempt to isolate Jesus from any honorable form of legitimation, certainly from any effort to claim authorization from the Torah or the temple.

When challenged, an honorable man does not answer the question or respond to implied charges but changes the terms of the debate and shifts its ground. Jesus responds by promising to answer the question but on his terms and after his opponents have answered his question. His demand is punctuated by two imperatives (*apokrithēte*, answer, vv. 29a, 30b). With his counterquestion, "Was the baptism of John from heaven or from humans?" (v. 30) and its associated demands, the spotlight shifts to the scribes, who are unexpectedly undermined and in a quandary. The question has exposed the Achilles heel of the scribes' implied argument, because Judeans have long recognized forms of prophetic authority that critique the Torah and those who abuse it, whether king or priest. John is but a recent example of a long tradition. The reference to John is well-chosen and may be even more germane than it first appears. If John the Baptist simply immersed, he would have been innocuous enough, but he "preached a baptism of repentance for the forgiveness of sins" (Mark 1:4; cf. Mark 1:4–6; Matt. 3:1–2a, 4–6; Luke 3:1–3; cf. also Q: Luke 3:7–9; Matt. 3:7–10). If this brokering of God's forgiveness through the offer of baptism or immersion anticipates Jesus' later practice, then John, no less than Jesus, posed a threat to the temple's hegemony. Was John providing baptism as a way to deal with sin and indebtedness without reference to the temple? Did those who underwent his baptism believe themselves no longer obligated to the temple? Both John and Jesus stepped into the role of prophetic broker of God's forgiveness and prophetic critic of the current authorities who claim a monopoly of that role for themselves. Jesus may well have first seen the role of broker lived out in John. So Jesus' choice of John is contextually appropriate.

Cornered by their own devices, the scribes "equivocate" (*dielogizonto*), to use Myers's translation. In Mark, at least, the verb indicates "ideological confusion" (cf. Mark 2:6, 8; 8:16f.; 9:33).[62] Their dilemma indicates how powerfully a dead prophet, revered by the people, controls the living, and their confusion testifies to the inherent weakness of the Judean ruling class that Goodman has described in detail.[63] The temple ruling class is "politically isolated, fearful of the very people it purportedly serves."[64] If they acknowledge that John's baptism was of divine origin, then they have conceded that they do not exercise unconditional control over the redemptive media and have, therefore, opened the door to Jesus' claims of prophetic legitimation. The very God who ordained the authority of the priests has also ordained the authority of the prophets in a divine version of a system of checks and balances. The living voice of the prophets and their continuing influence in public affairs makes Judea a dead prophets' society. In light of these widely held sentiments, it would be suicide to declare that John's baptism was anything less than ordained by heaven, which means ordained by God. To reduce it to a human activity would be to risk a riot at pilgrimage festival. So the weasels withdraw from the debate by refusing to answer the question. To refuse to answer is not a sign of total weakness. It could be accompanied by a status display that indicates the question was not worthy of a response because it was irrelevant to the matter at hand. To say, "We do not know," can mean, "We refuse to respond." The bottom line, in any case, is that Jesus wins the standoff. The expectation of victory accompanied the scribes as they went into action. Anything less than total victory is a defeat. Jesus' final retort, "Then neither will I tell you by what authority I do these things" (v. 33), closes the riposte by giving the impression that he is in control, refusing to reveal his secret because his adversaries have not met his conditions.

In his discussion of the entry into Jerusalem and cleansing of the temple, Ben Meyer takes note of the puzzling character of Jesus' actions and teaching: "Riddles and symbolic acts have in common a deliberately provocative aspect. . . . Though most of his riddles belonged to esoteric teaching, there were also those spoken in public."[65] The question about John's baptism and Jesus' final refusal to answer fit this description. Jesus walks on the edge of revealing his great secret. The authority of heaven is once again afoot in the land. The reign of God is coming near, so close that one could almost reach out and touch it, so near that is at the very gates (Mark 1:15; Matt. 4:17). Hultgren puts it in more traditional language: "it is the eschatological *exousia* of God that is coming into being in these actions which appear disruptive, illegitimate, and unauthorized."[66] Jesus' refusal fools no one; the crowd knows that John's baptism was "from heaven," and now they know that Jesus' authority comes from the same source.

The debate over authority confirms Jesus' recalcitrant stance. He is opposed to the temple and, if his movement succeeds, it could seriously undermine the authority and prestige of the temple. By his words and deeds, he has indeed threatened to destroy the temple. His course of action could not remain unchallenged. Jesus and the temple were on a collision course. The only question was when the collision would occur. All of this means that the chief priests, the elders, and their scribes were right to press charges against Jesus. He was a threat to the temple.

"Are You the Messiah, the Son of the Blesssed One?"

The third charge is that Jesus claimed to be "ruler of the Judeans" or messiah. This charge seems best understood in the context of popular kingship.[67] At the time of Herod the Great's death, a number of figures rose to claim the empty throne. His own servant, Simon, crowned himself and led a band of his followers across the countryside, looting and burning royal residences. He was eventually defeated and beheaded (*Ant.* 17.273–76). Athronges, an obscure shepherd, attempted to revive the legend of David by conducting guerrilla warfare against the Romans. After a period of relative success he too was defeated and executed (*Ant.* 17.278–85). Like Simon, Athronges seems to have appointed himself king, although both men were able to attract a following. In Galilee, Judas, son of Hezekias, raided the palace at Sepphoris, confiscated weapons, armed his followers, and conducted warfare against other rivals for the throne (*Ant.* 17.271–72; *War* 2.56). All three men cut imposing figures and, at least for a time, showed military skill and leadership. They appear to have wanted to rid the land of the Romans as a prelude to assuming the throne.

Horsley and Hanson speculate that the tradition of popular kingship traces to the period of the judges, when "mighty men of valor" (Judg. 6:12) were anointed to lead the people through a political or military crisis. Like the judges of old, the popular kings were charismatic figures, able to command a following and conduct a limited military campaign. They were of humble origin, not from royal lineage. Their followers were primarily peasants or the disaffected urban poor, an indication, perhaps, that the people of the land were no longer looking to their aristocratic masters for leadership. The movements shared a common goal:

> The principal goal of these movements was to overthrow Herodian and Roman domination and to restore the traditional ideals of a free and egalitarian society. . . . Besides attacking both Ro-

man and royalist forces, they also raided and destroyed the mansions of the gentry along with royal residences. We can reasonably infer a certain resentment at prolonged social-economic inequity and exploitation, as well as a spirit of egalitarian anarchism, typical among peasant uprisings.[68]

Similar outbreaks of popular kingship would also occur at the time of the First Jewish Revolt, when they took on a more clearly messianic character.

The Gospels contain echoes and allusions to kingship as associated with Jesus. The Gospel of John records a strange incident in which the multitude, who have just been fed the loaves and fish, first declare Jesus the fulfillment of the prophet promised in Deuteronomy 18:15 and then try to highjack him and make him king (John 6:15). In the Synoptic Gospels, Jesus is greeted as a messianic king during his entry into Jerusalem. The acclamation of the crowd is clearly messianic (Mark 11:9–10; Matt. 21:9; Luke 19:38; John 12:13). The manner of the entry is in such marked contrast to the expectations of the crowd that it is entirely possible that Jesus is lampooning their messianic expectations by riding a donkey into the city, rather than riding a war horse or driving a chariot like a Roman general enjoying a "triumph," although some elements of the procession (palm branches and shouts of praise) do recall the triumphal entry of Simon Maccabeus into Jerusalem (1 Macc. 13:51). The overall impression is more akin to what Myers calls "political street theatre."[69] The allusion to Zechariah strengthens this impression. Zechariah's oracle (9:9–17) is not so much a war oracle as a vision of the ingathering of God's people and the initiation of an age of peace. Applied to Jesus, the oracle fits, for Jesus' public work has been dedicated to gathering in the outcasts to participate in the covenant community.

If the argument of this study is to be taken into consideration, it would weigh against Jesus making a claim to popular kingship. His proclamation of the reign of God was not a coded way of staking his claim to the throne. If related to this issue in any way, it was a rejection of kingship because its abuses proved to be ineradicable. In a study of the parables, I argued that the parable of the unmerciful servant (Matt. 18:23–35) could be read as a rejection of the messianic ideal, because any messiah who did ascend the throne would be caught in the systemic realities of kingship in agrarian societies and aristocratic empires. Every king is captive of kingship, including the messiah![70] The short history of the Hasmonaean dynasty could be invoked to make the same point.

It seems unlikely that Jesus either staked a claim to kingship or allowed himself to be anointed as a messianic king. The third charge against Jesus was, on the face of it, false. At another level, Jesus was subversive to colonized rulers and colonial masters alike. Even if he did not employ the tool of messianic kingship, he did form a threat no less real. The prophet could be involved in the rise and fall of political leaders.

Up to this point, I have argued in this chapter that the charges against Jesus were sustainable. He did not accede to paying tribute, and he did threaten to destroy the temple system. Since Rome viewed any threat to its tributary supply lines as a threat to the empire, the Romans had a reason to condone the execution of Jesus. Since the temple was the symbolic center and focus of loyal dedication for many Judeans and Galileans, a threat to the temple was a credible threat to be reckoned with. Even if Jesus made no claims to kingship, he was a subversive leader and friend neither to temple nor the Roman occupying power. Therefore, in some sense, every charge against Jesus had some basis in reality. He was not crucified by accident, nor was his crucifixion the result of a case of mistaken identity.

THE SHOW TRIAL IN JERUSALEM

Jesus was never tried to determine his innocence or guilt. There never was a "trial of Jesus."[71] To speak of a trial is an anachronism, for, more often than not, it assumes that modern canons of jurisprudence applied to the first century. A trial in our society involves bringing charges, providing for a prosecutor and a defense attorney, introducing evidence and weighing its relevance, impaneling a jury of peers, adhering to a code of law, following court procedures designed to protect the rights of all involved, determining innocence or guilt only as the outcome of the legal process, allowing appeals, and regarding the accused innocent until proven guilty, to name just a few. In relationship to the executive and legislative branches, the judicial branch of government exists within the framework of a system of checks and balances to prevent one branch from being forced to serve the interests of the others. The entire system attempts to live up to the ideal of blind justice or equal justice before the law. None of this applies to the show trial of Jesus.

A show trial is a form of political theater. In her work on theaters in the Roman world, Mary Boatwright has noted that, in addition to their use for plays and musical and athletic festivals, theaters also "were used as venues for public trials or meetings."[72] In a show trial, the guilt of the person being "tried" has already been determined. There is no effort to weigh evidence, nor is there a defense of the offender. Show trials are conducted under the firm control of the state; there is no independent judiciary. The procedure does not conform to laws but follows the expedient will of power elites. Some ad hoc body of accusers stands in place of a jury, and its members belong to the same ruling class as the accusers. A show trial is not a legal process but a political process whose purpose is the public degradation and humiliation of an enemy of the state before his foreordained execution.

It was one thing for Jesus to engage the local elites in Galilee and Judea, but when he came to Jerusalem, he confronted the elites who defined the public life of Judea and represented the interests of Rome. The high priests formed the most powerful interest group in Judea, and along with the Herodians who controlled Galilee, made the rules that governed the political game. As Malina and Neyrey note, "Interest group members frequently function as rule creators for the society at large. And these rule creators likewise command rule enforcers."[73] This is what was at stake in the arguments over the Torah. In the Torah, the high-priestly rule creators found a convenient means for enforcing their governance of Judea and the peasants of Galilee: their rules were really God's rules, just as the temple was the "temple of God." It was left to the rule enforcers (most likely, scribes and Pharisees) to expose deviance and punish it. When Jesus undermined the temple and called its legitimacy into question, he threatened the most powerful group in Judea. If, as M. Goodman has suggested, their hold on power was more precarious than that of elites in other areas of the empire, they would have been particularly sensitive to any challenges to their hegemony. This is why Malina and Neyrey are right to observe about the debate over authority, "The essence of this confrontation consists in a factual, political question about Jesus' authority, not an academic or theoretical question about Torah."[74] When Jesus refused to concede ground on the question of authority, he set himself against a political interest group that could not tolerate his challenge.

The first phase of opposition involved "negative labeling." The Synoptic traditions contain numerous examples of this tactic. For example, Jesus is accused of being in league with Beelzebul and colluding with Satan (Mark 3:22–26; Matt. 12:22–30; Luke 11:14–23), of befriending toll collectors and sinners (Mark 2:16; Matt. 9:11; Luke 5:30), and of uttering blasphemy (Mark 2:7; Matt. 9:3; Luke 5:21). Presumably, the scribes and Pharisees come down from Jerusalem to confirm Jesus' deviance so that they can disseminate his standing in the eyes of the high-priestly caste.

Once Jesus is in the custody of his enemies, the negative labeling escalates as "witnesses" come forward to denounce him (Mark 14:57–58; Matt. 26:61). The charges now include blasphemy (Mark 14:63–64; Matt. 26:65) and threatening to destroy the temple (Mark 14:58; Matt. 26:61). It is during this process that an ad hoc power group could be convened to serve as a "deviance processing agency" and give an appearance of legitimacy to the process. They lend their aristocratic respectability to the show trial and, as prominent figures, lend their endorsement to the proceedings, thus enhancing the aura of authority surrounding the show trial.[75] Their scribes work as "imputation specialists" who create the record on which the deviant will be executed. There is no evidence that such a record was prepared during the trial of Jesus, probably because he was a poor, insignificant peasant, and his judges deemed him unworthy of such attention. Even without a written record, the intention of the procedure remained the same, namely, to reduce the person on display to a stereotype of a criminal: "the person accused of deviance must be made to be an instance of what she or he is alleged to have done: from devious doer to deviant; from crime perpetrator to criminal."[76] The purpose of denunciation is to destroy the person's identity and establish a new, more sinister identity in its place. Although told through the eyes of a defensive early church, the process of denunciation is portrayed in Mark 14:55–65 and Matthew 26:59–68.

The outcome of the process of negative labeling and denunciation is to create a "retrospective interpretation" of the deviant's life. A retrospective interpretation is an attempt to fashion

> A "biography" of the alleged deviant to show that the offensive behavior is not just a single instance of deviant activity but that it represents a total identity, a long standing pattern or an incontrovertible indicator of a totally perverse character.[77]

In the process of creating such an interpretation, the goal is to assign a "master status" to the person on trial. In Jesus' case, "The specific charges made in the trial are not isolated incidents for he has always behaved in deviant fashion. Jesus' master status, then, is that of a deviant, a blaspheming temple-profaner and a presumptious fraud."[78]

One rhetorical strategy employed to stigmatize the criminal is to apply honorable labels in an ironic fashion. So Jesus is mocked as both a "prophet" (Mark 14:65; Matt. 26:67–68; Luke 22:64) and a "king of the Judeans" (Mark 15:17–19; Matt. 27:28–30). But the master label that captured the retrospective interpretation of Jesus' life was summarized on the titulus, "The King of the Judeans" (Mark 15:26; Matt. 27:37; Luke 23:38; John 19:19). Again, it is interesting to note that the charge eventually used to interpret Jesus retrospectively was probably the only charge brought against him that was not true. If the titulus was to serve as a shorthand for the "biography" of the deviant, it most likely evoked a story line, in this case the story line of popular kingship. What all of the aspirants to the throne have in common is their humble origins and their violent end. All are captured and executed.[79] Jesus is being cast in their image as he hangs on the cross, a warning to others with similar ambitions. Crossan describes crucifixion as a form of "state terrorism" whose goal was deterrence, especially among the poor.[80] The point of the crucifixion is to exhibit what happens to those who step out of their station and claim a role for which they were not authorized.

The show trial and execution serve as a "status degradation ritual."[81] The show trial is one means of shaming and dehumanizing the deviant so that he becomes an example of what is being condemned. "The work of denunciation effects the recasting of the objective character of the perceived other. The other person becomes in the eyes of his condemners literally a different and new person. . . . He is reconstituted."[82] The prophet must be transformed into the false prophet (Mark 14:65), and the reputational leader of a prophetic movement must be transformed into a false messiah leading the people down the path to ruin and chaos (Luke 23:2, 4–5; Mark 15:17–20a; Matt. 27:28–31a; John 19:1–2). The figure popular with the masses must be degraded before the crowd and turned into a mockery of what they hoped he would be.

The status degradation ritual includes the meetings of the ad hoc consultative body that served as a kangaroo court and was mistakenly identified as the Sanhedrin by the Gospel writers, the public exchange with Pilate, and the public condemnation. The humiliation and torture conducted by the soldiers is also part of the ritual, which culminated in crucifixion, the most brutal, painful, and shameful death imaginable in the Roman Empire.[83] Crossan is surely correct to suggest that "it is hard for us . . . to bring our imagination down low enough to see the casual brutality with which he was probably taken and executed."[84]

But who set the process in motion? The Gospel writers speak of the Sanhedrin (Mark 14:55; Matt. 26:59; Luke 22:66). But it is highly unlikely that the Sanhedrin participated in the process. James McLaren has studied twenty-one episodes, ranging from the Hasmonaean period through the Jewish Revolt, in which Jews were involved in political decision making. His analysis of the trial of Jesus is especially useful.[85] McLaren divides the actors in the trial into three categories:

> certain: chief priests; Caiaphas; Pilate
> probable: the elders, rulers, or scribes; captain of the temple; high priest's father-in-law
> doubtful: Pharisees; Antipas; the Sanhedrin. (91–94)

No formal trial took place. Rather, the power elite worked in concert with Pilate to execute Jesus. McLaren's conclusion coheres with the reading proposed here:

> It is important to acknowledge that the execution of Jesus was instigated by a powerful, select group of Jews. The action was formal and legitimate because the Jewish protagonists were influential men of high public standing, able to manipulate the situation to their advantage, and obtaining Roman support. (97)

But they acted as urban elites would have been expected to act in order to protect themselves from a perceived threat and to please their Roman overlords. In this sense, Ellis Rivkin has perceived correctly how much the Roman imperial system dominated the process. Shifting the question from "who crucified Jesus" to "what crucified Jesus," Rivkin concludes:

> For it emerges with great clarity, both from Josephus and the Gospels, that the culprit is not the Jews, but the Roman imperial system. It was the Roman emperor who appointed the procurator; it was the procurator who appointed the high priest; and it was the high priest who convoked the privy council. It was the Roman imperial system which exacted harsh tribute. It was the actions of Roman procurators which drove the people wild and stirred Judea with convulsive violence.[86]

The results of this study are contiguous with Rivkin's findings, although the approach advocated here does highlight the stake that the Judean leaders held in the execution of Jesus. Rivkin is surely right to emphasize the pressure placed on them by the Roman demand for a pacified province. If the reconstruction proposed here is in any way reflective of what happened historically, then it finesses the question of the Sanhedrin's role and changes the character of the participation of the Jerusalem elites. There is no need to pursue Solomon Zeitlin's proposal that there were two Sanhedrins, a religious one and a political one.[87]

This reading also changes the character of the debate between Raymond Brown and Crossan.[88] In particular, Crossan's solution—that the Gospel accounts of the trial of Jesus are "prophecy historicized" rather than "history remembered"[89]—risks erasing the political dimension of the events in Jerusalem and threatens a solution compatible with the Orwellian historians in *1984*, always rewriting the past to reflect contemporary concerns and needs. Embarrassment need not lead to erasure of memory and denial of the past. Not even the abuse of the past should lead to its eradication as history.

McLaren's analysis of other instances of political decision making reinforce the pattern discerned in studying Jesus' trial, a pattern in which power elites work to enhance their own self-interests with their colonial masters. They use bodies like the Sanhedrin only when it conveniently serves their interests and contributes to their strategies. This means that rulers or ruling cliques make political decisions on their own before consulting ad hoc power groups, mainly to confirm what they have determined. This pattern is clear in Jesus' trial. What the Gospel writers call a "sanhedrin" was most likely such an informal but powerful body, convened for the purpose of legitimating what had already been decided by the high priests and, perhaps, the elders, the landed aristocrats who ruled with them. But they were not convened to preside over a trial. Luke's language suggests this construal of the situation, because he uses a variety of phrases to describe the ad hoc group overseeing the elimination of Jesus. He identifies them as "the elders of the people" (*to presbyterion tou laou*), chief priests (*archiereis*), scribes (*grammateis*, 22:66), "rulers of the people (*archontas ton laon*, 23:13), and "the principal men of the people" (*hoi prōtoi tou laou*, 19:47). McLaren is right in observing that all the groups identified have one thing in common: they all possess power and privilege. They are the shakers and movers of the city and, in this role, they perform their functions. If there is confusion about their identity, it is understandable, because power elites often stayed out of public view, preferring to rule in relative anonymity and let their retainers take the brunt of popular hostility and resentment at their oppressive policies.

In none of this is there a hint that the leaders acted because they were "Jews." They were first-century Judeans, caught in the grip of imperial Rome, collaborating with a prefect to ensure the pacification of the province. The dynamics of the show trial, status degradation ritual, and execution could have been repeated in a variety of contexts with virtually identical results. On the basis of this reading, there is nothing to support the mean and abusive uses to which the show trial of Jesus has been put. Crossan is surely right to connect his concern for interpreting the trial of Jesus to the problem of anti-Semiticism. This study shares his concern, if not his drastic solution.

CONCLUSION

I have argued that Jesus was charged with three crimes: (1) he opposed the payment of tribute to Caesar; (2) he threatened to destroy the temple, which was a blasphemous act, because the temple was "the temple of God" (Matt. 26:61), and therefore any action against the temple was an act of aggression against God; (3) he claimed to be a messianic king. Further, I have argued that the first two claims were essentially true. Jesus declared that "the sons [and daughters] are free" of the temple tribute (Matt. 17:26), and, in an argument over what belongs to Caesar and what to God, Jesus undermined the basis for the payment of tribute to Rome (Mark 12:13–17). In a clash with the scribes, Jesus asserted his counterauthority as a prophet, legitimated "from heaven." His refusal to concede ground to the priestly class and its control of the temple earned him their lasting animosity. The third charge, namely, that Jesus claimed to be a messianic king, was false, although he was a subversive power whose actions threatened to disrupt the hieratic hierarchy of the temple and the colonial control of Rome.

It was his potential threat to these political interest groups that led to Jesus' arrest. The show trial and status degradation ritual to which he was subjected represented the attempt of both temple and Roman leaders to exterminate the deviant and utterly discredit his movement. Jesus' prophetic lament over Jerusalem (Q: Luke 13:34–35 = Matt. 23:37–39) provided a glimpse of the fate that awaited him. At the end of the day now known as Good Friday, it appeared for all the world as though the ruling priests, landed aristocrats, and Roman rulers had prevailed again. The show trial and execution of Jesus demonstrated once again how firm was their hold on power and how foolish it was to question their authority. The cross had put Jesus in his place, a degraded form of punishment for a disgraced peasant who presumed to criticize the temple ordained by God and the Torah as the oracle of God.

Crossan has argued forcibly that crucifixion did not end with the death of the deviant on the cross. The body was left to rot away and serve as carrion for the dogs at the foot of the cross and the vultures gathering at its pinacle. "But what we often forget about crucifixion is the carrion crow and the scavenger dog who respectively croak above and growl below the dead or dying body."[90] For Crossan, this aspect of crucifixion explains why we have recovered so few remains of those who were crucified. It explains one other feature of the accounts of Jesus' death that Crossan failed to observe. Why would the women have remained "looking on from afar" at Jesus' dying on the cross? (Mark 15:40–41; Matt. 27:55–56; Luke 23:49). In light of Hengel's and Crossan's work, one answer comes readily to mind. They remained in the vicinity of the cross to protect Jesus' body from the scavengers. It was their final act of piety. Perhaps they knew of Joseph's plan to seek the body, or perhaps they did not know but were simply trying to salvage some shred of honor for the dying man they had so admired. But they were not there as disinterested spectators. Their presence was a mark of respect for the prophet who had brought the reign of God so close that they thought they had almost been able to reach out and touch it.

11

A Concluding Unhistorical Postscript

This final chapter deals briefly with two matters. The first is the meaning and status of the resurrection for understanding the historical Jesus. The second is the relationship between the historical Jesus and the Christology that emerged out of the resurrection.

WHY SEEK THE LIVING AMONG THE DEAD?

The resurrection changed everything. By the end of the day on which he was crucified, Jesus hung in shame on the cross, although his body would be claimed before it became carrion. But a decent burial, important as it was for the sake of honor, could not erase the shame of the show trial, public spectacle, torture, and execution. When the sun set on what would be called Good Friday, it cast a fading light on the hopes of the disciples before leaving them enveloped in darkness. Their dying hope is perfectly captured in the lament of the disciples on the Emmaus Road, "but we had hoped that he was the one to redeem Israel" (Luke 24:21). More to the point for the political atmosphere, the rulers had once again prevailed over the ruled. The urban elites of Jerusalem had gained an even tighter control of temple and Torah, and by making an example out of the unauthorized peasant prophet they had reinforced the intimidation, fear, and violence by which they continued their domination. Yet, by dawn of the first day of the week, the situation was changing.

The resurrection was confusing, because it combined experiences of absence and presence. It was first experienced as absence, the absence of the historical Jesus (Mark 16:1–8; Matt. 28:1–8; Luke 24:1–11; John 20:1–13). This is why the question of the body is important. The absence of the body first intimated the resurrection. The disciples were the first doubters (Luke 24:11) as well as the first believers (Matt. 28:8). Then the resurrection was experienced as presence, the presence of the Risen Christ in what appeared to be bodily form but was not. The Risen One was unrecognizable and recognizable at the same time (Matt. 28:9–10, 16–20; Luke 24:13–35, 36–43; John 20:11–18, 19–29; 21:1–14). The presence of the Risen One, almost as a bodily apparition, was encouraging (Luke 24:30–35), empowering, and commissioning (Matt. 28:16–20; John 19:21–23). Unlike other messianic movements, the Jesus movement neither disbanded nor looked for a new messiah when its leader was violently executed.[1] The movement refused to go away because of "the one who did not go away."[2]

Although, at times in the past century of quests for the historical Jesus, scholars have been reserved about dealing with the resurrection, in more recent times, they have not been hesitant to comment on the resurrection as part of their research into the historical Jesus, even if only to dismiss it. Opinion continues to vary as to whether it is proper to discuss a theological belief like resurrection in a historical study of Jesus. Both Sanders and Meyer, for example, simply ignore the resurrection as part of their account of Jesus' life.[3] Funk reports the "hilarity" and scorn expressed by the members of the Jesus Seminar when asked to comment on the following proposition: "The resurrection was an event in the life of Jesus."[4] It was considered to be a "meaningless" formulation, since "we all assume . . . that Jesus' life ended with his crucifixion and death."[5]

Whatever the resurrection refers to, it could not have been captured by a video camera on Easter morning. Borg, a member of the seminar, has tried to nuance his understanding of the resurrection while fundamentally sharing the skepticism of the seminar. "Though the story of the historical Jesus ends with his death on a Friday in A.D. 30," he writes, "the story of Jesus does not end there."[6] This allows Borg to distinguish between a pre-Easter Jesus and a post-Easter Jesus, the former being the historical Jesus while the latter refers to "the Jesus of Christian tradition and experience."[7] Put a bit differently, Easter leads to two equally important affirmations, "Jesus lives, and Jesus is Lord," both of which mean that "Jesus was experienced after his death, and that he is both Lord and Christ."[8]

None of this careful explanation should be taken to mean that the body of Jesus is important for understanding the resurrection. The fate of Jesus' body is utterly irrelevant to the meaning of resurrection. In their joint discussion of the resurrection, the major difference between Borg and Wright seems to be their disagreement on this point (111–42). Wright insists that, "once you allow that something remarkable happened to his body that morning," then all of the riddles and puzzlements of the resurrection fall into place. But once this is denied, "you are driven to ever more complex and fantastic hypotheses to explain the data" (124). In spite of his advocacy that Jesus' body was transformed as the prelude to Easter, Wright is no mere literalist; he is aware of the metaphorical layers of the stories. At heart, they serve to validate Jesus' messianic claim, to reveal that the cross was a triumph, not a tragedy, and to intimate the coming of a new creation.

> When Jesus emerged, transformed, from the tomb on Easter morning, the event was heavy with symbolic significance, to which the evangelists drew attention, without wishing to detract from [its] historical nature. . . . It was the first day of God's new week, the moment of sunrise after the long night, the time of new meetings, new meals, of reconciliation and new commissioning. It was the beginning of the new creation. (126)

One of the questions that continues to divide scholars is the significance of empty tomb. Was Jesus' body lost, tossed into the garbage dump in the Hinnom Valley, eaten by dogs and vultures, or transformed by the power of God?

Pursuing the literary option more fully, Crossan conceives of Easter as a metaphor for unfolding Christian experience, as implied by his chapter heading, "How many years was Easter Sunday?"[9] His point is that what we now know as Easter was formed over a long time during which traditional meanings were assimilated and consolidated into a theological synthesis, at times assuming story form. As in his treatment of the Emmaus story, he could say, "Easter never happened; Easter always happens," a position implied in his remark, "my thesis, remember, is that Christian faith was not Easter faith. It was there as soon as anyone saw God in Jesus."[10] The resurrection stories, like the Emmaus Road story, are metaphorical narratives evoking the journey of faith and the moments of recognition in that journey. "Emmaus never happened; Emmaus always happens." This is all part of a pattern Crossan has discerned in the Gospel and early church narratives: "a dialectical process of past/present and then/now in which those twin elements interpenetrate and interweave. . . . Jesus-past acts and speaks as Christ-present; Jesus-then acts and speaks as Lord-now."[11] For Crossan, the resurrection stories are essentially no different from any other stories able to evoke the experience of faith, that moment when one sees God at work in Jesus. An earlier generation of scholars, who saw difficulties between the postresurrection stories and the message they were being asked to bear, interpreted the situation differently. Reginald Fuller noted how difficult it was to express in narrative form the eschatological encounters narrated in the resurrection stories. He even judged the stories in Luke and John to be less helpful than the earlier stories (e.g., the appearance to Mary in Matthew) because they failed to capture "the resurrection faith of the earliest community, conceived in apocalyptic terms as transformation into an entirely new (eschatological) mode of existence."[12] In his study of the resurrection, Brown identified the same problem.

> If the various Gospel accounts thus betray the difficulty of framing the eschatological encounter with the Risen Jesus in the categories of space and time, they also hint at the radically changed status of the one who appears. The post-resurrectional confession is not simply "We have seen Jesus" but "We have seen *the Lord*.[13]

For Funk and the Jesus Seminar, the appeal to eschatology was nothing more than a clever ploy "to keep the resurrection of Jesus out of reach" and "out of range for empirical and historical investigation."[14]

Being surrounded by so great a cloud of divergent and dissident witnesses, I recognize the importance of articulating my own position. The resurrection did not signal an absolute discontinuity between the historical one and the Risen One, but defined the relationship between the two. The resurrection is the link that joins the historical Jesus with the Risen Christ. The two are one; the resurrection interprets the discontinuity in the midst of the continuity that joins the historical one to the Risen One. It was "Jesus of Nazareth, a man attested to you by God with deeds of power and wonders, and signs that God did through him" who was both crucified and raised up. This man "God raised up, having freed him from death" (Acts 2:22–24). It is the specificity and particularity of the resurrection that must not be lost. Therein resides its glory and its scandal. It was the status elevation ritual that put the status degradation ritual of the show trial and execution in a different perspective.[15] When God honored Jesus by means of resurrection, transforming his hideous death into honorable life, it was God's way of saying, "the quislings and the executioners got it wrong. My kid got it right. Go thou and do likewise." The resurrection, then, was the validation of Jesus' work and the confirmation of Jesus' way, and, because of that, the historical Jesus has no less relevance for the life of faith than the Risen Christ. The resurrection places God's stamp of approval on the ministry of the prophet of the justice of the reign of God. Jesus so embodied that reign that his risen presence is the continuing presence of the reign of God and the constant call for justice "on earth, as it is in heaven."

To say that God raised Jesus of Nazareth from the dead is to acknowledge that the resurrection is indeed an event that happened to Jesus. In this the language of the Gospels concur, especially the verb *egeirein*.

> The subject of *egeirein* is always God, or else the verb is used in the passive, which then always has the sense 'raised by God'. This establishes the resurrection as an act of God towards Jesus, and hence the theocentric character of the whole gospel.[16]

If the resurrection is God's act of honoring Jesus, then it is not a collective hallucination of the early church, nor is it the determination of the early disciples not to let Jesus be forgotten, nor the rising of Jesus into the kerygma of the early church. Resurrection is the raising of Jesus by the power of God into a transformed existence beyond our reckoning. Its importance for discipleship is considerable, both because of the one who was raised and because of the substance of his public work. The resurrection is not only an abstract possibility pointing to life in the reign of God (although it does do that); it is God's way of validating what Jesus incarnated and embodied in his life, including his practice of justice. Therefore, the choice to become a justice people is not primarily a political decision but a christological commitment informing our discipleship as we align ourselves with the way of God revealed in the historical Jesus and the will of God confirmed in the Risen Christ. Social ethics is finally rooted in Christology, just as Christology is rooted in the resurrection. To confess "Jesus is Lord" is to confess a desire to pursue the vision of justice that informed Jesus' work.

JESUS AND CHRISTOLOGY

Every "historical Jesus" is a Christ in disguise. In this regard, Crossan's wariness is justified. "It is impossible to avoid the suspicion that historical Jesus research is a very safe place to do theology and call it history, to do autobiography and call it biography."[17] With his insight, Crossan once again confirms the lasting truth of Schweitzer's insights. It is impossible to study the historical Jesus without doing Christology, whether the form of that Christology is compatible with church teaching or a radical denial of it. This conviction may seem, at first glance, to be out of place, even ill-conceived, since Christology is a branch of theology while the quest for the historical Jesus is a branch of historical study, and never the twain shall meet. Indeed, scholars engaged in historical Jesus research seem to fear nothing so much as being accused and convicted of doing theology. Therefore, they make every effort to strain out the gnat of doing theology disguised as history, while swallowing the camel of believing that they can study the historical Jesus without theological investments.

When separated from the reality of Jesus of Nazareth, Christology is reduced to abstractions unrelated to the incarnation and the questions of justice that drove Jesus' ministry. When separated from Christology, the historical Jesus becomes a dessicated figure reduced to the size of the investigator's hostility toward the church. Sobrino puts it this way:

> It is impossible to write a history of Jesus without producing theology about him, but it is also true—and this is the specific contribution of the Gospels—that it is impossible to produce a

theology about Jesus without writing a history of him. . . . There are two important lessons that Latin American Christology learns from the Gospels. The first is that we cannot turn the figure of Jesus into theology without turning him into history and telling the story of his life and fate. Without this, faith has no history. The second is that we cannot turn Jesus into history without turning him into theology as good news and so an essential reference for the communities. Without this, history has no faith.[18]

All of this would seem to argue that Martin Kähler was right after all: It is as utterly impossible to separate the Jesus of history from the Christ of faith as it is to unscramble an omelette, a position more recently reiterated by Luke Johnson.[19] If they are christologically correct, then it would be useless to initiate any quest for the historical Jesus. The exercise is misguided and futile, doomed from the start. Why bother attempting what cannot be done?

Fortunately, the Gospel writers did not share this pessimism. No matter how completely they blended the historical Jesus with the Christ of faith, all four evangelists believed that it was important to present the work of Jesus before the resurrection, even if, in their view, that work could not be fully comprehended until after the resurrection. No one confuses the Gospel of Mark with the Apostles' Creed, the Gospel of Matthew with the Nicene Creed, or the Gospel of Luke with the Chalcedonian Creed. The Gospels are not just creeds in disguise. The Gospels are historical narratives infused with the postresurrection perspective, just as Josephus's *Jewish War* is a historical narrative informed by a perspective gained by knowing the outcome of the conflict before writing his account of it.

The Gospels are incarnate visions. Each evangelist fashioned the story of Jesus to speak to the events and crises of his own day. Did the church canonize the historical moments when the Gospels were written as well as their four portraits of Jesus? If we accept the logic of Kähler's position, this would seem to be the case. But suppose the canon includes not only the final form of the texts but also all the traditions that contribute to that final form. Suppose the Gospels were meant to model what every generation of Christians must do, namely, present the historical work of Jesus as a framework for understanding our own historical vocation as his disciples.

This reaches to the hermeneutical heart of the matter. The very existence of a quest for the historical Jesus implies that the portraits of Jesus in the Gospels are not final portrayals but first prototypes of an ongoing task. To acknowledge that the historical Jesus is both more than and, in some important ways, other than the portraits of Jesus in the Gospels is to concede that the interpretive project is never done. Those who believe that they can short-circuit this process by claiming that they believe in the Jesus of the Gospels have not solved the problem either, since they usually mean that they accept some interpretation of the Jesus (or Jesuses) presented in the Gospels. Everyone has an interpretive template. The quest for the historical Jesus puts us all on the same footing, encouraging us, as it does, to acknowledge that we are scrutinizing the materials of the Gospels in order to construe and construct other readings of Jesus hidden in the subversive memory of the Jesus traditions. It does no good to retreat to Kähler's or Johnson's position; they have done little more than restate the problem.

A Prophet? Yes, I Tell You, and More Than a Prophet

This effort to study the historical Jesus as a prophet of the justice of the reign of God raises the same question posed by other similar studies. How is it possible to get from this portrayal of Jesus to the christological issues of the early church? How could this portrait of Jesus serve as the basis for christological development, or is the interpretation of Jesus advanced here simply impossible to connect to Christology? Is Jesus simply political, without theology?

This work has argued that Jesus claimed the role of broker of God's forgiveness and that he brokered God's forgiveness through his words and deeds, especially his healings. In this role, Jesus canceled the debts peasants owed the temple and offered them a new lease on life. This role as broker was found in the healing of the paralytic (Mark 2:1–12). When Jesus claimed to broker God's *charis,* or favor, he placed himself in direct competition with the temple hierarchy who had claimed that role for themselves and controlled access to it,[20] but it was a conflict that he accepted and escalated, when the occasion demanded it. As he acquired honor in challenge-riposte encounters, Jesus came to be seen as a figure of power, a figure who mediated God's covenant love, God's justice, and God's healing power. If this reconstruction is arguable, it lays the foundation for a fuller christological elaboration of Jesus as exclusive mediator of God's beneficence. So the writer of 1 Timothy could write, "For there is one God; there is also one mediator between God and human beings, Christ Jesus, himself human, who gave himself a ransom for all" (2:5–6). In similar fashion, the writer of Hebrews speaks of Jesus as "the mediator of a new covenant" (9:15; 12:24). In this case, the word for broker and mediator is the same (*mesitēs*), but its meaning has been nuanced.

Much of the christological language applied to Jesus can be seen as tracing to a Jesus like the one portrayed in this work. When Jesus healed the bent woman, he acted as a redeemer. He entered Satan's prison where the woman was bound and loosed her bonds (Luke 13:10–17). Similarly,

Jesus' exorcisms were examples of entering the strong man's house and binding the strong man so that the imprisoned could go free (Mark 3:27; cf. Luke 4:16–30). His prophetic activity became the basis for christological affirmations of his work. The role of mediator would be interwoven with other images of Jesus as savior and redeemer, which, taken together, formed the raw material from which a Christology could be refined. In these actions, Jesus acted like Yahweh, who had gone to Egypt to redeem his people from their bondage.

Jesus' actions and announcement of forgiveness were also expanded to cover human sin and other forms of indebtedness to God. The Paulinist who wrote Colossians can, therefore, speak of Christ "in whom we have redemption, the forgiveness of sins" (1:14), and the writer of Ephesians speaks eloquently of "the forgiveness of our trespasses, according to the riches of his grace" (1:7). In similar fashion, the writer of Acts speaks of the forgiveness made possible through Jesus as a theological article of faith (Acts 2:38; 5:31; 10:43; 13:38–39; 26:17–18). The importance of forgiveness of debt was also retained in the Lord's Prayer as the model prayer for Matthew's church (Matt. 6:9–13). The meaning of forgiveness may have become unmoored from its more specific reference to "cancellation of debt" and been expanded into a metaphor describing a general human need, but it does connect to the roots suggested in this study. As this occurred, Jesus became more of a cosmic figure and less the historical Jesus of Nazareth whose public work mattered, but this theological development reflects the postresurrectional context in which it occurred.

Lurking behind Jesus' practice of justice was a view of God as father, rather than king. The God proclaimed by Jesus and implied through his brokering was a God who canceled debt and included the outcast, especially those who were deemed hopelessly lost. The early church captured this theology in its use of "abba" (Gal. 4:6; Rom. 8:15; Mark 14:36). Paul's effort to create a community in which there would be "neither Jew nor Greek, neither slave nor free, neither male nor female" (Gal. 3:28) reflects a similar vision in the recontextualized setting of the preindustrial city. In fairness, it should be said that Jesus' anti-monarchic view of God did not inform the theological reflection of the early church because it had no context in the Roman Empire.

Jesus' symbolic destruction of the temple would seem to have been forgotten by the early church, which centered its life in Jerusalem under the leadership of James, who was pious and devout in his temple obligations. However, the early chapters of Acts also contain traditions of Peter and John being arrested for preaching in the temple area and then refusing to abide by the efforts of the Sanhedrin to silence them (3:1–4:41). Similarly, Stephen's anti-temple speech (6:8–7:60), which leads to his execution, is a clear indication of an anti-temple strain of thought in the early church.

Not only did the Gentile church abandon loyalty to the temple, but the early church turned the temple into a metaphor for the Christian's own body as well as the community as the body of Christ (1 Cor. 3:16–17; 6:19; 8:10; 9:13; 2 Cor. 6:16; Eph. 2:21–22). It did not take the church long to identify the "something greater than the temple" that had arrived, and, with a touch of irony, they kept the term "temple" but turned it into a metaphor for the "something greater" that was here. The subversion of the temple was complete. It no longer identified an exclusive institution but described an inclusive community, loyal to the vision of Isaiah 56.

Jesus was an authoritative interpreter of the Torah. Like a prophet in the Deuteronomic tradition, he discerned the will of God through reading Torah, and he warned of the consequences that would attend any neglect of the Torah. In time, Jesus the interpreter of God's Word would become Jesus the embodiment of God's Word, and the authority of Jesus' words would rival those of the Torah itself (e.g., the five discourses in the Gospel of Matthew). The renewal of the covenant that Jesus proclaimed became, in time, the new covenant found in Jesus (1 Cor. 11:25). Even more importantly, the reign of God proclaimed by Jesus came increasingly to be associated with Jesus, until the return of Jesus (*parousia*) became almost inseparable from the hope expressed in the Lord's Prayer, "thy kingdom come, thy will be done on earth as it is in heaven" (Matt. 6:10). The coming kingdom would also bring the coming of Christ (1 Thess. 4:13–5:11).

In general, the teachings of Jesus were increasingly applied to Jesus, and as that happened, the message of the justice of the reign of God was subordinated to other concerns. This became increasingly true as the church began to take on a life of its own beyond the synagogue and required documents able to provide a foundation history and symbolic universe adequate to its new vision. The process of christological reflection was also continuing. None of these developments was necessarily misguided, but neither were these developments conducive to the recovery of the historical Jesus. Yet the Gospels retained materials that bore witness to the historical Jesus, even when those stories and sayings might prove embarrassing or failed to cohere with the growing theological concerns of the church.

CONCLUSION

In the final analysis, the Gospels preserved more than enough material to encourage the unfinished task of reconstructing the historical Jesus from one age to the next and from one generation to the next. Out of the maze of parables, riddles, aphorisms, conflicts, healings, exorcisms, charges, questions, counterquestions, Torah disputes, temple incidents, the drama of a show trial, and courage under fire, a shadowy figure begins to emerge from the mists of the first century, standing on a far shore, beckoning the inquirer to come closer. Try as we might, we cannot approach the shore, but remain at sea, on the face of the deep, too far removed for a closer look. The mists thicken, and the figure disappears, leaving only the memory of his appearing. It is all we have to work with, but it is enough to encourage us to cast off from the distant shore and risk the voyage once again.

If this study has enabled anyone to catch a fleeting glimpse of the shadowy figure on the distant shore of history, it will have served a useful purpose.

NOTES

Introduction

1. See Gerd Theissen, *Sociology of Early Palestinian Christianity*, trans. John Bowden (Philadelphia: Fortress, 1978), 7–30.
2. This is essentially the message of Robert Funk, *Honest to Jesus: Jesus for a New Millennium* (San Francisco: HarperCollins, 1996), 297–314.
3. Albert Schweitzer, *The Quest of the Historical Jesus*, trans. W. Montgomery (New York: Macmillan Co., 1956; German original, 1906), 1–12.

Chapter 1. The "Third Quest" in Context

1. See Ben Witherington III, *The Jesus Quest: The Third Search for the Jew of Nazareth* (Downers Grove, Ill.: InterVarsity, 1995); N. T. Wright, *Jesus and the Victory of God* (Minneapolis: Fortress, 1996), 83ff.
2. Schweitzer, *Quest.*
3. See John Reumann, "Introduction" to Joachim Jeremias, *The Problem of the Historical Jesus* (Philadelphia: Fortress, 1964), vii; W. Barnes Tatum, *In Quest of Jesus: A Guidebook* (Atlanta: John Knox, 1982), 71–74; Marcus Borg, *Jesus in Contemporary Scholarship* (Valley Forge: Trinity Press International, 1994), 3–5.
4. The best summary of the movement is found in James M. Robinson, *A New Quest of the Historical Jesus* (London: SCM Press, 1959).
5. Schweitzer, *Quest,* 13; Hermann Samuel Reimarus, *The Goal of Jesus and His Disciples,* introduction and translation by George Wesley Buchanan (Leiden: Brill, 1970); Wilhelm Wrede, *The Messianic Secret in the Gospels,* trans. J. C. G. Grieg (Cambridge: James Clarke, 1971; German original, 1901).
6. Schweitzer, *Quest,* 238.
7. For formulations of the criterion, see: Rudolf Bultmann, *History of the Synoptic Tradition,* trans. John Marsh (Oxford: Blackwell, 1963; German original, 1921), 205 (hereafter known as *HST*); cf. also Norman Perrin, *Rediscovering the Teaching of Jesus* (New York: Harper & Row, 1967), 39–49.
8. Schweitzer, *Quest,* 6–7.

9. See David Dungan, "Reconsidering Albert Schweitzer," *Christian Century,* Oct. 8, 1975, 874–80; idem, "Albert Schweitzer's Disillusionment with the Reconstruction of the Life of Jesus," *PJ* (1976): 27–48, esp. 34.

10. Dungan, "Schweitzer's Disillusionment," 40–41.

11. For different reasons and with a different purpose, Martin Kähler came to essentially the same conclusion. No conception of the historical Jesus could do justice to the biblical Christ because all historical portrayals needed to contain Jesus within the bounds of ordinary human psychology. Martin Kähler, *The So-Called Historical Jesus and the Historic, Biblical Christ,* trans. Carl Braaten (Philadelphia: Fortress, 1964; German original, 1892). For comments on Kähler's contribution, see David Cairns, "The Motives and Scope of Historical Inquiry about Jesus," *SJT* 29 (1976): 339–44.

12. Martin Dibelius, *From Tradition to Gospel,* trans. Bertram Lee Woolf (New York: Scribner's, 1934); Bultmann, *HST.*

13. Karl L. Schmidt, *Der Rahmen der Geschichte Jesu* (Berlin: Karl Ludwig, 1919).

14. Dibelius, *From Tradition to Gospel,* 1–8.

15. C. H. Dodd, "The Framework of the Gospel Narrative," in C. H. Dodd, *New Testament Studies* (Manchester: Manchester University Press, 1953), 11. The article was first published in the *Expository Times* in 1932. For a response, see D. E. Nineham, "The Order of Events in St. Mark's Gospel—an Examination of Dr. Dodd's Hypothesis," in D. E. Nineham, ed., *Studies in the Gospels* (London: Blackwell, 1957).

16. For discussions of the kerygma, see Robinson, *New Quest;* Carl Braaten and Roy Harrisville, eds., *The Historical Jesus and the Kerygmatic Christ* (New York: Abingdon, 1964); Gerhard Ebling, *Theology and Proclamation: A Discussion with Rudolf Bultmann,* trans. John Riches (London: Collins, 1966).

17. Ernst Käsemann, "The Problem of the Historical Jesus," in Ernst Käsemann, *Essays on New Testament Themes,* trans. W. J. Montague (London: SCM Press, 1964), 20. The essay was first given as a lecture in 1953.

18. Rudolf Bultmann, *Jesus and the Word,* trans. L. P. Smith and E. H. Lantero (New York: Scribner's, 1934).

19. Quoted in Robinson, *New Quest,* 188.

20. William Manson, *Jesus the Messiah: The Synoptic Tradition of the Revelation of God in Christ, with Special Reference to Form Criticism* (London: Hodder & Stoughton, 1943); Vincent Taylor, *The Life and Ministry of Jesus* (London: Macmillan & Co., 1953). For others, see, e.g., A. M. Hunter, *The Work and Words of Jesus* (Philadelphia: Westminster, 1950; rev. ed., 1973). Hunter devotes two chapters to a "Sketch of the Ministry" (pp. 51–68) before organizing Jesus' teachings in thematic form. T. W. Manson, *The Servant Messiah: A Study of the Public Ministry of Jesus* (Cambridge: Cambridge University Press, 1953; rev. ed., 1961), followed a similar format.

21. Joachim Jeremias, *The Parables of Jesus,* 6th ed., trans. S. H. Hooke (New York: Scribner's, 1963). The German first ed. was published in 1947. All quotations are from the 6th ed.
22. Ibid., 22.
23. C. H. Dodd, *The Parables of the Kingdom* (London: Nisbet & Co., 1935).
24. The remarks were published in Käsemann, *Essays on New Testament Themes,* 15–47.
25. The lecture was included in Ernst Fuchs, *Studies of the Historical Jesus,* trans. A. Scobie (London: SCM Press, 1964), 11–31.
26. Günther Bornkamm, *Jesus of Nazareth,* trans. I. and F. McLuskey with James Robinson (New York: Harper & Row, 1960). The German original, *Jesus von Nazareth,* was published in 1956. All references are to the English edition.
27. Robinson, *New Quest.*
28. The periodical literature of the period is replete with commentary on the "new quest." The following sample will indicate the many channels of discussion stimulated by the "new questers." William Farmer and Norman Perrin, "The Kerygmatic Theology and the Question of the Historical Jesus," *RL* 29:1 (1959–1960): 86–97; Werner G. Kümmel, "Kerygma, Selfhood, or Historical Fact: A Review Article on the Problem of the Historical Jesus," *Encounter* 21:2 (1960): 232–34; Hugh Anderson, "The Historical Jesus and the Origins of Christianity," *SJT* 13:2 (1960): 113–36; Allan Barr, "More Quests of the Historical Jesus," *SJT* 13:4 (1960): 394–409; Oscar Cullmann, "Out of Season Remarks on the 'Historical Jesus' of the Bultmann School," *USQR* 16:2 (1961): 131–48; Paul J. Achtemeier, "The Historical Jesus: A Dilemma," *T&L* 4:2 (1961): 107–19; Dwight Marion Beck, "The Never-Ending Quest for the Historical Jesus (A Review Article of Bornkamm's *Jesus of Nazareth*)," *JBibRel* 19:3 (1961): 227–31; James M. Robinson, "The Recent Debate on the 'New Quest'," *JBibRel* 30:3 (1962): 198–208; Schubert Ogden, "Bultmann and the 'New Quest'," *JBibRel* 30:3 (1962): 209–18; Lou H. Silberman, "The New Quest for the Historical Jesus," *Judaism* 11:3 (1962): 260–67; J. Benjamin Bedenbaugh, "The First Decade of the New Quest for the Historical Jesus," *LuthQ* 16 (1964): 239–67; Dan O. Via, Jr., "The Necessary Complement to the Kerygma," *JR* 45 (1965): 30–38; John H. Elliott, "The Historical Jesus, the Kerygmatic Christ, and the Eschatological Community," *Concordia Theological Monthly* 37:8 (1966): 470–91.
29. I have adapted the phrase "third quest" from the title of the survey by Ben Witherington III. See Witherington, *Jesus Quest;* N. T. Wright also uses the phrase "third quest," though in a more restricted sense, in N. T. Wright, *Jesus and the Victory of God* (Minneapolis: Fortress, 1996), 83–124.
30. Leander Keck, *A Future for the Historical Jesus: The Place of Jesus in Preaching and Theology* (New York: Abingdon, 1971), 9.

31. S. G. F. Brandon, *Jesus and the Zealots* (New York: Scribner's, 1967), 1–25, 322–58.
32. Ibid., 283–321.
33. Ibid., 331–36, for Brandon on the "cleansing of the temple."
34. Oscar Cullmann, *Jesus and the Revolutionaries,* trans. G. Putnam (New York: Harper & Row, 1970); Martin Hengel, *Was Jesus a Revolutionist?* trans. W. Klassen (Philadelphia: Fortress, 1971); idem, *Victory over Violence: Jesus and the Revolutionists,* trans. D. Green (Philadelphia: Fortress, 1973).
35. Martin Hengel, *The Zealots: Investigations into the Jewish Freedom Movement in the Period from Herod until 70 A.D.,* trans. D. Smith (Edinburgh: T. & T. Clark, 1989). The German original was published in 1961, revised and expanded in 1976.
36. Ibid., Parts 5 and 6.
37. Cullmann, *Revolutionaries,* 12 et passim.
38. Ibid., 35.
39. Ibid., 39f.
40. Hegel, *Victory,* 47.
41. John Howard Yoder, *The Politics of Jesus* (Grand Rapids: Eerdmans, 1972); André Trocmé, *Jesus and the Nonviolent Revolution,* trans. M. H. Shank (Scottsdale, Pa.: Herald, 1973). The French original was published in 1961.
42. Yoder, *Politics,* 90–93.
43. Ibid., 64–77.
44. Sean Freyne, *Galilee from Alexander the Great to Hadrian, 323 B.C.E. to 135 C.E.* (Notre Dame: University of Notre Dame Press, 1980).
45. James Charlesworth, "From Barren Mazes to Gentle Rappings: The Emergence of Jesus Research," *PrinSemBull* 7 (1986): 221–30; p. 221.
46. It would consume too much space to present an exhaustive list of journal articles and books. The following is a sample of periodical literature from the 1980s and 1990s in chronological order. Paul Hollenbach, "Recent Historical Jesus Studies and the Social Sciences," SBLSP (1983): 61–78; Irvin W. Batdorf, "Interpreting Jesus Since Bultmann: Selected Paradigms and Their Hermeneutical Matrix," SBLSP (1984): 187–215; James Charlesworth, "Research on the Historical Jesus Today: Jesus and the Pseudepigrapha, the Dead Sea Scrolls, the Nag Hammadi Codices, Josephus and Archaeology," *PrinSemBull* 6 (1985): 98–115; Marcus Borg, "A Renaissance in Jesus Studies," *TheolToday* 45:3 (1988): 280–92; Stephen Fowl, "Reconstructing and Deconstructing the Quest of the Historical Jesus," *SJT* 42 (1989): 319–33; Paul Hollenbach, "The Historical Jesus Question in North America Today," *BTB* 19:1 (1989): 11–22; John Dominic Crossan, "The Life of a Mediterranean Jewish Peasant," *Christian Century,* Dec. 18–25, 1991: 1194–1204; Tony Kelly, "The Historical Jesus and Human Subjectivity: A Response to John Meier," *Pacifica* 4:2 (1991): 202–28; Marcus Borg, "Portraits of Jesus in Contemporary North American Scholarship (with Addendum)," *HTR* 84:1 (1991): 1–22; Walter F. Taylor, Jr.,

"New Quests for the Historical Jesus," *TrinitySemRev* 15:2 (1993): 69–83; Thomas Long, ed., *TheolToday* 52 (1995), entire issue, which includes articles by Marcus Borg, Howard Clark Kee, Stephen J. Patterson, Pheme Perkins, James D. G. Dunn, and Paula Fredrickson; Luke T. Johnson, "The Search for (the Wrong) Jesus," *BR* 11:4 (1995): 20–25, 44; John Dominic Crossan, "A Response," *BR* 12:1 (1996): 35–38, 42–45; N. T. Wright, "How Jesus Saw Himself," *BR* 12:3 (June 1996): 22–29; Bruce Chilton, "The Son of Man—Who Was He?" *BR* 12:4 (1996): 34–39, 45–46; Robert J. Miller, "The Jesus of Orthodoxy and the Jesuses of the Gospels: A Critique of Luke Timothy Johnson's *The Real Jesus,*" *JSNT* 68 (1997): 101–20; idem, "History Is Not Optional: A Response to 'The Real Jesus' by Luke Timothy Johnson," *BTB* 28:1 (1998): 27–34.

Various studies have surveyed various aspects of the emergence of historical Jesus research: W. Barnes Tatum, *In Quest of Jesus: A Guidebook* (Atlanta: John Knox, 1982); Bruce Chilton and Craig A. Evans, eds., *Studying the Historical Jesus: Evaluations of the State of Current Research* (Leiden: Brill, 1994); Witherington, *Jesus Quest;* Gerd Theissen and Annette Merz, *The Historical Jesus: A Comprehensive Guide,* trans. John Bowden (Minneapolis: Fortress, 1996).

47. John Bowker, *Jesus and the Pharisees* (Cambridge: Cambridge University Press, 1973); James H. Charlesworth, *Jesus within Judaism: New Light from Exciting Archaeological Discoveries* (New York: Doubleday, 1988); idem, ed., *Jesus' Jewishness: Exploring the Place of Jesus in Early Judaism* (New York: Crossroad, 1991); idem, ed., *Jesus and the Dead Sea Scrolls: The Controversy Resolved* (New York: Doubleday, 1992); Bruce Chilton, *A Galilean Rabbi and His Bible: Jesus' Use of the Interpreted Scripture of His Time* (Wilmington, Del.: Glazier, 1984); David Flusser, *Jesus,* trans. R. Walls (New York: Herder & Herder, 1969); Donald Hagner, *The Jewish Reclamation of Jesus: An Analysis and Critique of the Modern Jewish Study of Jesus* (Grand Rapids: Zondervan, 1984); Ben F. Meyer, *The Aims of Jesus* (London: SCM Press, 1979); John Riches, *Jesus and the Transformation of Judaism* (New York: Seabury, 1982); Ellis Rivkin, *What Crucified Jesus? The Political Execution of a Charismatic* (Nashville: Abingdon, 1984); E. P. Sanders, *Jesus and Judaism* (Philadelphia: Fortress, 1985); idem, *The Historical Figure of Jesus* (London: Penguin, 1993); Geza Vermes, *Jesus the Jew: A Historian's Reading of the Gospels* (Philadelphia: Fortress, 1973); idem, *Jesus and the World of Judaism* (Philadelphia: Fortress, 1983); idem, *The Religion of Jesus the Jew* (Minneapolis: Fortress, 1993); Irving Zeitlin, *Jesus and the Judaism of His Time* (Cambridge: Polity, 1988).

48. Sanders, *Jesus and Judaism;* idem, *Historical Figure.*

49. Sanders, *Jesus and Judaism,* 11.

50. Sanders, *Historical Figure,* 10–11.

51. Sanders, *Jesus and Judaism,* 77–119, for the elements of restoration eschatology.

52. Ibid., 245–69.
53. Sanders, *Historical Figure,* 15–32.
54. K. C. Hanson and Douglas Oakman, *Palestine in the Time of Jesus* (Minneapolis: Fortress, 1998), 131–59.
55. See the three works of Geza Vermes cited in n. 47.
56. Vermes, *Jesus the Jew,* 46.
57. Vermes, *Religion of Jesus the Jew,* 11–75.
58. The following list will provide a sample of studies dealing with the political aspects of the historical Jesus: Ernst Bammel and C. F. D. Moule, eds., *Jesus and the Politics of His Day* (Cambridge: Cambridge University Press, 1984); Marcus J. Borg, *Conflict, Holiness and Politics in the Teachings of Jesus* (Harrisburg, Pa.: Trinity Press International, 1998; original edition, 1984); Hugo Echegaray, *The Practice of Jesus,* trans. Matthew O'Connell (Maryknoll, N.Y.: Orbis, 1984); Hanson and Oakman, *Palestine in the Time of Jesus;* William R. Herzog II, *Parables as Subversive Speech: Jesus as Pedgogue of the Oppressed* (Louisville, Ky.: Westminster John Knox, 1994); Richard A. Horsley and John S. Hanson, *Bandits, Prophets, and Messiahs: Popular Movements at the Time of Jesus* (New York: Winston, 1985); Richard Horsley, *Jesus and the Spiral of Violence: Popular Jewish Resistance in Roman Palestine* (San Francisco: Harper & Row, 1987); idem, *Galilee: History, Politics, People* (Valley Forge, Pa.: Trinity Press International, 1995); R. David Kaylor, *Jesus the Prophet: His Vision of the Kingdom on Earth* (Louisville, Ky.: Westminster John Knox, 1994); Albert Nolan, *Jesus before Christianity* (Maryknoll, N.Y.: Orbis, 1978); Douglas Oakman, *Jesus and the Economic Questions of His Day* (Lewiston: Edwin Mellen, 1986); Luise Schottroff, *Jesus and the Hope of the Poor,* trans. Matthew O'Connell (Maryknoll, N.Y.: Orbis, 1986); Juan Luis Segundo, *The Historical Jesus of the Synoptics,* trans. John Drury (Maryknoll, N.Y.: Orbis, 1985); Jon Sobrino, *Jesus the Liberator: A Historical-Theological View,* trans. Paul Burns and Francis McDonagh (Maryknoll, N.Y.: Orbis, 1993).
59. Ernst Bammel, "The Revolution Theory from Reimarus to Brandon," in Bammel and Moule, *Jesus and Politics,* 11–68.
60. Horsley, *Spiral of Violence,* 209–85; 147–66.
61. Ibid., 167–208.
62. Marcus Borg, "The Jesus Seminar and the Church," in Borg, *Jesus in Contemporary Scholarship,* 162.
63. Luke Timothy Johnson, *The Real Jesus: The Misguided Quest for the Historical Jesus and the Truth of the Traditional Gospels* (San Francisco: HarperCollins, 1996), 1–27.
64. Witherington, *Jesus Quest,* 42–57; Robert Funk, "The Issue of Jesus," *Forum* 1:1 (1985): 7–12.
65. Quoted in Johnson, *Real Jesus,* 12.
66. Ibid., 13.
67. Witherington, *Jesus Quest,* 56. See also the critique by Richard B. Hays, "The Corrected Jesus," *First Things* 43 (May 1994): 43–48, which identifies the same problem.

68. Schweitzer, *Quest*, 4.
69. Marcus Borg, "An Orthodoxy Reconsidered: The 'End-of-the-World Jesus'," in L. D. Hurst and N. T. Wright, eds., *The Glory of Christ in the New Testament: Studies in Christology* (Caird Memorial Volume) (Oxford: Clarendon, 1987), 207–17.
70. Marcus Borg, "A Temperate Case for a Non-Eschatological Jesus," *Forum* 2:3 (1986): 81–102.
71. Marcus Borg, "Jesus and Eschatology: Current Reflections," in Borg, *Jesus in Contemporary Scholarship*, 80.
72. Sanders, *Jesus and Judaism*, 11.
73. John Dominic Crossan, *The Historical Jesus: The Life of a Mediterranean Jewish Peasant* (San Francisco: HarperCollins, 1991), 333–37; idem, *Jesus: A Revolutionary Biography* (San Francisco: HarperCollins, 1994), 108–10.
74. Quoted in Borg, *Jesus in Contemporary Scholarship*, 7.
75. John Gager, *Kingdom and Community: The Social World of Early Christianity* (Englewood Cliffs, N.J.: Prentice-Hall, 1975).
76. Freyne, *Galilee*.
77. John P. Meier, *A Marginal Jew: Rethinking the Historical Jesus,* vol. 2: *Mentor, Message, Miracles* (New York: Doubleday, 1994), 4–5.
78. Ibid., 1.

Chapter 2. Models and Methods in the Quest for the Historical Jesus

1. These materials include the canonical Gospels, their sources, other Gospel-like documents existing outside the canon, and scattered materials in which sayings of Jesus are embedded. One of the significant achievements of the Jesus Seminar was to collect these materials into a data base.

   Raymond Brown, *An Introduction to the New Testament* (New York: Doubleday, 1997), 100–1, notes that many of the the so-called apocryphal gospels do not carry that title. "The title 'gospel' has been used to refer to noncanonical works independently of their self-designation." In fairness, the same could be said of the canonical Gospels with the exception of Mark. Brown seems to be reacting to the baptism of noncanonical Gospels by the Jesus Seminar, and his warning is still important to heed. Not every document that appears to be a "gospel" may be one.

2. The Gospel of Thomas is a document found at Nag Hammadi in Upper Egypt. Written in Coptic and showing evidences of Gnostic influence, it was usually placed in the second century until the Jesus Seminar reconsidered the matter and placed it much earlier. The Gospel is a collection of 114 sayings, without a narrative framework. Some of the sayings obviously parallel materials in the Synoptic tradition; others are completely different.

3. See Crossan, *Historical Jesus,* xxvii–xxxiv, for a statement of method, and 427–34, for his stratigraphy of sources.

4. See Burton L. Mack, *The Lost Gospel: The Book of Q and Christian Origins* (New York: HarperCollins, 1993); Crossan, *Historical Jesus,* 421–22, for summary statement; idem, *Revolutionary Biography,* 102–22.

5. Robert W. Funk, "Rules of Evidence," in Robert W. Funk with Mahlon H. Smith, *The Gospel of Mark: Red Letter Edition* (Sonoma, Calif.: Polebridge, 1991), 29–52.

6. Marcus Borg, *Meeting Jesus Again for the First Time: The Historical Jesus and the Heart of Contemporary Faith* (San Francisco: Harper-Collins, 1994), 69–95. See also Bernard Brandon Scott, "Jesus as Sage: An Innovating Voice in Common Wisdom," in John G. Gammie and Leo G. Perdue, eds., *The Sage in Israel and the Ancient Near East* (Winona Lake, Ind.: Eisenbrauns, 1990), 399–415.

7. For development of the idea of a "little tradition" and its larger social matrix, see Robert Redfield, *The Little Community* (Chicago: University of Chicago Press, 1955); idem, *Peasant Society and Culture* (Chicago: University of Chicago Press, 1956).

8. Dennis Polkow, "Method and Criteria for Historical Jesus Research," SBLSP (1987): 336–56.

9. Ibid., 342, for a more detailed version of the diagram.

10. Bultmann, *HST,* 205.

11. Norman Perrin, *Rediscovering the Teaching of Jesus* (New York: Harper & Row, 1967), 39.

12. Polkow, "Method and Criteria," 348.

13. Ibid., 351–55.

14. Charles E. Carlston, "A Positive Criterion of Authenticity?" *BibRes* 7 (1951): 34. Quoted by Polkow, "Method and Criteria," 353.

15. Jeremias, *Prayers of Jesus;* see appendix: "The Characteristics of the *ipsissima vox Jesu*," 108–15.

16. James Breech, *The Silence of Jesus* (Philadelphia: Fortress, 1983), 81–85.

17. This was noted long ago by Walter Wink, *The Bible in Human Transformation* (Philadelphia: Fortress, 1974). Each generation of scholars, Wink noted, consumes the assured results of its predecessors the way a guppie swallows her own children.

18. Bernard Brandon Scott, *Hear Then the Parable: A Commentary on the Parables of Jesus* (Minneapolis: Fortress, 1989), 18.

19. Funk, "Rules of Evidence," 35–36.

20. Schweitzer, *Quest,* 7.

21. Ibid.

22. Meier, *Marginal Jew,* 2:4–5.

23. Ibid., 4.

24. Marcus Borg, "Jesus and Eschatology: Current Reflections," in *Jesus in Contemporary Scholarship,* 80–84; esp. p. 80.

25. Ibid.

26. Johnson, *Real Jesus,* 141–66.

27. For a critique of this pattern, see Miller, "Jesus of Orthodoxy," 103–16.

28. Johnson, *Real Jesus,* 124–25.
29. Ibid., 100.
30. John Dominic Crossan, "The Historical Jesus," *BR* 12:1 (1996): 45.
31. For discussions of the world-maintaining and world-subverting roles of religion, see Peter Berger, *The Sacred Canopy: Elements of a Sociological Theory of Religion* (New York: Doubleday (Anchor Books), 1969), 3–101; Peter Berger and Thomas Luckmann, *The Social Construction of Reality: A Treatise in the Sociology of Knowledge* (New York: Doubleday (Anchor Books), 1967), 147–63.

Chapter 3. Prophet of the Justice of the Reign of God

1. Herzog, *Parables as Subversive Speech.*
2. For a recent treatment, see Kaylor, *Jesus the Prophet.* For a summary of the relationship between Jesus the prophet and his eschatology, see Theissen and Merz, *Historical Jesus Guide,* 240–80. In his summary of the third quest, Witherington (*Jesus Quest,* 137–60) summarizes recent work on Jesus as "prophet of social change."
3. Wright, *Jesus and the Victory of God,* 162.
4. Rebecca Gray, *Prophetic Figures in Late Second Temple Jewish Palestine: The Evidence from Josephus* (New York: Oxford University Press, 1993), 128.
5. See Joan E. Taylor, *The Immerser: John the Baptist within Second Temple Judaism* (Grand Rapids: Eerdmans, 1997), for a recent study of John the Baptist in relation to the movements of his time.
6. Gerd Theissen, *The Gospels in Context: Social and Political History in the Synoptic Tradition,* trans. Linda Maloney (Minneapolis: Fortress, 1991), 26–42.
7. Morna D. Hooker, *The Signs of a Prophet: The Prophetic Actions of Jesus* (Harrisburg, Pa.: Trinity Press International, 1997), 19–21.
8. For an extensive word study of "prophet," see Helmut Krämer et al., "prophētēs," in Gerhard Friedrich, ed., *TDNT,* 6, trans. Geoffrey Bromiley (Grand Rapids: Eerdmans, 1968), 781–861.
9. Robert L. Webb, *John the Baptizer and Prophet: A Socio-Historical Study,* JSNT Supplemental Series, 62 (Sheffield: Sheffield Academic Press, 1991), 307–48.
10. Gray, *Prophetic Figures,* 110.
11. Webb, *Baptizer and Prophet,* 333–42.
12. "Sign prophets": P. W. Barnett, "The Jewish Sign Prophets—A.D. 40–70: Their Intention and Origin," *NTS* 27 (1980): 679–97. "Popular prophets": Horsley and Hanson, *Bandits, Prophets and Messiahs,* 135–89.
13. Horsley and Hanson, *Bandits, Prophets, and Messiahs,* 135–36.
14. For a fuller description of time orientation, see Bruce Malina, "Christ and Time: Swiss or Mediterranean," *CBQ* 51 (1989): 1–31. Reprinted in Bruce Malina, *The Social World of Jesus and the Gospels* (London: Routledge, 1996), 179–214. References are to the reprinted article.

15. Ibid., see diagram on p. 208.
16. Ibid., 192–93.
17. Ibid., see chart, p. 186.
18. Gray, *Prophetic Figures,* 138.
19. Webb, *Baptizer and Prophet,* 342.
20. Horsley and Hanson, *Bandits, Prophets and Messiahs,* 139.
21. Cf. Malina, "Christ and Time," 209, for relationship of antecedent and forthcoming to the present.
22. Horsley and Hanson, *Bandits, Prophets and Messiahs,* 137.
23. Ibid.
24. Gray, *Prophetic Figures,* 113, 133–43.
25. Ibid., 125–30.
26. Ibid., 127.
27. For a general discussion of the issue, see Ben Witherington III, *Women in the Ministry of Jesus* (Cambridge: Cambridge University Press, 1984), 116–18, for a discussion of Luke 8:1–3.
28. It is possible to view the feedings as other than so-called nature miracles. They are modeled on the provision of manna in the wilderness and may admit to a more social reading.
29. Gray, *Prophetic Figures,* 140.
30. Sanders, *Jesus and Judaism,* 296, quoted in Gray, *Prophetic Figures,* 138.
31. See, e.g., the work of James C. Scott. James C. Scott, *The Moral Economy of the Peasant: Rebellion and Subsistence in Southeast Asia* (New Haven, Conn.: Yale University Press, 1976); idem, *Weapons of the Weak: Everyday Forms of Peasant Resistance* (New Haven, Conn.: Yale University Press, 1985); idem, *Domination and the Arts of Resistance: Hidden Transcripts* (New Haven, Conn.: Yale University Press, 1990).
32. Much of this section is indebted to Joseph Blenkinsopp, *Sage, Priest, Prophet: Religious and Intellectual Leadership in Ancient Israel* (Louisville, Ky.: Westminster John Knox, 1995), 115–65.
33. Ibid., 120. Blenkinsopp also observes that the prophet interprets the fall of the divided kingdom as the judgment of Yahweh and, therefore, justifies the course of events while articulating a theodicy that justifies the ways of God to the people. "The prophetic task is therefore to proclaim the law, to predict the consequences of ignoring or contravening it, and, by so doing, to exonerate the Deity of responsibility for bringing about these disasters," ibid., 121.
34. Ibid., 120–22.
35. Lester L. Grabbe, *Priests, Prophets, Diviners, Sages: A Socio-Historical Study of Religious Specialists in Ancient Israel* (Valley Forge, Pa.: Trinity Press International, 1995), 71.
36. Ibid., 72.
37. Blenkinsopp, *Sage, Priest, Prophet,* 138–54.
38. Ibid., 147.
39. Ibid., 154.

40. Chap. 4 will deal with these matters in more detail.
41. Blenkinsopp, *Sage, Priest, Prophet,* 139.
42. Horsley, *Galilee,* 19–33.
43. See, e.g.: R. A. Batey, *Jesus and the Forgotten City: New Light on Sepphoris and the Urban World of Jesus* (Grand Rapids: Baker, 1991); Shirley Jackson Case, "Jesus and Sepphoris" *JBL* 65 (1926): 14–22; Thomas W. Longstaff, "Nazareth and Sepphoris: Insights into Christian Origins," *ATR* Supp. Series 11 (1990): 8–15; Stuart S. Miller, "Sepphoris, the Well-Remembered City," *BA* (June 1992): 74–83.
44. This point is also emphasized by N. T. Wright, who also views Jesus as a prophet. See N. T. Wright, *Jesus and the Victory of God,* Part 2: "Profile of a Prophet," 147–474.
45. Kaylor, *Jesus the Prophet;* Wright, *Jesus and the Victory of God,* Part 2. Their efforts have many precedents. See, e.g., Morton Scott Enslin, *The Prophet from Nazareth* (New York: Schocken, 1961), for a liberal approach to the topic. Many other current researchers have touched on Jesus' prophetic role. Borg, *Jesus,* 150–71, speaks of Jesus' prophetic role in a changing social world. Sanders, *Jesus and Judaism,* portrays Jesus as a prophet of a restoration eschatology. Sobrino, *Jesus the Liberator,* 160–79, explores Jesus' prophetic praxis. Most recently, Dale Allison, *Jesus of Nazareth: Millenarian Prophet* (Minneapolis: Fortress, 1998), explores Jesus as a millenarian ascetic. The choice of Kaylor and Wright is meant to frame my interpretation of Jesus.
46. Kaylor, *Jesus the Prophet,* 3, 4.
47. Two scholars have provided balanced and judicious summaries of Wright's work. See Witherington, *Jesus Quest,* 219–32; Mark Allan Powell, *Jesus as a Figure in History: How Modern Historians View the Man from Galilee.* Louisville, Ky.: Westminster John Knox, 1998), 150–66.
48. One of Wright's distinctive contentions is that the Jewish people in the first century viewed themselves as still in exile.
49. Wright, *Jesus and the Victory of God,* 219.
50. See John Dominic Crossan, *In Parables: The Challenge of the Historical Jesus* (New York: Harper & Row, 1973), 23–36.
51. Ibid., 27.
52. Ibid., 35.
53. I explored the same alternative way of addressing the question of eschatology in two articles: William R. Herzog II, "Apocalyptic and the Historical Jesus," *PacTheolRev* 18:1 (1984): 17–25; idem, "The Quest of the Historical Jesus and the Discovery of the Apocalyptic Jesus," *PacTheolRev* 19:1 (1985): 25–39.
54. See Berger and Luckmann, *Social Construction of Reality.*
55. On colonial occupation, see, e.g., Albert Memmi, *The Colonizer and the Colonized,* trans. Howard Greenfield (Boston: Beacon, 1965); Frantz Fanon, *The Wretched of the Earth* (New York: Grove, 1963). On Roman, Herodian, and temple domination, see, e.g., Horsley, *Jesus and Spiral of Violence,* 1–58; idem, *Galilee,* 111–85; Horsley and

Hanson, *Bandits, Prophets and Messiahs,* 88–243; Crossan, *Historical Jesus,* 3–88.

56. Grabbe, *Priests, Prophets, Diviners, Sages,* 95.
57. See Herzog, *Parables as Subversive Speech,* 16–29.
58. Scott D. Hill, "The Local Hero in Palestine in Comparative Perspective," in Robert B. Coote, ed., *Elijah and Elisha in Socioliterary Perspective* (Atlanta: Scholars, 1992), 39.
59. Ibid., 52. Compare the role of the local hero with the figure Peter Brown calls "the holy man in late antiquity." See Peter Brown, "The Rise and Function of the Holy Man in Late Antiquity," *JRS* 61 (1971): 80–101. Brown sees the holy man of the fifth and sixth centuries acting as village patron and mediator between the village and the larger world as well as settling disputes within the village. He was a "hinge man" who could "place his *dynamis,* his know-how and (let us not forget) his culture and values at the disposal of the villagers." Though some of the similarities are intriguing, the holy man of late antiquity does not provide a good analogy to Jesus' public work.
60. Grabbe, *Priests, Prophets, Diviners, Sages,* 107, 116.
61. Blenkinsopp, *Sage, Priest, Prophet,* 115–19.
62. For information on dyadic societies and honor and shame, see Bruce J. Malina, *The New Testament World: Insights from Cultural Anthropology,* rev. ed. (Louisville, Ky.: Westminster/John Knox, 1993), chaps. 2, 3. See also Halvor Moxnes, "Honor and Shame," and Bruce Malina, "Understanding New Testament Persons," in Richard L. Rohrbaugh, ed., *The Social Sciences and New Testament Interpretation* (Peabody, Mass.: Hendrickson, 1996), chaps. 1, 2.
63. Bruce J. Malina, "Jesus as Charismatic Leader?" *BTB* 14 (1984): 55–62, reprinted as "Was Jesus a Charismatic Leader?" in Malina, *Social World of Jesus and the Gospels,* 123–42. All references are to this version of the article.
64. Ibid. For a summary of Malina's argument, see his chart on p. 130 comparing a Weberian charismatic leader with a reputational leader. The traits discussed here are taken from this chart.
65. For the fullest discussion of what we can either know or infer about Jesus' roots, see Meier, *Marginal Jew,* chaps. 8–10 (205–371).

Chapter 4. The Search for a Usable Context

1. The two classic texts that launched form criticism in New Testament studies are: Martin Dibelius, *Die Formgeschichte des Evangeliums* (Tübingen: Mohr, 1919; English translation: *From Tradition to Gospel* [New York: Scribner's, 1934]); and Rudolf Bultmann, *Die Geschichte der synoptischen Tradition* (Göttingen: Vandenhoeck & Ruprecht, 1921; English translation: *History of the Synoptic Tradition* [New York: Harper & Row, 1963]). A popular presentation of the basic tenets of form criticism was published in English in 1934: Rudolf Bultmann and Karl Knudsin, *Form Criticism: Two Essays on New Testament Re-*

search, trans. F. C. Grant (New York: Harper Torchbooks, 1962 [1934]). For British treatments of form criticism, see Vincent Taylor, *The Formation of the Gospel Tradition* (London: Macmillan & Co., 1933], and C. H. Dodd, *More New Testament Studies* (Grand Rapids: Eerdmans, 1968). The most influential use of form criticism in biblical studies may have been Jeremias's *Parables of Jesus* (see chap. 2, n. 21). A programmatic introduction to the method can be found in Klaus Koch, *The Growth of the Biblical Tradition: The Form-Critical Method*, trans. S. M. Cupitt (New York: Scribner's, 1969). A brief introduction can be found in Edgar V. McKnight, *What Is Form Criticism?* Guides to Biblical Scholarship (Philadelphia: Fortress, 1969). The evolution of the discipline was marked by the publication of Erhardt Guttgemanns, *Candid Questions Concerning Gospel Form Criticism*, trans. William Doty (Pittsburgh: Pickwick, 1979; German ed., 1971).

2. Hans Dieter Betz, "The Cleansing of the Ten Lepers (Luke 17:11–19)," *JBL* 90:3 (1971): 314–28.

3. An "apophthegm" is a story that leads to a memorable saying. See Bultmann, *HST,* 11–69. Dibelius called them "paradigms" (Dibelius, *From Tradition to Gospel,* 37–69), and Vincent Taylor called them "pronouncement stories" (Taylor, *Formation of the Gospel Tradition,* 63–87). More recently, these brief stories have been called "chreia," using a term from the rhetoric of the Hellenistic world that refers to a short anecdote (Mack, *Myth of Innocence,* 172–207).

4. Joachim Jeremias, *Die Gleichnisse Jesu* (Zurich: Verlag, 1947). The 4th ed. was translated by S. H. Hooke as *The Parables of Jesus* (see chap. 1, n. 21). All quotations are from the 6th ed.

5. Ibid., "Message of the Parables," 115–229.

6. See Theodore J. Weeden, Sr., "Recovering the Parabolic Intent in the Parable of the Sower," *JAAR* 47:1 (1979): 97–120.

7. See chap. 1 above.

8. Dodd, *Parables of the Kingdom;* Taylor, *Formation;* Vincent Taylor, *The Gospel According to St. Mark,* 2d ed. (New York: Macmillan, 1966). The first ed. was published in 1952.

9. William Manson, *Jesus the Messiah: The Synoptic Tradition of the Revelation of God in Christ: With Special Reference to Form Criticism* (London: Hodder & Stoughton, 1943); T. W. Manson, *The Sayings of Jesus* (London: SCM Press, 1949). Originally published as Part 2 of *The Life and Mission of Jesus* in 1937.

10. See Rudolf Bultmann, *Jesus* (Berlin: Deutsche Bibliothek, 1936), trans. L. P. Smith and E. H. Lantero, *Jesus and the Word* (New York: Scribner's, 1934 [1958]). The perduring influence of Bultmann on his pupils can be seen in the only full-length study of Jesus to come out of the "new quest for the historical Jesus," Günther Bornkamm, *Jesus von Nazareth* (Stuttgart: Verlag W. Kohlhammer, 1956), trans. Irene and Fraser McLuskey with James M. Robinson, *Jesus of Nazareth* (New York: Harper & Row, 1960). Bornkamm portrayed Jesus in essentially the same terms as Bultmann.

11. Bultmann, *HST,* 66, 136–37.
12. Günther Bornkamm, Gerhard Barth, and Heinz Joachim Held, *Tradition and Interpretation in Matthew,* trans. Percy Scott (Philadelphia: Westminster, 1963). The work contains articles and work that had appeared between 1948 and 1957.
13. Willi Marxsen, *Mark the Evangelist: Studies on the Redaction History of the Gospel,* trans. J. Boyce; D. Juel; W. Poehlmann with Roy Harrisville (Nashville: Abingdon, 1969). The German original appeared in 1956.
14. Hans Conzelmann, *The Theology of St. Luke,* trans. Geoffrey Buswell (New York: Harper & Row, 1960). The German original bore the title *Die Mitte der Zeit* and was published in 1953.
15. In 1962, Joachim Rohde submitted a dissertation chronicling the shift from form criticism to redaction criticism. It was published subsequently in 1966 and translated into English in 1968. Joachim Rohde, *Rediscovering the Teaching of the Evangelists,* trans. Dorothea Barton (Philadelphia: Westminster, 1968). A brief introduction to redaction criticism was published about the same time. Norman Perrin, *What Is Redaction Criticism?* Guides to Biblical Scholarship (Philadelphia: Fortress, 1969).

 Each Gospel attracted redactional critical studies. A few typical studies are listed below to give a sense of the scope of the work.

 The Gospel of Matthew: W. D. Davies, *The Setting of the Sermon on the Mount* (New York: Cambridge University Press, 1964). Jack Dean Kingsbury, *The Parables of Jesus in Matthew 13: A Study in Redaction-Criticism* (London: SPCK, 1969). Idem, *Matthew: Structure, Christology, Kingdom* (Philadelphia: Fortress, 1975).

 The Gospel of Mark: Ernest Best, *The Temptation and the Passion: The Marcan Soteriology* (New York: Cambridge University Press, 1965). Werner Kelber, *The Kingdom in Mark: A New Place and a New Time* (Philadelphia: Fortress, 1974). Werner Kelber, ed., *The Passion in Mark: Studies on Mark 14–16* (Philadelphia: Fortress, 1976).

 The Gospel of Luke: H. Flender, *St. Luke: Theologian of Redemptive History,* trans. R. H. and Ilsa Fuller (Philadelphia: Fortress, 1967). Leander Keck and J. Louis Martyn, eds., *Studies in Luke-Acts: Essays Presented in Honor of Paul Schubert* (Nashville: Abingdon, 1966). Charles Talbert, ed., *Perspectives on Luke-Acts,* Perspectives in Religious Studies, 5. (Danville, Va.: Association of Baptist Professors of Religion, 1978).

 The periodical literature from the period 1960–1980 is filled with examples of redaction-critical studies or studies in conversation with redaction criticism.
16. The two-source hypothsis refers to the consensus solution to the Synoptic problem. Mark was the earliest Gospel, and both Matthew and Luke used Mark as a source, although they did not know each other. The second source was a collection of sayings called Q (from the German, *Quelle,* which means "source"). Q accounts for the material

shared by Matthew and Luke but not found in Mark. If Matthew and Luke did not use each other but shared common material not found in Mark, they must have gleaned it from another source. This source is called Q. Mark and Q, therefore, became the two sources referred to in the "two-source hypothesis." It should be said that Q is a hypothetical construction without any manuscript evidence to confirm its existence. It is a logical inference from the assumptions about the relationships among the Synoptic Gospels outlined above.

17. E.g., see Paul Achtemeier, "Towards the Isolation of Pre-Markan Miracle Catenae," *JBL* 89 (1970): 265–91, and "The Origin and Function of the Pre-Markan Miracle Catenae," *JBL* 91 (1972): 198–221. See also the section on Markan sources in Howard Clark Kee, *Community of the New Age: Studies in Mark's Gospel* (Philadelphia: Westminster, 1977). C. Clifton Black wrote an extensive critique of the application of redaction criticism to Mark's Gospel in C. Clifton Black, *The Disciples According to Mark: Markan Redaction in Current Debate* JSNT Supp. Series, 27 (Sheffield: Sheffield Academic Press, 1989).

18. Theodore J. Weeden, *Mark: Traditions in Conflict* (Philadelphia: Fortress, 1971); Jack Dean Kingsbury, *The Christology of Mark's Gospel* (Philadelphia: Fortress, 1983).

19. See the survey of three options in Black, *Disciples*. See also the following articles: Robert C. Tannehill, "The Disciples in Mark: The Function of a Narrative Role," *JR* 57 (1977): 386–405; Elizabeth Struthers Malbon, "Fallible Followers: Women and Men in the Gospel of Mark," *Semeia* 28 (1983): 29–48; idem, "Disciples/Crowds/Whoever: Markan Characters and Readers," *NovT* 28:2 (1986): 104–30. All three articles cited move from redaction critical to literary forms of analysis in an effort to break the impasse noted by Black.

20. See Davies, *Sermon on the Mount*, chap. 2.

21. See Michael J. Cook, *Mark's Treatment of Jewish Leaders* (Leiden: Brill, 1978).

22. Kingsbury, *Parables*. The same point is made by Mary Ann Tolbert, *Perspectives on the Parables: An Approach to Multiple Interpretations* (Philadelphia: Fortress, 1979), chap. 1.

23. Two examples of the genre are: Howard Clark Kee, *Jesus in History: An Approach to the Synoptic Gospels* (New York: Harcourt, Brace & World, 1970); Jack Dean Kingsbury, *Jesus Christ in Matthew, Mark and Luke*, Proclamation Commentaries (Philadelphia: Fortress, 1981).

24. Robert Gundry, *Matthew: A Commentary on His Literary and Theological Art* (Grand Rapids: Eerdmans, 1982), 157.

25. This review will not focus on structural interpretation, which was popular in the mid-1970s but was soon eclipsed by other forms of literary criticism. For an introduction, see Daniel Patte, *What Is Structural Exegesis?* Guides to Biblical Scholarship (Philadelphia: Fortress, 1976); Edgar V. McKnight, *Meaning in Texts: The Historical Shaping of a Narrative Hermeneutics* (Philadelphia: Fortress, 1978). Examples of structural interpretation in use can be found in Daniel and Aline Patte,

Structural Exegesis: From Theory to Practice (Philadelphia: Fortress, 1978), and Elizabeth Struthers Malbon, *Narrative Space and Mythic Meaning in Mark* (San Francisco: Harper & Row, 1986).

26. See David Rhoads and Donald Michie, *Mark as Story: An Introduction to the Narrative of a Gospel* (Philadelphia: Fortress, 1982), for an introduction to the elements of narrative. Three years earlier Werner Kelber had attempted to comprehend the Gospel of Mark as a unified story in Werner Kelber, *Mark's Story of Jesus* (Philadelphia: Fortress, 1979). Kingsbury would apply literary approaches to both Matthew and Mark. See Jack Dean Kingsbury, *Matthew as Story* (Philadelphia: Fortress, 1986; rev. ed., 1988); idem, *Conflict in Mark: Jesus, Authorities, Disciples* (Philadelphia: Fortress, 1989).

27. For a compendium of literary approaches applied to one Gospel, see Janice Capel Anderson and Stephen D. Moore, *Mark and Method: New Approaches in Biblical Studies* (Minneapolis: Fortress, 1992).

28. Kingsbury, *Conflict in Mark*, 63–88.

29. Malbon, "Narrative Criticism: How Does the Story Mean?" in Anderson and Moore, *Mark and Method*, 42–43.

30. Mary Ann Tolbert, *Sowing the Gospel: Mark's World in Literary-Historical Perspective* (Minneapolis: Fortress, 1989).

31. Norman K. Gottwald, *The Tribes of Yahweh: Sociology of the Religion of Liberated Israel* (Maryknoll, N.Y.: Orbis, 1979).

32. Gerd Theissen, *Sociology of Early Palestinian Christianity*, trans. John Bowden (Philadelphia: Fortress, 1978; German original, 1977).

33. John H. Elliott, *A Home for the Homeless: A Sociological Exegesis of 1 Peter, Its Situation and Strategy* (Philadelphia: Fortress, 1981); Malina, *New Testament World* (see chap. 3, n. 62).

34. It would require a small monograph to cover this field adequately. The following works are limited to those that bear on this study or provide overviews of the subject. Some of the major works would include: Fernando Belo, *A Materialist Reading of the Gospel of Mark*, trans. Matthew J. O'Connell (Maryknoll, N.Y.: Orbis, 1981); Thomas F. Best, "The Sociological Study of the New Testament: Promise and Peril of a New Discipline," *SJT* 36 (1983): 181–94; O. C. Edwards, "Sociology as a Tool for Interpreting the New Testament," *TheolRev* 65 (1983): 431–38; John Elliott, ed., *Social-Scientific Criticism of the New Testament and Its Social World*, Semeia 35 (Decatur, Ga.: Scholars Press, 1986); Philip Esler, *The First Christians in Their Social Worlds: Social-Scientific Approaches to New Testament Interpretation* (London: Routledge, 1994); Elisabeth Schüssler Fiorenza, *In Memory of Her: A Feminist Theological Reconstruction of Christian Origins* (New York: Crossroad, 1983); John Gager, *Kingdom and Community: The Social World of Early Christianity* (Englewood Cliffs, N.J.: Prentice Hall, 1975); Hanson and Oakman, *Palestine in the Time of Jesus;* Daniel Harrington, "Sociological Concepts and the Early Church: A Decade of Research," *TS* 41 (1980): 181–90; Paul Hollenbach, "Jesus, Demoniacs and Public Authorities: A Socio-Historical Study," *JAAR* 49 (1981):

567–88; idem, "Recent Historical Jesus Studies and the Social Sciences," SBLSP (1983): 61–78; Richard Horsley, *Sociology and the Jesus Movement* (New York: Continuum, 1989; 2d ed., 1994); Sheldon Isenberg, "Millenarism in Greco-Roman Palestine," *Religion* 4 (1974): 26–46; idem, "Power through Temple and Torah in Greco-Roman Palestine," in Jacob Neusner, ed., *Christianity, Judaism and Other Greco-Roman Cults,* part 2 (Leiden: Brill, 1975), 24–52; Bruce Malina, *Christian Origins and Cultural Anthropology: Practical Models for Biblical Interpretation* (Atlanta: John Knox, 1986); idem, *Windows on the World of Jesus: Time Travel to Ancient Judea* (Louisville, Ky.: Westminster/John Knox, 1993); Bruce Malina and Jerome Neyrey, *Calling Jesus Names: The Social Value of Labels in Matthew* (Sonoma, Calif.: Polebridge, 1988); Bruce Malina and Richard Rohrbaugh, *Social-Science Commentary on the Synoptic Gospels* (Minneapolis: Fortress, 1992); Itumeleng Mosala, *Biblical Hermeneutics and Black Theology in South Africa* (Grand Rapids: Eerdmans, 1989); Halvor Moxnes, *The Economy of the Kingdom: Social Conflict and Economic Relations in Luke's Gospel* (Philadelphia: Fortress, 1988); Ched Myers, *Binding the Strong Man: A Political Reading of Mark's Story of Jesus* (Maryknoll, N.Y.: Orbis, 1988); Jerome Neyrey, *Honor and Shame in the Gospel of Matthew* (Louisville, Ky.: Westminster John Knox, 1998); idem, ed., *The Social World of Luke-Acts: Models for Interpretation* (Peabody, Mass.: Hendrickson, 1991); John J. Pilch and Bruce J. Malina., eds., *Biblical Social Values and Their Meanings: A Handbook* (Peabody, Mass.: Hendrickson, 1993); Richard Rohrbaugh, ed., *The Social Sciences and New Testament Interpretation* (Peabody, Mass.: Hendrickson, 1996); Luise Schottroff, *Let the Oppressed Go Free: Feminist Perspectives on the New Testament,* trans. Annemarie Kidder (Louisville, Ky.: Westminster/John Knox, 1993); Willy Schottroff and Wolfgang Stegemann, eds., *God of the Lowly: Socio-Historical Interpretations of the Bible,* trans. Matthew O'Connell (Maryknoll, N.Y.: Orbis, 1984).

I have not included in this brief bibliography works already mentioned in other chapters of this study, such as the work of Horsley on the historical Jesus. The reader is referred to the notes in other chapters to find related material.

35. For studies of the Mediterranean and the methodological discussion, see the following works: Jeremy Boissevain, et al., "Toward an Anthropology of the Mediterranean," *CA* 20 (1979): 81–93; Fernand Braudel, *The Mediterranean and the Mediterranean World in the Age of Philip II,* vol. 1, 2, trans. Sian Reynolds (New York: Harper & Row, 1972; French original, 1966); John Davis, *People of the Mediterranean: An Essay in Comparative Social Anthropology* (London: Routledge & Kegan Paul, 1977); David Gilmore, *Honor and Shame and the Unity of the Mediterranean* (Washington, D.C.: AMA, 1987); idem, "Anthropology of the Mediterranean Area," *ARA* 11 (1982): 175–205; J. G. Peristiany, *Honor and Shame: The Values of the Mediterranean* (Chicago: University of Chicago Press, 1966); Julian

Pitt-Rivers, *The People of the Sierra* (Chicago: University of Chicago Press, 1954); idem, *The Fate of Shechem or the Politics of Sex: Six Essays in the Anthropology of the Mediterranean* (Cambridge: Cambridge University Press, 1971). For a summary of the discussion, see Crossan, *Historical Jesus,* 3–15.

36. Kenneth Bailey, *Poet and Peasant: A Literary Cultural Approach to the Parables in Luke* (Grand Rapids: Eerdmans, 1976), 27–43.

37. Ibid., 31. Bailey is quoting Henry Ayrout.

38. For a related discussion of the importance of models, see John H. Elliott, "Social-Scientific Criticism of the New Testament: More on Models and Methods," in Elliott, *Social-Scientific Criticism,* 1–33.

39. For a summary of the discussion, see Jan Lambrecht, "Jesus and the Law: An Investigation of Mk 7, 1–23," *Ephemerides Theologicae Lovanienses* 53 (1977): 24–79, and Roger P. Booth, *Jesus and the Laws of Purity: Tradition History and Legal History in Mark 7* (Sheffield: JSOT, 1986). This text will be dealt with in chap. 7.

40. Jerome Neyrey, "Idea of Purity in Mark's Gospel," in Elliott, *Social-Scientific Criticism,* 91–128.

41. See chap. 1, "Jesus and the Zealots: A Preview of Coming Attractions."

Chapter 5. The Quest for the Historical Jesus and the Quest for the Historical Galilee

1. On advanced agrarian societies, see Gerhard Lenski and Jean Lenski, *Human Societies: An Introduction to Macrosociology,* 4th ed. (New York: McGraw-Hill, 1982), chap. 7; Gerhard Lenski, *Power and Privilege: A Theory of Social Stratification* (New York: McGraw-Hill, 1966), chaps. 8, 9. On aristocratic empires, see John Kautsky, *The Politics of Aristocratic Empires* (Chapel Hill: University of North Carolina Press, 1982).

2. Lenski, *Power and Privilege,* 220–24.

3. Peter Garnsey and Richard Saller, *The Roman Empire: Economy, Society and Culture* (London: Duckworth, 1987), 151–53.

4. Joachim Jeremias, *Jerusalem in the Time of Jesus,* trans. F. H. and C. H. Cave (Philadelphia: Fortress, 1969), 181–99.

5. For discussions of the bureaucratic nature of empires, see Samuel Eisenstadt, *The Political System of Empires* (New York: Free Press, 1963); Kautsky, *Aristocratic Empires.*

6. The most thorough analysis of this systemic exploitation and the social structures that made it necessary is found in G. M. E. de Ste. Croix, *The Class Struggle in the Ancient Greek World from the Archaic Age to the Arab Conquests* (Ithaca, N.Y.: Cornell University Press, 1981).

7. See G. Lenski, *Power and Privilege,* 210–30.

8. Ibid., 231–42.

9. Ibid., 214–19.

10. Freyne, *Galilee,* 163–65; Horsley, *Galilee,* 213.

11. Kautsky, *Aristocratic Empires,* 211.

12. Michelle Corbier, "City, Territory and Taxation," in John Rich and Andrew Wallace-Hadrill, eds., *City and Country in the Ancient World,* (London: Routledge, 1991), 211.
13. Ibid., 234.
14. Garnsey and Saller, *Roman Empire,* 56.
15. Ian W. J. Hopkins, "The City Region in Roman Palestine," *PEQ* 112 (1980): 19–32.
16. Horsley, *Galilee,* 54.
17. Richard Fox, *Urban Anthropology: Cities in Their Cultural Setting* (Englewood Cliffs, N.J.: Prentice-Hall, 1977), 10–11.
18. See Sean Freyne, "Urban-Rural Relations in First-Century Galilee: Some Suggestions from the Literary Sources," in Lee I. Levine, ed., *The Galilee in Late Antiquity* (New York: Jewish Theological Seminary of America, 1992), 75–91.
19. Freyne, *Galilee,* 71.
20. Ibid., 125; see esp. 122–28.
21. Ibid., 129.
22. Fox, *Urban Anthropology,* chaps. 3 and 4.
23. Ibid., 53; see 41–54.
24. Horsley, *Galilee,* 171; Douglas Edwards, "The Socio-Economic and Cultural Ethos of the Lower Galilee in the First Century: Implications for the Nascent Jesus Movement," in Levine, *Galilee in Late Antiquity,* 68.
25. Ibid., 67.
26. Freyne, "Urban-Rural Relations," 83.
27. Ibid., 84.
28. G. Lenski, *Power and Privilege,* 243–48.
29. Tom Carney, *The Shape of the Past: Models and Antiquity* (Lawrence, Kans.: Coronado, 1975), 52.
30. Freyne, *Galilee,* 132.
31. Horsley, *Galilee,* 78–79.
32. Ibid., 47, 54–55.
33. Eisenstadt, *Political Systems of Empires,* 65.
34. Ibid., 266–78.
35. Horsley, *Galilee;* see esp. chap. 1, "The Roots of Galilean Independence," 19–33.
36. Freyne, *Galilee,* 44. On this point Horsley agrees. See Horsley, *Galilee,* 34.
37. Horsley, *Galilee,* 46–51.
38. Ibid., 148–49.
39. Freyne, *Galilee,* 16.
40. The following chronological list will indicate the contours of the discussion: Eric Meyers, "Galilean Regionalism as a Factor in Historical Reconstruction," *BASOR* 21 (1976): 93–101; idem, "The Cultural Setting of Galilee: The Case of Regionalism and Early Judaism," *ANRW* 2:19.1 (1979): 686–702; Ian W. J. Hopkins, "The City Region in Roman Palestine," *PEQ* 112 (1980): 19–32; Eric M. Meyers and James F.

Strange, *Archaeology, the Rabbis, and Early Christianity* (Nashville: Abingdon, 1981); Eric Meyers, "Galilean Regionalism: A Reappraisal," in William Scott Green, ed., *Approaches to Ancient Judaism*, vol. 5: *Studies in Judaism in Its Greco-Roman Context* (Atlanta: Scholars, 1985), 115–31; David Adan-Bayewitz, "Kefer Hananya, 1986," *IEJ* 37.2/3 (1987): 170–85; J. Andrew Overman, "Who Were the First Urban Christians?" SBLSP (1988): 160–68; Douglas R. Edwards, "First-Century Urban/Rural Relations in Lower Galilee: Exploring the Archaeological and Literary Evidence," SBLSP (1988): 169–82; Richard Horsley, "Bandits, Messiahs and Longshoremen: Popular Unrest in Galilee around the Time of Jesus," SBLSP (1988): 183–99; Thomas R. W. Longstaff, "Nazareth and Sepphoris: Insights into Christian Origins," *ATR Supp. Series 11* (1990): 8–15; David Adan-Bayewitz, "The Local Trade of Sepphoris in the Roman Period," *IEJ* 40 (1990): 153–72; R. A. Batey, *Jesus and the Forgotten City: New Light on Sepphoris and the Urban World of Jesus* (Grand Rapids: Baker, 1991); Miller, "Sepphoris, the Well-Remembered City," BA (1992): 74–83.

41. See the works cited in n. 40 above by Adan-Bayewitz, Edwards, Hopkins, Longstaff, Meyers, Miller, and Overman.
42. See works by Adan-Bayewitz and Edwards cited in n. 40.
43. Edwards, "First-Century Urban/Rural Relations," 174.
44. Ibid., 176.
45. From K. Hopkins, "Economic Growth and Towns in Classical Antiquity," in Philip Abrams and E. A. Wrigley, eds., *Towns in Societies: Essays in Economic History and Historical Sociology* (Cambridge: Cambridge University Press, 1978), 75. It is quoted in Edwards, "Urban/Rural Relations," 176.
46. Edwards, "Urban/Rural Relations," 178–79.
47. Martin Millett, "Roman Towns and Their Territories: An Archaeological Perspective," in John Rich and Andrew Wallace-Hadrill, eds., *City and Country in the Ancient World* (London: Routledge, 1991), 169.
48. Ibid.
49. For an overview of the nature of the ancient economy and reference to the major figures who have reconstructed the difference between modern economies and their ancient predecessors, see Douglas Oakman, "The Ancient Economy in the Bible," *BTB* 21 (1991): 34–39.
50. J. Scott, *Moral Economy of the Peasant*, 26, 57–62.
51. Kautsky, *Aristocratic Empires*, 110–11.
52. Ibid., 121–23.
53. G. Lenski, *Power and Privilege*, 50–56.
54. Ibid., 53.
55. A. H. M. Jones, *Cities of the Eastern Roman Provinces*, 2d ed. (Oxford: Oxford University Press, 1971; original ed. 1937), 294.
56. Garnsey and Saller, *Roman Empire*, 20.
57. Ibid., 20–26.
58. Kautsky, *Aristocratic Empires*, 124.

59. Martin Goodman, *The Ruling Class of Judea: The Origins of the Jewish Revolt against Rome, A.D. 66–70* (Cambridge: Cambridge University Press, 1987), 27–133.

60. Ibid., 57; see also idem, "The First Jewish Revolt: Social Conflict and the Problem of Debt," *JJS* 33 (1982): 417–27; Douglas Oakman, "Jesus and Agrarian Palestine: The Factor of Debt," SBLSP 24 (1985): 57–73.

61. Horsley, *Galilee*, 146.

62. Ibid.

63. Richard Horsley, "Popular Prophetic Movements at the Time of Jesus: Their Principal Features and Social Origins," *JSNT* 26 (1986): 3–27.

64. David A. Fiensy, *The Social History of Palestine in the Herodian Period: The Land Is Mine* (Lewiston, N.Y.: Edwin Mellen, 1991), 119–53; Shimon Dar, *Landscape and Pattern: An Archaeological Survey of Samaria, 800 B.C.E.–636 C.E.* (Oxford: BAR, 1986), 7, 77–79.

65. Shimon Applebaum, "Judaea as a Roman Province: The Countryside as a Political and Economic Factor," *ANRW* 2.8 (1977): 361–79.

66. Eric Wolf, *Peasants* (Englewood Cliffs, N.J.: Prentice-Hall, 1966), 70–73.

67. Horsley, *Galilee*, chap. 2, emphasizes the presence of social banditry in Galilee, whereas Freyne, *Galilee*, chap. 3, thinks that Hezekias was a disaffected Hasmonaean nobleman and attributes opposition to Herod to a remnant that remained loyal to the Hasmonaean line.

68. On social banditry, see Eric Hobsbawm, *Primitive Rebels: Studies in Archaic Forms of Social Movement in the Nineteenth and Twentieth Centuries* (New York: Norton, 1959); idem, *Bandits*, rev. ed. (New York: Pantheon, 1981 [1969]).

69. Horsley, *Spiral of Violence*, 209–84.

70. M. Goodman, *Ruling Class of Judaea*, 58.

71. The text is taken from Jacob Neusner, *The Rabbinic Traditions about the Pharisees before 70; Part 1: The Masters* (Leiden: Brill, 1971), 217–20.

72. Ibid., 217.

73. Appelbaum, "Judaea as a Roman Province," 370.

74. De Ste. Croix, *Class Struggle*, 125. See also the works of Paulo Freire, especially *Pedagogy of the Oppressed*, trans. Myra Bergman Ramos (New York: Seabury, 1973).

Chapter 6. "Something Greater than the Temple Is Here"

1. Sanders, *Jesus and Judaism*, 61–90 (see chap. 1, n. 47); idem, *Historical Figure of Jesus*, 249–64.

2. Sanders, *Jesus and Judaism*, 75.

3. For a summary of scholarship on the incident, see William R. Herzog II, "Temple Cleansing," in Joel Green and Scot McKnight, eds., *Dictionary of Jesus and the Gospels* (Downers Grove, Ill.: InterVarsity, 1992), 850.

4. Lenski and Lenski, *Human Societies*.
5. Hanson and Oakman (*Palestine in the Time of Jesus*, chap. 5), elaborate this point.
6. See G. Lenski, *Power and Privilege*, 256–66.
7. Ibid., 50–58.
8. John M. Lundquist, "The Legitimizing Role of the Temple in the Origin of the State," SBLSP 21 (1982): 271–97.
9. Ibid., 279. Lundquist is quoting the work of Henri J. M. Claessen and Peter Skalnik, eds., *The Early State: Studies in the Social Sciences*, 32 (The Hague: Mouten, 1978).
10. Ibid., 274–77, outlines the "typology" of the temple. All phrases in quotation marks are taken from this section of Lundquist's article unless otherwise indicated.
11. E. P. Sanders, *Judaism: Practice and Belief, 63 BCE–66 CE* (Philadelphia: Trinity Press International, 1992), 113.
12. Jacob Neusner, *From Politics to Piety: The Emergence of Pharisaic Judaism*, 2d ed. (New York: KTAV, 1979), 67–96.
13. Herbert Danby, *The Mishnah*, trans. H. Danby (Oxford: Oxford University Press, 1933), 605–6.
14. Neyrey, "Idea of Purity in Mark," 95–96.
15. Ibid., 96.
16. Jeremias, *Jerusalem in the Time of Jesus*, 272; 217–74.
17. This case is argued by James S. McLaren, *Power and Politics in Palestine: The Jews and the Governing of Their Land, 100 BC–70 AD* (Sheffield: JSOT, 1991).
18. Sheldon R. Isenberg, "Power through Temple and Torah in Greco-Roman Palestine," in Jacob Neusner, ed., *Christianity, Judaism, and Other Greco-Roman Cults, Part 2: Early Christianity* (Leiden: Brill, 1975), 24–52.
19. Sanders, *Judaism*, 166–69.
20. Horsley, *Spiral of Violence*, 29–33; idem, *Galilee*, 137–44; Borg, *Conflict, Holiness and Politics*, 47–49.
21. Sanders, *Judaism*, 157–69.
22. Freyne, *Galilee*, 293–97. Note his references to Haggai 1:7–11; 2:10–19; Zechariah 14:16–17, where the connection between land and temple is explicitly mentioned.
23. T. H. Gaster, "Sacrifices," *IDB* 4 (1962): 151.
24. Ibid., 152.
25. Isenberg, "Power through Temple and Torah," 28.
26. The conflict stories or "controversy dialogues" are one form of the larger category called variously "apophthegms" (Bultmann), "paradigms" (Dibelius), "pronouncement stories" (Taylor), "chreia" (Mack), or "conflict stories" (Hultgren). They vary in length from very brief to more extended narratives, and they have been seen as largely creations of the early church.
27. Perrin, *Rediscovering the Teaching of Jesus*, 29.
28. See Funk, "Rules of Evidence," 36–37.

29. Bultmann, *HST,* 15.
30. Ibid., 47.
31. Arland Hultgren, *Jesus and His Adversaries: The Form and Function of the Conflict Stories in the Synoptic Tradition* (Minneapolis: Augsburg, 1979), 107.
32. Vincent Taylor, *The Gospel according to St. Mark,* 2d ed. (London: Macmillan, 1966), 191–92; Joachim Jeremias, *Theology of the New Testament,* vol. 1: *The Proclamation of Jesus* (Philadelphia: Fortress, 1971), 89–90; Meier, *Marginal Jew,* 2:679.
33. Taylor, *Gospel According to St. Mark,* 192; Meier, *Marginal Jew,* 2:680, 726.
34. Bultmann, *HST,* 15.
35. Manson, *Jesus the Messiah,* 41.
36. Bultmann, *HST,* 15.
37. Jeremias, *Theology,* 114.
38. Bultmann, *HST,* 15.
39. Gerd Theissen, *The Miracle Stories of the Early Christian Tradition,* trans. Francis McDonagh (Philadelphia: Fortress, 1983; German original, 1974), 322; 113.
40. Ibid., 111.
41. Meier, *Marginal Jew,* 2:680.
42. Belo, *Materialist Reading,* 108.
43. Taylor, *Gospel According to St. Mark,* 195.
44. John H. Elliott, "Patronage and Clientage," in Rohrbaugh, *Social Sciences,* 144–56; Malina and Rohrbaugh, *Social-Science Commentary,* 235–37; Halvor Moxnes, "Patron-Client Relations and the New Community in Luke-Acts," in Neyrey, *Social World of Luke-Acts,* 241–68.
45. I have applied this perspective to the parable in Matt. 18:23–35. See Herzog, *Parables as Subversive Speech,* 131–49.
46. Bruce J. Malina, "Patron and Client: The Analogy Behind Synoptic Theology," *Forum* 4:1 (1988), reprinted in Malina, *Social World of Jesus,* 143–75.
47. Isenberg, "Power through Temple and Torah," 28.
48. Ibid., 29.
49. See William Ryan, *Blaming the Victim,* rev. ed. (New York: Vintage, 1976).
50. Crossan, *Historical Jesus,* 324.
51. Malina and Rohrbaugh, *Social-Science Commentary,* 185.
52. Ibid., 211; John J. Pilch, "Healing in Mark: A Social Science Analysis," *BTB* 15 (1985): 142–50; idem, "The Health Care System in Matthew: A Social Science Analysis," *BTB* 16 (1986): 102–6; idem, "Understanding Biblical Healing: Selecting the Appropriate Model," *BTB* 18 (1988): 60–66; idem, "Sickness and Healing in Luke-Acts," in Neyrey, *Social World of Luke-Acts,* 181–209.
53. Taylor, *Gospel according to St. Mark,* 196.
54. Malina and Rohrbaugh, *Social-Science Commentary,* 187.
55. Joachim Gnilka, *Jesus of Nazareth: Message and History,* trans.

Siegfried Schatzmann (Peabody, Mass.: Hendrickson, 1997), 116–17; Jeremias, *Theology*, 86.

56. Wright, *Jesus and the Victory of God*, 192.
57. See Joseph Fitzmyer, *A Wandering Aramean: Collected Aramaic Essays*, SBL Monograph 25 (Missoula, Mont.: Scholars, 1979); Vermes, *Jesus the Jew*, 160–91; idem, *Jesus and the World of Judaism*, 89–99.
58. Barnabus Lindars, *The Son of Man: A Fresh Examination of the Son of Man Sayings in the Gospels* (Grand Rapids: Eerdmans, 1984); C. F. D. Moule, *The Origins of Christology* (Cambridge: Cambridge University Press, 1977).
59. Joseph A. Fitzmyer, *The Gospel According to Luke (X–XXIV)* (Garden City, N.Y.: Doubleday, 1985), 1260.
60. Sanders, *Jesus and Judaism*, 62–63.
61. Ibid., 65.
62. Taylor, *Gospel according to St. Mark*, 462.
63. Richard H. Hiers, "Purification of the Temple: Preparation for the Kingdom of God," *JBL* 90 (1971): 82–90.
64. Ibid., 87.
65. Sanders, *Jesus and Judaism*, 67.
66. Gundry, *Matthew*, 413.
67. Eduard Schweizer, *The Good News According to Mark*, trans. Donald Madvig (Richmond: John Knox, 1970), 232.
68. Ibid., 234.
69. Taylor, *Gospel according to St. Mark*, 464.
70. Brandon, *Jesus and the Zealots*.
71. David Daube, *Civil Disobedience in Antiquity* (Edinburgh: University Press, 1972), 101–9.
72. Horsley, *Galilee*, 258–59; idem, *Spiral of Violence*, x–xi, 77–89.
73. Cecil Roth, "The Cleansing of the Temple and Zechariah," *NovT* 4 (1960): 174–81; quotations are from p. 181.
74. George Wesley Buchanan, "Mark 11:15–19: Brigands in the Temple," *HUCA* 30 (1959): 169–77.
75. Bultmann, *HST*, 36.
76. Ibid., 56.
77. Crossan, *Historical Jesus*, 359.
78. J. Duncan M. Derrett, "No Stone upon Another: Leprosy and the Temple," *JSNT* 30 (1987): 3–20.
79. Ibid., 5, 6.
80. Neill Q. Hamilton, "Temple Cleansing and Temple Bank," *JBL* 83 (1964): 365–72.
81. Martin Goodman, "The First Jewish Revolt: Social Conflict and the Problem of Debt," *JJS* 33 (1982): 418–19.
82. M. Goodman, *Ruling Class of Judaea*, 57.
83. Nathan Avigad, *Discovering Jerusalem* (Oxford: Oxford University Press, 1984).
84. Meier, *Marginal Jew*, 2:628.
85. John Bright, *History of Israel*, 3d ed. (Philadelphia: Westminster,

1981), 324–26; J. Maxwell Miller and John Hayes, *A History of Ancient Israel and Judah* (Louisville, Ky.: Westminster/John Knox, 1986), 403–6.

86. John Bright, *Jeremiah,* Anchor Bible (Garden City, N.Y.: Doubleday, 1965), 56.
87. For more on social bandits, see the work of Hobsbawm, cited in chap. 5, n. 68.
88. Frederick J. Gaiser, "A New Word on Homosexuality? Isaiah 56:1–8 as Case Study," *Word and World* 14 (1994): 280–93; see 283.
89. Ibid., 287.
90. C. Myers, *Binding the Strong Man,* 302.
91. Horsley, *Spiral of Violence,* 300.
92. C. Myers, *Binding the Strong Man,* 300–1.
93. Jacob Neusner, "Money-Changers in the Temple: The Mishnah's Explanation," *NTS* 35 (1989): 287–90.
94. Malina and Rohrbaugh, *Social-Science Commentary,* 249–52; Kaylor, *Jesus the Prophet,* 60–63.
95. Malina and Rohrbaugh, *Social-Science Commentary,* 252.

Chapter 7. "What Is Written? How Do You Read?"

1. Howard Clark Kee, "Early Christianity in the Galilee," in Levine, *Galilee in Late Antiquity,* 3–22. In the same volume, see Lee I. Levine, "The Sages and the Synagogue in Late Antiquity: The Evidence of the Galilee," 201–22; Gideon Foerster, "The Ancient Synagogues of the Galilee," 289–316.
2. Joseph Gutmann, "Prolegomena" in idem, ed., *The Synagogue: Studies in Origins, Archaeology and Architecture* (New York: Jewish Theological Seminary of America, 1975), xiii–xiv.
3. S. B. Honig, "The Ancient City-Square: The Forerunner of the Synagogue," *ANRW* 2.19.1 (1979): 453.
4. Gutmann, "Prolegomena," xiii–xiv.
5. Kee, "Early Christianity in Galilee," 11–12.
6. Ibid., 12.
7. Honig, "Ancient City-Square," 448–76.
8. Horsley, *Galilee,* 227–30.
9. For the importance of market days in the Roman Empire and a survey of the wide variety of activities occurring on them, see Ramsey MacMullen, "Market-Days in the Roman Empire," *Phoenix* 24:4 (1970): 333–41.
10. Horsley, *Galilee,* 232.
11. Ibid.
12. For the variety of ways in which this phrase was used, see A'haron Oppenheimer, *The 'am-ha-aretz: A Study in the Social History of the Jewish People in the Hellenistic-Roman Period* (Leiden: Brill, 1977).
13. Horsley, *Galilee,* 234.
14. Neusner, *From Politics to Piety,* 67.

15. Anthony J. Saldarini, *Pharisees, Scribes and Sadduccees in Palestinian Society* (Wilmington, Del.: Glazier, 1988), 63–106.

16. See Bryan Wilson, *Magic and the Millenium: A Sociological Study of Religious Movements of Protest among Tribal and Third-World Peoples* (London: Heinemann, 1973), 16–26.

17. Neusner, *From Politics to Piety*, 67–80.

18. Ibid., 74.

19. Saldarini, *Pharisees, Scribes and Sadduccees*, 149.

20. See Berger and Luckmann, *Social Construction of Reality*.

21. Isenberg, "Power through Temple and Torah," 42.

22. James C. Scott, "Protest and Profanation: Agrarian Revolt and the Little Tradition, Part I," *Theory and Society* 4 (1977): 1–38; p. 4.

23. Freyne, *Galilee*, 71.

24. J. Scott, "Protest and Profanation," 10.

25. Freyne, *Galilee*, 132.

26. J. Scott, "Protest and Profanation," 15.

27. Freyne, *Galilee*, 16.

28. Ibid.

29. J. Scott, "Protest and Profanation," 21.

30. Neusner, *From Politics to Piety*, 89–90.

31. Ibid., 90.

32. J. Scott, "Protest and Profanation," 29.

33. On the role of labeling, see Bruce J. Malina and Jerome H. Neyrey, *Calling Jesus Names: The Social Value of Labels in Matthew* (Sonoma, Calif.: Polebridge, 1988).

34. Horsley, *Galilee*, 129.

35. Freyne, *Galilee*, 257–304.

36. Ibid., 293–97.

37. Horsley, *Galilee*, 128–57.

38. Belo, *Materialist Reading*, 37–59.

39. L. William Countryman, *Dirt, Greed, and Sex: Sexual Ethics in the New Testament and Their Implications for Today* (Philadelphia: Fortress, 1988), 25–26.

40. Belo, *Materialist Reading*, 39.

41. Kenneth E. Bailey, *Through Peasant Eyes: More Lukan Parables, Their Culture and Style* (Grand Rapids: Eerdmans, 1980), 161–63.

42. Ibid., 162.

43. Taylor, *Gospel according to St. Mark*, 425.

44. Malina and Rohrbaugh, *Social-Science Commentary*, 244.

45. Ibid.

46. BAGD, 99.

47. Ibid.

48. On limited good, see George M. Foster, "Peasant Society and the Image of Limited Good," in Jack M. Potter, May N. Diaz, and George Foster, eds., *Peasant Society: A Reader* (Boston: Little Brown, 1967), 300–23; Bruce J. Malina, "Limited Good and the Social World of Early Christianity," *BTB* 8 (1978): 162–76.

49. F. Hauck, "*mamōnas*," in *TDNT*, 4:388.
50. Ibid., 389.
51. Malina and Rohrbaugh, *Social-Science Commentary*, 251–52.
52. Wright, *Jesus and the Victory of God*, 302.
53. Bailey, *Through Peasant Eyes*, 163.
54. Bultmann, *HST*, 22; 48.
55. Horsley, *Spiral of Violence*, 248–49.

Chapter 8. Resistance and Conflict

1. See the earlier discussion in chap. 3, in the section "Israel's Prophetic Tradition."
2. For a full discussion of Jesus' birth and early years, see Meier, *Marginal Jew*, 1:205–371.
3. Ibid., 274.
4. For a thorough discussion of the many proposals regarding Markan redaction, see Jan Lambrecht, "Jesus and the Law: An Investigation of Mk 7, 1–23," *Ephemerides Theologicae Lovanienses* 53 (1977): 24–79.
5. Ibid., 39–73.
6. Bultmann, *HST*, 47; see also 17–18.
7. Hultgren, *Jesus and His Adversaries*, 116–17; see his more literal translation of the LXX and MT versions of Isaiah 29:13 on p. 117. Roger P. Booth, *Jesus and the Laws of Purity: Tradition History and Legal History in Mark 7* (Sheffield: JSOT, 1986), 92–94.
8. The phrase is from Bruce J. Malina, "A Conflict Approach to Mark 7," *Forum* 4 (1988): 3–30.
9. Ibid., 8.
10. Freyne, *Galilee*, 321.
11. Ibid.
12. Sanders, *Jesus and Judaism*, 265.
13. Wright, *Jesus and the Victory of God*, 391–92.
14. Lawrence H. Schiffman, "Was There a Galilean Halakah?" in Levine, *Galilee in Late Antiquity*, 143–56; see p. 156.
15. Ibid., 145–48; Freyne, *Galilee*, 317–18.
16. Malina, "A Conflict Approach," 12.
17. See Neusner, *From Politics to Piety*, 67–96.
18. For a fuller description of how the purity system is operative in the encounter, see Jerome H. Neyrey, "A Symbolic Approach to Mark 7," *Forum* 4 (1988): 63–91.
19. On profanation, see J. Scott, "Profanation and Protest," 224–40.
20. C. H. Dodd, *According to the Scriptures: The Sub-Structure of New Testament Theology* (London: Collins, 1965).
21. John J. Pilch, "A Structural Functional Analysis of Mark 7," *Forum* 4 (1988): 34. See also Joseph Fitzmyer, "The Aramaic *qorban* Inscription from Jebel Hallett et-Turi and Mark 7:22/Matt 15:5," in idem, *Essays on the Semitic Background of the New Testament* (London: Geoffrey Chapman, 1971), 93–100.

22. Pilch, "Structural Functional Analysis," 34.
23. Neyrey, "Symbolic Approach," 66. He is using the work of cultural anthropologist Mary Douglas. See Mary Douglas, *Purity and Danger* (London: Routledge & Kegan Paul, 1966), and idem, *Natural Symbols* (New York: Pantheon, 1982).
24. Borg (*Conflict, Holiness and Politics,* 135–55) came to a similar conclusion.
25. Neyrey, "Symbolic Approach," 80.
26. See Joanna Dewey, *Markan Public Debate: Literary Technique, Concentric Structure and Theology in Mark 2:1–3:6* (Chico, Calif.: Scholars, 1980).
27. Hultgren, *Jesus and His Adversaries*, 82–84; Meier, *Marginal Jew*, 2:681–84. See the discussion in Robert Banks, *Jesus and the Law in the Synoptic Tradition* (London: Cambridge University Press, 1975), 113–31.
28. Borg, *Conflict, Holiness and Politics,* 168.
29. Meier, *Marginal Jew,* 2:683.
30. Sanders, *Jesus and Judaism,* 266.
31. Sanders, *Historical Figure of Jesus,* 214–16.
32. Gundry, *Matthew,* 226–27.
33. Meier, *Marginal Jew,* 2:630.
34. Ibid., 646–772.
35. Freire, *Pedagogy of the Oppressed,* 36.
36. Sanders, *Historical Figure of Jesus,* 215.
37. Malina and Rohrbaugh, *Social-Science Commentary,* 95.
38. See Batey, *Jesus and the Forgotten City*; Richard A. Batey, "Jesus and the Theatre," *NTS* 30 (1984): 563–74; Miller, "Sepphoris, the Well-Remembered City" 76; BAGD, 845.
39. Malina and Rohrbaugh, *Social-Science Commentary,* 363.
40. Sanders, *Historical Figure of Jesus,* 214. See also idem, *Jesus and Judaism,* 265.
41. Schweizer, *Mark,* 70.
42. Hultgren, *Jesus and His Adversaries,* 111–15.
43. Schweizer, *Mark,* 71.
44. Sanders, *Jesus and Judaism,* 265.
45. Bultmann, *HST,* 39.
46. Dar, *Landscape and Pattern* (Oxford: BAR, 1986); D. H. K. Amiran, "Sites of Settlements in the Mountains of Lower Galilee," *IEJ* 6 (1956): 69–77; M. W. Prausnitz, "The First Agricultural Settlements in Galilee," *IEJ* 9 (1959): 166–74. B. Golomb and Y. Kedar, "Ancient Agriculture in the Galilee Mountains," *IEJ* 21 (1971): 136–40.
47. Eric Meyers, "Galilean Regionalism as a Factor in Historical Reconstruction," *BASOR* 221 (1976): 93–101; idem, "The Cultural Setting of Galilee: The Case of Regionalism and Early Judaism," *ANRW* 2.19.1 (1979): 686–702; idem, "Galilean Regionalism: A Reappraisal," in William Scott Green, ed., *Approaches to Ancient Judaism,* vol. 5 *Studies in Judaism and Its Greco-Roman Context* (Atlanta: Scholars, 1985), 115–31.

48. Dar, *Landscape and Pattern*, 230–313.
49. J. Duncan M. Derrett, "Judaica in St. Mark," in idem, *Studies in the New Testament*, vol. 1 (Leiden: Brill, 1977), 89.
50. C. Myers, *Binding the Strong Man*, 160.
51. Banks, *Jesus and the Law*, 115.
52. Derrett, *Studies in the New Testament*, 1:91–92.
53. Walter Brueggemann, *David's Truth in Israel's Imagination and Memory* (Minneapolis: Fortress, 1985), 19–39.
54. Ibid., 21.
55. See Norman K. Gottwald, *The Tribes of Yahweh: A Sociology of the Religion of Liberated Israel, 1250–1050 B.C.E.* (Maryknoll, N.Y.: Orbis, 1979.

Chapter 9. The Temple, the Land, and the Reign of God

1. Horsley, *Spiral of Violence*, 1–58.
2. W. D. Davies, *The Gospel and the Land* (Berkeley, Calif.: University of California Press, 1974), 15–53.
3. Cited by David Fiensy, *Social History of Palestine*, 1. The citation is from H. G. Kippenberg, *Religion und Klassenbildung im antiken Judaea* (Gottingen: Vandenhoeck & Ruprecht, 1978), 154–55.
4. Freyne, *Galilee*, 275–97.
5. Ibid., 294, 295.
6. Herzog, *Parables as Subversive Speech*, 9–29.
7. J. Scott, *Domination and the Arts of Resistance*, 1–44.
8. Dodd, *Parables of the Kingdom*, 142.
9. Jeremias, *Parables of Jesus*, 151.
10. Crossan, *In Parables*, 84–85.
11. Bultmann, *HST*, 200.
12. Ibid., 172–73.
13. Bernard Brendan Scott, *Hear Then the Parable: A Commentary on the Parables of Jesus* (Minneapolis: Fortress, 1989), 368.
14. BAGD, 122.
15. Crossan, *In Parables*, 34.
16. Ibid., 83.
17. Jeremias, *Parables of Jesus*, 200–1.
18. B. Scott, *Hear Then the Parable*, 402–3 (see 389–403).
19. Gundry, *Matthew*, 275–78.
20. Johannes Weiss, *Jesus' Proclamation of the Kingdom of God*, trans. and ed. Richard Hiers and D. Larrimore Holland (Philadelphia: Fortress, 1971; German original, 1892).
21. Schweitzer, *Quest*, 238.
22. See the following two essays by Marcus Borg, "A Temperate Case for a Non-Eschatological Jesus" and "Jesus and Eschatology: Current Reflections," in Marcus Borg, *Jesus in Contemporary Scholarship* (Valley Forge, Pa.: Trinity Press International, 1994), 47–96.
23. See Crossan, *Historical Jesus*, 265–302; idem, *Jesus*, 54–74.
24. Crossan, *Historical Jesus*, 290.

25. Ibid., 303–53.
26. See Sanders, *Jesus and Judaism*, 222–41; idem, *Historical Figure of Jesus*, 169–204.
27. Sanders, *Jesus and Judaism*, 229.
28. Meyer, *Aims of Jesus*, 174–222.
29. Wright, *Jesus and the Victory of God*, 208.
30. Horsley, *Spiral of Violence*, 157, 159.
31. Ibid., 172.
32. BAGD, 431.
33. Gerhard Friedrich, "kērux, etc." in *TDNT* 3:687–88.
34. Wright, *Jesus and the Victory of God*, 241.
35. B. Scott, *Hear Then the Parable*, 7–76.
36. Funk, *Honest to Jesus*, 157.
37. Crossan, *In Parables*, 51.
38. Crossan, *Historical Jesus*, 276–79; idem, *Jesus*, 64–66.
39. Crossan, *Historical Jesus*, 278.
40. See B. Scott, *Hear Then the Parable*, 321–29; Crossan, *Historical Jesus*, 280–81.
41. Jeremias, *Parables*, 147.
42. Wright, *Jesus and the Victory of God*, 241–42.
43. Freire, *Pedagogy of the Oppressed*, 36.
44. Paul Hollenbach, "Jesus, Demoniacs and Public Authorities," *JAAR* 49 (1981): 567–88.
45. See the final paragraph of chap. 5 above for a discussion of the Lord's Prayer in a village setting.
46. The following reading is indebted to Bailey, *Through Peasant Eyes*, 1–21.
47. Luke speaks of a "woman of the city" (*en tē polei*), but he is notorious for using the word "city" to describe towns and villages as well. See Richard Rohrbaugh, "The Pre-industrial City in Luke-Acts: Urban Social Relations," in Neyrey, *Social World of Luke-Acts*, 125–49.
48. Bailey, *Through Peasant Eyes*, 8.
49. Malina and Rohrbaugh, *Social-Science Commentary*, 246.
50. John Dominic Crossan, *Raid on the Articulate: Comic Eschatology in Jesus and Borges* (New York: Harper & Row, 1976), 67.
51. Ibid., 66.
52. Jane Schneider, "Of Vigilance and Virgins: Honor, Shame, and Access to Resources in Mediterranean Societies," *Ethnology* 9:20, 18. Quoted in Crossan, *Historical Jesus*, 14.
53. See Malina, *New Testament World*, 28–62, 117–48; Hanson and Oakman, *Palestine in the Time of Jesus*, 19–61.

Chapter 10. The "Show Trial" in Jerusalem

1. Bultmann, *HST*, 34–35.
2. Ibid., 34.
3. Meier, *Marginal Jew*, 2:880–884; Gundry, *Matthew*, 355–57. "The

diction, grammatical constructions, stylistic features, and use of OT phraseology show that Matthew himself composed the story."

4. Meier, *Marginal Jew,* 2:881–83.
5. Ibid., 883. Meier argues essentially the same point.
6. Fiensy, *Social History of Palestine,* 100–1.
7. Banks, *Jesus and the Law,* 92.
8. Ibid., 92–93.
9. Meier, *Marginal Jew,* 2:883.
10. See John Donahue, "Tax Collectors and Sinners: An Attempt at Identification," *CBQ* 33 (1971): 39–61. Donahue notes that the *telōnēs* is a toll collector, not the "tax farmer" or tax collector. They are the lowly subordinates who collect at toll booths and absorb the hostility of the people by fronting for more powerful and richer figures. I will translate *telōnēs* as "toll collector."
11. Funk, *Honest to Jesus,* 208.
12. Crossan, *Historical Jesus,* 263; cf. 261–64.
13. Ibid., 263.
14. Bultmann, *HST,* 26.
15. Taylor, *Gospel according to St. Mark,* 478.
16. J. Scott, *Domination and the Arts of Resistance.*
17. The phrase is from Kautsky, *Aristocratic Empires,* 202.
18. J. Scott, *Domination and the Arts of Resistance,* 2–4.
19. J. Scott, *Weapons of the Weak,* 29.
20. Ibid., 33.
21. J. Duncan M. Derrett, "Luke's Perspective on Tribute to Caesar," in Richard J. Cassidy and Philip Scharper, eds., *Political Issues in Luke-Acts* (Maryknoll, N.Y.: Orbis, 1983), 39.
22. Ibid., 40.
23. Fiensy, *Social History of Palestine,* 100.
24. Ibid., 101.
25. Malina and Rohrbaugh, *Social Science Commentary,* 256.
26. Ibid.
27. Myers, *Binding the Strong Man,* 311.
28. Ibid., 310–11.
29. Paul C. Finney, "The Rabbi and the Coin Portrait (Mark 12:15b, 16): Rigorism Manqué," *JBL* 112 (1993): 632.
30. F. F. Bruce, "Render to Caesar," in Bammel and Moule, *Jesus and the Politics of His Day,* 254–55.
31. Ibid., 255–56; cf. I. Abrahams, *Studies in Pharisaism and the Gospels* (Cambridge: Cambridge University Press, 1917), 62–65.
32. Myers, *Binding the Strong Man,* 310.
33. H. St. J. Hart, "The Coin of 'Render unto Caesar . . .' (A Note on Some Aspects of Mark 12:13–17; Matt 22:15–22; Luke 20:20–26)," in Bammel and Moule, *Jesus and the Politics of His Day,* 242–44; Stauffer, *Christ and the Caesars,* 122–28.
34. Stauffer, *Christ and the Caesars,* 124.
35. See Belo, *Materialist Reading,* 187; Bruce, "Render to Caesar," 259–61;

Finney, "Rabbi and the Coin Portrait," 631–32; J. S. Kennard, *Render to God* (New York: Oxford University Press, 1950), 73–102; C. Myers, *Binding the Strong Man,* 311; Stauffer, *Christ and the Caesars,* 121–28.

36. Finney, "Rabbi and the Coin Portrait," 631.
37. This is how Finney, "Rabbi and the Coin Portrait," 631, and Taylor, *Gospel according to St. Mark,* 479, read the passage.
38. Belo, *Materialist Reading,* 187.
39. Kennard, *Render to God,* 113–20.
40. Bruce, "Render to Caesar," 260.
41. Stauffer, *Christ and the Caesars,* 129–34.
42. Kennard, *Render to God,* 113–19.
43. Abrahams, *Studies in Pharisaism and the Gospels,* 62–65.
44. Robert Tannehill, *The Sword of His Mouth* (Philadelphia: Fortress, 1975), 173–76.
45. Belo, *Materialist Reading,* 187.
46. Horsley, *Spiral of Violence,* 308–14.
47. Ibid., 309.
48. G. Lenski, *Power and Privilege,* 214–19.
49. Kautsky, *Aristocratic Empires,* 152.
50. Horsley, *Spiral of Violence,* 309, 311–14.
51. Kennard, *Render to God,* 123–25.
52. Belo, *Materialist Reading,* 187.
53. See chaps. 6 and 9 above.
54. Hultgren, *Jesus and His Adversaries,* 70.
55. Bultmann, *HST,* 20.
56. Hultgren, *Jesus and His Adversaries,* 73.
57. Malina and Neyrey, *Calling Jesus Names,* 78.
58. For a discussion of the primitive sequence, see Hultgren, *Jesus and His Adversaries,* 71. He is discussing the proposal put forward by D. Nineham, *Saint Mark* (Baltimore: Penguin, 1967), 300.
59. Malina and Rohrbaugh, *Social Science Commentary,* 132.
60. Ibid.
61. Hultgren, *Jesus and His Adversaries,* 69–70.
62. C. Myers, *Binding the Strong Man,* 307.
63. M. Goodman, *Ruling Class of Judaea.*
64. C. Myers, *Binding the Strong Man,* 307.
65. Meyer, *The Aims of Jesus,* 168.
66. Hultgren, *Jesus and His Adversaries,* 73.
67. See Horsley and Hanson, *Bandits, Prophets, and Messiahs,* 88–134.
68. Ibid., 116.
69. C. Myers, *Binding the Strong Man,* 294.
70. Herzog, *Parables as Subversive Speech,* 131–49.
71. The literature on the trial of Jesus is immense, and this section of one chapter cannot begin to do justice to it. The purpose of this section is to sketch a framework for understanding the show trial of Jesus. It is indebted to many works on the trial of Jesus. To mention just a few: Ernst Bammel, ed., *The Trial of Jesus* (SBT, second series, 13);

(Naperville, Ill.: Allenson, 1970); S. G. F. Brandon, *The Trial of Jesus of Nazareth* (New York: Stern & Day, 1968); Raymond Brown, *The Death of the Messiah: From Gethsemane to the Grave*, 2 vols. (New York: Doubleday, 1994); John Dominic Crossan, *Who Killed Jesus: Exposing the Roots of Anti-Semiticism in the Gospel Story of the Death of Jesus* (San Francisco: HarperCollins, 1995); Ellis Rivkin, *What Crucified Jesus? The Political Execution of a Charismatic* (Nashville: Abingdon, 1984); Paul Winter, *On The Trial of Jesus* (Berlin: Walter de Gruyter, 1961); Solomon Zeitlin, *Who Crucified Jesus?* 4th ed. (New York: Bloch, 1964; original, 1942).

72. Mary T. Boatwright, "Theatres in the Roman Empire," *BA* (1990): 184 (see 184–92).
73. Malina and Neyrey, *Calling Jesus Names*, 73.
74. Ibid., 75.
75. Ibid., 85–86, on "borrowing respectability" and "endorsements from prominent figures."
76. Bruce Malina, "Interpreting the New Testament Anthropologically: Some Examples," paper presented to a meeting of the seminar on "Social Sciences and New Testament Interpretation" of the Catholic Biblical Association, 17. See also Erdwin Pfuhl, Jr., *The Deviance Process* (New York: D. Van Norstand, 1980), 160–99.
77. Malina and Neyrey, *Calling Jesus Names*, 86; cf. Pfuhl, *Deviance Process*, 176–78.
78. Ibid., 88.
79. Horsley and Hanson, *Bandits, Prophets, and Messiahs*, 88–134.
80. Crossan, *Jesus*, 127.
81. See Malina and Neyrey, *Calling Jesus Names*, 69–91.
82. Harold Garfinkel, "Conditions of Successful Degradation Ceremonies," *AJS* 61 (1956): 421–22. Quoted in Pfuhl, *Deviance Process*, 180.
83. Martin Hengel, *Crucifixion in the Ancient World and the Folly of the Message of the Cross*, trans. John Bowden (Philadelphia: Fortress, 1977).
84. Crossan, *Jesus*, 152.
85. McLaren, *Power and Politics in Palestine*, 88–101.
86. Rivkin, *What Crucified Jesus?* 117.
87. Zeitlin, *Who Crucified Jesus?*
88. Brown, *Death of the Messiah*; Crossan, *Historical Jesus*, 354–94; idem, *Jesus*, 123–58; elaborated more fully in *Who Killed Jesus?*
89. Crossan, *Who Killed Jesus?* 1–38.
90. Crossan, *Jesus*, 127.

Chapter 11. A Concluding Unhistorical Postscript

1. Wright makes this point in Marcus Borg and N. T. Wright, *The Meaning of Jesus: Two Visions* (San Francisco: HarperCollins, 1999), 111.
2. Crossan, *Jesus*, 199. The phrase is a title of one of the subsections of the epilogue.

3. Sanders, *Jesus and Judaism*; Meyer, *Aims of Jesus*. Sanders does include an epilogue on the resurrection in *Historical Figure of Jesus*, 276–81.
4. Funk, *Honest to Jesus*, 258.
5. Ibid.
6. Borg, *Jesus*, 184.
7. Marcus Borg, "Portraits of Jesus," in Herschel Shanks, ed., *The Search for Jesus: Modern Scholarship Looks at the Gospels* (Washington: Biblical Archaeology Society, 1994), 86.
8. Borg and Wright, *Meaning of Jesus*, 129.
9. Crossan, *Jesus*, 159–201.
10. Crossan, *Search for Jesus*, 132.
11. Crossan, "Historical Jesus," *BR* 12 (1996): 44.
12. Reginald Fuller, *The Formation of the Resurrection Narratives* (Philadelphia: Fortress, 1971), 173.
13. Raymond Brown, *The Virginal Conception and Bodily Resurrection of Jesus* (New York: Paulist, 1973), 112.
14. Funk, *Honest to Jesus*, 258.
15. On prominence theory and status elevation rituals, see Malina and Neyrey, *Calling Jesus Names*, 94–131.
16. C. F. Evans, *Resurrection and the New Testament* (London: SCM Press, 1970), 21.
17. Crossan, *Historical Jesus*, xxviii.
18. Sobrino, *Jesus the Liberator*, 60, 63.
19. Kähler, *The So-Called Historical Jesus and the Historic Biblical Christ*, 1896; Johnson, *Real Jesus*, 1996.
20. For the role of broker, see Bruce Malina, "Patron and Client: The Analogy Behind Synoptic Theology," in Malina, *Social World of Jesus*, 143–75.

BIBLIOGRAPHY

Reference Works

Aland, Kurt, Matthew Black, Carlo M. Martini, Bruce M. Metzger, and Allen Wikgren, eds. *The Greek New Testament,* 4th ed., revised. Munster: United Bible Societies, 1993.

Aland, Kurt, ed. *Synopsis of the Four Gospels* (Greek-English ed.). Stuttgart: United Bible Societies, 1975.

Alt, A., O. Eissfeldt, P. Kahle, R. Kittel, eds. *Biblia Hebraica Stuttgartensia.* Stuttgart: Deutsche Bibelgesellschaft, 1984.

Arndt, William F., Walter Bauer, Frederick W. Danker, F. Wilbur Gingrich. *A Greek English Lexicon of the New Testament and Other Early Christian Literature.* 2d ed., revised and augmented. Chicago: University of Chicago Press, 1979.

Danby, Herbert, ed. *The Mishnah.* Trans. H. Danby. Oxford: Oxford University Press, 1933.

Josephus. *The Jewish War, I–III.* Trans. H. St. J. Thackeray. Cambridge, Mass.: Harvard University Press, 1976. (LCL=Loeb Classical Library)

———. *The Jewish War, IV–VII.* Trans. H. St. J. Thackeray. Cambridge, Mass.: Harvard University Press, 1979. (LCL)

———. *Jewish Antiquities, IX–XI.* Trans. Ralph Marcus. Cambridge, Mass.: Harvard University Press, 1978. (LCL)

———. *Jewish Antiquities, XII–XIV.* Trans. Ralph Marcus. Cambridge, Mass.: Harvard University Press, 1976. (LCL)

———. *Jewish Antiquities, XV–XVII.* Trans. Ralph Marcus and Allen Wikgren. Cambridge, Mass.: Harvard University Press, 1980. (LCL)

———. *Jewish Antiquities, XVIII–XIX.* Trans. L. H. Feldman. Cambridge, Mass.: Harvard University Press, 1981. (LCL)

———. *Jewish Antiquities, XVIII–XX.* Trans. L. H. Feldman. Cambridge, Mass.: Harvard University Press, 1965. (LCL)

———. *Life.* Trans. H. St. J. Thackeray. Cambridge, Mass.: Harvard University Press, 1926. (LCL)

Rahlfs, Alfred, ed. *Septuaginta*. Stuttgart: Deutsche Bibelgesellschaft, 1979.

Secondary Sources

Abrahams, I. *Studies in Pharisaism and the Gospels*. Cambridge: Cambridge University Press, 1917.

Abrams, Philip. and E. A. Wrigley, eds. *Towns in Societies: Essays in Economic History and Historical Sociology*. Cambridge: Cambridge University Press, 1978.

Achtemeier, Paul. "The Historical Jesus: A Dilemma." *T&L* 4 (1961): 107–19.

———. "Towards the Isolation of Pre-Markan Miracle Catenae." *JBL* 89 (1970): 265–91.

———. "The Origin and Function of the Pre-Markan Miracle Catenae." *JBL* 91 (1972): 198–221.

Adan-Bayewitz, David. "Kefer Hananya, 1986." *IEJ* 37 (1987): 178–79.

———. "The Local Trade of Sepphoris in the Roman Period." *IEJ* 40 (1990): 153–72.

Allison, Dale. *Jesus of Nazareth: Millenarian Prophet*. Minneapolis: Fortress Press, 1998.

Amiran, D. H. K. "Sites of Settlements in the Mountains of Lower Galilee." *IEJ* 6 (1956): 69–77.

Anderson, Hugh. "The Historical Jesus and the Origins of Christianity." *SJT* 13 (1960): 113–36.

Appelbaum, Shimon. "Judaea as a Roman Province: The Countryside as a Political and Economic Factor." *ANRW* 2.8 (1977): 361–79.

Anderson, Janice Capel, and Stephen D. Moore. *Mark and Method: New Approaches to Biblical Studies*. Minneapolis: Fortress Press, 1992.

Avigad, Nathan. *Discovering Jerusalem*. Oxford: Oxford University Press, 1984.

Bailey, Kenneth. *Poet and Peasant: A Literary Cultural Approach to the Parables*. Grand Rapids: Wm. B. Eerdmans Publishing Co., 1976.

———. *Through Peasant Eyes: More Lukan Parables, Their Culture and Style*. Grand Rapids: Wm. B. Eerdmans Publishing Co., 1980.

Bammel, Ernst, ed. *The Trial of Jesus*. Naperville, Ill.: Allenson, 1970.

Bammel, Ernst, and C. F. D. Moule, eds. *Jesus and the Politics of His Day*. Cambridge: Cambridge University Press, 1984.

Banks, Robert. *Jesus and the Law in the Synoptic Tradition*. London: Cambridge University Press, 1975.

Barnett, P. W. "The Jewish Sign Prophets—A.D. 40–70: Their Intention and Origin." *NTS* 27 (1980): 679–97.

Barr, Allen. "More Quests of the Historical Jesus." *SJT* 13 (1960): 394–409.

Batdorf, Irvin W. "Interpreting Jesus since Bultmann: Selected Paradigms and Their Hermeneutical Matrix." *SBLSP* (1983): 187–215.

Batey, Richard A. "Jesus and the Theatre." *NTS* 30 (1984): 563–74.

————. *Jesus and the Forgotten City: New Light on Sepphoris and the Urban World of Jesus*. Grand Rapids: Baker Book House, 1991.

Beck, Dwight Marion. "The Never-Ending Quest for the Historical Jesus (A Review Article of Bornkamm's *Jesus of Nazareth*)." *JBibRel* 19 (1961): 227–31.

Bedenbaugh, J. Benjamin. "The First Decade of the New Quest for the Historical Jesus." *Lutheran Quarterly* 16 (1964): 239–67.

Belo, Fernando. *A Materialist Reading of the Gospel of Mark*. Translated by Matthew J. O'Donnell. Maryknoll, N.Y.: Orbis Books, 1981.

Berger, Peter. *The Sacred Canopy: Elements of a Sociological Theory of Religion*. New York: Doubleday (Anchor Books), 1969.

Berger, Peter, and Thomas Luckmann. *The Social Construction of Reality: A Treatise in the Sociology of Knowledge*. New York: Doubleday (Anchor Books), 1967.

Best, Ernest. *The Temptation and the Passion: The Marcan Soteriology*. New York: Cambridge University Press, 1965.

Best, Thomas F. "The Sociological Study of the New Testament: Promise and Peril of a New Discipline." *SJT* 36 (1983): 181–94.

Betz, Hans Dieter. "The Cleansing of the Ten Lepers (Luke 17:11–19)." *JBL* 90 (1971): 314–28.

Black, C. Clifton. *The Disciples according to Mark: Markan Redaction in Current Debate*. Sheffield: Sheffield Academic Press, 1989.

Blenkinsopp, Joseph. *Sage, Priest, Prophet: Religious and Intellectual Leadership in Ancient Israel*. Louisville, Ky.: Westminster/John Knox Press, 1995.

Boatwright, Mary T. "Theatres in the Roman Empire." *BA* 53 (1990): 184–92.

Boissevain, Jeremy. "Toward an Anthropology of the Mediterranean." *CA* 20 (1979): 81–93.

Booth, Roger. *Jesus and the Laws of Purity: Tradition and Legal History in Mark 7*. Sheffield: JSOT Press, 1986.

Borg, Marcus. *Conflict, Holiness and Politics in the Teaching of Jesus*. Harrisburg: Trinity Press International, 1998. Original, 1984.

————. *Jesus: A New Vision; Spirit; Culture and the Life of Discipleship*. San Francisco: Harper & Row, 1987.

————. *Jesus in Contemporary Scholarship*. Valley Forge, Pa.: Trinity Press International, 1994.

————. *Meeting Jesus Again for the First Time: The Historical Jesus and the Heart of Contemporary Faith*. San Francisco: HarperCollins, 1994.

————. "A Temperate Case for a Non-Eschatological Jesus." *Forum* 2 (1986): 81–102.

————. "An Orthodoxy Reconsidered: The 'End-of-the-World Jesus.'" In *The Glory of Christ in the New Testament: Studies in Christology,* Caird Memorial Volume, ed. L. D. Hurst and N. T. Wright, 207–17. Oxford: Clarendon Press, 1987.

————. "A Renaissance in Jesus Studies." *TheolToday* 45 (1988): 280–92.

————. "Portraits of Jesus in Contemporary North American Scholarship (With Addendum)." *HTR* 84 (1991): 1–22.

Bornkamm, Günther. *Jesus of Nazareth.* Trans. I. and F. McLuskey with James Robinson. New York: Harper & Row, 1960.

Bornkamm, Günther, Gerhard Barth, and Heinz Joachim Held. *Tradition and Interpretation in Matthew.* Trans. Percy Scott. Philadelphia: Westminster Press, 1963.

Bowker, John. *Jesus and the Pharisees.* Cambridge: Cambridge University Press, 1973.

Braaten, Carl, and Roy A. Harrisville, eds. *The Historical Jesus and the Kerygmatic Christ.* New York: Abingdon Press, 1964.

Brandon, S. G. F. *Jesus and the Zealots: A Study of the Political Factor in Primitive Christianity.* New York: Charles Scribner's Sons, 1967.

————. *The Trial of Jesus of Nazareth.* New York: Stern & Day Publishers, 1968.

Braudel, Fernand. *The Mediterranean and the Mediterranean World in the Age of Philip II.* Vols. 1, 2. Trans. Sian Reynolds. New York: Harper & Row, 1972.

Breech, James. *The Silence of Jesus.* Philadelphia: Fortress Press, 1983.

Bright, John. *Jeremiah.* Anchor Bible. Garden City, N.Y.: Doubleday & Co., 1965.

————. *History of Israel.* 3d ed. Philadelphia: Westminster Press, 1981.

Brown, Peter. "The Rise and Function of the Holy Man in Late Antiquity." *JRS* 61 (1971): 80–101.

Brown, Raymond. *The Death of the Messiah: From Gethsemane to the Grave.* 2 vols. New York: Doubleday & Co., 1994.

————. *An Introduction to the New Testament.* New York: Doubleday, 1997.

Bruce, F. F. "Render to Caesar." In *Jesus and the Politics of His Day,* ed. F. Bammel and C. F. D. Moule. Cambridge: Cambridge University Press, 1984.

Brueggemann, Walter. *David's Truth in Israel's Imagination and Memory.* Minneapolis: Fortress Press, 1985.

Buchanan, George Wesley. "Mark 11:15–19: Brigands in the Temple." *HUCA* 30 (1959): 169–77.

Bultmann, Rudolf. *History of the Synoptic Tradition.* Trans. John Marsh. Oxford: Basil Blackwell Publisher, 1963. German original, 1921.

————. *Jesus and the Word.* Trans. L. P. Smith and E. H. Lantero. New York: Charles Scribner's Sons, 1934. German original, 1926.

Bultmann, Rudolf, and Karl Knudsin. *Form Criticism: Two Essays on New Testament Research.* Trans. F. C. Grant. New York: Harper Torchbooks, 1962.

Cairns, David. "The Motives and Scope of Historical Inquiry about Jesus." *SJT* 29 (1976): 339–44.

Carlston, Charles E. "A Positive Criterion of Authenticity?" *BibRes* 7 (1951): 25–39.

Carney, Tom. *The Shape of the Past: Models and Antiquity.* Lawrence, Kans.: Coronado Press, 1975.

Case, Shirley Jackson. "Jesus and Sepphoris." *JBL* 45 (1926): 14–22.

Charlesworth, James. "Research on the Historical Jesus Today: Jesus and the Pseudepigrapha, the Dead Sea Scrolls, the Nag Hammadi Codices, Josephus and Archaeology." *Prin Sem Bull* 6 (1985): 98–115.

————. "From Barren Mazes to Gentle Rappings: The Emergence of Jesus Research." *Prin Sem Bull* 7 (1986): 221–30.

————. *Jesus within Judaism: New Light from Exciting Archaeological Discoveries.* New York: Doubleday, 1988.

Charlesworth, James, ed. *Jesus' Jewishness: Exploring the Place of Jesus in Early Judaism.* New York: Crossroad, 1991.

————. *Jesus and the Dead Sea Scrolls: The Controversy Resolved.* New York: Doubleday, 1992.

Chilton, Bruce. *A Galilean Rabbi and His Bible: Jesus' Use of the Interpreted Scripture of His Time.* Wilmington, Del.: Michael Glazier, 1984.

————. "The Son of Man—Who Was He?" *BR* 12 (1996): 34–39, 45–46.

Chilton, Bruce, and Craig Evans, eds. *Studying the Historical Jesus: Evaluations of the State of Current Research.* Leiden: E. J. Brill, 1994.

Claessen, Henri J. M., and Peter Skalnik, eds. *The Early State: Studies in the Social Sciences,* 32. The Hague: Mouten, 1978.

Conzelmann, Hans. *The Theology of St. Luke.* Trans. Geoffrey Buswell. New York: Harper & Row, 1960.

Cook, Michael J. *Mark's Treatment of Jewish Leaders.* Leiden: E. J. Brill, 1978.

Corbier, Michelle. "City, Territory and Taxation." In *City and Country in the Ancient World,* ed. John Rich and Andrew Wallace-Hadrill. London: Routledge, 1991.

Countryman, L. William. *Dirt, Greed, and Sex: Sexual Ethics in the New Testament and Their Implications for Today.* Philadelphia: Fortress Press, 1988.

Crossan, John Dominic. *In Parables: The Challenge of the Historical Jesus.* New York: Harper & Row, 1973.

―――. *Raid on the Articulate: Comic Eschatology in Jesus and Borges.* New York: Harper & Row, 1976.

―――. *The Historical Jesus: The Life of a Mediterranean Peasant.* San Francisco: HarperCollins, 1991.

―――. "The Life of a Mediterranean Jewish Peasant." *Christian Century* (Dec. 18–25, 1991): 1194–1204.

―――. *Jesus: A Revolutionary Biography.* San Francisco: HarperCollins, 1994.

―――. *Who Killed Jesus? Exposing the Roots of Anti-Semiticism in the Gospel Story of the Death of Jesus.* San Francisco: HarperCollins, 1995.

―――. "A Response (To Luke Johnson)." *BR* 12 (1996): 35–38, 42–45.

Cullmann, Oscar. *Jesus and the Revolutionaries,* Trans. G. Putnam. New York: Harper & Row, 1970.

―――. "Out of Season Remarks on the 'Historical Jesus' of the Bultmann School." *USQR* 16 (1961): 131–48.

Dar, Shimon. *Landscape and Pattern: An Archaeological Survey of Samaria, 800 B.C.E.–636 C.E.* Oxford: BAR, 1986.

Daube, David. *Civil Disobedience in Antiquity.* Edinburgh: The University Press, 1972.

Davies, W. D. *The Setting of the Sermon on the Mount.* New York: Cambridge University Press, 1964.

Davis, John. *People of the Mediterranean: An Essay in Comparative Social Anthropology.* London: Routledge & Kegan Paul, 1977.

Derrett, J. Duncan M. "Judaica in St. Mark." In *Studies in the New Testament,* vol. 1, ed. J. Duncan M. Derrett. Leiden: E. J. Brill, 1977.

―――. "Luke's Perspective on Tribute to Caesar." In *Political Issues in Luke-Acts,* ed. Richard J. Cassidy and Phillip Scharper. Maryknoll, N.Y.: Orbis Books, 1983.

―――. "No Stone upon Another." *JSNT* 30 (1987): 3–20.

Dewey, Joanna. *Markan Public Debate: Literary Technique, Concentric Structure, and Theology in Mark 2:1–3:6.* Chico, Calif.: Scholars Press, 1980.

Dibelius, Martin. *From Tradition to Gospel.* Trans. Bertram Lee Woolf. New York: Charles Scribner's Sons, 1934. German original, 1919.

Dodd, C. H. *The Parables of the Kingdom.* London: Nisbet & Company, 1935.

―――. "The Framework of the Gospel Narrative." In *New Testament Studies,* ed. C. H. Dodd. Manchester: Manchester University Press, 1953.

————. *According to the Scriptures: The Sub-Structure of New Testament Theology.* London: Collins, 1965.

————. *More New Testament Studies.* Grand Rapids: Wm. B. Eerdmans Publishing Co., 1968.

Donahue, John. "Tax Collectors and Sinners: An Attempt at Identification." *CBQ* 33 (1971): 39–61.

Douglas, Mary. *Purity and Danger.* London: Routledge & Kegan Paul, 1966.

————. *Natural Symbols.* New York: Pantheon Books, 1982.

Dungan, David. "Reconsidering Albert Schweitzer." *Christian Century,* Oct. 8, 1975: 874–80.

————. "Albert Schweitzer's Disillusionment with the Reconstruction of the Life of Jesus." *PJ* (1976): 27–48.

Ebling, Gerhard. *Theology and Proclamation: A Discussion with Rudolf Bultmann.* Trans. John Riches. London: Collins, 1966.

Echegaray, Hugo. *The Practice of Jesus.* Trans. Matthew O'Connell. Maryknoll, N.Y.: Orbis Books, 1984.

Edwards, Douglas. "First-Century Urban/Rural Relations in Lower Galilee: Exploring the Archaeological and Literary Evidence." *SBLSP* (1988): 169–82.

————. "The Socio-Economic and Cultural Ethos of the Lower Galilee in the First Century: Implications for the Nascent Jesus Movement." In *The Galilee in Late Antiquity,* ed. Lee I. Levine. New York: Jewish Theological Seminary of America, 1992.

Edwards, O.C. "Sociology as a Tool for Interpreting the New Testament." *TheolRev* 65 (1983): 431–38.

Eisenstadt, Samuel Noah. *The Political System of Empires.* New York: Free Press, 1963.

Elliott, John H. *A Home for the Homeless: A Sociological Exegesis of I Peter, Its Situation and Strategy.* Philadelphia: Fortress Press, 1981.

————. "The Historical Jesus, the Kerygmatic Christ, and the Eschatological Community." *Concordia Theological Monthly* 37 (1966): 470–91.

Elliott, John H., ed., *Social-Scientific Criticism of the New Testament and Its Social World.* Semeia 35. Decatur, Ga.: Scholars Press, 1986.

Enslin, Morton Scott. *The Prophet from Nazareth.* New York: Schocken Books, 1961.

Esler, Philip. *The First Christians in Their Social Worlds: Social-Scientific Approaches to New Testament Interpretation.* London: Routledge, 1994.

Fanon, Franz. *The Wretched of the Earth.* New York: Grove Press, 1963.

Farmer, William, and Norman Perrin. "The Kerygmatic Theology and the Question of the Historical Jesus." *RL* 29 (1959–1960): 86–97.

Fiensy, David. *The Social History of Palestine in the Herodian Period: The Land Is Mine.* Lewiston, N.Y.: Edwin Mellen Press, 1991.

Finney, Paul C. "The Rabbi and the Coin Portrait (Mark 12:15b, 16): Rigorism Manqué." *JBL* 112 (1993): 629–44.

Fiorenza, Elisabeth Schüssler. *In Memory of Her: A Feminist Theological Reconstruction of Christian Origins.* New York: Crossroad, 1983.

Fitzmyer, Joseph. "The Aramaic *qorban* Inscription from Jebel Hallett et-Turi and Mark 7:22/Matt 15:5." In *Essays on the Semitic Background of the New Testament.* London: Geoffrey Chapman, 1971.

———. *A Wandering Aramean: Collected Aramaic Essays.* Missoula, Mont.: Scholars Press, 1979.

———. *The Gospel according to Luke (I–IX).* Garden City, N.Y.: Doubleday & Co., 1981.

———. *The Gospel according to Luke (X–XXIV).* Garden City, N.Y.: Doubleday & Co., 1985.

Flender, Helmut. *St. Luke, Theologian of Redemptive History.* Trans. R. H. and Ilsa Fuller. Philadelphia: Fortress Press, 1967.

Flusser, David. *Jesus.* Trans. R. Walls. New York: Herder & Herder, 1969.

Foerster, Gideon. "The Ancient Synagogues of the Galilee." In *The Galilee in Late Antiquity,* ed. Lee I. Levine. New York: The Jewish Theological Seminary of America, 1992.

Foster, George M. "Peasant Society and the Image of Limited Good." In *Peasant Society: A Reader,* ed. Jack M. Potter, May N. Diaz, and George Foster. Boston: Little Brown & Co., 1967.

Fowl, Stephen. "Reconstructing and Deconstructing the Quest of the Historical Jesus." *SJT* 42 (1989): 319–33.

Fox, Richard. *Urban Anthropology: Cities in Their Cultural Setting.* Englewood Cliffs, N.J.: Prentice-Hall, 1977.

Freire, Paulo. *Pedagogy of the Oppressed.* Trans. Myra Bergman Ramos. New York: Seabury Press, 1973.

Freyne, Sean. *Galilee from Alexander the Great to Hadrian, 323 B.C.E. to 135 C.E.* Notre Dame, Ind.: University of Notre Dame Press, 1980.

———. "Urban-Rural Relations in First Century Galilee: Some Suggestions from the Literary Sources." In *The Galilee in Late Antiquity* ed. Lee I. Levine, 72–91. New York: Jewish Theological Seminary of America, 1992.

Friedrich, Gerhard. "*Kērux,* etc." *TDNT* 3: 683–96.

Fuchs, Ernst. "The Quest of the Historical Jesus." In *Studies of the Historical Jesus,* 11–31. Trans. A. Scobie. London: SCM Press, 1964.

Funk, Robert. *Honest to Jesus: Jesus for a New Millenium.* San Francisco: HarperCollins/Polebridge Press, 1996.

———. "The Issue of Jesus." *Forum* 1 (1985): 7–12.

————. "Rules of Evidence." In *The Gospel of Mark: Red Letter Edition,* Robert Funk with Mahlon H. Smith, 29–52. Sonoma, Calif.: Polebridge Press, 1991.

Gager, John. *Kingdom and Community: The Social World of Early Christianity.* Englewood Cliffs, N.J.: Prentice-Hall, 1975.

Gaiser, Frederick J. "A New Word on Homosexuality? Isaiah 56:1–8 as Case Study." *Word & World* 14 (1994): 280–93.

Garfinkel, Harold. "Conditions of Successful Degradation Ceremonies." *AJS* 61 (1956): 421–22.

Garnsey, Peter and Richard Saller. *The Roman Empire: Economy, Society, Culture.* London: Gerald Duckworth & Co., 1987.

Gaster Theodore., "Sacrifices." *IDB* 4 (1962): 147–59.

Gilmore, David. *Honor and Shame and the Unity of the Mediterranean.* Washington, D.C.: AMA, 1987.

————. "Anthropology of the Mediterranean Area." *ARA* 11 (1982): 175–205.

Gnilka, Joachim. *Jesus of Nazareth: Message and History.* Trans. Siegfried Schatzmann. Peabody, Mass.: Hendrickson Publishers, 1997.

Golomb, B., and Y. Kedar. "Ancient Agriculture in the Galilee Mountains." *IEJ* 21 (1971): 136–40.

Goodman, Martin. "The First Jewish Revolt: Social Conflict and the Problem of Debt." *JJS* 33 (1982): 417–27.

————. *State and Society in Roman Galilee, A.D. 132–212.* Totowa, N.J.: Rowman & Allanheld Publishers, 1983.

————. *The Ruling Class of Judea: The Origin of the Jewish Revolt against Rome, A.D. 66–70.* Cambridge: Cambridge University Press, 1987.

Gottwald, Norman K. *The Tribes of Yahweh: Sociology of the Religion of Liberated Israel.* Maryknoll, N.Y.: Orbis Books, 1979.

Grabbe, Lester L. *Priests, Prophets, Diviners, Sages: A Socio-Historical Study of Religious Specialists in Ancient Israel.* Valley Forge, Pa.: Trinity Press International, 1995.

Gray, Rebecca. *Prophetic Figures in Late Second Temple Jewish Palestine: The Evidence from Josephus.* New York: Oxford University Press, 1993.

Gundry, Robert. *Matthew: A Commentary on His Literary and Theological Art.* Grand Rapids: Wm. B. Eerdmans Publishing Co., 1982.

Gutmann, Joseph, ed., *The Synagogue: Studies in Origins, Archaeology, and Architecture.* New York: KTAV, 1975.

Guttgemanns, Erhardt. *Candid Questions concerning Gospel Form Criticism.* Trans. William Doty. Pittsburgh: Pickwick Press, 1979.

Hagner, Donald. *The Jewish Reclamation of Jesus: An Analysis and Critique of the Modern Jewish Study of Jesus.* Grand Rapids: Zondervan Books, 1984.

Hamilton, Neill Q. "Temple Cleansing and Temple Bank." *JBL* 83 (1964): 365–72.

Hanson, K.C., and Douglas Oakman. *Palestine in the Time of Jesus: Social Structures and Social Conflicts.* Minneapolis: Fortress Press, 1998.

Harrington, Daniel. "Sociological Concepts and the Early Church: A Decade of Research." *TS* 41 (1980): 181–90.

Hart, H. St. J. "The Coin of 'Render unto Caesar . . . ' (A Note on Some Aspects of Mark 12:13–17; Matt 22:15–22; Luke 20:20–26)." In *Jesus and the Politics of His Day,* ed. E. Bammel and C. F. D. Moule. Cambridge: Cambridge University Press, 1984.

Hays, Richard B. "The Corrected Jesus." *First Things* 43 (1994): 43–48.

Hengel, Martin. *The Zealots: Investigations into the Jewish Freedom Movement in the Period from Herod until 70 A.D.* Trans. D. Smith. Edinburgh: T. & T. Clark, 1989. German original, 1961; rev. and expanded in 1976.

———. *Was Jesus a Revolutionist?* Trans. W. Klassen. Philadelphia: Fortress Press, 1971.

———. *Victory over Violence: Jesus and the Revolutionists.* Trans. David Green. Philadelphia: Fortress Press, 1973.

———. *Crucifixion in the Ancient World and the Folly of the Message of the Cross.* Trans. John Bowden. Philadelphia: Fortress Press, 1977.

Herzog, William R., II. *Parables as Subversive Speech: Jesus as Pedagogue of the Oppressed.* Louisville: Ky., Westminster/John Knox Press, 1994.

———. "Apocalyptic and the Historical Jesus." *PacTheolRev* 18 (1984): 17–25.

———. "The Quest of the Historical Jesus and the Discovery of the Apocalyptic Jesus." *PacTheolRev* 19 (1985): 25–39.

Hiers, Richard. "Purification of the Temple: Preparation for the Kingdom of God." *JBL* 90 (1971): 82–90.

Hill, Scott D. "The Local Hero in Palestine in Comparative Perspective." In *Elijah and Elisha in Socioliterary Perspective,* ed. Robert B. Coote. Atlanta: Scholars Press, 1992.

Hobsbawm, Eric. *Primitive Rebels: Studies in Archaic Forms of Social Movements in the Nineteenth and Twentieth Centuries.* New York: W. W. Norton & Co., 1959.

———. *Bandits.* Rev. ed. New York: Pantheon Books, 1981.

Hollenbach, Paul. "Jesus, Demoniacs, and Public Authorities: A Socio-Historical Study." *JAAR* 49 (1981): 567–88.

———. "Recent Historical Jesus Studies and the Social Sciences." *SBLSP* (1983): 61–78.

———. "The Historical Jesus Question in North America Today." *BTB* 19 (1989): 11–22.

Honig, S. B. "The Ancient City-Square: The Forerunner of the Synagogue." *ANRW* 2.19.1 (1979): 448–76.

Hooker, Morna D. *The Signs of a Prophet: The Prophetic Actions of Jesus.* Harrisburg, Pa.: Trinity Press International, 1997.

Hopkins, Ian W. J. "The City Region in Roman Palestine." *PEQ* 112 (1980): 19–32.

Hopkins, K. "Economic Growth and Towns in Classical Antiquity." In *Towns in Societies: Essays in Economic History and Historical Sociology*, ed. Phillip Abrams and E. A. Wrigley. Cambridge: Cambridge University Press, 1978.

Horsley, Richard. "Popular Prophetic Movements in the Time of Jesus: Their Principal Features and Social Origins." *JSNT* 26 (1986): 3–27.

———. *Jesus and the Spiral of Violence: Popular Jewish Resistance in Roman Palestine.* San Francisco: Harper & Row, 1987.

———. "Bandits, Messiahs, and Longshoremen: Popular Unrest in Galilee around the Time of Jesus." *SBLSP* (1988): 183–99.

———. *Sociology and the Jesus Movement.* New York: Continuum, 1989. 2d ed., 1994.

———. *Galilee: History, Politics, People.* Valley Forge, Pa.: Trinity Press International, 1995.

Horsley, Richard, and John Hanson. *Bandits, Prophets, and Messiahs: Popular Movements at the Time of Jesus.* New York: Winston Press, 1985.

Hultgren, Arland. *Jesus and His Adversaries: The Form and Function of the Conflict Stories in the Synoptic Tradition.* Minneapolis: Augsburg, 1979.

Isenberg, Sheldon. "Millenarism in Greco-Roman Palestine." *Religion* 4 (1974): 26–46.

———. "Power through Temple and Torah in Greco-Roman Palestine." In *Christianity, Judaism, and Other Greco-Roman Cults,* Part 2, ed. Jacob Neusner, 24–52. Leiden: E. J. Brill, 1975.

Jeremias, Joachim. *The Parables of Jesus.* 6th ed. Trans. S. H. Hooke. New York: Charles Scribner's Sons, 1963. German first ed., 1947.

———. *The Problem of the Historical Jesus.* Trans. Norman Perrin, with an Introduction by John Reumann. Philadelphia: Fortress Press, 1964.

———. *The Prayers of Jesus.* Trans. John Bowden and John Reumann. London: SCM Press, 1967.

———. *Jerusalem in the Time of Jesus.* Trans. F. H. and C. H. Cave. Philadelphia: Fortress Press, 1969.

———. *Theology of the New Testament,* Vol. 1: *The Proclamation of Jesus.* Trans. John Bowden. Philadelphia: Fortress Press, 1971.

Johnson, Luke T. "The Search for the (Wrong) Jesus." *BR* 11 (1995): 20–25, 44.

Jones, A. H. M. *Cities of the Eastern Roman Provinces*. Oxford: Oxford University Press, 1937. 2d ed., 1971.

Kähler, Martin. *The So-Called Historical Jesus and the Historic Biblical Christ*. Trans. Carl Braaten. Philadelphia: Fortress Press, 1964. German original, 1892.

Käsemann, Ernst. "The Problem of the Historical Jesus." In *Essays on New Testament Themes*, trans. W. J. Montague. London: SCM Press, 1964.

Kautsky, John. *The Politics of Aristocratic Empires*. Chapel Hill: University of North Carolina Press, 1982.

Kaylor, R. David. *Jesus the Prophet: His Vision of the Kingdom on Earth*. Louisville, Ky.: Westminster/John Knox Press, 1994.

Keck, Leander. *A Future for the Historical Jesus: The Place of Jesus in Preaching and Theology*. Nashville: Abingdon Press, 1971.

Keck, Leander, and J. Louis Martyn, eds. *Studies in Luke-Acts*. Nashville: Abingdon Press, 1966.

Kee, Howard Clark. *Jesus in History: An Approach to the Synopic Gospels*. New York: Harcourt Brace Jovanovich, 1970.

———. *Community of the New Age: Studies in Mark's Gospel*. Philadelphia: Westminster Press, 1977.

———. "Early Christianity in Galilee." In *The Galilee in Late Antiquity*, ed. Lee I. Levine. New York: Jewish Theological Seminary of America, 1992.

Kelber, Werner. *The Kingdom in Mark: A New Place and a New Time*. Philadelphia: Fortress Press, 1974.

———. *Mark's Story of Jesus*. Philadelphia: Fortress Press, 1979.

Kelber, Werner, ed. *The Passion in Mark: Studies on Mark 14–16*. Philadelphia: Fortress Press, 1976.

Kelly, Tony. "The Historical Jesus and Human Subjectivity: A Response to John Meier." *Pacifica* 4 (1991): 202–28.

Kennard, J. S. *Render to God*. New York: Oxford University Press, 1950.

Kingsbury, Jack Dean. *The Parables in Matthew 13: A Study in Redaction-Criticism*. London: SPCK, 1969.

———. *Matthew: Structure, Christology, Kingdom*. Philadelphia: Fortress Press, 1975.

———. *Jesus Christ in Matthew, Mark, and Luke*. Philadelphia: Fortress Press, 1981.

———. *The Christology of Mark's Gospel*. Philadelphia: Fortress Press, 1983.

———. *Matthew as Story*. Rev. ed. Philadelphia: Fortress Press, 1988.

———. *Conflict in Mark: Jesus, Authorities, Disciples*. Philadelphia: Fortress Press, 1989.

Kippenberg, H. G. *Religion und Klassenbildung im antiken Judaea.* Gottingen: Vandenhoeck und Ruprecht, 1978.

Koch, Klaus. *The Growth of the Biblical Tradition: The Form-Critical Method* Trans. S. M. Cupitt. New York: Charles Scribner's Sons, 1969.

Krämer, Helmut. "*Prophētēs.*" *TDNT*, 6: 781–96.

Kümmel, Werner G. "Kerygma, Selfhood, or Historical Fact: A Review Article on the Problem of the Historical Jesus." *Encounter* 21 (1960): 232–34.

Lambrecht, Jan. "Jesus and the Law: An Investigation of Mk 7, 1–23." *Ephemerides Theologicae Lovanienses* 53 (1977): 24–79.

Lenski, Gerhard. *Power and Privilege: A Theory of Social Stratification.* New York: McGraw-Hill Book Co., 1966.

Lenski, Gerhard, and Jean Lenski. *Human Societies: An Introduction to Macrosociology.* 4th ed. New York: McGraw-Hill Book Co., 1982.

Lindars, Barnabus. *The Son of Man: A Fresh Examination of the Son of Man Sayings in the Gospels.* Grand Rapids: Wm. B. Eerdmans Publishing Co., 1984.

Long, Thomas, ed. *Theology Today* 52 (1995).

Longstaff, Thomas W. "Nazareth and Sepphoris: Insights into Christian Origins." *ATR* Supp. Series 11 (1990): 8–15.

Lundquist, John M. "The Legitimizing Role of the Temple in the Origin of the State." *SBLSP* 21 (1982): 271–97.

Mack, Burton. *The Lost Gospel: The Book of Q and Christian Origins.* New York: HarperCollins, 1993.

MacMullen, Ramsey. "Market-Days in the Roman Empire." *Phoenix* 24 (1970): 333–41.

Malbon, Elizabeth Struthers. *Narrative Space and Mythic Meaning in Mark.* San Francisco: Harper & Row, 1986.

―――. "Fallible Followers: Women and Men in the Gospel of Mark." *Semeia* 28 (1983): 29–48.

―――. "Disciples/Crowds/Whoever: Markan Characters and Readers." *NovT* 28 (1986): 104–30.

Malina, Bruce. "Limited Good and the Social World of Early Christianity." *BTB* 8 (1978): 162–78.

―――. "Jesus as Charismatic Leader?" *BTB* 14 (1984): 55–62.

―――. *Christian Origins and Cultural Anthropology: Practical Models for Biblical Interpretation.* Atlanta: John Knox Press, 1986.

―――. "Patron and Client: The Analogy behind Synoptic Theology." *Forum* 4 (1988): 2–32.

―――. "A Conflict Approach to Mark 7." *Forum* 4 (1988): 3–30.

————. "Christ and Time: Swiss or Mediterranean." *CBQ* 51 (1989): 1–31.

————. *The New Testament World: Insights from Cultural Anthropology.* Rev. ed. Louisville, Ky.: Westminster/John Knox Press, 1993.

————. *Windows on the World of Jesus: Time Travel to Ancient Judea.* Louisville, Ky.: Westminster/John Knox Press, 1993.

————. *The Social World of Jesus and the Gospels.* London: Routledge, 1996.

Malina, Bruce, and Jerome Neyrey. *Calling Jesus Names: The Social Value of Labels in Matthew.* Sonoma, Calif.: Polebridge Press, 1988.

Malina, Bruce, and Richard Rohrbaugh. *Social-Science Commentary on the Synoptic Gospels.* Minneapolis: Fortress Press, 1992.

Manson, T.W. *The Sayings of Jesus.* London: SCM Press, 1949.

Manson, William, *Jesus the Messiah: The Synoptic Tradition of the Revelation of God in Christ, with Special Reference to Form Criticism.* London: Hodder & Stoughton, 1943.

Marxsen, Willi. *Mark the Evangelist: Studies on the Redaction History of the Gospel.* Trans. J. Boyce, D. Juel, W. Poehlmann, with Roy Harrisville. Nashville: Abingdon Press, 1969.

McKnight, Edgar V. *What Is Form Criticism?* Guides to Biblical Scholarship. Philadelphia: Fortress Press, 1969.

————. *Meaning in Texts: The Historical Shaping of a Narrative Hermeneutics.* Philadelphia: Fortress Press, 1978.

McLaren, James S. *Power and Politics in Palestine: The Jews and the Governing of Their Land, 100 BC–70 AD.* Sheffield: JSOT Press, 1991.

Meier, John P. *A Marginal Jew: Rethinking the Historical Jesus,* Vol. 1: *The Roots of the Problem and the Person.* New York: Doubleday, 1991.

————. *A Marginal Jew: Rethinking the Historical Jesus,* Vol. 2: *Mentor, Message, Miracles.* New York: Doubleday, 1994.

Memmi, Albert. *The Colonizer and the Colonized.* Trans. Howard Greenfield. Boston: Beacon Press, 1965.

Meyer, Ben F. *The Aims of Jesus.* London: SCM Press, 1979.

Meyers, Eric. "Galilean Regionalism as a Factor in Historical Reconstruction." *BASOR* 21 (1976): 93–101.

————. "The Cultural Setting of Galilee: The Case of Regionalism and Early Judaism." *ANRW* 2:19.1 (1979): 686–702.

————. "Galilean Regionalism: A Reappraisal." In *Approaches to Ancient Judaism,* Vol. 5: *Studies in Judaism in Its Greco-Roman Context,* ed. William Scott Green. Atlanta: Scholars Press, 1985.

Meyers, Eric, and James F. Strange. *Archaeology, the Rabbis, and Early Christianity.* Nashville: Abingdon Press, 1981.

Miller, Robert. "The Jesus of Orthodoxy and the Jesuses of the Gospels: A

Critique of Luke Timothy Johnson's *The Real Jesus*." *JSNT* 68 (1997): 101–20.

———. "History Is Not Optional: A Response to 'The Real Jesus' by Luke Timothy Johnson." *BTB* 28 (1998): 27–34.

Miller, Stuart S. "Sepphoris, The Well-Remembered City." *BA* 55 (1992): 74–83.

Millett, Martin. "Roman Towns and Their Territories: An Archaeological Perspective." In *City and Country in the Ancient World*, ed. John Rich and Andrew Wallace-Hadrill. London: Routledge, 1991.

Mosala, Itumeleng. *Biblical Hermeneutics and Black Theology in South Africa*. Grand Rapids: Wm. B. Eerdmans Publishing Co., 1989.

Moule, C. F. D. *The Origins of Christology*. Cambridge: Cambridge University Press, 1977.

Moxnes, Halvor. *The Economy of the Kingdom: Social Conflict and Economic Relations in Luke's Gospel*. Philadelphia: Fortress Press, 1988.

Myers, Ched. *Binding the Strong Man: A Political Reading of Mark's Story of Jesus*. Maryknoll, N.Y.: Orbis Books, 1988.

Neusner, Jacob. *The Rabbinic Traditions about the Pharisees before 70, Part 1: The Masters*. Leiden: E. J. Brill, 1971.

———. *From Politics to Piety: The Emergence of Pharisaic Judaism*. 2d ed. New York: KTAV, 1979.

———. "Money Changers in the Temple: The Mishnah's Explanation." *NTS* 35 (1989): 287–90.

Neyrey, Jerome. "The Idea of Purity in Mark." In *Social-Scientific Criticism of the New Testament and Its Social World*, Semeia 35, ed. John H. Elliott. Decatur, Ga.: Scholars Press, 1986.

———. "A Symbolic Approach to Mark 7." *Forum* 4 (1988): 63–91.

———. *Honor and Shame in the Gospel of Matthew*. Louisville, Ky.: Westminster John Knox Press, 1998.

Neyrey, Jerome, ed. *The Social World of Luke-Acts: Models for Interpretation*. Peabody, Mass.: Hendrickson Publishers, 1991.

Nineham, D. E. "The Order of Events in St. Mark's Gospel—An Examination of Dr. Dodd's Hypothesis." In *Studies in the Gospels*, ed. D. E. Nineham. London: Basil Blackwell Publisher, 1957.

———. *Saint Mark*. Baltimore: Penguin Books, 1967.

Nolan, Albert. *Jesus before Christianity*. Maryknoll, N.Y.: Orbis Books, 1978.

Oakman, Douglas. "Jesus and Agrarian Palestine: The Factor of Debt." *SBLSP* (1985): 57–73.

———. *Jesus and the Economic Questions of His Day*. Lewiston, N.Y.: Edwin Mellen Press, 1986.

———. "The Ancient Economy in the Bible." *BTB* 21 (1991): 34–39.

Ogden, Schubert. "Bultmann and the 'New Quest'." *JBibRel* 30 (1962): 209–18.

Oppenheimer, A'haron. *The 'am-ha-aretz: A Study in the Social History of the Jewish People in the Hellenistic-Roman Period.* Leiden: E. J. Brill, 1977.

Overman, J. Andrew. "Who Were the First Urban Christians?" *SBLSP* (1988): 160–68.

Patte, Daniel. *What Is Structural Exegesis?* Guides to Biblical Scholarship. Philadelphia: Fortress Press, 1976.

Patte, Daniel, and Aline Patte. *Structural Exegesis: From Theory to Practice.* Philadelphia: Fortress Press, 1978.

Peristiany, J. G., ed. *Honor and Shame: The Values of the Mediterranean.* Chicago: University of Chicago Press, 1966.

Perrin, Norman. *Rediscovering the Teaching of Jesus.* New York: Harper & Row, 1967.

————. *What Is Redaction Criticism?* Guides to Biblical Scholarship. Philadelphia: Fortress Press, 1969.

Pfuhl, Erdwin. *The Deviance Process.* New York: D. Van Norstrand Co., 1980.

Pilch, John J. "Healing in Mark: A Social Science Analysis." *BTB* 15 (1985): 142–50.

————. "The Health Care System in Matthew: A Social Science Analysis." *BTB* 16 (1986): 102–6.

————. "Understanding Biblical Healing: Selecting the Appropriate Model." *BTB* 18 (1988): 60–66.

————. "A Structural Functional Analysis of Mark 7." *Forum* 4 (1988): 31–62.

————. "Sickness and Healing in Luke-Acts." In *The Social World of Luke-Acts: Models for Interpretation,* ed. Jerome Neyrey, 181–209. Peabody, Mass.: Hendrickson Publishers, 1991.

Pilch, John J., and Bruce Malina, eds. *Biblical Social Values and Their Meanings: A Handbook.* Peabody, Mass.: Hendrickson Publishers, 1993.

Pitt-Rivers, Julian. *The People of the Sierra.* Chicago: University of Chicago Press, 1954.

————. *The Fate of Shechem, or the Politics of Sex: Six Essays in the Anthropology of the Mediterranean.* Cambridge: Cambridge University Press, 1971.

Polkow, Dennis. "Method and Criteria for Historical Jesus Research." *SBLSP* (1987): 336–56.

Potter, Jack M., May N. Diaz, and George Foster, eds. *Peasant Society: A Reader.* Boston: Little Brown & Co., 1967.

Powell, Mark Allen. *Jesus as a Figure in History: How Modern Historians*

View the Man from Galilee. Louisville, Ky.: Westminster John Knox Press, 1998.

Prausnitz, M.W. "The First Agricultural Settlements in Galilee." *IEJ* 9 (1959): 166–74.

Redfield, Robert. *The Little Community*. Chicago: University of Chicago Press, 1955.

———. *Peasant Society and Culture*. Chicago: University of Chicago Press, 1956.

Reimarus, Hermann Samuel. *The Goal of Jesus and His Followers*. Translated and with an introduction by George W. Buchanan. Leiden: E. J. Brill, 1970.

Rhoads, David, and Donald Michie. *Mark as Story: An Introduction to the Narrative of a Gospel*. Philadelphia: Fortress Press, 1982.

Riches, John. *Jesus and the Transformation of Judaism*. New York: Seabury Press, 1982.

Rivkin, Ellis. *What Crucified Jesus? The Political Execution of a Charismatic*. Nashville: Abingdon Press, 1984.

Robinson, James M. *A New Quest of the Historical Jesus*. London: SCM Press, 1959.

———. "The Recent Debate on the 'New Quest'." *JBibRel* 30 (1962): 198–208.

Rohde, Joachin. *Rediscovering the Teaching of the Evangelists*. Trans. Dorothea Barton. Philadelphia: Westminster Press, 1968.

Rohrbaugh, Richard L., ed. *The Social Sciences and New Testament Interpretation*. Peabody, Mass.: Hendrickson Publishers, 1996.

Roth, Cecil. "The Cleansing of the Temple and Zechariah." *NovT* IV (1960): 174–81.

Ryan, William. *Blaming the Victim*. Rev. ed. New York: Vintage Books, 1976.

Saldarini, Anthony. *Pharisees, Scribes, and Sadduccees in Palestinian Society*. Wilmington, Del.: Michael Glazier, 1988.

Sanders, E. P. *Jesus and Judaism*. Philadelphia: Fortress Press, 1985.

———. *Judaism: Practice and Belief, 63 BCE–66 CE*. Philadelphia: Trinity Press International, 1992.

———. *The Historical Figure of Jesus*. London: Penguin Books, 1993.

Schiffman, Lawrence H. "Was There a Galilean Halakah?" In *The Galilee in Late Antiquity*, ed. Lee I. Levine. New York: Jewish Theological Seminary of America, 1992.

Schmidt, Karl L. *Der Rahmen der Geschichte Jesu*. Berlin: Karl Ludwig, 1919.

Schneider, Jane. "Of Vigilance and Virgins: Honor, Shame and Access to Resources in Mediterranean Studies." *Ethnology* 9 (1971): 1–24.

Schottroff, Luise. *Jesus and the Hope of the Poor.* Trans. Matthew O'Connell. Maryknoll, N.Y.: Orbis Books, 1986.

———. *Let the Oppressed Go Free: Feminist Perspectives on the New Testament.* Trans. Annemarie Kidder. Louisville, Ky.: Westminster/John Knox Press, 1993.

Schottroff, Willy, and Wolfgang Stegemann, eds. *God of the Lowly: Socio-Historical Intepretations of the Bible.* Trans. Matthew O'Connell. Maryknoll, N.Y.: Orbis Books, 1984.

Schweitzer, Albert. *The Quest for the Historical Jesus.* Trans. W. Montgomery. New York: Macmillan Co., 1956. German original, 1906; first English ed., 1910.

Schweizer, Eduard. *The Good News according to Mark.* Trans. Donald Madvig. Richmond: John Knox Press, 1970.

Scott, Bernard Brandon. *Hear Then the Parable: A Commentary on the Parables of Jesus.* Minneapolis: Fortress Press, 1989.

———. "Jesus as Sage: An Innovating Voice in Common Wisdom." In *The Sage in Israel and the Ancient Near East,* John G. Gammie and Leo G. Perdue, eds., 399–415. Winona Lake, Ind.: Eisenbrauns, 1990.

Scott, James C. *The Moral Economy of the Peasant: Rebellion and Subsistence in Southeast Asia.* New Haven, Conn.: Yale University Press, 1976.

———. "Protest and Profanation, Parts I and II." *Theory and Society* 4 (1977): 1–38, 211–46.

———. *Weapons of the Weak: Everyday Forms of Peasant Resistance.* New Haven, Conn.: Yale University Press, 1985.

———. *Domination and the Arts of Resistance: Hidden Transcripts.* New Haven, Conn.: Yale University Press, 1990.

Segundo, Juan Luis. *The Historical Jesus of the Synoptics.* Trans. John Drury. Maryknoll, N.Y.: Orbis Books, 1985.

Silberman, Lou. "The New Quest for the Historical Jesus." *Judaism* 11 (1962): 260–67.

Sobrino, Jon. *Jesus the Liberator: A Historical-Theological View.* Trans. Paul Burns and Francis McDonagh. Maryknoll, N.Y.: Orbis Books, 1993.

Stauffer, Ethelbert. *Christ and the Caesars.* Trans. K. & R. Gregor Smith. Philadelphia: Westminster Press, 1955.

Ste. Croix, G. M. E. de. *The Class Struggle in the Ancient Greek World from the Archaic Age to the Arab Conquests.* Ithaca, N.Y.: Cornell University Press, 1981.

Talbert, Charles, ed. *Perspectives on Luke-Acts.* Danville, Ky.: Association of Baptist Professors of Religion, 1978.

Tannehill, Robert C. *The Sword of His Mouth.* Philadelphia: Fortress Press, 1975.

————. "The Disciples in Mark: The Function of a Narrative Role." *JR* 57 (1977): 386–405.

Tatum, W. Barnes. *In Quest of Jesus: A Guidebook*. Atlanta: John Knox Press, 1982.

Taylor, Joan E. *The Immerser: John the Baptist within Second Temple Judaism*. Grand Rapids: Wm. B. Eerdmans Publishing Co., 1997.

Taylor, Vincent. *The Formation of the Gospel Tradition*. London: Macmillan & Co., 1933.

————. *The Life and Ministry of Jesus*. London: Macmillan & Co., 1954.

————. *The Gospel according to St. Mark*. 2d ed. New York: Macmillan & Co., 1966.

Taylor, William F. "New Quests for the Historical Jesus." *TrinitySemRev* 15 (1993): 69–83.

Theissen, Gerd. *Sociology of Early Palestinian Christianity*. Trans. John Bowden. Philadelphia: Fortress Press, 1978.

————. *The Miracle Stories of the Early Christian Tradition*. Trans. Francis McDonagh. Philadelphia: Fortress Press, 1983.

————. *The Gospels in Context: Social and Political History in the Synoptic Traditions*. Trans. Linda Maloney. Minneapolis: Fortress Press, 1991.

Theissen, Gerd, and Annette Merz. *The Historical Jesus: A Comprehensive Guide*. Trans. John Bowden. Minneapolis: Fortress Press, 1996.

Tolbert, Mary Ann. *Perspectives on the Parables: An Approach to Multiple Interpretations*. Philadelphia: Fortress Press, 1979.

————. *Sowing the Gospel: Mark's World in Literary-Historical Perspective*. Minneapolis: Fortress Press, 1989.

Trocmé, André. *Jesus and the Nonviolent Revolution*. Trans. M. Shank. Scottsdale, Pa.: Herald Press, 1973. French original, 1961.

Vermes, Geza. *Jesus the Jew: A Historian's Reading of the Gospels*. Philadelphia: Fortress Press, 1973.

————. *Jesus and the World of Judaism*. Philadelphia: Fortress Press, 1983.

————. *The Religion of Jesus the Jew*. Philadelphia: Fortress Press, 1993.

Via, Dan O. Jr. "The Necessary Complement to the Kerygma." *JR* 45 (1965): 30–38.

Webb, Robert L. *John the Baptizer and Prophet: A Socio-Historical Study*. Sheffield: Sheffield Academic Press, 1991.

Weeden, Theodore J. Sr. *Mark: Traditions in Conflict*. Philadelphia: Fortress Press, 1971.

————. "Rediscovering the Parabolic Intent in the Parable of the Sower." *JAAR* 47 (1979): 97–120.

Weiss, Johannes. *Jesus' Proclamation of the Kingdom of God*. Trans. and ed. Richard Hiers and D. Lattimore Holland. Philadelphia: Fortress Press, 1971.

Wilson, Bryan. *Magic and the Millenium: A Sociological Study of Religious Movements of Protest among Tribal and Third-World Peoples.* London: William Heinemann, 1973.

Wink, Walter. *The Bible in Human Transformation.* Philadelphia: Fortress Press, 1974.

Winter, Paul. *On the Trial of Jesus.* Berlin: Walter de Gruyter & Co., 1961.

Witherington, Ben III. *The Jesus Quest: The Third Search for the Jew of Nazareth.* Downers Grove, Ill.: InterVarsity Press, 1995.

———. *Women in the Ministry of Jesus.* Cambridge: Cambridge University Press, 1984.

Wolf, Eric. *Peasants.* Englewood Cliffs, N.J.: Prentice-Hall, 1966.

Wrede, Wilhelm. *The Messianic Secret in the Gospels.* Trans. J. C. G. Grieg. Cambridge: James Clarke, 1971. German original, 1901.

Wright, N. T. *Jesus and the Victory of God.* Minneapolis: Fortress Press, 1996.

———. "How Jesus Saw Himself." *BR* 12 (1996): 22–29.

Yoder, John Howard. *The Politics of Jesus.* Grand Rapids: Wm. B. Eerdmans Publishing Co., 1972.

Zeitlin, Irvin. *Jesus and the Judaism of His Time.* Cambridge: Polity Press, 1988.

Zeitlin, Solomon. *Who Crucified Jesus?* 4th ed. New York: Bloch, 1964.

INDEX OF SCRIPTURE AND OTHER ANCIENT SOURCES